BIRMINGHAM GUNMAKERS

BIRMINGHAM GUNMAKERS

A COMPLETE OVERVIEW OF THE BIRMINGHAM
GUN TRADE AND ITS HISTORY AS WELL AS A
LISTING OF THE BIRMINGHAM GUNMAKERS

BY

DOUGLAS TATE

Safari Press Inc.
Essex, Connecticut

Safari Press Inc.

An imprint of Globe Pequot, the trade division of
The Rowman & Littlefield Publishing Group, Inc.
4501 Forbes Boulevard, Suite 200
Lanham, Maryland 20706

Distributed by NATIONAL BOOK NETWORK

Tate, Douglas
Second edition

ISBN 978-1-57157-055-0

Library of Congress Catalog Card Number 96-70048

Printed in India

TABLE OF
❋ CONTENTS ❋

Preface VII

Acknowledgments IX

PART 1: THE RISE OF THE BIRMINGHAM GUN TRADE

In The Beginning 4

The Newdigate Contract 7

The Africa Trade 9

Industrial Revolution, Colonial Expansion, and
    the War with France 14

The Interchangeable Concept and the Introduction
    of the Breechloader 17

PART 2: HISTORIES OF THE FAMOUS FIRMS

William Baker 24

Bentley & Playfair 26

C. G. Bonehill 29

A. A. Brown & Sons 32

B. S. A. 37

William Cashmore 40

J. P. Clabrough 42

William Ford 44

W. W. Greener 48

John Harper 66

John Harris 69

Holloway & Naughton 71

Arthur Ilsley 76

William Palmer Jones 77

G. E. Lewis 79

Daniel Leonard 84

Joseph Needham 87

Charles Osbourne 89

William Powell 92

Charles Rosson 98

Skimin & Wood 100

Henry Tolley 104

J. & W. Tolley 106

Thomas Turner 107

Rowland Watson & Thomas Wild 110

Webley & Scott 113

P. Webley & Son 114

W. C. Scott & Son 116

Westley Richards 127

Tony R. White 145

PART 3: Birmingham Guns and Industries

Portal into the Past: The Birmingham Gun Barrel Proof House,
     by Vic Venters 152

Buying Birmingham Guns 159

Valuing Birmingham Guns, by Don Gustine 162

PART 4: Appendices and Reference

Appendix I: The Manufacture of Sporting Guns & Rifles 169

Appendix II: Birmingham Industries (The Gun Trade) 174

Glossary of Gunmakers, Terms 182

Bibliography 187

❊ PREFACE ❊

This book grew from two sources: The first was a series of telephone calls from owners of relatively obscure British shotguns, who wanted to know something about the guns they owned. The typical caller—perhaps because I am British and import guns into the United States—assumed a depth of knowledge I simply didn't have. I researched this book so that I would be better able to answer their questions.

It was also my original intention to write a book about William Rochester Pape, a gunmaker from Newcastle upon Tyne, my home town. But the more I discovered about Pape the more I came to realize how heavily he depended upon the Birmingham gun trade. Although he started by designing and making his own guns in 1858, he came to rely more and more on Birmingham until most of his guns were being made there on designs patented by Birmingham men. It became clear that a book about Pape's North of England Gun Works would actually have to be about the Midland city of Birmingham.

My interest is in sporting breechloading shotguns, and this book reflects that interest. It is essentially about the "birding" gun after 1850. The date is important because in the mid-nineteenth century the breechloader was introduced from France and gun manufacturing machinery was introduced from America. The breechloader made shooting simpler, and it consequently became more popular. The effect of gun manufacturing machinery was much more permanent; slowly machines became responsible for the production of military weapons while sporting shotguns became the province of intensive craft labor. Before machines, Birmingham made both kinds of guns; after the advent of machines, this was increasingly less the case. Eventually—with the exception of companies documented in this book—only handmade sporting shotguns were built in the traditional gun quarter. That is what this book is about.

The book is divided into two parts: The second is about the various firms who built sporting shotguns after 1850 and is an attempt to answer the questions asked by the telephone callers referred to above. While writing the chapters on those firms, I realized that a historical overview of the trade up until 1850 was essential to understanding what happened after that date. The first part of this book is just that—a broad overview up until mid-century. Wherever possible, I have let the gunmakers tell the story in their own words, or at least the words of their contemporaries. In these cases I have left their idiosyncratic spellings intact in order to retain some of the historical and cultural flavor. Otherwise, standard American spelling is used.

Descriptions of the mechanical operation of various gun designs are tedious and have consequently been kept to a minimum. However, patent specifications (in parentheses so as not to disrupt the narrative) are included so that serious scholars may research further. All patent numbers are British unless otherwise stated. Throughout, it is my hope to share with you the pleasure of owning, shooting, and enjoying quality Birmingham guns but also to convey the rich sense of history and craft embodied by them.

Douglas Tate

❊ ACKNOWLEDGMENTS ❊

Unlike the novel that springs from a writer's fertile imagination, no work of this kind can be the work of a single person. Hundreds of people helped make this book possible, and I would like to thank them all, though remembering every single one will not be easy. Prime among my accomplices are my wife, Bonny Hawley; my partner, Don Gustine; and his wife, Jaime, without whose forbearance none of this would have been written.

Vic Venters of *Shooting Sportsman* provided resources and made numerous useful suggestions. Mike Newland at the Birmingham Museum of Science & Industry made available to me his notes on his home town's gunmakers.

Birmingham's gunmakers were, perhaps as might be expected, a source of invaluable information: Robin and his dad, Sidney, of A. A. Brown; Alan Thornton of William Ford Ltd; Graham Greener of W. W. Greener; John, Brian, Colin, and Frank Wiseman of Holloway & Naughton; John Harris of G. E. Lewis; Peter Powell of William Powell & Son Ltd.; Barry King of Rowland Watson and Thomas Wild; Anthony B. Alborough-Tregear of Westley Richards; and Tony White, Belinda White, John Chandler, and Ted Atkinson of Tony R. White.

Those who once worked in the Birmingham gun quarter but who now toil in North America were also a great help: Nick Makinson, Kirk Merrington, Jack Rowe, and Dale Tate.

Other accomplices included: Jason Abbot and Jim Buchanan for copies of old gunmakers' catalogues. The staffs at the patent office, Birmingham's and Wolverhampton's public libraries, and David Penn at The Imperial War Museum. A. G. Scott and R. J. Hancox, past and present Proof Masters at the Birmingham Proof House. Dr. G. L. Sturgess of Weller & Dufty, the Birmingham Auction House.

Dr. Paul G. Brown for his help with John Harper, John A. Crawford for all the help with the Webley & Scott chapter, Lawrence P. Shelton for permission to use research he did on Clabrough, Golcher & Co, and Alistair Kissack and Richard Schreiber for their help with the two-inch 12-bore.

The photographs that illustrate this book came from many sources, and I would like to thank all of the following for their contributions: Adrian Weller at Sotheby's; Christopher Austyn and Sophie Caswell at Christie's; David Grant; Simon D. Clode at Westley Richards; Larry Barnes of Gunnerman Books; Martin

Westley; Mims Reed; Joe Hall at Matched Pairs; Nick Kenny; Dr. Paul Brown; Dave Williams III; Tim Crawford; Dave Jones; Peter Bush; Michael Howarth; Jeff Bird; and Keith Flannery.

❋ DEDICATION ❋

Dedicated to Geoffrey Boothroyd,
whose writing precipitated the current renaissance
in British gunmaking.

PART 1

The Rise of the Birmingham Gun Trade

The Rise of the Birmingham Gun Trade

In the Beginning

Gunpowder and gunmaking came late to Birmingham. Gunpowder and the weapons associated with it appear to have originated in the Far East and made their way to England via Italy and Germany, countries with a strong tradition of making armor.

The English had learned the lessons of weapons technology the hard way. During the Hundred Years War (1337-1453), the superiority of French cannon was a constant factor. As early as 1339, cannon helped save Cambrai from Edward III, and when Joan of Arc raised the siege of Orléans in 1429, she was aided by an immense cannon lent by the people of Metz.

The French did not have it all their own way, however. The records of the kings wardroom tell us that on 1 February 1345, Edward ordered *Gunnis cum pellotis* for the forthcoming campaign. The French chronicler Jean Froissart, in his *Chronique Abrigees*, tells us how these guns and pellets were put to use at the Battle of Crécy the following year. The English used "bombarbs," which made "discharges upon the Genoese who fell into a state of disorder when they heard them roar." But history is written by the winners, and the English winners at Crécy largely credited the yeoman and his longbow with the victory. The tried and tested longbow was retained while the newer weapon went relatively undeveloped.

English schoolboys may recall the glory of Crécy, but how many are familiar with the Battle of Castillon? This battle was the last engagement of the Hundred Years War and the first battle in history to be decided by artillery. In the spring of 1453, the French under Jean Bureau besieged Castillon, where they constructed and heavily defended an artillery park. The English forces under John Talbot, Earl of Shrewsbury, made the fatal decision to attack this stronghold and were utterly destroyed for their trouble. England, although forced from her French possessions except Calais, was slow to accept the superiority of cannon.

One reason for the English reluctance to adopt cannon was the danger inherent in the new technology. The capricious nature of these proto-cannon can be gauged by the death of James II of Scotland, killed in 1460 when a cannon—probably made in Mons, Belgium—exploded at Roxburgh. Firearms in the late Middle Ages were dangerous, expensive, and, above all else, foreign. Despite enormous resistance to them, however, they could no longer be ignored.

By the War of the Roses (1455-1485), cannon were in general use, and their appearance at a siege was usually sufficient to induce the defenders to surrender. The Lancastrians in their Northumbrian castles at Alnwick and Dunstanburgh waved white flags at the merest suggestion of siege trains equipped with cannon. The only exception was Sir Ralph Grey at Bamburgh, who could expect no mercy from the Yorkists because of his previous hostile activities. His refusal to surrender produced the only set siege with artillery of the entire war. The great cannon, which were so important that they were given their own names—Newcastle, London, etc.— soon pulverized the walls, and Sir Ralph was captured and beheaded.

About the same time, hand-held guns began to appear in England—first at the second Battle of St. Albans in the hands of Burgundian troops and again a decade later among Flemish troops under the command of Edward IV. English soldiers were not equipped with hand-held guns until the beginning of the Tudor Dynasty in 1485, when Henry VII organized a body of men as his Royal Guard. Even then he hedged his bets, equipping only half the men with arquebuses while the remainder retained their longbows. It was only after his son, Henry VIII, was crowned that the English began to make guns in any real numbers.

Henry's efforts to import and manufacture guns and the encouragement he gave for their use cannot be underestimated. His aspirations to the French throne caused him to spend huge sums on armaments. Initially, he bought his guns from Italy and the Lowlands, but later offered incentives to craftsmen from both places to relocate to London. Artisans from Mons, the capital of Hainaut in southwestern Belgium, arrived to make arquebuses while the Arcana family from Cesena, in Italy, are said to have traveled to England to cast cannon.

Henry's task in luring competent gunmakers to England seems have been made relatively easy by Draconian legislation aimed at gun founders who were not members of traditional guilds in continental Europe. Guilds of metalsmiths and armorers used their influence to pass legislation that prevented anyone but themselves from making arms. Anyone found making weapons outside this closed shop was subject to huge fines. These early efforts at monopoly stifled technical innovation and had the unintentional side effect of sending artisans, who would otherwise have been assets in times of war, fleeing to foreign enemies.

Henry VIII, the first English monarch to fully appreciate the potential of firearms, ordered his newly acquired gunmakers to arm his fleet with cannon. The roots of the Royal Navy, which came to dominate the world's oceans for hundreds of years, can be traced to this period. Indeed, Henry ordered so many guns to be placed on the decks of the fighting ship *Mary Rose* that their weight may have contributed to her sinking during a skirmish with the French fleet at Spithead in 1545.

After Henry VIII dissolved the monasteries and nunneries (1536-1540), the convent on his doorstep, called the Minories, soon became an armory. Sales of monastic land brought hundreds of thousands of pounds into the exchequer. This money was used to buy weapons and establish cannon foundries to further Henry's ambitions in Europe. His confidence in the new handgun technology was so complete that he enacted a statute requiring all "lords, knights, esquires and gentlemen, and all the inhabitants of cities, boroughs, and market towns, of this Realm of England, to shoot with any hand gun, demthake, or hagbut" [another name for arquebus] and "to have and keep in every of their houses such hand guns, of length of a whole yard . . . whereby . . . they may better aid and assist in the defense of this realm."

Ostensibly similar to modern Swiss legislation that requires all reservists (most of the adult population) to keep their service rifles at home, Henry's statute was in reality elitist. The "lords, knights, esquires, and gentlemen" were all required to be landowners whose rentals generated more than £100 per annum, which at the time meant only about the upper 10 percent of the population. Nevertheless, the English gunmaking industry had its beginnings in the reign of Henry VIII.

During Henry's time, gunmaking was centered in London, first at the Tower of London and later, when the Tower was no longer large enough to accommodate a bur-geoning industry, in the convent next door, a building that eventually gave its name to the entire London gunmaking quarter—the Minories. Toward the end of Henry's reign, cannon were also cast in Uckfield in Sussex. Because of its proximity to the channel ports and because of iron ore deposits of the Sussex Weald, Uckfield became England's first provincial gunmaking town.

In his classic work *The Gun and Its Development*, W. W. Greener, perhaps the most famous of all the Birmingham gunmakers, tells us that cannon were not made in Deriton, Birmingham, until about 1643 or at Bromsgrove (a town some twenty miles southwest of Birmingham) until the time of Commonwealth (1649-1660). Here in the West Midlands, the proximity of iron ore and coal deposits meant that the manufacture of ironware and nails were well-established trades. The demand for weapons during the English Civil War (1642-1651) appears to have changed the face of these trades, creating swordsmiths from plowshare-makers.

Birmingham supplied the Parliamentary forces with a large share of their swords, pikes, and possibly guns, and sympathized with the Puritan cause to the extent of jailing two of the king's agents sent to Birmingham to buy weapons—an act that stirred the wrath of the Royalists, who assaulted the town in 1643. A force of almost two thousand men under Prince Rupert occupied Birmingham, where "They beastly assaulted many Women's chastity and impudently made their brags of it afterwards, how many they had ravished; glorying in the shame . . . were outrageously lascivious and lecherous." After looting anything of value, they torched the town and left.

Despite the arms made for the Roundhead armies, it was not until the restoration of the monarchy in 1689 and the proclamation of William of Orange as King of England in 1689 that Birmingham became an important gun manufacturing center. And just as Henry VIII had single-handedly created the English firearms industry, one man was largely responsible for establishing the Birmingham gun trade. That man was Sir Richard Newdigate.

THE NEWDIGATE CONTRACT

Birmingham's first recorded gunmaker was probably a German. Richard Hanns made a wheel-lock pistol or "dag" with which Tom Colmore tried to shoot his uncle in 1603 during the reign of Queen Elizabeth I. However, there is little evidence to suggest that Hanns was anything other than a gunmaker working in relative isolation and none to indicate a gunmaking quarter or industry. That would take another eighty-six years, an international military crisis, and a rare individual. That individual was Sir Richard Newdigate and the year was 1689. To understand his contribution to the development of Birmingham, it's useful to take a quick look into the political problems of late seventeenth century Europe.

In 1689, Prince William of Orange, a Protestant, was crowned King of England. Louis XIV, a Catholic and William's implacable enemy, was king of France. Within a year, William would defeat the Jacobites, Louis's Catholic allies, at the Battle of the Boyne in Ireland. A few years later he would defeat Louis's armies at Namur in what is now Belgium. But in 1689, William was gearing up for a war on two fronts, and his gunmakers in London could not keep up with the demand for weapons. Some were purchased from William's native Holland, but not enough. Traditionally, when demand outstripped supply, English armies would turn to the old gunmaking towns of lowland Europe such as Mons or Liege. These towns now constituted the frontline between William's Protestant and Louis' Catholic armies and were therefore not a secure source of arms. As if this were not enough, William's problems were exacerbated by his need to replace the old matchlocks of the English army with the new pattern of flintlocks.

Member of Parliament Sir Richard Newdigate's novel solution to the dilemma was to suggest that his constituents in the Warwickshire town of Birmingham could fill the gap. After all, the town had a centuries-old tradition of metalwork, an industry that had developed in the West Midlands because of a rich supply of iron ore beneath the ground and an abundant supply of local coal with which to smelt it. Even though there is no evidence to suggest that Birmingham had any experience in making guns prior to 1689, Sir Richard was confident that the local "lorimers and naylors" could make the guns, if only they could be supplied with a pattern. Clearly, the emergency was great enough for the Board of Ordnance to try this unproven source of arms:

> For their Majesties service.
> To Sir Richard Newdigate at Arbury,
> near Warwick—These.

> Sir,-Pursuant to an order of this Board wee have directed the sending to you, by the Tamworth carrier, 2 snap hand musquettes of differing sorts of patterns, desiring you will please to cause them to be shewed to your Bermingham workmen; and upon your return of their ability and readiness to undertake the making and fixing them accordingly or the making barrells or locks only, together with the time a sufficient quantity of barrels can be made to answer the trouble and charge of sending an officer on purpose to prove the same according to the Tower proof-which is the equall weight of powder to one of the

bulletts alsoe sent to you; and their lowest price either for a compleat musquett ready fixt, or for a barrel or a lock, distinct or together as they will undertake to make them. We shall, therefore cause further directions to be given as shall be most beneficial for their Majesties service, with a thankfull acknowledgment of your great favour and trouble aforded us herein.

We are, Sir, Your most humble servants,

T. Gardiner,
Jos. Charlton,
Wm. Boulter.

Office of Ordnance
10th of January
1689.

Clearly, the Birmingham men filled this order to the satisfaction of the Board of Ordnance because the extant correspondence indicates a more extensive contract five years later:

CONTRACTED and agreed this fifth day of January Anno Dei 1693 and in the fifth year of the Reigne of our Soveraigne Lord and Lady King William and Queene Marye by the Grace of God [sovereigns of] England, Scotland, France, and Ireland, Defenders of the faith etc. By virtue of an order of the Right Honble. Henry Lord Viscount Sidney Master Genl. of their Maties. Ordnance and the board 4th. Novem Last Between the Honble. the principal Officers of the same on their Maties. behalfe of the one part and William Bourne, Tho. Moore, John West, Richd. Weston and Jacob Austin of Birmingham in the County of Warwick Gun Smithes of the other part as folls, viz.—

IMPRIMIS, The said William Bourne, Tho. Moore, John West, Richd. Weston and Jacob Austin do covenant and agree to and with the said principall Officers of their Maties. Ordnance on their behalf of themselves and the rest of the Gunmakers of Birmingham that they shall and will make and provide for their Maties. Service Two hundred Snaphance

Musquets every Month for the space of one Yeare from the Expiration of their last Contract Bearing Date the six and twentieth day of March 1692. And that one half of the said Musquets shall have flat locks engraven, and the other half Round Locks and that all of them shall have brass pipes cast and brass heel plates and all the stocks varnished, and to have six Good thrids in the Breech screws, and that all the said Gun Stocks shall be well made and Sustantiall and none of them Glewed.

AND ALSO that the said Musquet Barrells shall be Compleatly filed before they are proved and that they shall be proved at Birmingham according to the Tower proofe and a fitt person (who shall be impowered by this Office) shall inspect the same and marke them wth. the Office Marke, and (when finished) to survey them. And that powder and bullets shall be provided and sent down at the Charge of this Office for the proofe of the said Armes.

AND THE SAID principall officers of their Maties. Ordnance (for and on their Maties. behalfe) doe agree wth. the said William Bourne, Thomas Moore, John West, Richd. West, and Jacob Austin in behalfe of themselves and the rest of the Gun Makers of Birmingham, that they shall be paid for the said Armes in manner following, viz. for every one hundred severall Armes after the Rate of seventeene shillings per piece ready money by way of debenture wth. in one week after the delivery thereof into thir Maties stores in the tower of London or Any other place within this kingdome, as the Board shall order and direct, and also that they shall be paid and allowed three shillings for the carriage of every one hundred weight from Birmingham to the tower and so proportionally to any other place and that the money shall be paid to them without any charge or trouble as they shall direct and Returne the same from time to time to Birmingham.

IN WITNESS whereof the said parties to these prnts Interchangeably have set their hands and seals the day and year first above written.

> Tho Littleton   Sigillum O
> Jo, Charlton   Sigillum O
> Wm. Boulter   Sigillum O
>
> Sealed and delivered in the presence of Will Phelps

This contract and particularly the line "will make and provide for their Maties. Service Two hundred Snaphance Musquets every Month for the space of one Yeare from the Expiration of their last Contract . . ." suggest an earlier contract for which no documentary evidence can now be found. More significantly, it would indicate the establishment of a burgeoning gun trade where none had previously existed, a theory that bears fruit after reading the last of the contemporary correspondence:

> To the worshipful Sir Richard Newdigate, att Arbury, sent with a gunn.
> Bermingham, Nov. 4th, 1692
>
> WORTHY SIR,—Wee are much ashamed that we have been soe long silent of acknowledgements for the great kindness that your worship did us in helping us to the worke of making musketts for his Majtie in Bermingham; and we could not tell how to make your worship any part of sattisfaction for your great kindness that we have always received from you. Therefore, we beg your worships acceptance of a small token which wee have sent by the bearer, hopeing your worship will pardon this trouble, we remain,
> Ev your worships humble servants,
>
> THE COMPANY OF GUNMAKERS IN BERMINGHAM.

It is a fascinating speculation that the "gunn" presented to Sir Richard with this testimonial may have been the first sporting gun made by the Birmingham men. Sporting guns would not become a mainstay of the trade for another 150 years. The Newdigate contracts were for army weapons, but contractors are notoriously fickle masters. The problem for Birmingham was that military contracts are by nature a boom-and-bust venture. What was needed was a more stable or regular demand. That demand came from a strange quarter: traders who bought cheap guns to exchange for slaves on the west coast of Africa.

THE AFRICA TRADE

It was once said of Liverpool, which flourished with the slave trade, that "every brick of this infernal town is cemented with an African's blood." The same thing could be said of Birmingham. With the Treaty of Ryswick, signed in 1697, France recognized William III as King of England, and a series of five lucrative contracts, for which the Birmingham gunmakers supplied a total of 11,036 completed firearms to the Board of Ordnance, came to an abrupt end. It is likely that the Birmingham gun trade would have died with the signing of the peace treaty were it not for the slave trade, which was beginning as the war was ending. The first order for African flintlock muskets was executed in 1698, and with it Birmingham became part of the Triangular Trade, a market that sent rum from Bristol, cloth from Manchester, and guns from Birmingham to Africa in exchange for slaves. The slaves were shipped to the West Indies and Britain's thirteen American colonies, where they were swapped for molasses, cotton, and tobacco. Those goods in turn were sent back to England, where the molasses was turned into rum and the cotton woven into cloth, and both were sent to Africa along with guns to trade for slaves.

In 1672, the Royal Africa Company of England was granted a charter for the exclusive trading rights to the west coast of Africa and all the way south to the Cape of Good Hope.

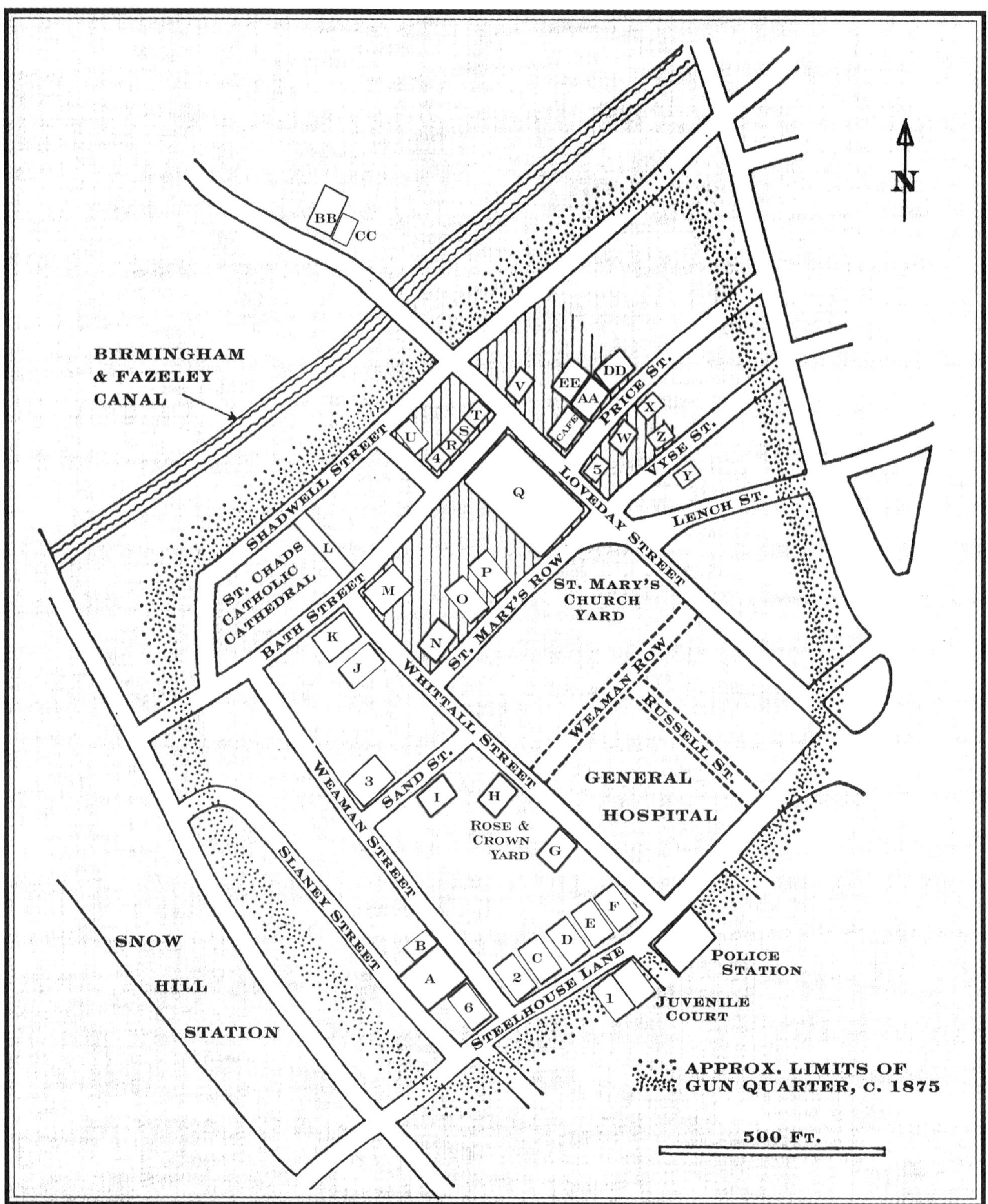

~ BIRMINGHAM GUN QUARTER ~

CIRCA 1946

BY JACK ROWE, A FORMER BIRMINGHAM GUNMAKER

THIS MAP MADE FROM HIS RECOLLECTIONS ON 23 NOVEMBER 1989

KEY TO MAP
GUNMAKERS

A	WEBLEY
B	PHILLIPSON & NEPHEW ACTION MACHINISTS
C	GEORGE BATE
D	C.H. SMITH & COMPANY
E	ROWLAND KEEN & COMPANY
F	LINCOLN JEFFRIES
G	PALMER JONES
H	T. WILD & R. WATSON
I	A.A. BROWN
J	PARKER-HALE & CHEQUERER EDGAR PERKES
K	WALKER'S TOOL SHOP
L	MIDLAND GUN COMPANY
M	MIDLAND GUN COMPANY OFFICE
N	ARCO JIG & TOOL
O	MULLERITE CARTRIDGE COMPANY
P	WILLIAM FORD & J. CARR
Q	W.W. GREENER & B.H. POTTIER
R	SMITH'S VACUUM COMPANY
S	S. WRIGHT & SON
T	JOSEPH BOURNE
U	MITCHELL-BOSLEY & STANDARD GUN COMPANY-MONTREAUX & COMPANY
V	RODGERS GUN PARTS ETC.
W	BONEHILL
X	G & S HOLLOWAY
Y	J. ASTBURY ACTION MACHINISTS
Z	HOLLOWAY & NAUGHTON & SKIMMIN & WOOD
AA	BILLY WOODWARD & RAY ST.LEDGER POLISHERS AND HARDENERS
BB	G.E. LEWIS
CC	ALBERT & JOHN HARRISON
DD	T. YATES BARREL BORER
EE	NEW BUILDINGS YARD

PUBLIC HOUSES

1	GOLDEN CROSS
2	GREEN DRAGON
3	GREEN MAN
4	GUNMAKER'S ARMS
5	BULL'S HEAD
6	GANMONT THEATER

When the company lost its exclusive rights and the trade was opened up (1698), the Birmingham gun industry increased enormously.

There can be no doubt that the trade was lucrative. In 1708, the Africa company sought to reestablish its monopoly but was met with a great deal of resistance. Parliament was petitioned from all corners of the country. The Birmingham gun trade alone sent two petitions, the first in 1707:

A petition of the Gun makers, Cutlers, and other Artificers of Birmingham in the County of Warwick, Manufacturers of Wrought Iron, was presented to the House and read: Setting forth that since the age of 9, Willielmi, for laying open the trade to Africa, the Manufacturers of all sorts have been made and exported by several Trades in greater Quantities than was ever known before; and praying that the said trade may not be monopolised to any Persons in a Joint Stock.

Two years later the appeal was repeated and presented to the House of Commons:

Inhabitants of the Town of Birmingham and Places adjacent . . . that the Manufacture of Cutlers Ware, Gun barrels, and many other Sorts of Wrought Iron, have been very much improved and increased in this Town and Places adjacent since the trade to Africa was laid open by act of Parliament in the Year 1698, by reason of the Great Demand for Exportation by the Merchants trading to that Coast, which affords employment for great numbers of Poor Families in and about the said Town and who must otherwise fall to the Parish: That your Petitioners understand the said trade now lies under great Discouragement from the repeated Attempts of the African Company, and the Creditors, to engross the whole Trade in a Joint Stock Company, exclusive of all others, whereby your Petitioners would be confined to sell their work but to one buyer, and at what price such Buyer pleased; which would prove a Monopoly very grevious to this Town, and much lessen, if not totally impoverish the Poor, and hinder the Progress of the said Manufactures. And pray that the African Trade may continue open and free to all Her Majesty's subjects, and be discharged from all Discouragement.

The petitioners were successful, and on 8 June 1713 a bill was passed that laid the west African coast "free and open to all Her Majesty's subjects of Great Britain and the Plantations."

Below is a single example, from the ledgers of the Royal Africa Company, of what may have been a typical trade:

> At Cape Coast Castle. July 17th 1732.
> Bartered for 2 Men and 1 Woman:-
> 8 Horse Pistols.
> 4 Trading Guns.
> 1 Tankard.
> Scarlet Cloth.
> Basins.
> 1 White Felt Hat.
> 2 Gallons Rum etc. etc.

The guns were of the cheapest type, often garishly painted to appeal to the coastal tribes who sold their enemies into slavery. The locks were bought for pennies in the Black Country towns of Wednesbury and Darlaston, the barrels were crudely welded four-foot-long iron tubes of the quality used in gas pipes, and the stocks were beech wood from Herefordshire and Gloucestershire stained magenta or vermilion. The arms were given names like Long Danes, Buccaneer Guns, or Bonny Guns but were called Park Palings or simply Gas Pipes in the trade. If they were proofed at all, it was with water and not powder—"which if they are capable of holding, without permitting to ooze through the pores, they are sufficiently qualified to discharge their duty," as Morfitt wrote in his *Sketch of Birmingham* in 1802.

Of the firms that made fortunes from the slave trade, perhaps the Galton company is most famous. In 1746, Samuel Galton formed a partnership with James Farmer, who had inherited a barrel-making company from his father, Joseph Farmer, and the two men traded as Farmer & Galton. The partnership started when Galton married Farmer's sister, Mary, and ended with Farmer's death on 6 June 1773. The following year, Galton's son, Samuel John Galton, became a partner, and the firm traded as Galton & Son until 1796, when it became Samuel Galton. In 1795, the old man retired, and Samuel John Galton ran the firm until 1804, when he handed it over to a third-generation relative, Samuel Tertius Galton, who ran the business until 1818, when it closed.

The Galtons owned a barrel-grinding mill at Duddeston on the Rea and bought their locks in Darlaston and Wednesbury, but they assembled or "set up" their guns in Steelhouse Lane, Birmingham. Galton also erected a proof house on Weaman Street, where "he proved his own barrels and those of any gunmaker who chose to send them to him for that purpose." It may be due to Galton's influence in attracting other gunmakers to the neighborhood that the Snow Hill, Steelhouse Lane, and Weaman Street area became the center of the gunmaking industry. Certainly we can accurately trace the origin of the present gun quarter to the period in the 1740s when Farmer and Galton erected their factory in this area.

During 1751, a total of seventy-one slave ships left Liverpool for West Africa. Birmingham's gunmakers had so many orders that they had trouble keeping up with the demand. Letters from Samuel Galton to James Farmer, dating from 1748 to 1760 and preserved among the Galton papers in the Birmingham Reference Library, shed some light on their difficulties. "Every gun manufacturer is pricing the workmen for locks. Willets [John Willets of Wednesbury, who supplied the Board of Ordnance with gun locks used in the Seven Years' War, 1756-1763] sent to Darlaston to let the workmen know he'd give 14d. each for the musket locks."⁺ This was an increase of almost 30 percent over what had previously been paid. Farmer & Galton was involved in the lucrative trade between Portugal and her colonies in Africa and Brazil at the time and offered the Wednesbury lockmakers an extra ½ d [one-half penny] for locks from which Angola muskets were assembled, but their competition was prepared to pay more. On 16 March 1754 Galton wrote to Farmer that "Yesterday we collected but 146 Angola muskets at Wednesbury."

The partners were assembling 500 or 600 guns a week in 1754 but were still not keeping up with the demand. In December of 1754, they received an order for 1,400 guns for the slave-trading ship *Castleton* at Lancaster, an order for 450 guns for the *Swan* at Liverpool, another for 300 from the *Phenix* at Bristol, and one for 600 from a slaver in the port of London. Samuel Galton was so overrun he asked the Darlaston lockmakers to work during their annual June holidays.

Most of these Birmingham guns were "female" guns, which could be traded for a female slave. Male slaves could be had for a weapon of better quality such as an old British Army service rifle brightly painted to appeal to the local market. However, the price varied with locality and year. The slave trade, after all, lasted over 100 years. In 1721, a man could be bought on the West African coast for eight guns, two cases of distilled liquor, and twenty-eight cotton sheets.

The Galton family invested its fortunes in the new turnpikes and canals, which, along with the railways, helped define the Industrial Revolution. The Galtons appear to have been motivated by the profits inherent in these improved transportation systems but seem also to have been looking for quicker ways to get their guns to the slaving ports.

They were Quakers and were formally dismissed from the Birmingham Society of Friends for "fabricating instruments for the destruction of mankind." Samuel John Galton, who neither stopped making guns nor stopped attending Friends meetings, was unrepentant: "My grandfather, afterwards my uncle, then my father and uncle and finally myself have been engaged in this manufacture for a period of 70 years."

The slave trade was abolished in 1807, but trade for other merchandise such as palm oil continued until at least the First World War. Proofs for "African" gun barrels declined from 612 in 1916 to none at all in 1917, though the trade with West Africa almost certainly revived with the armistice. J. W. Ward, who succeeded Charles Playfair as chairman of the Proof House Guardians in 1898, was the last of the Birmingham gunmakers to make the African or "Long Dane" guns, and he was still trading in 1921!

For the entire period of the Africa trade, low-quality flintlocks were the gun of choice. A catalogue published in 1865 by a maker of gun flints, W. Curson of Brandon in Suffolk, offered "For the American, South American, Indian, West Indian, African, and Cape of Good Hope Markets" gun flints including African gun flint at 1s. & 9d. or 2s. [one shilling, 9 pence or two shillings] per thousand. John Dent Goodman, writing in 1866, sixty years after the abolition of the African slave trade, had this to say in "The Birmingham Gun Trade," a chapter from Samuel Timmins' *Birmingham and the Midland Hardware District:*

> The taste of the African is fickle in the matter of beads; a shade of colour which is in demand one season may be unsalable the next; but it is not so with guns, wherein he rejects all improvements, and rigidly adheres to the old flint musket, with its bright barrel, which his father and his grandfather used before him.

Goodman added, "Probably 100,000 to 150,000 of these guns, made in Birmingham, are annually exported."

During the period from the opening of the slave trade in 1698 to its abolition in 1807, Birmingham grew dramatically. In his *History of England,* Thomas Macaulay tells us the population of Birmingham in 1685 was only 4,000. By 1801, it had exploded to 71,000, and the gun trade under the impetus of slavery was largely responsible for the growth.

When the slave trade ended at the turn of the nineteenth century, Britain was embarked on a policy of unprecedented colonial expansion fueled in part by a need to find markets for the produce of the Industrial Revolution. Colonialism and the changes of the Machine Age would have long-term effects on Birmingham gun trade.

Industrial Revolution, Colonial Expansion and the War With France

When the slave trade ended in 1807, Birmingham's gunmakers may have worried that they would experience a period of economic depression. Indeed, they may have had cause for concern were it not for one important development: The peace of Amiens, signed between Britain and France in 1802, had failed and the world's two great powers were once again at war. From 1803, the war continued almost without interruption until 1815. In essence it was a continuation of the Anglo-French conflict of the previous century in which the superpowers of their day fought to see who could accumulate the most Imperial possessions. Britain made certain of gaining Canada for her empire when Wolfe defeated Montcalm at Quebec in 1759, and the Jewel in the Crown was also assured by 1763, when France was eliminated as a rival in

India. Britain didn't have it all her own way, however When the thirteen colonies rebelled in 1776, France supported the rebels and compelled Great Britain to recognize American independence in the Treaty of Versailles (1783). Gun locks stamped "T. Ketland & Co." for Thomas Ketland, a gun factor with premises in Weaman Row, Birmingham, were used by both sides in the American War of Independence.

France never abandoned hope of recovering her overseas empire, and Napoleon's expedition to Egypt (1798-99) was intended to open the back door to India. Other plans for restoring France's position in North America were thwarted by Nelson's victory at Trafalgar (1805), and Napoleon's fate eventually was sealed at Waterloo (1815).

During the war, Birmingham's gunmakers produced unprecedented amounts of pistols, carbines, rifles, and muskets. Between 1804 and 1815, the Birmingham gun trade made a total of 1,682,610 small arms for the Board of Ordnance alone. In the same period they also made 2,774,346 gun barrels and 2,646,228 gun locks to be made into guns by the London trade for the Board. To this must also be added approximately one million guns for the East India Company and perhaps as many as 500,000 sporting guns—bringing the total to almost five million guns.

In the same period, all of the French armories combined did not produce half as many firearms. The Birmingham firms enjoyed several real advantages. First, they were located in one place close to iron and coal deposits, whereas the manufactories of France were spread across the entire country. Second, the degree of specialization among its gunmakers permitted men from other metalworking trades to be trained quickly, giving Birmingham a wonderful elasticity. And third, by the early nineteenth century, Britain in general and

Birmingham in particular were in the throws of the Industrial Revolution.

The Industrial Revolution, which began in England in the reign of George III, was the catalyst of the modern world. It lasted until 1900, and throughout this period Britain was the workshop for the globe. The industrial strength that enabled Britain to dominate world markets accounts for its preeminence in the age of imperialism. Several factors account for Great Britain's strength. Not only was it well endowed with coal and iron ore but it was also spared the ravages of warfare on its own soil—unlike most of continental Europe during the Revolutionary and Napoleonic wars. Trade barriers within the union of England, Scotland, and Wales were nonexistent, so Britain functioned as a single economic unit in which men and material moved without hindrance. Britain also enjoyed a favorable position in the lucrative Atlantic trade: Because it is an island, Britain developed strong naval traditions, which quickly incorporated any improvements in seafaring techniques or equipment and turned them into real advantages for trade. Her major ports, such as Liverpool and Bristol, are also closer to potential markets in Africa, Asia, and the New World than the ports of Germany or Russia. Other conditions, such as the enclosure of common land, released a rural workforce for industrial labor. Also, good communications created by paving roads and building canals dramatically reduced the cost of transporting goods.

However, the most significant single development of the Industrial Revolution as far as Birmingham was concerned was the invention of James Watt's steam engine. It was developed during the 1770s, perfected in 1782, and initially installed—with the help of Matthew Boulton, Birmingham's most famous engineer, silversmith, and entrepre-

neur—into a cotton spinning factory in Papplewick in Nottinghamshire in 1785.

Birmingham's gunmakers, and particularly the barrel makers, quickly saw the superiority of a machine that could be located anywhere. The previous generation of barrel-grinding machines had relied on water power and were therefore located on rivers, like Galton's mill on the Rea at Duddeston. Now barrels could be made anywhere, and the steam engine must have contributed to the consolidation of the gun quarter in the area around St. Mary's church when Thomas Ketland installed a Boulton and Watt engine in his Whittal Street factory—allegedly the first to do so. Not that Birmingham was the only site for gunmaking in the West Midlands. Shaw in his *History of Staffordshire* (1801) tells us:

> That the population of the hamlet of Smethwick had much increased of late years by the canal passing through it to Birmingham . . . on which canal a Mr. Whateley [probably John or Thomas Whateley, both listed as gun barrel makers at about this time] has established a large manufactory of gun barrels, which were forged and bored by the aid of a steam engine.

The introduction of machinery inevitably followed the invention of the steam engine, and in 1800 Thomas Gill of Bartholomew Chapel, Birmingham, who was a sword cutler to the government, patented a machine for cutting rifling into gun barrels. Over the next decade, patents were granted to John Jones (1806-09), Benjamin Cook (1808), John Bradley (1811), and Henry James and John Jones (1811), all for machines that used grooved rollers for gun-barrel manufacture. A slightly different and more colorful story is told by John Dent Goodman in "The Birmingham Gun Trade," an article published in *The Resources, Products and Industrial History of Birmingham and the Midland Hardware District*, edited by Samuel Timmins in 1866:

The invention of making gun barrels by means of grooved rolls is due to a Birmingham manufacturer of the name of Osborne. It was on the occasion of a strike of the barrel welders that he was led to make an experiment. He was not allowed to introduce his system without opposition, for no sooner were his rolls set to work than twelve hundred barrel welders, each armed with his forge hammer, proceeded, to the private residence of Mr. Osborne, in the Stratford Road, threatening its destruction. The Military were called out before the disturbance could be quelled, and for many days afterward a guard was placed over the mill in which the work was carried on.

This tale dates from 1812, the year Wellington entered Madrid and Napoleon entered Moscow. Regardless of whether Goodman's story is absolutely true in every detail, it cannot be denied that machinery—developed as a result of the Industrial Revolution—played a major role in making the guns which armed the force that ultimately defeated Napoleon.

In the years following Napoleon's defeat at Waterloo, the Birmingham gun trade was hit hard by an eight-year-long economic depression. The slump was one of many that marked the history of an industry whose fortunes over 150 years was dependent on the vicissitudes of military contracts. Despair deepened when Birmingham's inhabitants learned that despite their having supplied the government with an average of over 1,000 muskets a day during the war with France, the Board of Ordnance now planned to make its own arms at a state-run factory closer to London in either Lewisham or Enfield.

The Birmingham gunmakers petitioned their Member of Parliament, who in turn appealed to the Duke of Wellington, the hero of Waterloo but also the "Master General of Ordnance":

I can assure Your Grace, that not only the gentlemen concerned in the Manufacture, but every person interested in the general welfare and trade of Birmingham feels the greatest apprehension of alarm from so serious a blow to the principal article of trade in this Town.

The Iron Duke passed the matter to the Board of Ordnance, which in turn handed it to the Master Furbisher of Arms at the Tower of London, one Mr. Bellis. Mr. Bellis produced a damning report on the inferiority and bad workmanship of the Birmingham weapons received by the Board during the war. He maintained that many were "very unsound" and "very badly case hardened" and that "great numbers of limbs break when put into action," adding that arms should never again be assembled in Birmingham "without some absolute necessity existed."

The report was sent to Stratford Dugdale, Esq., the Member representing the gunmakers. Dugdale responded sarcastically that he did not wish:

. . . for the Board to receive articles of an inferior quality—nor am I indeed aware that such can be introduced into the magazines as I have always understood that every article is examined and passed by a person employed expressly for that purpose.

Indeed, every musket went through eleven different inspections by a total of fifty-eight "viewers" appointed by the board in Birmingham to make sure British troops never received poor-quality arms. The Board had appointed a Colonel Miller as Officer in charge of the View and Proof of Arms, and he had rented rooms where the inspections could take place. The rooms were open from six in the morning until six at night. In theory at least, it was impossible for any substandard arm to sneak through.

Eventually the Duke of Wellington ordered an inquiry:

. . . to ascertain the mode in which the transactions of the Ordnance were carried out at Birmingham during the war and whether the bad quality of the arms supplied is to be attributed to the manner in which the business of the Ordnance is carried on, or to the deficiencies of the workmen.

Two colonels and a major arrived in Birmingham to conduct the inquiry on 12 April 1824. What they found was that corruption among the viewers had been widespread during the war. Two rough stock viewers named Nellum and Blake had been dismissed in 1810 because they insisted on bribes for viewing work. Their refusal to pass perfectly good work unless bribed led some gunmakers to confront the Ordnance Board's solicitors, Spurrier and Ingleby, with accounts kept by one of the stocker's wives of bribes paid to Blake. Nellum and Blake were fired, but the abuses continued.

Contractors continued to have perfectly good weapons rejected, but the independent gunmakers who actually did the work took it upon themselves to pay the necessary bribes. Rejections mysteriously ceased, with the inevitable long-term result that quality declined.

However, corrupt viewers were only part of a greater problem. During the war, the demand for weapons was so great that everyone—contractors, workers, and viewers—was overworked. The unprecedented demand stretched Birmingham's famed elasticity to the limits; carpenters were offered premiums to take up gunstocking, and the tradesmen who soldered candle snuffers were offered inducements to become lockmakers. Children too were taken into the gunmaking trade, and as a well-known contractor, John Dent Goodman, would say about a later generation, "We regret to say that many are employed in this work too

young for the burdens they are called upon to bear."

None of this was good for the Birmingham trade, which was elevated from the depths of depression only by the Burmese War of 1824 and an order of 140,000 arms from France in 1830. In 1839, the British government eventually began to adopt the percussion system of ignition, and converting flintlocks to percussion-action guns appears to have provided a brief respite for the Birmingham trade. Real prosperity would not return until the Crimean War began in 1853, but by then other events were under way that would change the face of the Birmingham gun trade forever.

THE INTERCHANGEABLE CONCEPT AND THE INTRODUCTION OF THE BREECHLOADER

In 1851, two events occurred that would monumentally affect the Birmingham gun trade: The Ordnance Board sent the first of a series of delegations to the United States to look at American rifle making machinery, and French gunmakers introduced the breechloading sporting shotgun to Britain at the Great Exhibition. The first event precipitated the end of Birmingham as a military supplier while the second suggested the possibility of new stimulus for the Birmingham trade.

That year was also significant because it was the year in which the rifle superseded the smoothbore musket as the general service arm in England. In 1851, Birmingham contributed 5,167 of a total of 7,731 gunsmiths and workers in the kingdom, or 67 percent. But in that year:

The production of guns themselves owed practically nothing to machinery. Certain parts were made under the 'kick stamp,' the military barrels were rolled and ground by steam driven plant, but the rest of the process was performed entirely by hand.

Or so wrote G. C. Allen in *The Industrial Development of Birmingham and the Black Country 1860-1927*, first published in 1929. Allen reiterates the same point a few pages later:

> . . . trade was essentially a skilled handicraft, and over the greater part of the industry the stamp and the foot-lathe were the only machines employed.

But by mid-century, the Ordnance Board was aware that changes were afoot, particularly in America. W. W. Greener tells us:

> The idea of making guns on the interchangeable system by the aid of machinery originated with the French during the latter part of the eighteenth century. The process of stamping instead of forging the various parts of a gun was the only successful result, and the honour of working out the system to a successful issue is due to the Americans.

Certainly all the important developments leading to interchangeable-part, machine-made guns appear to have originated in America. Eli Whitney, the American who invented the cotton gin, secured a contract for 10,000 guns, which he manufactured from stampings, using machinery for shaping and finishing parts. He also developed a system of gauges and templates that ensured a standardization, and hence interchangeability of parts. John H. Hall of Harpers Ferry, West Virginia, refined the interchangeable system and introduced it into U.S. government workshops. A certain Blanchard of Middlebury, Massachusetts, adapted lathes for the turning of gun barrels and stocks, and Greener records that he needed seventeen different machines for the shaping of his stocks. Col. Samuel Colt was questioned by a committee of the House of Commons on the possibility of making guns on the interchangeable plan, and on the strength of his evidence a committee was sent to the United States.

In 1853, a Royal Commission headed by Sir Joseph Whitworth, the engineer who had proposed the standard screw thread a decade earlier and a man who would ultimately develop fluid gun barrel steel, set off for America. Birmingham was represented by George Wallis, who had been the headmaster of the Birmingham School of Art, although why a schoolteacher rather than a gunmaker was sent remains a mystery. They visited the New York exhibition and the U.S. Government Arms Factory at Springfield, Massachusetts, where they watched ten muskets—each made in a different year from 1844 to 1853 inclusive—be taken apart and the parts mixed together. They then asked the arms assembler to put them together while they, the committee, handed him parts randomly. The muskets were assembled using only a screwdriver, and when the operation was complete the committee concluded:

> All the parts were as close, and the muskets as efficient, as they were before the interchange took place. . . . The experiment of interchanging was also tried on three locks with the most perfect success, the parts fitting closely and working as freely after as before the interchange had taken place.

Their report convinced the British government to establish a factory in Middlesex on the same lines as the one in Massachusetts.

The Enfield factory became a contentious issue in the House of Commons, with Mr. Newdigate (no doubt a descendent of Sir Richard Newdigate, founder of the Birmingham gun trade) arguing against the government's entering into competition with the private trade of the country. The outbreak of the Crimean War sealed the issue, however, and the factory was erected on a grander scale than originally conceived.

Another commission, consisting of two officers of the Royal Artillery and a Mr. Anderson, the Ordnance Inspector of Machinery, was sent to the U.S. with instructions to inspect gun factories and to purchase machinery for the proposed factory at Enfield. Their report is worth quoting in part:

> In consequence of the scarcity and high price of labour in the United States, and the extreme desire manifested by masters and workmen to adopt all labour saving appliances, from the conviction of such being for their mutual interest, a considerable number of different trades are carried on in the same way as the cotton manufacture in England, viz: in large factories, with machinery applied to every process.

It went on:

> Americans display an amount of ingenuity, combined with undaunted energy, which, as a nation, we would do well to imitate, if we mean to hold our present position in the great market of the world.

The commission eventually bought machinery from Robbins and Lawrence of Windsor, Vermont, and Ames Manufacturing Company of Chicopee Falls, Massachusetts. By 1858, the Enfield factory was turning out 2,000 rifles each week—to the chagrin of the Birmingham trade. Although Birmingham had always made a large amount of sporting shotguns, it was the military weapon that had ensured the prosperity of the town, and the gunmakers now organized themselves to compete with the government factory.

The Birmingham Small Arms Company Limited (B.S.A.) was formed in 1861 by about a dozen of the town's larger gun factories. A resolution was passed "to form a company to make guns by machinery" and "to order without delay, from America, the machinery necessary for the making of the woodwork of the rifles." After surviving a catastrophic slump precipitated by the cancellation of significant American arms contracts in 1863, B.S.A. won an order for Short Enfield rifles with interchangeable parts for the Ottoman Turks.

One of the original shareholders was John Dent Goodman, who wrote in 1865 at a time of economic depression:

> The termination of the war in America [the U.S. Civil War, 1861-65] will restore the demand for sporting guns in the United States market, which has always been one of the most important for our trade; but the employment which may be looked for with the greatest expectation, will arise from the demand for military arms, when a decision shall have been arrived at respecting the merits of the best breech loaders.

In 1866, B.S.A. won part of an order to convert muzzleloaders to the new Snider breechloading system, and in 1871 it was awarded part of a contract for the new Martini-Henry rifle. But even as the company began to compete with the government factory at Enfield, the split between the military and sporting sections of the trade was becoming more apparent. Or as C. G. Allen explained:

> In 1860 there was no sharp contrast between the methods of production pursued in those two branches; but by the end of the decade, while sporting goods continued to be made by traditional methods in little workshops, a great part of the military trade was being conducted in large factories equipped with plants of complex machinery. The manufacture of military rifles, in fact, was ceasing to be the concern of the craftsman and was becoming a task for the engineer. By 1870 the change was not complete, for the factories were not yet capable of satisfying the entire demand. But

the old Birmingham gun trade had lost what only a short time previously had been its chief source of profit.

For almost 200 years the small independent gunmakers of Birmingham had depended on military contracts for their livelihood. With the introduction of interchangeable-parts guns and the building of machine-equipped factories, they would never again make arms for British soldiers. However, relief was on the way, albeit from an unlikely source—France.

During 1851, the Great Exhibition was held at the Crystal Palace in Hyde Park, London. Its rationale was to "unite the industry and art of all the nations of the earth." The gunmakers' art was certainly well represented, with almost 140 entries from all over the world. The aforementioned Robbins and Lawrence from Windsor, Vermont, was present, offering "rifles with their various parts made to interchange." More than a dozen representatives of the Birmingham trade were there as well, but it was the French contingent that caused the biggest bang.

The official catalogue describes W. & J. Needham of 26 Piccadilly as exhibiting "double and single guns to load at the breech," and also tells us that Montigny & Fusnot of Brussels showed three infantry guns on the Montigny system, also a breech-loading design. But it was a gun displayed by M. Casimir Lefaucheux of Paris that would eventually transform the British sporting shotgun. All three were breech-loaders, but the Needham and Montigny guns were rigid while the Lefaucheux hinged so that the muzzles pointed down and the breech ends tipped up to reveal a pair of self-contained pin-fire cartridges. It was this tip-up feature, or *system de bascule* to use the French term, which would eventually gain the gun wide currency, but at the

time of the Great Exhibition, few saw the Lefaucheux's potential.

A handful of London gunmakers— Joseph Lang, John Blanch, and George H. Daw—acquired examples and began efforts to improve and particularly to strengthen the system by which the gun was bolted rigid when made ready to fire. Success was not immediate, and the tip-up breechloader was considered by most to be a dangerous novelty. As Colonel Hawker remarked, "Let me caution the whole world against using firearms that are opened and loaded at the breech end—a horrid ancient invention revived by foreign makers." The Colonel harbored no love for the French after being wounded at the Battle of Talavera in the Peninsula War almost half a century earlier. Despite resistance, by 1858 the breechloading shotgun was in wide enough use that John Henry Walsh, editor of *The Field* magazine, organized a trial pitting the new gun against the more established muzzleloader. Significantly, none of the three London advocates of the breechloader—Lang, Blanch, or Daw—entered guns.

The muzzleloaders emerged triumphant, which only provided ammunition for the detractors of breechloaders. William Greener, one of Birmingham's most famous gunmakers, lambasted the newcomer. Writing in the immediate wake of the trial, he had this to say:

> The French system of breechloading firearms is a specious pretence, the supposed advantages of which have been loudly boasted of; but none of these advantages have as yet been established by its most strenuous advocates. How it is that the British sportsman has become the dupe of certain men who set themselves up for reputable gunmakers I know not. . . . With regard to the safety of these guns, they display an utter want of the most ordinary judgement.

He went on:

> First, there is no possibility of a breech loader ever shooting equal to a well constructed muzzle loader; secondly, the gun is unsafe and becomes more and more unsafe from the first time it is used; and, thirdly it is a very costly affair, both as regards the gun and ammunition.

Greener eventually concluded, "no fear need be entertained that the use of breechloaders will become general. . . ."

However, by the 1860s the use of the breechloader was general, and it helped popularize shooting. Previously, gentlemen had walked up their birds, slowly recharging their muzzleloaders after each flush. Now it was the beaters who did the walking, flushing birds over standing guns and making really large bags possible. For many it was the rapidity of fire that made driven shooting so attractive, and this fast-fire mode was in itself made possible by matched pairs of breechloading guns and a man to reload them. Shooting was transformed, and it became a fashionable pursuit with Royals, who were society leaders. Many followed the Royal example, and shooting became immensely popular.

It was the introduction of the split breechloader from France that stimulated the success of the driven shoot, but it was the Birmingham gun trade that would reap the benefit. Gentlemen may have bought the guns they needed to participate in the new sport from provincial makers in their home towns, but after 1870 these guns were increasingly made in Birmingham. Provincial makers simply could not compete with a trade as concentrated and organized as the one in the St. Mary's district. William Greener had once worked as a gunmaker in Newcastle upon Tyne but found gunmaking more profitable after moving his business to Birmingham. London makers built best guns for their affluent clientele, but they too had recourse to the Birmingham trade for guns of second and third quality. A second tier of London gunmakers, such as Army & Navy and W. J. Jeffery, appears to have had most of their guns made in Birmingham. By the 1870s the city that had armed the British forces for almost two-hundred years was supplying the country gentleman with his shotguns and the big-game hunter with his double rifle.

PART 2

HISTORIES OF THE FAMOUS FIRMS

HISTORIES OF THE FAMOUS FIRMS

WILLIAM BAKER

Of all the Birmingham gunmakers, William Baker is probably the greatest of them all; he is also the least well known. Baker, who was born in Handsworth in 1858 and died at the same place in 1934, identified himself as a "gun action manufacturer" but is best remembered as one of the gun trade's most prodigious inventors. He successfully obtained thirty-five patents, including some that are still being used, but because most of the guns he designed and built were signed by other gunmakers, he is today largely forgotten.

William Baker may have learned his trade with David Bentley, a gun and pistol maker at the Tower Works at 45 Aston Road, Birmingham; certainly he took out his earliest patent with Bentley. It was for a single-trigger mechanism, an idea that preoccupied Baker for twenty years but ultimately brought him little in the way of revenue or recognition. Despite patenting five single-trigger mechanisms—one with David Bentley, two with William Palmer Jones, and two by himself—Baker never developed a system that was widely adopted or could be called successful.

In one respect his was a radical departure from the traditional trigger, and this may have been the reason for its failure. Instead of the normal bow, starting at the top center of the guard and extending back and down in a graceful curve, the Baker trigger in its final incarnation was a push-me, pull-you arrangement reminiscent of two triggers welded together with one in the rear of the guard and one in the front. It was pulled in the normal way if the right barrel was required to fire first, or pushed forward and then pulled if the left was required. Gun buyers are a conservative lot, and something as unusual as this would have been a difficult sell.

The patent record shows that Baker also appears to have been engrossed by ejectors, coil springs, over-unders, and, ultimately, over-unders with coil-spring ejectors. He patented his earliest ejector mechanism in 1889 together with William Philipson, and his final over-under with coil-spring ejectors thirty-five years later in 1924. In between, he built guns based on his own patents for the London and provincial trade from workshops first at 87 Snow Hill and later from 7 Bath Street. The most commonly encountered are sidelock side-by-sides with inexpensive coil-spring lockwork built for Vickers of Crayford and J. P. Hodgson of Louth. Less frequently, over-unders built for Harrison & Hussey and G. & S. Holloway come to light.

The coil-spring sidelocks enjoyed a modest success at the lower to middle end of the trade because they were well adapted to inexpensive machine manufacture, but the over-unders seem scarcely to have been built. The reason is that though Baker dispensed with the Purdey underbolt in favor of a sidebolting system in an effort to reduce the depth of the action, he retained an underhinge instead of going with side hinges like Boss or Woodward. The result was that Baker's over-unders never achieved the elegance of line enjoyed by the two London-made guns and were consequently never built in anything like the numbers of those two other makers.

William Baker eventually developed two related mechanisms that were widely adopted, though it's doubtful he ever benefited to any great extent from them. It began in 1890, when Baker patented an ejector powered by a coil spring housed in a cylindrical tube that pivoted at the front of the ejector kicker. The system appears to have been moderately well accepted and in terms of remuneration was probably one of Baker's greatest successes.

Its real significance is that it seems to have inspired a pair of similar patents in 1900 and 1903 which, while they both feature flat rather than coil springs, have the springs contained on a plate in the earlier version and in a box in the later. Ejector mechanisms are often compared with gunlocks because they contain the same basic components and fulfill a similar function. Indeed, the contemporary descriptions occasionally refer to ejectors as "ejector locks." It is hardly surprising then that Baker saw the potential of his evolving ejector concept for its use as a firing mechanism. And in 1906 he patented a gunlock in which the mainspring was contained in a box that hinged at the rear of the action. Advertisements in *The Sporting Guns Review* claimed reliability and strength for the new action, which was an almost exact echo of the claims Baker made for his ejector mechanism just a few years earlier. Incidentally, neither advertisement contained an address, strongly suggesting that Baker worked exclusively for the trade.

The box containing the mainspring projected back into the angle of the lockplate, which was the opposite of most sidelocks in which the mainspring lay forward in the bar. In traditional sidelocks, steel is removed from the bar to accommodate the mainspring. This insetting reduces strength, and as a consequence the bar must be robust and heavy. In the Baker design, the need to remove metal is eliminated and the bar of the action can be reduced in size and therefore in weight without threatening the structural integrity of the gun.

The result is a trim 12-bore that weighs less than six pounds and yet has exceptional sectional strength. Like the Boss over-under or the Dickson round-action, the design also has a certain intangible quality that is sometimes—though inadequately—described as good handling characteristics.

This is a very sophisticated design in which the tumbler is cocked as the gun opens, but the mainspring is not compressed until the gun is closed. Thus it is, in practice, an assisted opener, which eliminates the wrist-breaking difficulties associated with the true self-opener. An additional advantage is that the springs are at rest when the gun is not in use.

Baker's action was ingenious in concept and required a great deal of time and skill to build. Nevertheless it was widely adopted by Britain's best gunmakers: William Powell in Birmingham, E. J. Churchill in London, and Lindsey Brothers in the provincial city of Leeds all offered them, as did Harrison and Hussey, Stephan Grant, and Charles Lancaster.

Stephan Grant called its version the "Lightweight," but it was the Lancaster variant known as the "12/20" that captured the largest audience. The Lancaster guns are built no better than any of the others—indeed, it is likely that Baker built most of them—but they consistently outsold identical guns by other makers. It seems the Lancaster firm simply did a better job of promotion, offering the gun as a 12-bore that weighed as little as a 20.

Lancaster adopted the design in 1924, some eighteen years after it had been patented, suggesting that the firm may have been waiting for the patent to lapse in order to avoid paying royalties. So it would seem that William Baker, despite having designed and built one of the finest shotguns of all time, was denied not only the recognition he deserved—today the 12/20 is synonymous with the Lancaster name—but also his full financial due.

William Baker died on 16 February 1934 at his home in Handsworth, and the company bearing his name carried on for only a few more years before disappearing sometime at the end of the decade—apparently unable to survive the death of one of the Birmingham gun trade's cleverest inventors.

BENTLEY & PLAYFAIR

The British gun trade in the Victorian era abounds with mysteries for the modern researcher. Which Mr. Bentley for example, made up half of the firm of Bentley & Playfair? That is perhaps the most perplexing of all the puzzles pertaining to the Birmingham trade.

Playfair is fairly well documented. He was Charles Playfair, a gunmaker of Aberdeen, Scotland, who founded a small dynasty that endured well into the 1950s in the granite city. In 1846 Playfair's son, also named Charles, entered into a partnership with a certain Mr. Bentley in Birmingham. Bentley & Playfair advertising always claimed, "Established 1840," but that was the date Bentley began the business; he wasn't joined by Charles Playfair until 1846.

The problem is that at the time of the partnership a number of Bentleys were working in the Birmingham gun quarter. Of these, David Bentley of New Church Street is the most famous because of his semi-hammerless gun action (Patent Number 17,037 of 1884), which was widely licensed throughout the trade. But the only two serious candidates for Playfair's partner are Joseph Bentley of 11 Steelhouse Lane, who also had premises in Liverpool, and Thomas Bentley, who with his brother Charles occupied a workshop at 315 Summer Lane.

Bailey and Nie in their directory, *English Gunmakers*, under the entry for Bentley & Playfair, state: "Partnership of Joseph Bentley

THE WILLIAM BAKER PATENTS

DATE	NO.	DESCRIPTION	DATE	NO.	DESCRIPTION
1882	4,766	Single trigger with D. Bentley	1911	4,440	Gun action (coil springs) with exterior projection for hand cocking
1883	5,292	Gun action with D. Bentley			
1889	8,323	Ejectors with Wm. Philipson	1912	4,922	Pierced spindle for o/u
1889	18,781	Ejectors with Wm. Philipson	1912	15,605	Ejector for o/u
1890	17,292	Ejectors (coil spring in tube)	1912	9,768	Bolting for o/u
1895	1,844	Single trigger with W. P. Jones	1913	16,788	Cocking mechanism for o/u (coil springs)
1895	5,543	Single trigger with W. P. Jones	1915	1,507	Single-barrel gun action (coil springs)
1898	2,931	Boxlock action (coil springs)			
1900	2,650	Single trigger	1915	5,045	Air gun
1900	8,183	Ejector	1916	101,562	Air gun
1901	19,430	Single trigger	1919	158,420	Spindle with Birmingham Gun Makers Ltd.
1902	2,899	Sidelock action (coil springs)	1920	160,057	Air gun with A. H. Marsh
1903	16,814	Ejector	1920	162,923	Air gun with A. H. Marsh
1905	21,967	Ejector	1920	167,050	Cocking slide with J.D. Thompson
1906	26,903	Sidelock action (12/20)			
1907	6,162	Improvement to cocking mechanism for 12/20	1920	167,117	Spindle with J. D. Thompson
1910	6,223	Pierced spindle	1922	194,118	Single-barrel gun action (coil springs)
1910	28,806	Improvement to 12/20	1923	224,712	Ejector for o/u
1911	3,708	Ejector	1924	237,708	Ejector for single barrel and o/u

and Charles Playfair. "On the other hand, in an obituary for T. C. Bentley dated 15 July 1916, *The Sporting Goods Review* says: "The late Mr. Bentley was a member of the firm of Bentley and Playfair, founded in 1846, when Mr. Thomas Bentley, who died in March, 1902, first joined forces with the late Mr. Playfair." The conundrum is compounded when one considers the further evidence: In 1868 the following advertisement appeared:

BENTLEY & PLAYFAIR, 315 and 316, Summer Lane Birmingham, Manufacturers of Every Description of Military and Sporting Rifles, Guns, Pistols and Revolvers, and of the most Improved Breech Loaders. Sole Manufacturers of Baker's Patent Central Fire Breech Loader, Walker's Patent Snap-Action Breech Loader, & Erskine's Patent Eccentric-Action Breech Loader, all of which are adapted to Eley's ordinary Central Fire and Pin Cartridges. Contractors to Her Majesty's War Department.

The address of "315 and 316, Summer Lane" had in part been occupied previously by the Bentley Brothers, strongly suggesting that Thomas was the Playfair partner. But the mention of revolvers points to Joseph Bentley, who had been granted a series of revolver patents throughout the 1850s and whose ads indicate he made a specialty of them. What's more, the reference to "Erskine's Patent Eccentric Action Breech Loader" may also point to Joseph: The Erskine in question was James Erskine of Newton Stewart, Wigtownshire in southwest Scotland, and the gun action was a slide-and-drop-down system similar to the more familiar MacNaughton. Apart from the obvious Scottish connection, a tribute to Erskine published in *The Field* in 1891 at the time of his death recounts how he "gained much professional knowledge in a house in Liverpool." Since Joseph Bentley occupied premises in Liverpool, it is tempting to infer that the "house in Liverpool" was the shop of Joseph Bentley and that this Bentley was the Playfair partner.

Some 150 years later we may never know the truth about which Bentley established the company. What we do know is that the firm he founded was a success. Operating from the "Colmore Works" in Birmingham, Bentley & Playfair soon opened a shop at 60 Queen Victoria Street, London, and advertised that it had outlets in Paris, Capetown, and Melbourne. Their stock in trade appears to have been good-quality boxlocks, often with sideplates identical to those seen on Windsor-grade Charles Hellis guns. That fact has led at least one enthusiast to conclude that the Hellis guns—or at least the ones made in this particular grade—were built by Bentley & Playfair.

Bentley & Playfair was prominent in forming the gun-trade trophy at the exhibition of 1862. Since no engraving was made, I can only assume that the trophy was similar to the one W. & C. Scott created for Queen Victoria's visit to Birmingham four years earlier. It took the form of a triumphal arch bedecked with royal and military standards and garlanded with floral bunting.

The previous year saw Bentley & Playfair, or at least Charles Playfair, investing £24,500 to become one of the original shareholders in the Birmingham Small Arms Company, Ltd., or B.S.A. as it has become known. B.S.A. was created to manufacture standardized military weapons when it was realized that the next major war would be fought with machine-made guns. A resolution was passed in June 1861 "to form a company to make guns by machinery," just one month before the first battle of Bull Run in Virginia.

Charles Playfair continued to be active in the trade, becoming chairman of the Guardians of Birmingham Proof House in 1892. When he died in 1898, his son, Captain Charles Playfair, took his place as head of the firm. In 1908, that Playfair developed a humane killer (Patent Number 2,447 of 1908) that the patent specifications refer to as a "slaughtering gun." The same year, he moved the firm's London premises from Queen Victoria Street to Holborn Viaduct. On 1 May 1914, the younger Playfair, who was by that time a Major, became Proof Master after first visiting the Belgian Proof House in preparation for his new position. In the collection of the Birmingham Proof House there is a delightful little 2-inch 12-bore J. W. Tolley, Serial Number 84040, which has a brass plaque attached to the stock that reads, "Presented in 1934 by the Guardians of the Birmingham Proof House to Lt. Col. C. Playfair J. P. Proof Master 1913-1941."

With the introduction of machine-made military guns, Bentley & Playfair concentrated its efforts on the sporting gun market. But shotguns too were being manufactured on machinery, and this factor, plus stiff import tariffs from nations that traditionally bought Birmingham's best, resulted in an amalgamation in 1911 between Bentley & Playfair and another old, established Birmingham gunmaking firm, Isaac Hollis & Sons.

Hollis, which claimed it was established in 1814, had a lengthy history of making military weapons, but catalogs dating from the approximate time of its incorporation featured a high percentage of trap and live-pigeon guns. Hollis, Bentley & Playfair traded from 16 & 17 Loveday Street and advertised "wholesale only" in trade journals between the wars. Although these ads feature sporting guns, they also offer more rifles than was typical, perhaps suggesting a degree of specialization. The firm, like so many companies, ceased trading when the inner-ring road-development scheme tore the heart out of Birmingham's gun quarter in the early 1960s.

C. G. BONEHILL

Until the middle of the last century, both military rifles and sporting guns were made by a legion of Birmingham firms that specialized in neither. The same work force, techniques, and materials were used for both army weapons and birding guns. The only differences were that the price was lower for one while the standard was higher for the other. Around the time of the Crimean War, an irreversible dichotomy occurred that had its roots in the previous century.

As early as 1795, George Bolton, a mathematician who had been tutor to George III, developed a simple, screwless gunlock that could be mass-produced by hand and had corresponding components so similar as to be interchangeable. The advantages were obvious: For one, a soldier in the field could mend broken locks using spare parts. Then, in the early part of the nineteenth century, when American companies based in New England developed machinery for manufacturing guns, the fate of handmade military weapons was sealed forever. The Birmingham men, who had previously hand-built army rifles in much the same way as today's craftsmen hand-build sporting shotguns, realized that machines could manufacture rifles cheaper and quicker than ever before. Those who could afford to do so invested in the new machinery, and many made fortunes in a period of unprecedented global warfare.

One of those who must have watched these developments with enormous interest was Christopher George Bonehill. Born in Birmingham in 1831 to a family that had once been Warwickshire farmers but had prospered during the Industrial Revolution as wholesale ironmongers and manufacturers, Bonehill was indentured to a Mr. Aston, a gunmaker and government contractor. This was probably Joseph Aston of 8 Upper Priory, Birmingham, who advertised himself as:

Manufacturer of Gun Locks, steel mountings, military ramrods, ribs, rings, springs, nails, triggers, swivels, screws, loops, sights, bolts, nipples, wrenches, turnscrews and worms to the Honourable Board of Ordnance and East India Company.

Bonehill must have learned his business well, for when he eventually emerged from his apprenticeship and his master asked him if he felt that he had thoroughly learned the trade and could conduct a business for himself, he not only responded in the affirmative but also set up a workshop and forge and began working for himself.

His earliest work, starting in 1851 at age twenty, was supplying rifle components to military contractors. A succession of colonial wars and international conflicts throughout the next few decades assured his success, and he moved from his St. George's workshop into larger premises at 33 Charlotte Street, taking additional space in Morville Street in 1873. By 1877, Bonehill's business had outgrown both premises, and he eventually occupied a factory in Belmont Row previously owned by The National Arms and Ammunition Company.

What made this expansion possible was a series of military contracts, including one from France—during the Franco-Prussian War—for 25,000 rifles. The French provided Bonehill with a guarantee of £8,000 and a pattern of the rifle as a standard of quality below which his product must not fall. During the war, the Senate in Paris was so satisfied that it complimented Bonehill on his punctuality and efficiency. But when a peace settlement was agreed upon, France began returning rifles as not being up to the specified standard. Bonehill's response was to submit the original pattern, pretending it was a rifle of his own manufacture. When this was also rejected and Bonehill pointed out the error, it is said that within two weeks the French had accepted all of the remaining rifles.

Bonehill's next contract was from the British War Office for 2,000 Snider cavalry carbines. Though only five of the Sniders failed to pass government inspection, military orders stopped coming. This was not unusual in nineteenth century Birmingham, which frequently weathered cycles of boom and bust. Before this time, a degree of flexibility was inherent in the nature of the trade. In time of work, some craftsmen were lured from other metalworking trades with the promise of higher wages and returned to those trades when the boom was over. Others went back to making sporting guns when military orders ceased.

By the late 1870s or early 1880s, however, the dichotomy was complete. Military arms would ever more be made on production lines. Furthermore, those production facilities were no longer in private hands but were state-owned, like the government factory at Enfield. Bonehill's dilemma was that he owned a modern manufacturing plant but could no longer find the military orders to maintain it. His answer was to begin manufacturing double-barreled sporting shotguns using machine methods.

Throughout this period Bonehill patented a series of gun actions and innovations that appear to have been developed cheaply, simply, and with machine manufacturing in mind. In 1877, he introduced a top lever gun (Number 3,718 of 1877) that could be made cheaply and sent a salesman to the United States with samples to sound out the market. The following year, he patented an action (Number 2,323 of 1878) that became the basis of one version of what became known as the "Interchangeable" gun. Throughout the next four years, Bonehill's son, Christopher George Bonehill Jr., traveled to America securing orders. Orders for 7,000 guns were taken in 1880 and 12,000 in 1881 for the "improved-top lever gun."

This may have been a reference to an action (Number 1,952 of 1880) Bonehill patented with a toolmaker, W. J. Mathews. Three other patents were taken out in 1884, the first for a "through lump" (Number 8,469 of 1884) made "from one piece of metal suitably forged and shaped," the second (Number 8,471 of 1884) for a fore-end and action, and the third (Number 12,586 of 1884), shared by the works manager, C. G. Simpson, featuring a gun action and appearing to be an effort at simplification.

By 1887, Bonehill's machine-made, double-barreled sporting shotgun had become a hammerless boxlock design and was known as the "Belmont" interchangeable. It was an established Birmingham tradition to allow other makers to market a successful design under their own names for a fee, but Bonehill resisted this concept. Instead, he offered the Belmont solely under his own name and retailed it through iron mongers. It's tempting to speculate that this was a distribution system Bonehill was familiar with from his father's days. The move was unpopular with traditional retailers, who threatened to boycott other Bonehill products. And judging from the size of his catalogs, which are as thick as Bibles, there were many items to boycott.

The McKinley tariff of 1890 delivered a staggering blow to Bonehill's still-growing enterprise. The tariff of 35 percent plus six dollars was intended to protect a nascent American sporting arms industry and to some degree was responsible for the success of such machine-made guns as the Fox and Parker. Bonehill never again found a large market for his inexpensive interchangeable guns and instead appears to have concentrated his efforts on rifles and particularly air rifles. In 1895, he patented a Martini-action rifle (Number 12,578 of 1895) with A. Tunstall that later became the basis of the famous W. W. Greener "GP" series of single-barreled shotguns. A rear sight suitable for "a rifle or air gun" followed (Number 22,658 of 1905) and in 1907 and 1908, working with H. Horner, he patented (Number 15,917 for 1907 and Number 13,567 for 1908) what would become his "Britannia" air rifle. The Britannia was said to be so powerful that it would literally blow apart a .177 pellet.

During the First World War, the "Belmont Firearms & Gun Barrel Works" produced luminous sights for Lewis machine guns, demonstration-model magazine rifles, and airplane engine parts. Bonehill was also asked to manufacture .303 rifle barrels but insisted on guarantees similar to those he had extracted from the French government almost half a century earlier. The Ministry of Munitions refused and confiscated his boring machines for use elsewhere until after the war.

Christopher George Bonehill died on the 14 January 1920 in the affluent Birmingham suburb of Edgbaston. He was eighty-nine years old and had only retired the previous July. (An earlier attempt at retirement, when he was forty, had ended in failure when he became bored with the gentleman farmer's life after a few years.) The *Sporting Goods Review* called him the "father of the Birmingham gun trade" on account of his seniority and the length of his career. The business was carried on by two of Bonehill's sons, the eldest of his sixteen children.

In 1928, the sons, A. A. and C. G. Bonehill, together with a Mr. A. Tunstall, patented an ejector (Number 323,726) that became an extractor when a button was pressed. The three men came together again in 1930, when they patented (Number 338,800) a single-barreled semi-hammerless shotgun that was probably intended for machine manufacture. Sometime in the early 1940s, C. G. Bonehill occupied smaller premises in Price Street before disappearing entirely.

A. A. BROWN & SONS

Only a handful of Birmingham gunmakers survived the Great Depression, the Second World War, and the period of austerity that followed. But one was established, survived, and ultimately succeeded during this difficult period for the trade.

Albert Arthur Brown was the son of John Joseph Brown, a gunmaker who had at one time worked for Webley & Scott, B.S.A., and W. W. Greener and who ended his working career as resident caretaker with Greener. A. A. Brown was an action filer who carved the leaf fences for the Birmingham trade. Although English gunmakers are a conservative lot by nature, not given to decorating their products with the bas-relief so familiar on Teutonic weapons, better-quality sidelocks are occasionally found with ivy, fern, and oak leaves chased to the fences. It is difficult, demanding work requiring a hammer and chisel instead of the normal hand-held graver, but Albert Arthur Brown was considered one of the few men capable of executing it.

In 1930, after working for F. E. & H. Rogers in Loveday Street and just a few months after the collapse of the U. S. Stock Exchange precipitated the world's worst economic crisis, Albert Arthur established his own business at 27 Whittal Street in what was then the heart of the gun quarter.

A very wealthy few managed to breeze through the Depression in magnificent style, ordering best guns as usual. Since A. A. Brown made a specialty of building high-quality guns that were ultimately signed by more prestigious firms, he appears to have survived by virtue of the trickle-down effect.

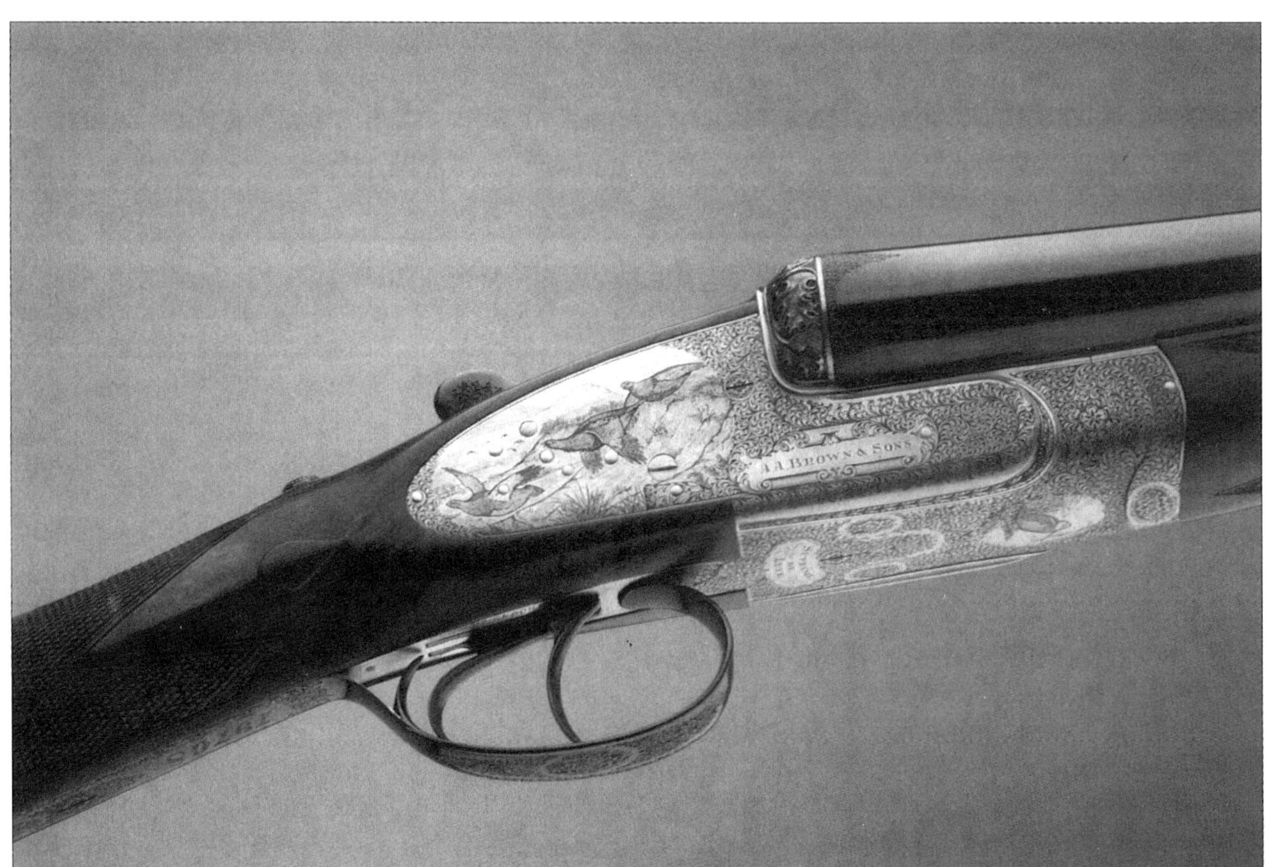

The rounded underside is a signature feature of A. A. Brown guns. (A. A. Brown & Sons)

On the eve of the Second World War, Albert Arthur was joined by his eldest son, Albert Henry, born in 1913. A few months later a second son, Sidney Charles, born in 1916, also came on board.

During the Second World War, when sport shooting was largely suspended, the family firm worked on weapons components for the War Department and made machine tools for that era's ultimate weapon, the Spitfire.

Due to Hermann Goering's redevelopment of Whittal Street, A. A. Brown moved around the corner to 4 Sand Street in the mid '40s. And during the austere period immediately after the war, when the steel tubes used to make shotgun barrels were unavailable, the Browns once again developed a strategy for survival. It is worth mentioning that Britain's industries were on a wartime footing for many years after Germany's surrender, and steel tubing that had been an important element of the armament's procurement took a long time to be rerouted into what were considered nonessential, leisure-oriented crafts like the building of sporting guns.

In 1945, Curry & Keen purchased the name, workshop, tools, and components of the established E. Anson & Co. on Steelhouse Lane. Among the materials purchased were parts for an air pistol, the Anson Star, now considered a rare collector's item, which Joe Curry asked the Browns to assemble. It was temporary work but appears to have provided the inspiration for an air pistol of the company's own design.

The "Abas Major" was of concentric design like the Anson Star, which inspired it. This means the compression cylinder envel-

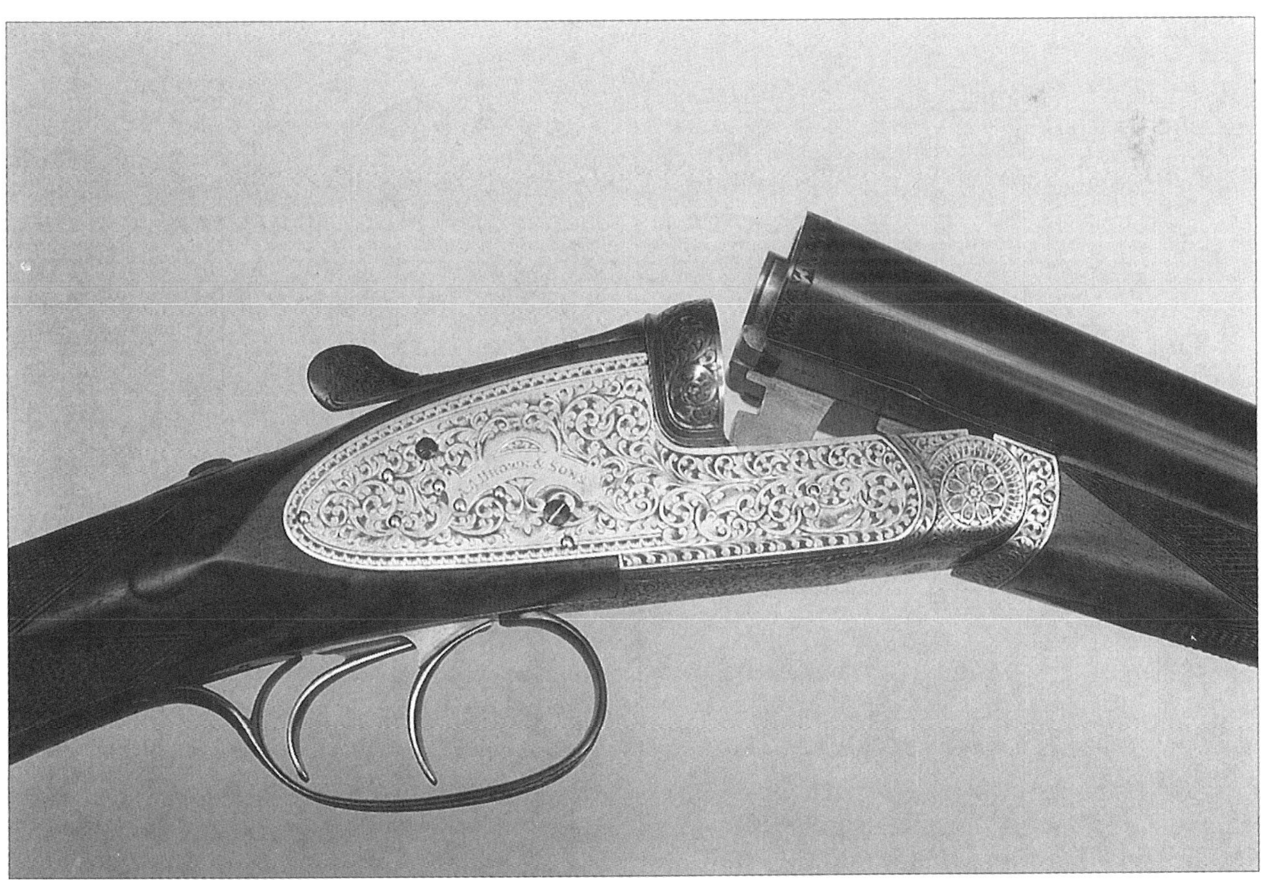

One of a pair of Supreme sidelock ejectors with cutaway scroll engraving by Les Jones, built in 1970. (Keith Flannery)

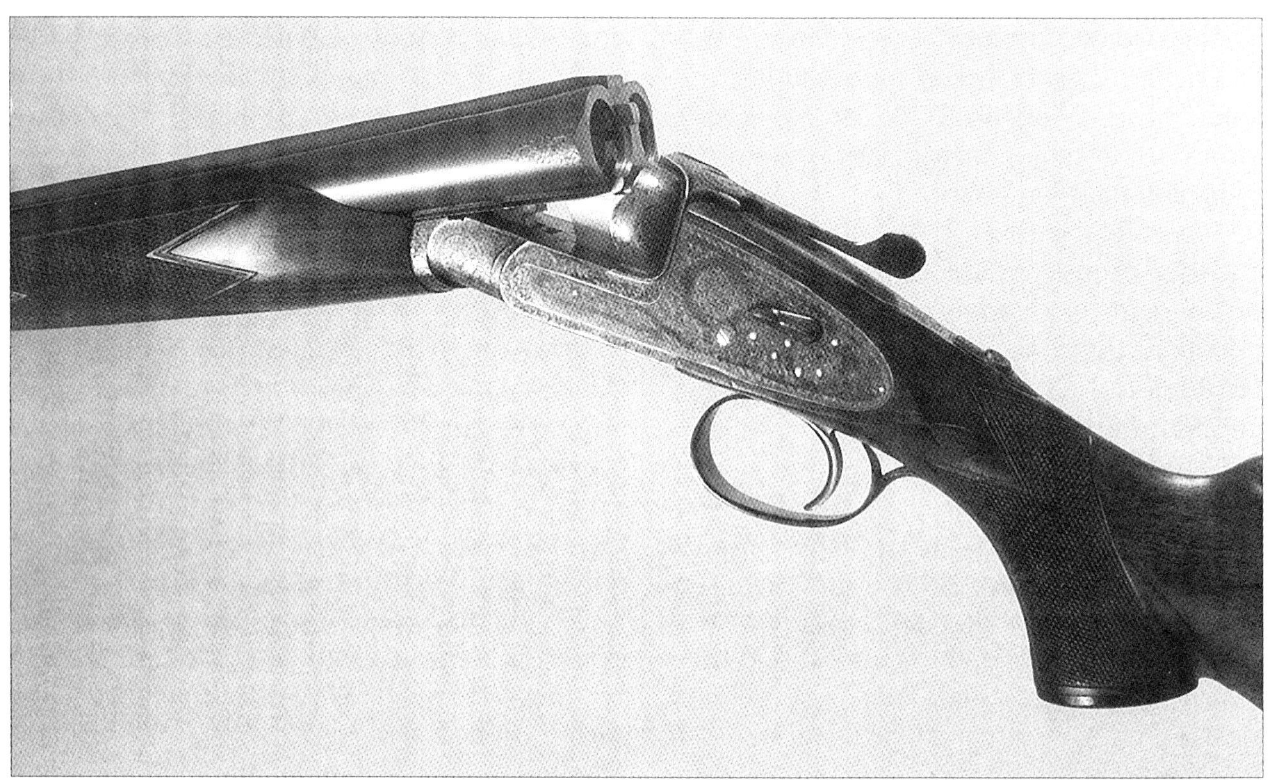

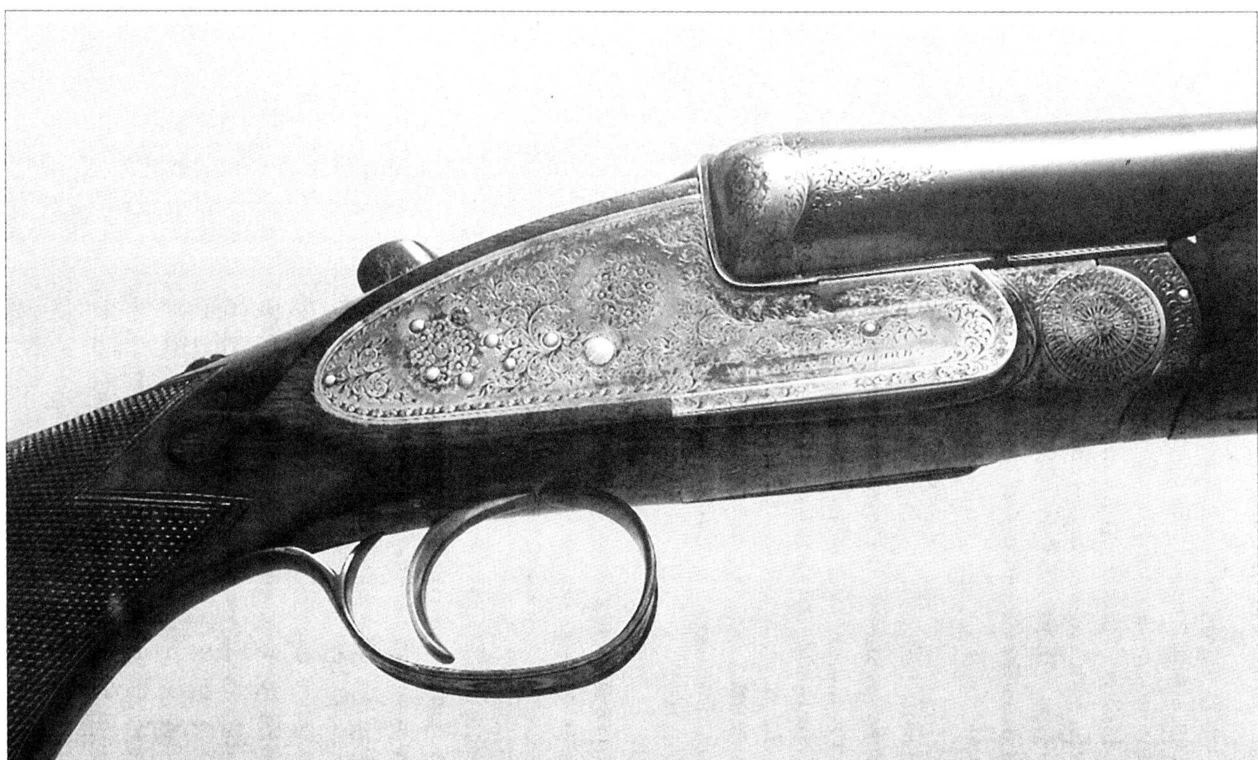

A Westley Richards single-trigger target gun built by A. A. Brown and Sons during its tenure at Bournebrook. The gun is something of a hybrid, with Holland & Holland-type hand-detachable locks, Purdey-like engraving, and the ABAS trademark. (Vic Venters)

ops the barrels, providing a compact design. In his classic tome *Gas, Air and Spring Guns of the World*, W. H. B. Smith calls the Abas Major "a better air pistol than most of the designs currently being made in Germany today. . . ." The visitor to Brown's current premises at 1 Snake Lane, Alverchurch, can see an example of the Abas Major fully engraved in bold foliate scroll in the manner of a Holland & Holland "Royal." It is the highest-quality British air pistol most visitors will ever see.

In 1948 tubes once more became available and the company ran down air-pistol production to again build shotguns. The firm's record books for the 1950s and '60s are replete with guns made by A. A. Brown & Sons for other makers. A recent visitor was shown entries for Holland & Holland, John Harper, and even Alex Martin "ribless" guns. Robin Brown explained that the Browns had made "many of the ribless guns for Alex Martin" and many of the XXVs sold by E. J. Churchill.

Alex Martin advertised that its ribless guns were "lighter, stronger and better balanced than guns of ordinary construction." Other advantages claimed were:

> 1) A quarter pound of useless metal is removed.
> 2) Removing this weight from the barrels makes the gun lighter forward, giving the left arm less work, more control, and an easier swing.
> 3) The usual hollow space between the barrels in which corrosion can take place undetected is eliminated.

Guns in which the barrels were constructed with spacers at the breech, muzzle, and mid-barrel have a long tradition with Scotland's gunmakers—both Daniel Fraser and James MacNaughton made them. It is therefore a little ironic that by the early 1950s Alexander Martin, like most of the provincial British gun trade, was having its guns made in Birmingham.

Robin Brown explained how the Churchill firm would order guns of identical specifications from different makers—Baker, Wrights, or Brown—that were engraved and finished except that the stock, though inletted and attached, remained in a rough and unfinished state. When a pair of guns was needed, Robert Churchill would select two likely candidates from the rack and have a stocker set about carving the wood to fit the customer. Robin's father, Sidney, said it was "pure hell" for the woodworker, but it meant finished guns could be ready in four or five weeks. On 9 January 1931, the Prince of Wales ordered a pair of Churchill "Premier" XXVs, and the guns were miraculously delivered five days later. Robin and Sidney Brown's explanation of how Churchill guns were made would account for the short delivery time.

Throughout the postwar period the Browns continued to build guns for the trade. Perhaps because they were industrious at a time when much of Britain wanted to rest after the exhausting task of defeating Hitler's Germany—or perhaps because they had a mature, highly skilled workforce dedicated to building the finest guns available—they flourished where others had failed. When Joseph Asbury, which machined many of the actions for the trade, went under, A. A. Brown acquired its machinery, giving Brown the capacity to machine its own actions from the raw forging.

Albert Arthur Brown retired in 1957, but new blood arrived four years later when Sidney's son, Robin, joined the family firm as an apprentice stocker.

In the early 1960s, much of the gun quarter was redeveloped to make way for Birmingham's inner-ring road. It was a time of turmoil for the trade: Shooting was unfashionable, and apprentices were hard to

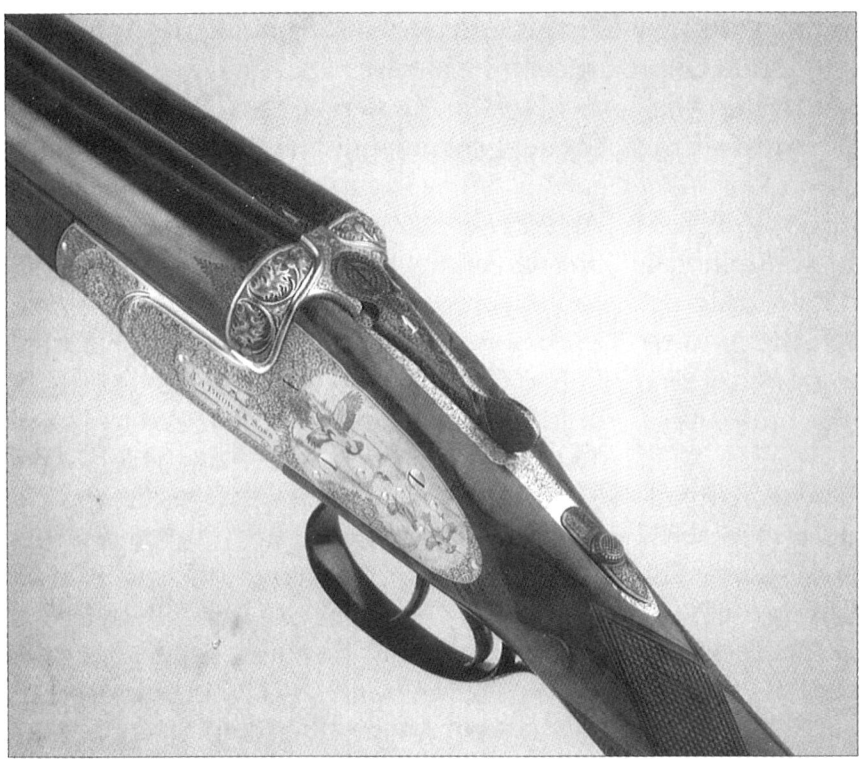

One of a trio of Supreme Deluxe game guns with game-scene engraving by Keith Thomas. (A. A. Brown & Sons)

find. Many well-known names—R. B. Rodda & Co., Bentley & Playfair, and Clabrough & Johnstone—disappeared rather than face the challenges of finding new premises, markets, and a work force. A. A. Brown's Sand Street premises became a multilevel parking structure, but the company found a new home within the Westley Richards firm out at Bournebrook. Westley Richards continued to build its own Anson and Deeley designed guns, particularly the hand-detachable lock model known to American collectors as the "droplock." However, for approximately fourteen years A. A. Brown built the Westley Richards best sidelock ejector gun.

Another change of premises in 1974—this time to the country village of Alvechurch, fourteen miles south of Birmingham—gave Brown an opportunity to change direction. Rather than continue to build a range of guns for the trade, A. A. Brown would henceforth make only best-grade sidelock ejectors, plus the occasional best boxlock, with a view to

capturing a share of the bespoke or custom market. This is not a decision the Browns can take full credit for. It was partly a result of the Trade Description Act passed into law by the British government, which demands accuracy in product identification. The Browns interpreted this law to mean that they would no longer be allowed to build guns to which other makers put their names. However, the practice of well-known makers having guns built in the trade continues to this day, with outworkers apparently enjoying the same legal status as subcontractors.

The decision to leave an urban gunmaking center for a village mentioned in the Doomsday book (circa 1085-86) was a courageous one back in 1974. However, the Browns held an advantage: Most of the work on their guns was done in-house. Only the tubes were bought in and only the engraving was farmed out—and only some of that, because they had a house engraver named Les Jones. Today, other independent gunmakers such as Alan Crew, Peter Chapman, and Peter Nelson have followed Brown's example, realizing that in the age of phone and fax, proximity is no longer essential to good gunmaking.

The decision to build only best guns to clients' specifications has also proven prescient. With most of the "off-the-shelf "guns today coming from Italy or Japan, the remains of the Birmingham trade are polarized between repairs on the one hand and building best bespoke guns on the other, with the latter doing better than the former. Brown's best gun is the model Supreme Deluxe, which uses a self-opening system similar to the Holland & Holland and a method of hand-detachable sidelocks like the Holland & Holland "Royal."

If the mechanics of the Supreme Deluxe are similar to a Holland & Holland, the aesthetic is entirely A. A. Brown. The semi-rounded body of the Supreme Deluxe developed out of a customer's request for a gun that was "already worn." Slightly domed lock plates and a double bar to the action add to the effect of a rounded gun. It is this roundness that gives A. A. Brown guns their organic feel and distinctive appearance. Apart from the engraving and the rough barrel tubes, virtually all of the work, including lockmaking, is done in-house by Sidney and his son Robin. They are aided by Harold Scandrett, a veteran gunmaker with more than forty years of experience with the firm. The Supreme Deluxe is built entirely to customer specifications, using chopper lump barrels, actions hand-filed from a solid forging, and exhibition-grade walnut of either French or Turkish origin. Best-gun features include disc set strikers and gold plating of the lockwork and the self-opening mechanism. This is not done for cosmetic reasons, but rather for corrosion control and ease of maintenance. Engraving in the past was executed in-house by Les Jones. Today, engraving on Brown guns is the work of modern master Keith Thomas, but clients can elect to go with any one of a stable of British engravers. Customers have a choice of case-hardened or polished finish, with any combination of bouquet and scroll or game-scene engraving.

Brown will build the Supreme Deluxe in any standard gauge in three weights: as a standard game gun, as a lightweight game gun, or as a slightly heavier pigeon gun. On average, Brown builds six to ten guns per year. In the past, the firm has also built several com- memorative pieces—a 28-bore for the Queen's Silver Jubilee, a pair of 20-bores for the same event, and a magnificent pair of 20-bores commemorating Matthew Boulton, an important figure in the Industrial Revolution and Birmingham's most famous silversmith. Prices start at about £20,000 for the standard game gun, and delivery time is about two years. Significantly, about 80 percent of Brown's guns are purchased within Britain, traditionally a market where intrinsic quality at a fair price has been more important than a prestigious name. Most of the remaining 20 percent are sold to buyers in the United States.

All of the guns made in Alvechurch are recognizable by the ABAS trademark found on the action flats; first used as the name for an air pistol, it is an acronym for A. Brown and Sons. The ABAS markings are also a reliable, but not foolproof, way to tell whether your gun, ostensibly by another maker, was actually made by A. A. Brown. The method isn't foolproof because in the past some retailers insisted that Brown omit the ABAS mark in order to create the impression that they—the retailers—built the gun.

A. A. Brown & Sons has come a long way since the days it made airguns, and the quality of its workmanship has continued to rise throughout the '70s, '80s, and into the '90s. Because so few are made, the emphasis is on making every gun the best yet. As long as there are customers who have the taste and resources to invest £24,000 in a Supreme Deluxe, A. A. Brown will not only survive but prosper.

B. S. A.

Until the Industrial Revolution, all guns were made by hand; then, in the last century, a schism occurred: The huge demand for weapons with interchangeable parts, together with the development of machine tools, combined to make possible the mass-produced gun.

Not surprisingly, the martial potential for this method of manufacture was quickly exploited. Most military weapons have been mass-produced ever since. High-quality hunting guns, on the other hand, have continued to be built one at a time by craftsmen.

In the early 1800s, Birmingham's gunmakers began to see that in the future the army's weapons would be made with the aid of machine tools, much as they were in the United States. Men who had previously worked on government contracts in times of war and sporting guns in times of peace saw that change was inevitable. Small independent gunmakers who had once been awarded lucrative contracts from the Board of Ordnance watched as the British government built its own gun factory at Enfield.

Slowly, a change came about: Military contracts came less often as the government made more of its own weapons. Clearly, what was needed was a factory in Birmingham on the same scale as the one in Enfield that could compete for government work.

In 1861, a dozen or so independent gunmakers came together in a company incorporated as The Birmingham Small Arms Company Limited (B.S.A.). B.S.A. had its origins in an association known as The Birmingham Gun Trade, organized in 1854 to negotiate collectively on behalf of the city's gunmakers for government work.

According to an unsigned and, as far as I know, previously unpublished manuscript in the Birmingham City Library, the:

> Birmingham Small Arms Trade Association attempted to counter the competition of the machine made arms by telling each other how very much superior hand made arms really were. It required a combination of unpleasant facts—an alarming diminution in trade and a shortage of skilled labor, consequent upon an eight months strike—to convince the master gunsmiths of Birmingham that they must either invest in machinery or go out of business. Eventually the trade association took the plunge. A meeting was held in June 1861, and a resolution was passed 'to form a company to make guns by machinery' and 'to order without delay, from America, the machinery necessary for the making of the woodwork of rifles . . .'

Thus was the Birmingham Small Arms Company born. The original shareholders were:

Joseph Bourne (sixty shares)
Joseph Rock Cooper (forty-eight shares)
John Dent Goodman (forty-seven shares)
Issac Hollis (ninety-five shares)
Charles Playfair (thirty shares)
John Field Swinburn (110 shares)
William Tranter (forty-five shares)
Thomas Turner (ninety-five shares)
Thomas Wilson (sixty shares)
Benjamin Woodward (twenty shares)
Henry Woodward (twenty shares)

After raising capital of £50,000, divided into 2,000 shares worth £25 each, the company bought twenty-five acres of land at Small Heath near Birmingham. Within two years the factory was operating at full capacity, and "within ten years the manufacture of army rifles by the traditional hand methods had virtually ceased." The quote is from Clive Harris's useful little book *The History of the Birmingham Gun Barrel Proof House*, which also says the company was forced to diversify into bicycles and cycles, owing to the "fluctuating character" of War Office work.

Harris's comments are understatement: B.S.A. was threatened with catastrophe every time peace broke out but managed to survive through a series of reorganizations and amalgamations. The cycle of boom and bust started in 1863 with the cancellation of a huge order from the U.S., which was almost immediately made up by a contract for Short Enfield rifles for the Ottoman Turks. Throughout the late nineteenth century, B.S.A. won government contracts for the Snider rifle in 1869, the Martini Henry in 1871, and the Lee Metford in 1892. In between orders the company appears to have survived by manufacturing bicycles.

The trends of the nineteenth century continued for the first half of the twentieth, when B.S.A. had full orders during World War I for Lewis machine guns and World War II, when they built, among other things, the Browning machine gun. In between they suffered the same problem they'd had previously: insufficient orders. The Twenties may have roared, but not for B.S.A.

To overcome its economic problems the company introduced a motorcycle and a cheap machine-made sporting shotgun. The shotgun had probably been planned before World War I; certainly it was based on a design patented in 1911. In that year a prolific designer named G. Norman, who worked for B.S.A. and held dozens of firearms patents, registered a design (Patent Number 15, 697 of 1911) in which the barrels were secured together by a "part circular dovetailed or like projection on one barrel engaging corresponding recess in the other barrel." Like most of Norman's patents, it was registered jointly with B.S.A. and no doubt employer and employee shared the remuneration it generated. The specifications went on to describe how "The parts may be further locked together by a screw . . . passing through the halves of the lump, and, as an additional security, the parts may be soft soldered."

Writing about the design in 1931, Major Sir Gerald Burrard made the point that:

> . . . the cost of cutting out the dovetails to an accurate fit by hand would be altogether excessive. Where mass production is carried out, special machinery can be installed for doing this work, but it would not pay the ordinary gunmaker to set up such costly machines, as he would not turn out enough guns to get back sufficient capital on the

machine, and he would be working all the time at a dead loss. So, from the point of view of economic manufacture, this method is only suitable for a factory where guns are manufactured in great numbers.

B.S.A. had the capacity to produce the gun, and they held the patent; the only additional requirement was to create the market. In 1922, the company took out advertising in the *Daily Mail, The Daily Mirror,* and the *Sunday Chronicle,* together with a full-page ad in the Christmas issue of *The Sporting Goods Review,* offering the basic model for eleven guineas, or less than half what a basic handmade gun cost at the time. This same ad told potential retailers, "Blocks for your advertising in local papers will also be supplied, free of charge, if requested." Advertisements later appeared in *Game and Gun* that ended with the suggestion, "Please write for catalog. "

The catalog featured five models of the Non-Ejector model at thirteen guineas each, the Ejector model at sixteen guineas, the Ejector model-de-lux at nineteen guineas, the Special Game model fitted with 25-inch barrels at £22, ten shillings, and the Wildfowling model with a choice of non-ejector at fourteen guineas or ejector at seventeen guineas. Illustrative diagrams showed the method of dovetailing the barrels together, and much was made of the metallurgy. The catalog emphasized the use of various types of steel thought appropriate for different tasks. The barrels were made of Jessop's fluid pressed steel from Sheffield; the body was of nickel steel; the cocking lever, sears, and tumblers were of chrome vanadium steel; and the springs were of special high-tension steel. A diagram showed the method of locking the barrels to the action, which was a conventional Purdey underbolt operated by the normal Scott spindle and top lever. All of the examples I have seen were stamped with the piled-arms trademark of B.S.A. and have a plain blued finish rather than the conventional color case-hardening.

The gun appears to have been a modest success in the colonies, but it never really caught on in England. This may have been, as Major Burrard pointed out, because "the thickness of the metal necessary for an efficient dovetail results in the inside walls of the barrels being very thick, which means wide barrels and a clumsy gun. . . ." The B.S.A. was a coarse and clunky gun that must have caused some muffled tittering among the sophisticates on driven shoots, but it did generate one successful imitator. The design for joining the barrels and the blued action was adopted by Winchester in the U.S. for its Model 21, which became a great favorite of wildfowlers and trapshooters.

WILLIAM CASHMORE

Before the development and popularization of machine-made, mass-marketed guns, Birmingham was gunmaker to the world. From a one-quarter square mile of grubby real estate close to the heart of central Birmingham, a few dozen small gunmakers dominated the global market. Some made a special effort in a specific area and came to dominate a very regional market: R. B. Rodda of Stafford Street sold a great many guns from its shop in Calcutta, which was then the capital of British India; J. P. Clabrough of Price Street controlled the lucrative San Francisco trade; William Cashmore of Steelhouse Lane concentrated on the burgeoning communities of southeast Australia.

William Cashmore was the most successful member of a dynasty of gunmaking Cashmores who thrived in Birmingham and West Bromwich in the nineteenth century. Mike Newland of the Birmingham Museum of Science & Industry writes, "I have been able to trace no less than eleven, most, if not all of these, I believe to be related in some way." The earliest was Edward Cashmore, a pistol maker of Virgins End, West Bromwich. Also

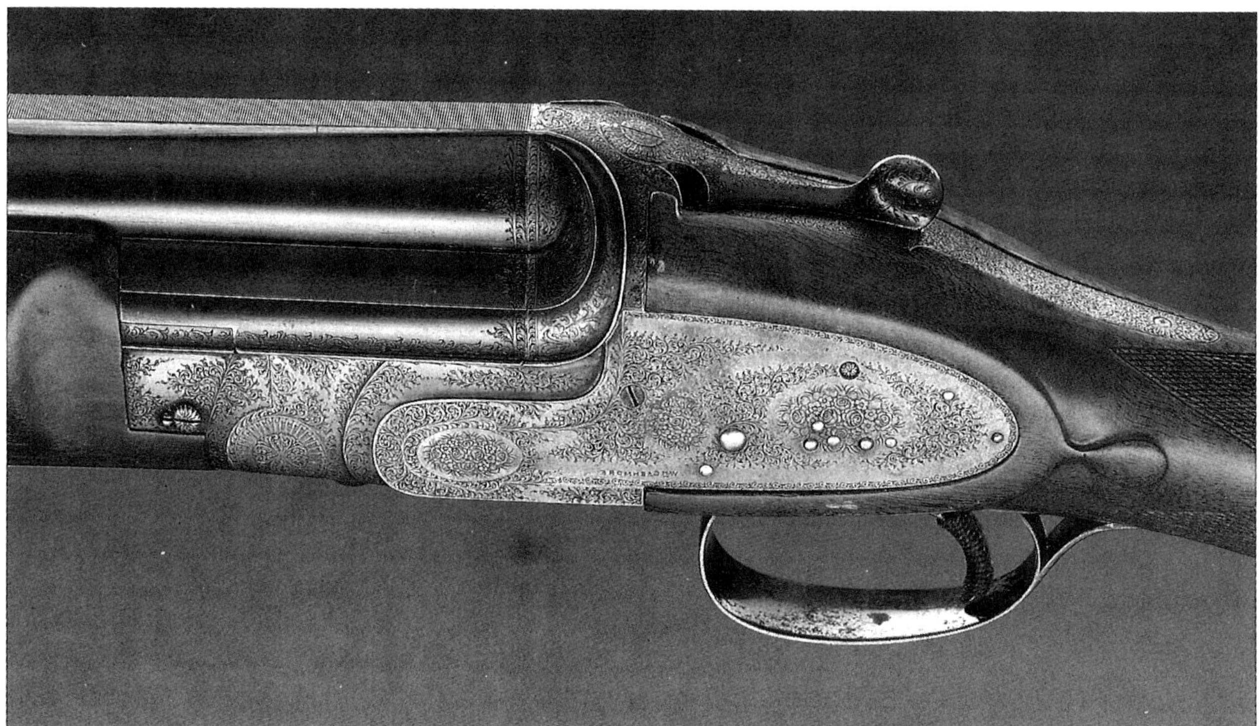

This over-and-under with phallic bar to the action may have been made in Germany for William Cashmore.

of West Bromwich was Mrs. Elizabeth Cashmore, who was registered as a gun and pistol maker in Reform Street during 1871-72.

Unfortunately, no obvious connection is apparent between the West Bromwich Cashmores and William Cashmore, who learned his trade with Benjamin Swift. Swift is something of a mystery, despite having been called a "leading member of the trade" by *The Sporting Goods Review*. William Cashmore started on his own account in 1835 with premises in Newton Street, on a site later occupied by the Birmingham County Court. Cashmore lived on the premises, and it was here that the second William Cashmore was born in 1857.

The following year the company moved to Steelhouse Lane, and it was here that the second William Cashmore entered his father's employment in the early 1870s to be followed by his younger brother, Arthur, approximately ten years later. In the last quarter of the nineteenth century there was a strong worldwide interest in live-pigeon and "inanimate bird" or clay-pigeon shooting. The target shots of the day demanded, and got, heavy guns capable of firing oversize charges. Every company in Birmingham and many located elsewhere built guns to meet the demand. By the late 1880s and certainly by the early 1890s, Messrs. Cashmore were building live-pigeon and heavy trap guns and concentrating their sales efforts in New South Wales, Victoria, South Australia, and Tasmania.

The Australian venture was the work of eldest son, William Cashmore II, who sailed to Sydney and started an agency for his father's firm. It must have been successful because Messrs. Cashmore were awarded first-prize medals at exhibitions in Adelaide in 1887-88, Melbourne in 1888-89, and Tasmania in 1891-92. The firm considered these prizes for quality of workmanship sufficiently important that they became decorations on its trade label. Shooting honors

too were forthcoming in the region, with Cashmore guns in the hands of the winners at the championship of Australasia, the Canonite trophy in Melbourne, and the championship of New South Wales. Even the celebrated Dr. Carver used a Cashmore when he defeated L. Clarke at Brighton, Victoria, on 1 December 1891.

At about this time, nitro or "semi-smokeless" powders were being introduced from Germany, and their advantages of increased velocity and better visibility for a second shot were quickly appreciated by money shots like Dr. Carver. What was required was a gun design of unprecedented strength capable of handling the powerful new loads.

In 1894, Samuel Mills, an action filer of 83 Prince Albert Street, Small Heath, Birmingham, patented an action (Number 19,300 of 1894) that had a conventional Purdey underbolt except that only the forward lump was utilized while the rear lump was dispensed with in favor of a pair of pivoted, hook-shaped pawls that hung on the outside of the action and engaged a pair of flanges on the rear of the barrels. It was just what William Cashmore was looking for.

Though not exactly elegant, these Mills guns are extremely strong, with the stress being distributed over a wide area. In 1895 William Cashmore patented an improvement to the Mills system (Number 17,040 of 1895) in which a pair of "lumps or projections" were added to the sides of the action body behind the joint pin that butted against the flanges on the rear of the barrels. The inventor claimed these additions would "very greatly assist the said front joint pin in resisting the longitudinal pressure of the explosion and thus prevent undue wear and strain on the said joint pin."

This new incarnation of the Mills system was promoted as the "Cashmore Nitro" shotgun; it must have created confidence at a time when the gun-buying public was unsure whether their guns could withstand the high pressures of the new nitro powders. The gun was such a success that it was the only model mentioned by name in William Cashmore's obituary when he died in 1920. It was built in what today would be considered magnum configurations, with 12-bore guns chambered for 3-inch and even 3¼-inch cases in an age when the standard game gun had 2½-inch chambers and even a live-pigeon gun had chambers of only 2¾ inches.

The same year Cashmore patented his improvements to the Mills system, he also introduced a single trigger (Patent Number 24,426 of 1995) that pivoted sideways and could be pushed to the right and pulled to fire the right barrel or pushed to the left and pulled to fire the left barrel. The following year, together with one G. Brazier, he patented a safety (Number 25,994 of 1896) in which a second safety sear engaged a bent in the main sear to effectively halve the chance of an accidental discharge.

William Cashmore was elected guardian of the Birmingham Proof House in 1893 and served as treasurer from 1913 until his retirement to the seaside town of Weston-super-Mare about 1918. He died there on 19 January 1920 and was succeeded by Albert Cashmore. The company survived the Great Depression and World War II, only to succumb sometime in the 1960s.

J. P. CLABROUGH

The casual student of the Birmingham trade could be forgiven for thinking the gunmaking gene was passed from father to son as surely as is eye color. Most of the city's gunmakers were the sons of gunmakers, even when their origins were provincial. William Wellington Greener and Charles Playfair both founded dynasties in "the city of a thousand trades" after apprenticing with their fathers in North British cities—Newcastle and Aberdeen, respectively. Another northerner who appears to fit in this same mold was John Plumb Clabrough. The only difference was that Clabrough came to Birmingham from Yorkshire via San Francisco.

When J. P. Clabrough was a young man, he emigrated to the United States, crossed the entire country, and immediately found work in a San Francisco gun shop. The ease with which he gained employment suggests that he may have previously acquired gunmaking experience. In 1862, when Wilson & Evans of Sacramento opened a store in San Francisco, Clabrough was taken on as a gunsmith. He was twenty-eight at the time, and though he may have gained some of his knowledge in America, it is likely that he'd served an apprenticeship in England. Throughout his life, Clabrough claimed Yorkshire as his birthplace, and the Post Office Directory shows an M. Carlton Clabrough working as a gunmaker in Selby, Yorkshire, in 1857. Perhaps this was J. P.'s father and the young man learned his trade in Selby before setting out to make his fortune in the New World.

In any event, he found himself in San Francisco, first working for Wilson & Evans and in 1864-1866 for Robert Liddle & Co. The Liddle company enjoyed a local reputation for shotguns that won awards at the San Francisco Mechanics Fair; however, it is impossible to know just how much Clabrough contributed to Liddle's success.

San Francisco in the third quarter of the nineteenth century was one of the fastest-growing cities in the fastest-growing country on the planet. Millionaires were being created daily, and the newly rich took up the fashionable sport of live-pigeon shooting and the recently introduced inanimate-bird shooting. Meanwhile, market gunners shot the ducks and shore birds that wintered in San Francisco Bay for the city's restaurants and hotels, and quail were sent by train from as far away as Arizona. Both the wealthy sportsman and the meat hunter needed shotguns, and the demand must have been enormous.

No doubt realizing the potential, Clabrough opened his own shop at 630 Montgomery Street in 1867. Initially, he shared the premises with a jeweler, but when business increased, he acquired the entire store. In 1870, Clabrough invited his brother, Joseph, to join him and the firm became "Clabrough and Bro." The following year, the brothers returned to England while a third brother, George, managed the store.

In England the brothers established a workshop in the heart of the Birmingham gun quarter with which to supply their San Francisco demand. By the mid 1870s, the Clabrough brothers had two factories—one at 8 Whittal Street and the second at 15 St. Mary's Row—from which they supplied over 1,000 guns a year to depots in New York, Philadelphia, Chicago, and San Francisco.

Sometime in the late '70s, George Clabrough died, leaving the San Francisco operation without a manager. Fortunately, John Clabrough had met William Golcher, the son of a Darlaston lockmaker, who had emigrated to Philadelphia with his father when he was only a boy. In 1877, Golcher had retired from gunmaking and was on a visit to Birmingham when he met John Clabrough. No doubt because of their shared experience as emigrant gunmakers, the two men quickly became friends. When Golcher agreed to come out of retirement to manage the San Francisco store, it became "Clabrough & Golcher."

By the late 1870s, it was becoming increasingly clear that the hammerless gun was more than just a novelty. In 1878, John Plumb Clabrough patented a hammerless gun action (Number 3,611 of 1878) with a coil-spring bolting system and hammers and mainsprings attached to the trigger plate. Though

J.P. CLABROUGH COMPANIES

YEAR	COMPANY NAME	ADDRESS
1871	J. P. CLABROUGH	5 NEW BLDGS, PRICE ST.
1873	J. P. CLABROUGH & BROTHERS	8 WHITTAL ST.
1880	CLABROUGH BROTHERS	15 ST. MARY'S ROW
1893-99	J. P. CLABROUGH & BROTHERS & JOHNSTONE	8 WHITTAL ST.
1900-01	J. P. CLABROUGH & JOHNSTONE	7½ ST. MARY'S ROW
1902-14	J. P. CLABROUGH & JOHNSTONE	3 PRICE ST.
1915-31	J. P. CLABROUGH & JOHNSTONE	16 & 17 LOVEDAY ST.
1932-37	J. P. CLABROUGH & JOHNSTONE	91 & 92 LOWER LOVEDAY ST.

Clabrough patented the design in England, it was actually the work of Julius Bluemel. Bluemel, an employee of the Clabroughs at their San Francisco shop, patented the design in his own name in the U.S. (Number 210,905 of 1878.) In England, the patent never went beyond provisional status, which may be some indication of its worth.

An even greater measure of the Bluemel patent's value, or lack of it, might be the fact that in 1882, Clabrough purchased the exclusive U.S. rights to another hammerless action. This was the Richard Ellis and Henry Scott (Number 2,816 of 1879) action in which "the hammers are raised to the cocked position by pressing a thumb plate," which in the patent drawings appears identical to a modern tang safety. This action was registered in the U.S. in the name of Henry Scott (Number 252,703 of 1882) and assigned to J. P. Clabrough but it appears to have been no more successful than the previous one. Always in search of commercial success, Clabrough purchased the American rights to yet another action, but this time he hit the jackpot.

In the previous year, two brothers, John Thomas Rogers and John Rogers, action filers of 78 Lower Tower Street, Birmingham, had protected an idea (Patent Number 397 of 1881) of "cocking levers bearing directly against the barrels and turning upon another centre than that upon which the barrels hinge." This time the quote is not from the patent specifications but from W. W. Greener's tome *The Gun and its Development*, which went on to compare the Rogers patent with the Anson and Deeley, adding:

> This permits detachable locks of the ordinary type being used, and is consequently much employed by those gunmakers who prefer the lock mechanism when arranged upon a side plate than when fitted into the breech action body as in the Anson and Deeley gun.

The Rogers patent became the standard British gun-trade method of cocking a sidelock. It was widely adopted by the trade for use in bar-action as well as back-action guns and generated considerable royalties for the Rogers brothers. The patent drawings show a flat back action with back-acting mainsprings and leg of mutton lockplates. This exact configuration was adopted by Clabrough and became a paradigm for the company's hammerless guns. All of the hammerless guns built by J. P. Clabrough or Clabrough Brothers encountered today are built on this action, and it was without a doubt the firm's most successful design.

In 1890, the U. S. government introduced the punitive McKinley tariff (35 percent plus six dollars per gun), which, while nurturing a nascent domestic gun trade, effectively destroyed the business between Birmingham and San Francisco. In 1893 John Plumb Clabrough sold his Birmingham workshops to Douglas V. Johnstone, and retired to San Francisco, where he died two years later at age sixty-one.

Johnstone continued on in Birmingham, and in 1910 he and a prolific inventor named A. H. Hill, trading as Clabrough and Johnstone and using the "TENGO" trademark, patented a means of attaching the lockplates to a gun (Patent Number 26,071 of 1910). A note in the *Sporting Goods Review* the following year introduced the new hand-detachable locks, which could be removed cocked or uncocked. They don't appear to have been a great success, but Johnstone soldiered on, making guns under the Clabrough name, eventually succumbing in 1937 at the height of the Great Depression.

WILLIAM FORD

By the mid nineteenth century, the Birmingham gun quarter was a warren of

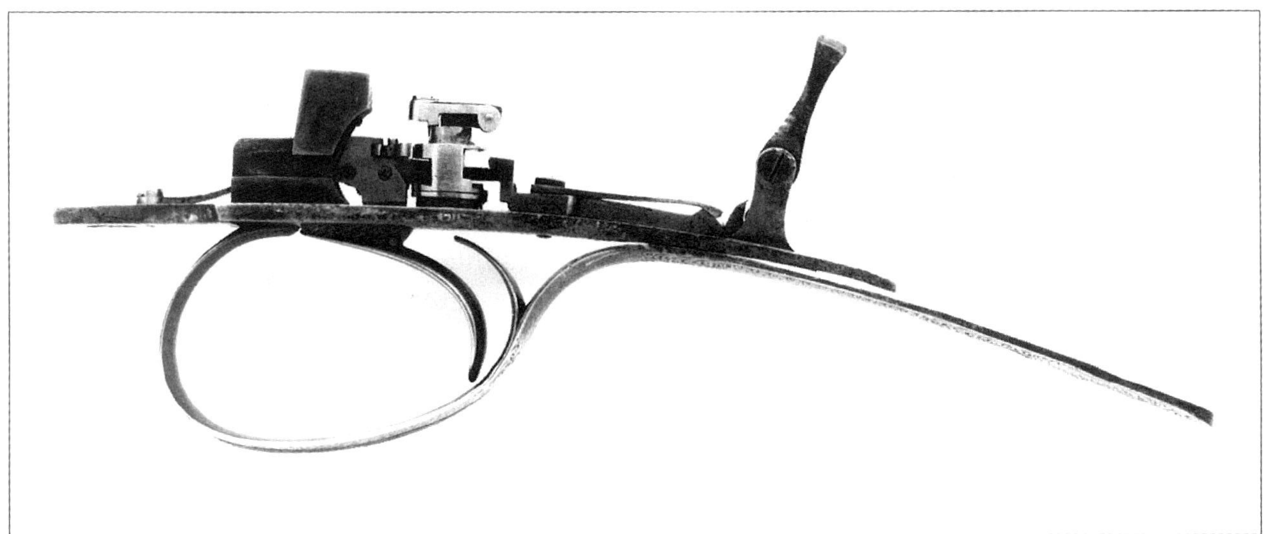

Boss single trigger fitted to Ford boxlock overleaf. (Christie's)

specialists. Locks, stocks, and barrels were all made by individuals who worked on nothing else. Locks were more often than not imported from companies such as Chilton and Brazier in the nearby towns of Darlaston and Wolverhampton. Stocks were finished by skilled woodworkers who bought their blanks from wood dealers located in the heart of the quarter, and barrels were bored by men who knew no other trade.

William Ford was one of the latter, a barrel borer who learned his trade, or at least polished his skills, working for W. W. Greener in the 1870s. Ford, obsessed with the internal ballistics of breechloading shotguns and their cartridge components, first came to the notice of the trade when he bored the barrels of the winning guns in *"The Field"* trials of 1875.

Those trials were ostensibly about pitting the new choke-bore guns against the old cyl-

This London-pattern William Ford sidelock ejector sold at Weller & Dufty in May 1994 for £3,200. (Weller & Dufty)

inder bores, but in the time needed to organize them, advantages of chokes had become obvious. All that was left to know was who bored the tightest-choked guns.

Up until this time, W. R. Pape, a gunmaker from Newcastle upon Tyne, had been the leading exponent of choke boring. He had introduced and patented the idea in 1866 and won previous *Field* trials by decisive margins. His only serious rival was another Novo Castrian named W. W. Greener, who some years earlier had moved to Birmingham with his father, also a gunmaker. (As an aside, the curious reader may wonder why the Newcastle gunmakers should be so interested in tight-shooting guns. The answer appears to have been a great regional interest in live-pigeon and even sparrow shooting among the affluent coal-mine owners.)

Although a Pape gun was second in the class for choke-bored 12-gauge guns, W. W. Greener swept the field, winning in classes for 20-, 12-, and 8-bores. Greener was also first and second with two 10-bores entered in the 8-bore class. Based on this success, William Ford was later able to claim in his advertising, "Borer of five Winning Guns at the Great London Trials in 1875."

This appears to have inspired some independence in Ford, and he soon opened his own premises at 4a Weaman Street, St. Mary's Row, Birmingham. Soon Ford's barrel-boring abilities were once again being sought by more established names. This time, though, the gunmaker, Lincoln Jeffries, then of 31 Whittall Street in Birmingham, was unwilling to credit Ford. After winning *"The Field"* trial in 1879, he advertised himself as "Winner of the *'FIELD'* 20 guinea Prize for Choke Bores, London, 1879 (My own work)."

Greener may have employed Ford's skills, but he never claimed they were all "my own work." Litigation followed, and here the narrative dims, but it appears that Ford won and was awarded a medal by Jeffries acknowledging that it was he, Ford, who had bored the barrels of the winning guns in 1879. Ford used this in his advertising and even added a small engraving of himself "at his boring bench."

In the 1880s, Ford's barrel skills were once again in demand. This time, though, it

A lightweight 12-bore boxlock ejector by William Ford, fitted with a Boss selective single trigger. (Christie's)

wasn't an established gunmaker who needed help but an inventor, surgeon, and all-round renaissance figure named Charles Joseph Heath, F.R.C.S. Heath was a serious wildfowler who designed a relatively light-weight gun (about 8½ pounds) that was capable of firing a heavy load of shot (up to 2 ounces). Low-pressure loads were used to keep recoil to a minimum, and striking energy was maintained by going to a larger shot size. The key to the entire system, however, was the use of thin brass cartridge cases in a gun that had the chambers removed—or, to put it another way, a gun in which chamber and bore were the same diameter. A tight gas seal was achieved by the use of oversize wads, and a thin brass case of 12-bore could be loaded with the components of a standard 10-bore cartridge. The Kynoch cartridge company manufactured the ammunition, which it called "Perfect" cases.

Several gunmakers built guns on the Heath chamberless system—including John Ross and F. T. Baker, both of London—but most had their barrels bored by William Ford of Birmingham. Ford even offered an "Excelsior" game and wildfowl gun that "is bored to shoot both paper and perfect cases and will fire a charge of from 3 to 4½ drams of power and from 1 to 2 ounces of shot, thus doing away with the necessity of gentlemen carrying a battery of guns." Unfortunately, the contemporary literature does not tell us how this was achieved. In 1990, while researching Charles Heath, I received a letter from Alan Thornton, then a director of William Ford Ltd., which has since become defunct. I had asked about the Heath system, and Alan's letter is worth quoting: "Chamberless guns … now being obsolete, we have converted a number of 12 bore brass case guns to 10 bore standard paper cases." Which, I think, gives some indication of the lack of popularity if not the lack of success of the system.

Alan Thornton's letter gives some indication of just how important a research tool gunmakers' records are. Without them we wouldn't know of the chamberless guns that were returned to William Ford to have conventional barrels built. The Ford records also feature a number of guns with short 22- and 24-inch barrels that were jug-choked and sent out to India and Africa for crocodile shooting.

The rise in popularity of driven shooting throughout the last quarter of the nineteenth century created a demand for enhanced firepower. One of the ways in which this was met was by the introduction of ejectors. Ejectors meant guns could be reloaded and consequently fired faster. Every gunmaker in Britain realized that whoever developed a consistent and reliable method of ejecting spent cases would sell a lot of guns. Many good minds competed to create the perfect mechanism. One of these was William Ford, who registered four designs with the patent office between 1887 and 1894. In chronological order they are:

8,841 of 1887

2,622 of 1888

9,348 of 1888, together with James Clifford

2,658 of 1894, together with R. Hill

None appears to have been widely adopted.

In 1890, Ford patented (Number 8,621 of 1890) a try gun that could no doubt be used at his two shooting schools, one at Crabtree Lane, Clayton, Manchester, and the other at Small Heath near Birmingham. The Birmingham school offered live targets such as rabbits, pigeons, and "American blackbirds," which were almost certainly American robins (*turdus migratorius*), though where Ford found these in sufficient numbers is a mystery.

In the 1890s he developed a "patented anti-recoil wad and cartridge rim protector," a "patented ignition tube," and a "force gauge" that he felt "should be more extensively used by his fellow gunmakers . . . without any charge whatever."

When William Ford died 9 December 1909, his son, A. F. Ford, took over management of the firm. In 1953, the Ford firm incorporated James Carr & Sons, another small family-owned concern, and eventually faded from the scene sometime in the early '90s.

W. W. GREENER

THE OLD MAN

The great Birmingham gunmakers lived in an age when the entrepreneur as inventor was crucial to the concept of capitalism. No one could become a business success simply by buying companies and stripping them of their assets. Even buying low and selling high had serious limitations. What was required of Victorian businessmen was that they manufacture something—take raw materials like wood and iron and fashion them into implements for which there was a demand. In an inventive age, William Greener grasped the creative zeitgeist lock, stock, and barrel.

He was born in 1806 at Felling, then a village on the outskirts of the industrial center of Newcastle upon Tyne in the northeast of England. Greener apprenticed as a gunmaker with Richard Burnand at the foot of Pilgrim Street—then, as now, one of Newcastle's major shopping thoroughfares. Later he worked in London for John Manton, younger brother of Joe Manton, king of the gunmakers. Greener thought highly of both the Manton brothers but saved his highest praise for the elder:

> Joseph Manton is entitled to the gratitude, not only of the present generation of the gunmaking fraternity, but of all the succeeding ones, for this reason—he not only gave character to English guns, but he raised the English artisan along with himself and left them the acme of mechanics.

The quote is often repeated and frequently, but erroneously, attributed to Colonel Peter Hawker; however, it is without a doubt the words of William Greener. He married in London at age twenty-three and returned to Newcastle, where he established his own gunmaking business.

Writing after his death, his son, William Wellington Greener, called him:

> . . . a man of undoubted genius and had his inventive qualities been allied more closely to pertinacity, he would have certainly achieved a greater name and in all probability have amassed a large fortune. His fertility of ideas led him to seek renown in diverse fields and while many of his discoveries were so far in advance of his time that it was difficult to convince others of their merits, they may truly be said to mark epochs in the development of many industries and were later the source of considerable profit to others who benefited by his inventions.

Much of the elder Greener's creativity was inspired by the events taking place around him in Newcastle, then a booming coal-mining town in the throes of the Industrial Revolution. When Greener was eight, George Stephenson developed the world's first steam locomotive to carry coal from a mine in Killingsworth to ships in the Tyne. When he was nine, Sir Humphrey Davey invented the world's first miner's safety lamp. And when he was nineteen, Stephenson inaugurated the world's first steam train passenger service between Stockton and Darlington. No inventive mind could have failed to be stimulated by the spirit of such times, and Greener responded with an improvement to Davey's lamp and a design for "a mechanical contrivance by means of which the four gates at Railway Crossways could be worked simultaneously," which won him a prize.

In 1842, when Greener was thirty-six, a young woman named Grace Darling singlehandedly rowed out to a shipwreck and saved nine of the crew. Although this took place just up the coast from Newcastle, Grace Darling's fame was more than regional. Her heroism was celebrated throughout the British Empire, and her fame was so great that public houses were named after her as far away as Melbourne, Australia. Shipwrecks were common enough at that time, but the worldwide publicity of the affair drew attention to the lack of a coastal rescue organization. The disaster would eventually lead to a national lifeboat system that covered the entire coastline, but its immediate impact was to inspire William Greener to invent a self-righting lifeboat.

A few years later, he, along with William Edward Staite of Peckham, London, developed an electric light (Patent Number 11,076 of 1846) in which the "illumination was effected by means of solid prisms or cylinders enclosed in [an] air tight vessel of glass or other transparent substance and rendered luminous by [a] current of voltaic or magnetic electricity." It is perhaps just a coincidence that when Sir Joseph W. Swan devised the first practical light bulb thirty-four years later, he did so in premises at the foot of Pilgrim Street, Newcastle upon Tyne, in the same location as Greener's old gun shop!

Of all his father's inventions, the one William Wellington Greener considered the most significant was the expanding bullet:

His most important invention, destined to revolutionize rifle shooting, was introduced in 1835, thus the first expansive rifle bullet was submitted to the British government and although the results of the trials far surpassed the expectations of the military experts and the invention was favourably reported upon by them, it was rejected on the grounds that the bullet was a compound one. Later the British Government awarded £20,000 to a Frenchman for a bullet upon the identical

principle and it was not until 1857 that my father's claim to priority was admitted and the act of injustice was partially righted when the government granted him £1,000 "for the first public suggestion of the principle of the expansive bullet commonly called the Minié principle in 1836."

The expanding bullet was tested at Tynemouth by a party of the 60th Rifles under a Major Walcot in August 1836. It loaded as easily as a conventional musket ball but retained the range and accuracy of a rifle. Fifty rounds were fired, and when these were recovered they were found to bear the "impress of the grooves exactly, thus proving that the expansion was complete." It was clearly a source of irritation for Greener that his bullet was ignored while similar ideas developed by M. Delvigne and M. Minié saw broad use. Greener grew up in the Francophobic atmosphere of the post- Napoleonic war years, and it must have been particularly irksome when the British government adopted the ideas of a Frenchman over his own. Writing in *Gunnery 1858*, he had this to say:

. . . that there is no evidence that either Delvigne or Minié had any profound knowledge of the science of gunnery; and that their knowledge of the principles of expansive bullets was so meager as to justify the assumption that their only connection with its production was that of copying from the *Times*, or from my works, published in 1842 and 1846.

William Greener had previously published a book called *The Gun* in 1834, which he dedicated to the Duke of Wellington. The Iron Duke, who had defeated Napoleon nineteen years earlier, was a personal hero for Greener, and when his wife bore him a son in 1834, he named the boy William Wellington Greener after the great man. Years later, W. W. Greener would recall that book's effect on business:

This work and his subsequent writings proved of considerable value to him as they attracted such world wide attention that many new customers were by their means introduced to him from abroad, particularly officers of the Indian guide Corps, who in the days of the Honorable Company were allowed personally to purchase the equipments for their Companies and many substantial orders for Carbines were given by them to my father.

The way in which these gun books promoted his father's business was a lesson the younger Greener never forgot. In later years he too became an author with the ulterior motive of marketing the next generation of Greener guns. However, he always claimed writing was forced upon him when he was compelled to write *Modern Sporting Gunnery* so as not to disappoint his father's readers, who were anticipating a new book from the old man when he died in 1869. Unfortunately, the younger Greener's books are so single-mindedly self-serving that they must be read eclectically to have any value at all. Their biggest fault is one of omission: W. W. Greener fails to credit his competition, even when—some would say especially when—their contribution to gunmaking is as significant as his own. They also lack any kind of biographical information.

Fortunately, the younger Greener left a fifteen page, unpublished biography that tells us quite a bit about his early life in Newcastle:

I was the third of five sons and was born at Newcastle upon Tyne, near where the Central Station now stands, on 16th September 1834. I was given my father's name of William in addition to that of Wellington, the latter being in remembrance of the Iron Duke for whom my father had a profound respect. My earliest recollections are of guns and munitions of war and I have a distinct remembrance of much that occurred at my father's workshop at the back of his house—No. 60, Pilgrim Street, opposite the Queens Hotel—which was at that time an important house of call for the mail coaches from London to Edinburgh.

William Wellington Greener's childhood memories are revealing for what they tell us about the variety of tasks the nineteenth century provincial gunmakers performed in order to stay in business:

At times all the workmen would be engaged in scouring the rust off musket barrels sent in after a long sea voyage while my mother would be superintending the manufacture of ball cartridges for use on board the ships. Again a consignment of muskets, pistols and cutlasses would arrive from Birmingham all of which would have to be carried by the men and boys, myself amongst the latter, on board the boats lying in the Tyne or all would be engaged in cleaning and browning the muskets used by the soldiers stationed at the barracks. Then the manufacture of Harpoon and Whaling guns for the Dundee Whalers was a steady and profitable source of income, while on one occasion the whole of the workmen were engaged in the manufacture of a large machine for making Ship's Biscuits.

One of W. W. Greener's memories reveals something of his sense of humor:

An amusing reminiscence relates to the testing of a shot gun in my father's garden situated some distance from the town. My father was at Birmingham and in his absence one of the workmen took a gun to shoot at a large target which was fixed up in the garden. A man in the next garden was nailing up a tree so close to the target that the workman asked him to move from what he thought was a dangerous position. The man refused to do so and as a result received a stray shot in the back. Although not seriously hurt he had the workman up before the Magistrates who sentenced him to seven days' imprisonment. When he reached the gaol the Governor gave him a pair of duelling pistols to clean which he did so thoroughly that it occupied the whole of his time in prison, and in fact he treated the affair as a huge joke. This man—David Griffith—by the way, was the only one of my father's workmen who came to Birmingham with him. He traveled from Newcastle to Birmingham in a third class carriage, which in those days resembled a modern open cattle truck. The journey was made in November in bitterly cold weather and he often said that he found it less of a joke than his seven days' imprisonment.

Birmingham was the home of the British gun trade, and the senior Greener spent so much time there collecting guns and material that his long absences were proving harmful to his business in Newcastle. In 1844, he "removed" to Birmingham, where he was able to make guns quicker and cheaper than in Newcastle. In the short term, the move almost proved disastrous because he lost almost all his north-country sporting-gun connections. However, he managed to retain his trade with the Scottish whalers because his harpoon guns were so highly thought of. They set a record for 120 yards of flight at a public contest in the London dockyards in 1848, were awarded a prize medal at the Great Exhibition of 1851, and won a silver medal at the Paris exhibition of 1855.

In the long term, business increased and was so good by the early 1850s that the elder Greener was compelled to "requisition a horse and trap" to take his work from outworker to outworker. In 1858, he won a contract to supply John Hayton of Grahamstown, South Africa, with a quantity of two-grooved rifles of medium quality. William Wellington Greener was given the job of overseeing the work. He had trained as a barrel borer and was responsible for the boring of the Greener gun that placed fourth in *The Field* trial held on 9 and 10 April of the same year—all this

despite a serious attack of measles seven years earlier that had left him almost blind.

This exercise in gunmaking left its mark on the impressionable twenty-four-year old:

> My father, true to his old trade traditions, failed to recognize that there would be a good demand for a medium priced weapon of sound workmanship. Nothing but the best at this time merited his attention but I was given the opportunity of undertaking the manufacture of this special rifle and there learned the first great business lesson upon which my future career may be said to have been founded, that sound material and honest workmanship offered at a moderate price will always command a ready market. . . . These rifles as well as Combination Rifles and Shot Guns were made in large quantities, hundreds being ordered at a time. Orders of such magnitude for this class of weapon were unique in the History of the gun trade and this business may be looked upon as the turning point in the fortunes of the firm.

In 1859, William Greener erected a new factory at Rifle Hill, Aston, which G. T. Teasdale Buckell tells us was paid for "with the money obtained by the supply of South Africa with two groove rifles." William Wellington Greener claimed the new works increased the company's capacity "ten fold." No sooner was the factory established than the Confederates took Fort Sumter, signaling the start of the American Civil War. The Greener firm worked day and night making Enfield rifles for the forces of both sides, and W. W. Greener recalled it as a time when:

> . . . fortune favoured us. . . . Night saw no cessation from the day's work. Everyone was occupied, good prices were paid—as much as 60 shillings each for Enfield Rifles—and when the ships were taking cargo every hand would be employed throughout the night packing rifles and carrying the cases to the Railway Station. This was a time of plenty for the Gunworker and many are the

extravagant tales told of their reckless improvidence.

In mid-nineteenth century Britain, breechloading guns were virtually unknown despite their having been shown by several French gunmakers at the Great Exhibition in 1851. In 1855, William Wellington Greener and his friend William Middleditch Scott, then aged twenty-one and twenty respectively, traveled to France and:

> . . . there confirmed the impression received on my earlier visit by the rows upon rows of Breech loading guns exposed for sale in the windows of a Parisian gunshop. I was firmly convinced that the muzzleloading gun was doomed but my father still refused to recognise the merits of the new system and I decided to commence business on my own account, which I did in a small house in St. Mary's Row, towards the end of 1861.

W. W. Greener's account of his split with his father was written long after the elder Greener had died and when the son was old and somewhat mellow. At the time, their decision to go their separate ways was a generational rift fueled by acrimony. As might be expected from someone with such highly developed anti-Gallic sensibilities, the old man loathed "the French crutch gun" and wrote bitter and abusive denunciations of it in his book, *Gunnery 1858*:

> The French system of breech loading is a specious pretence, the supposed advantages of which have been loudly boasted of; but none of these advantages have as yet been established by its most strenuous advocates. How it is that the British Sportsman has become the dupe of certain men who set themselves up for reputable gunmakers I know not. It is certain, however, that by these acts they have forfeited all claims to the confidence of their too confiding customers, and that they never could have tested the shooting properties of their guns. With regard to the safety of

these guns, they display an utter want of the most ordinary judgement; and this is abundant proof that they consider neither the safety, nor (what is also of importance) the economy of the whole arrangement, as regards their manufacture or their use.

William Greener continued to enumerate the guns' faults:

> First, there is no possibility of a breech loader ever shooting equal to a well constructed muzzle loader; secondly, the gun is unsafe, and becomes more and more unsafe from the first time it is used; and, thirdly it is a very costly affair, both as regards the gun and ammunition. . . . No fear need be entertained that the use of the breech loaders will become general . . .

William Greener's prejudice is difficult to understand in the light of his past vision and inventiveness and becomes even more incomprehensible when one learns he had himself patented (Number 2,693 of 1854) a breechloader in 1854. However, Greener's views make some sense when we recall that the muzzleloader had reached near perfection while the breechloader was still in the developmental stage. Add to this the desire to check a rebellious son and those Francophobic tendencies, and perhaps an explanation is at hand.

Whatever the reasons, father and son parted company, with the old man retaining the Aston factory while the son acquired a small house in St. Mary's Row in the heart of the gun quarter toward the end of 1861. Both were at pains to broadcast the knowledge of their split and to stress that they no longer had any business connections whatsoever. William Greener died in 1869 at age sixty-three, but not before registering one last design with the patent office. It was for specially chambered barrels (Patent Number 2,349 of 1864) for—what else?—a muzzleloading gun!

THE SON

In 1869, when his father died, William Wellington Greener bought the Rifle Hill business—despite considering it unsuitable because it was so far from the gun quarter—and merged the two firms. He appears to have considered his father's legacy a double-edged blade: On the one hand he saw the value of the old man's inventiveness and the part his books had played in publicizing the firm. On the other, he retained his rebellious streak and continued to offer guns of "moderate price" and to import ideas from France.

To the casual observer, W. W. Greener's success is attributable to his emulating his father. Certainly, the son saw the value of creativity and writing, taking out four times the number of patents and publishing twice as many books as his father had. But he never forgot the disagreements either. He remembered how his father had "failed to recognise that there would be a good demand for a medium priced weapon of sound workmanship" and consequently built a career around the gun of "moderate price" like those he had so successfully overseen for the South African, John Hayton, back in 1858. He never forgot his father's prejudice against the French breechloader either and, in an act of open rebellion, appears to have actively looked to France for his gunmaking inspiration.

His first patent (Number 2,231 of 1863) was for an improvement of the French pinfire gun his father had so heartily loathed. The older Greener had criticized the bolting system of Lefaucheux's guns because it was so inherently weak. The younger Greener strengthened the lock-up by placing a rod-shaped bolt in the breakoff, where it engaged a circular hole below the top rib. He also built it so the hammers were raised to half-cock by an underlever, making it unnecessary to withdraw them by hand in order to open the gun.

In his next specification (Patent Number 1,339 of 1867), Greener took the same idea of a cylindrically shaped bolt and a circular bite and turned it ninety degrees. Here, the bolt working transversely in the breakoff engages a slot cut in a rib extension. The gun, illustrated in his *Modern Breech Loaders 1871*, is clearly the prototype for what Greener called his "Treble Wedge-Fast" and what the rest of us refer to as the "Greener Cross Bolt." In his brief memoir, Greener states that he "refrained from placing this on the market as another maker claimed that it infringed his existing patent." Years later, in his magnum opus *The Gun and its Development*, Greener published an engraving (page 107 in the classic ninth edition) of an old flintlock that was clearly the inspiration of the Treble Wedge Fast or Greener Cross Bolt. The great irony is that the flintlock was French!

France also appears to have been the inspiration for Greener's next effort. One problem in the era before rebounding locks was that when a gun was fired, the firing pin could remain in the forward position with the nose embedded in the primer, preventing the gun from being opened. In 1862, a Parisian named Louis Julien Gastinne patented a firing pin that engaged a slot on the inside of the hammer so that when the hammer was drawn back the pin was retracted. In the Greener version (Patent Number 800 of 1868) the pins are equipped with laterally projecting pegs that are engaged by horn-shaped notches filed into the breast of the hammers. When the hammers are drawn back, the notch engages the peg and retracts the pin or "piston" as Greener called it. Others called them "needles." This from the gentleman's newspaper *Land and Water*: "We observe the needles are much stronger than usual, and altogether the gun appears neat and durable, and the arrangement very simple. We consider it worthy of the notice of sportsmen."

In 1873, Greener improved (Patent Number 3,084 of 1873) upon his Cross Bolt gun by adding underbolts. The patent drawings show three versions: the first with a conventional Purdey underbolt that Greener called his "Treble Wedge-Fast Gun;" the second, equipped with a Jones rotary T-bolt and clearly intended for heavy work, called the "Treble Grip-Fast Action;" and the third, an over-and-under that was no more than an ordinary Greener Cross Bolt gun turned on its side, without any additional means of fastening barrels to action. In *The Gun and its Development,* Greener tells us that this last version was "only made as an experiment."

William Wellington Greener appears to have had more respect for Joseph Needham and his inventions than for most of his contemporaries. In 1874, Greener acquired the name, goodwill, and "Damascus Works" from J. V. Needham and continued trading as Needham from the Loveday Street factory. In his writing Greener frequently credited Needham with inventing the hammerless gun cocked by the fall of the barrels and the "split extractor ejector gun;" it is therefore slightly ironic that at a later date, Greener used the Needham name to market colonial-quality Anson & Deeley boxlocks. The likely explanation is that he saw the demand for the cheap A & D but was embarrassed to market a rival action in his own name, especially after his legal problems with Westley Richards (more of this later.)

In the same year he bought out Needham, Greener refined (Patent Number 3,039 of 1874) the Purdey underbolt version of his Cross Bolt gun and "perfected and introduced the modern system of choke boring." During December of 1874, he placed this advertisement in *The Field* newspaper:

W. W. G. is now prepared to manufacture Guns to order that will put on an average of 210 pellets, with 12 bores weighing under 7½ lbs., with a charge of

3 drachms powder, and 1⅛ oz. of No. 6 shot; and over that weight, 220 pellets. Guns of 10-bore, weighing 9 to 9½ lbs, with a charge of only 4 drachms powder and 1¼ oz. No. 6 shot, an average of 240 pellets. Closer shooting may be obtained if desired, and the penetration is also one third greater. By using only 2¼ drachms of powder better pattern and penetration can be obtained than from other guns with 3 drachms of powder and much less recoil. See special reporter's notice in *The Field* of January 9, who has tried the shooting of these guns, and states that the trial was highly satisfactory, and certainly proved that Mr. Greener has not overstated on paper the capabilities of his gun. References can be given to sportsmen who have killed game at over 100 yards.

These extravagant claims stirred a furor of debate among sportsmen that was settled only when Greener swept *The Field* gun trials of 1875, winning all three choke-bore classes: 8, 12, and 20. It should be remembered that Greener had entered guns in a previous trial held by *The Field:* "In 1866 I bored the guns for *The Field* trials on the same principle as that employed for my father's gun at the 1859 Trials," but on both those occasions he had been beaten by another Newcastle native, William Rochester Pape. Pape had patented choke-bored guns in 1866 (Number 1,501 of 1866) but failed to maintain patent coverage by the nonpayment of stamp duty. Greener appears to have taken the germ of Pape's idea and made it practical. The obvious question here is: Why were the Newcastle gunmakers so obsessed with close-shooting guns?

The answer is—at least for me—a fascinating piece of social history. The owners of coal mines in the Newcastle area became affluent when the Industrial Revolution demanded more and more coal. Understandably, these "black diamond gentry"— as Blaine called them in his *Rural Sports* of

1848—wished to pursue the pastimes of the more established aristocracy such as fox hunting, fishing, and particularly shooting. But the growing coal fields quickly turned a rural environment into an urban one— unsuitable to gamebirds. The colliers' response was to turn to live-pigeon shoot- ing, a discipline requiring close-shooting guns. Such guns were apparently common as early as 1835, if we can believe this quote from William Greener:

Thus made, they have put in from forty to forty-five shotcorns in a circle of four inches diameter; (at forty yards) a fact well known in this neighbourhood (Newcastle upon Tyne). In truth, I could pick out ten old colliers, in as many miles, who have done it frequently.

Live-pigeon shooting was so popular in the northeast of England that the bird suppli- ers could not keep up with the demand, and as a result some shooters began substituting

This contemporary Greener lockplate is engraved by Alan Brown with mallards. (David Grant)

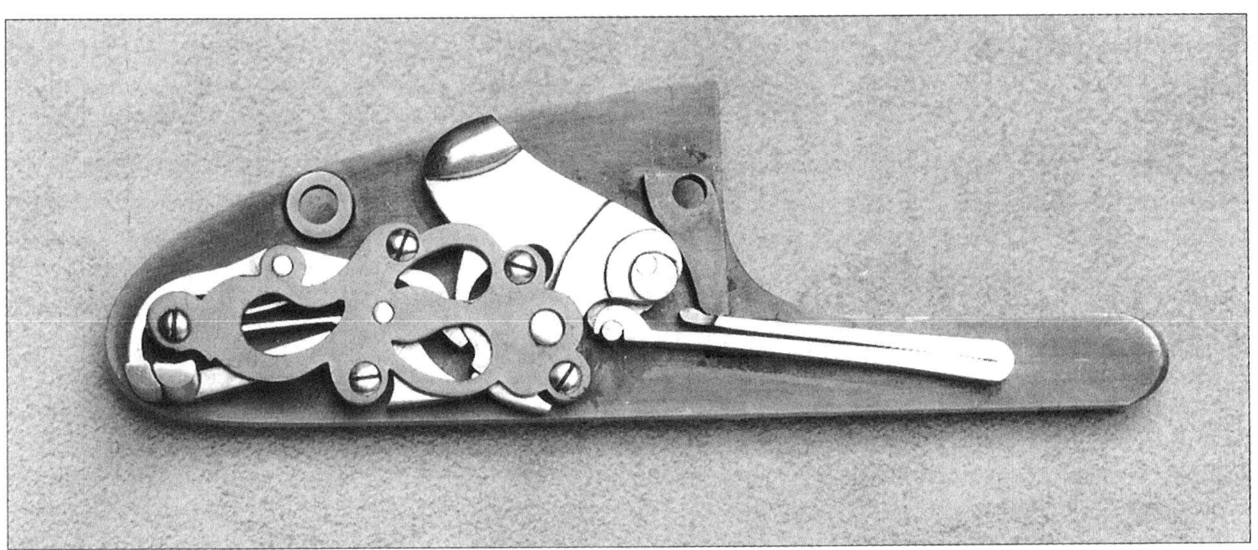

Harry Greener's 1914 patent sidelock with its unique eight-hole bridle. One pervasive fallacy about Greener was that the company made few sidelocks when in reality it made thousands. (David Grant)

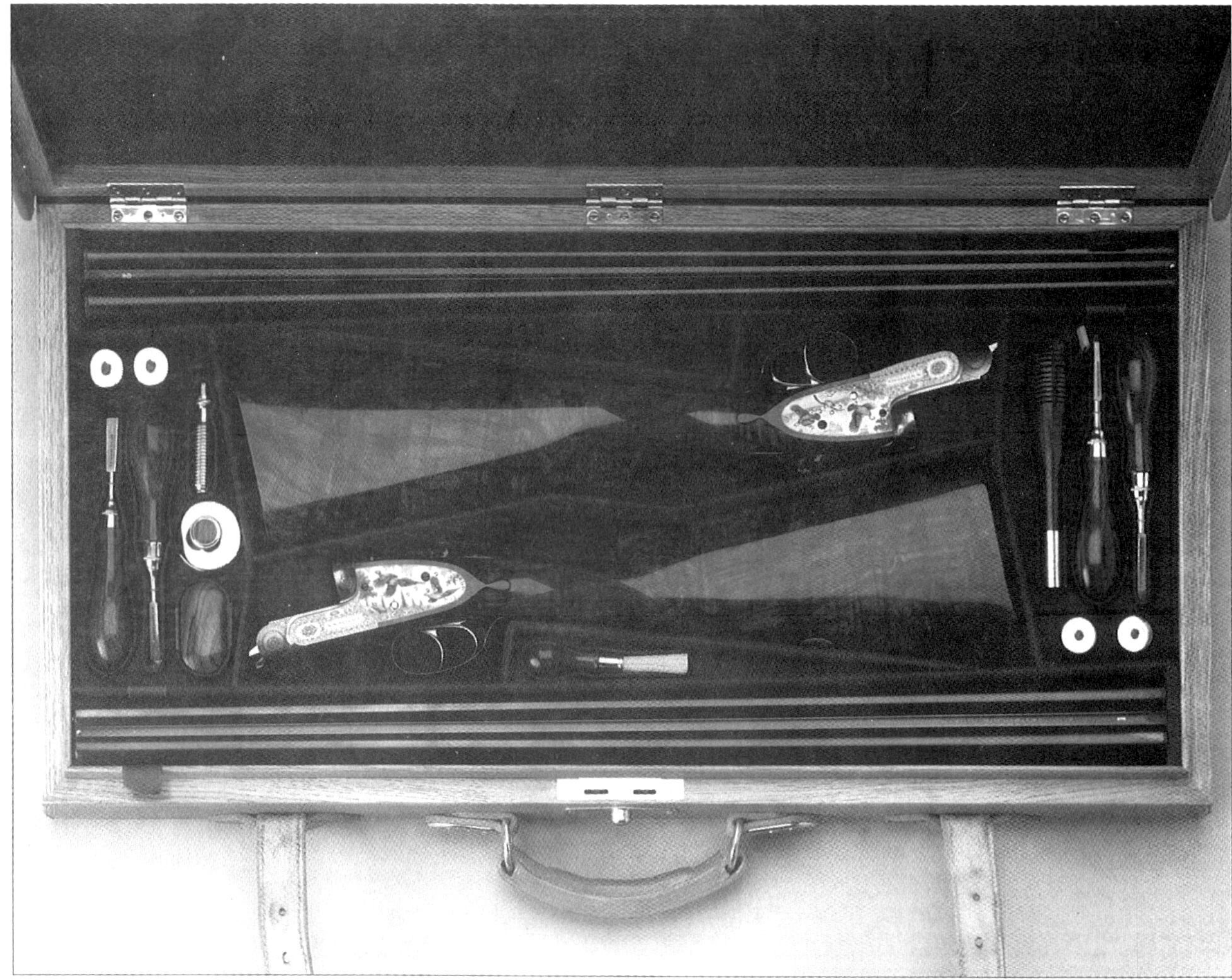

A cased pair of new very best sidelocks by W. W. Greener. (W. W. Greener)

sparrows. It is not difficult to imagine how tightly grouped a shot charge would have to be to prevent a bird as small as a sparrow from flying through it!

Pape's supporters attacked Greener in the sporting press, arguing that he was not the inventor of choke-bored guns. The charge prompted this response:

I have never claimed this distinction which I believe to be of American origin, but *The Field* trials which were the most exhaustive and perfectly impartial trials ever held, in this or any other country, proved conclusively that guns bored upon my improved system of choke boring gave results far superior to anything previously obtained and the position then gained by

my guns has been maintained until this day throughout the world, by pigeon shooters and others to whom close regular shooting is a sine qua non. The history of choke boring and the capabilities of shot guns is treated upon fully in my latest book *The History of Shooting of Choke Bore Guns* in which a detailed account of *The Field* gun trials and the incidents leading up to them are clearly given. One of my guns made upon the under and over principle—that is one barrel superimposed upon the other, instead of side by side as usual—was used in the 1875 trial and favourably commented upon in *The Field*. These successes added greatly to my reputation as a gunmaker and contributed largely to my later success.

In 1877 W. W. Greener patented his famous side safety (Number 1,623 of 1877), which bolted only the triggers and was awkward to use. Although frequently found on Greener guns, where it provides another signature feature to an already idiosyncratic firearm, the Greener safety was not widely adopted. The exception is on German drillings, where the conventional tang safety is replaced by a barrel selector. Greener considered the system appropriate for high-powered rifles because it left more wood in the head of the stock, "keeping the grip of the stock as strong as possible." Another safety featured in the same specifications frees the triggers when the user's shoulder activates a rod running through the stock. The same patent also covers a double-barreled over-and-under gun of falling-block design.

In 1878, Greener opened an agency in Paris and purchased the business of Theophilus Murcott, "the inventor of the Hammerless gun, and thus acquired a London Shop." For reasons unknown he then refined (Patent Number 769 of 1879) the Murcott gun, which by then must have been rendered obsolete by subsequent designs such as the Anson & Deeley. The next year Greener introduced his own boxlock design (Patent Number 930 of 1880) in direct competition with the Anson & Deeley and called it the "Facile Princep." To modern eyes, the Facile Princep, meaning "easily the boss," appears an effort to circumnavigate the Anson & Deeley patent. Westley Richards, which owned the patent rights to the A & D, thought so too.

In 1881, the first year *The Gun and its Development* appeared, Robert Edward Couchman, company secretary and a director of Westley Richards, and William Wellington Greener met in a courtroom, with the former claiming 15 shillings per gun plus damages of £5,000 from the latter. Greener

L. L. Greener's main showroom in London, circa 1900. (W.W. Greener)

won the first round and also a second round at the Court of Appeal, and when the case was eventually presented before the House of Lords, he won there too. This despite Greener's defense in which he claimed the Anson & Deeley patent was invalid because it had been anticipated by other patents— notably the John Henry Walsh patent of 1866 and the Joseph Needham patent of 1874, in which the fall of the barrels cocked the gun. The Lords ruled this point incidental and pointed out that Greener himself had accepted the validity of the A & D patent by manufacturing a small number of them under license before introducing the Facile Princep. The

Lords eventually ruled in Greener's favor because they felt that the two guns were fundamentally different even though Greener appears to have merely reshaped certain parts that were drawn in the Anson & Deeley patent. Greener, understandably, recalled the decision as a great victory:

> The introduction of my facile princeps Hammerless action caused much jealousy . . . Fortunately, after a lengthy trial lasting some years, judgment was given in the House of Lords in my favour when it was ruled that my system did not infringe the plaintiff's patent and I then proceeded with the manufacture of what is to-day still

A rare gun signed by David Dryhurst, the master gunmaker behind many of the modern Greener guns and a man many think is Birmingham's finest living gunmaker. (David Grant)

the simplest and most satisfactory ejecting mechanism made.

For the modern collector, the major difference between the two actions is aesthetic: In the Anson & Deeley, the tumblers run parallel, creating a boxy action, while in the Facile Princep, the tumblers curve together in order that they can be cocked by a single lever. This in turn allows the designer to create a distinctive rounded bar to the action, which gives so many Greener guns that distinctive "shouldered" look familiar to anyone who owns a Parker or a Fox.

In 1881, W. W. Greener patented ejector work (Number 2,003 of 1881) that was a combination of Joseph Needham's 1874 patent and his own Facile Princep. The following year he patented (Number 4,516 of 1882) another variant on the Facile Princep theme.

The Greener business prospered, and in 1884, W. W. erected a new factory fronting on St. Mary's Row. Later additions, which extended the property into Loveday and Bath Streets, allowed Greener to claim "the largest sporting gun factory in England."

In 1888, Greener wrote *Modern Shot Guns* and in the next year patented (Number 17,746 of 1889) a smooth choke for a rifled barrel: "To enable the same barrel to be used as a rifle and for firing small pellets, the rifling is stopped near the muzzle and an enlarged recess is formed, the remaining part of the bore being smooth." This was clearly a reversal of the famous Forsby rifled choke adopted by Holland & Holland as its "Paradox" ball and shot gun four years earlier. However, it was found that the recess or jug choke was insufficient to control the shot pattern after the disruption caused by the rifling, and Greener's system was never a success.

William Wellington Greener's two sons, Harry and Charles, became partners in 1890 after passing through the workshops and becoming thoroughly acquainted with the factory routine.

The Breechloader and how to use it, a reference for "all who wished to take up the art of shooting," first appeared in 1892, and the following year Greener patented another hammerless gun action (Number 18,558 of 1893) that had the novel feature of having a screw which, when turned, allowed ejectors to be turned into extractors. The same specification describes a gunstock that "is attached by a bolt which is screwed to the boss on the breech action, and is provided with recesses along its length to allow the stock to shrink without splitting."

His final patent (Number 228 of 1895) was a return to the familiar Greener Cross Bolt. This time he split the rib extension into "two tongues fitting recesses in the standing breech" and called it his "Improved Wedge-Fast Grip." The system was largely ignored by other British gunmakers but used extensively by German gunmakers on their over-and-unders when adapted as the "Kersten bolt."

In 1910 or 1911, Greener retired at age seventy-seven or seventy-eight and the firm continued under his sons, Harry and Charles. Looking back over his life in the gun trade, William Wellington Greener acknowledged the part the medium-priced gun had played in his success:

> I was the first to utilise steam power and while a best gun always will and must be hand made from the fact that only by this means can it receive that individuality resulting from the skilled craftsman's experience and the technical knowledge and oversight of a thoroughly trained gunmaker, yet the amount of machinery now employed has doubtless improved the quality of the medium priced gun and rendered it possible for the sportsman of to-day to procure a good gun at a figure which in the days of his grandfather would have purchased a gun of very mediocre quality and while figures

seem to prove that the gun trade of England is a declining industry yet I think that so long as there is game to be shot so long will the sportsmen of the world demand English guns and Birmingham will maintain its high position, not only as the home of the gun trade but as the place where the world's best guns are made.

THE LEGACY

When W. W. Greener retired, his sons Harry and Charles took over the everyday running of the company. Both had trained as practical gunmakers, and each embodied some aspect of the previous generation's appreciation of invention and publicity. Harry was the inventor, and the patent specifications record that he registered as many designs as his father, if not more. Charles, on the other hand, appears to have inherited the literary gift, sharing authorship of *The Causes of Decay in a British Industry* [i. e. the Birmingham gun trade] with W. O. Greener and also writing "Gun-making handicrafts" for the *Newcomen Society* magazine.

The list of patents attributed to Harry Greener cover a wide range of improvements, yet they broadly address ideas that interested all gunmakers in that period (1885-1914). Harry Greener took out patents for single triggers (Number 7,930 of 1899), pneumatic weapons (9,644 of 1903), and gun actions with helical springs (2,697 of 1891)—all ideas, that were very much *au courant*. He also patented the dovetail lump (Number 3,569 of 1911), which has since become the backbone of the mid-priced gun, and a humane killer (Number 6,491 of 1914):

> . . . a noiseless, smokeless shooting apparatus for killing cattle—the sound deadening principle of which anticipates to some extent the Maxim Silencer of which so much has most recently been "heard." The killer has been adopted by

H. M. Government for use in the Army and Navy and many thousands of butchers and veterinary surgeons, for whom a pocket cattle killer is made, now kill animals upon this humane and expeditious principle.

The words are those of William Wellington Greener.

Rifle shooting was a popular sport in Britain during the years leading up to World War I—so much so that German dispatches during that conflict frequently refer to the rapidity and accuracy of English fire. The Greener company profited from the sports appeal, and W. W. Greener wrote a couple of successful books on the subject: The first, published in 1900 and titled *Sharpshooting for Sport & War*, sold a phenomenal 20,000 copies; the second, *The British Miniature Rifle* published in 1908, did only half as well.

Small-bore rifles of middle quality sold well for Greener, and when W. W. Greener came to write about them, he did so in typical self-aggrandizing fashion:

> For nearly thirty years American rifle manufacturers controlled the sale of rifles of small calibre in this country but few, except rifles for rook shooting, being made in England. There was a considerable difficulty in drilling and rifling of the 22-bore barrel. The outbreak of the Anglo-Boer War led to the rapid formation of short range rifle clubs and in 1900, I introduced the .310 bore cartridge and designed a cheap but suitable rifle for it, which proved so satisfactory that it was adopted by the Commonwealth of Australia for the use of their cadets and I have made many thousands of these rifles for the Colonies. It has proved to be an ideal rifle for 'Club' use and the establishment of the Greener Competition at Bisley was not only a distinct success but resulted in some of the finest diagrams being made at 100 yards with the .310 rifle, the world's record for this range being made in 1901 while with the same type of rifle a 500 yards record

was established in 1908. With the rapid increase in short range rifle shooting came the necessity for rifles of lower power. This I met first by the manufacture in large quantities of the British made Air gun, here again opening up an immense industry to the British manufacturer, and also by the introduction of the new Miniature Club .22 bore rifle.

The gun featured in this embossed cardboard advertisement was referred to in Greener's catalogs as the "Saint George grade guns," though it appears only two were ever made. (Douglas Tate)

During this period, Greener issued many specialist rifle catalogs featuring fine line engravings of Harry Greener's patent rifle sights. The earliest of these sight patents (Number 6,096 of 1885) was for what the catalog called a "Vernier Markers, used as Elevator and Ventometer, price 8/-," and the last was for an improvement to Lyman's "orthoptic disk sight" (Number 21,516 of 1908) priced at 21 shillings. The catalogs contain novelties such as cuff links representing .22 caliber cartridges and also feature the Greener trademark of an elephant.

The story of how Greener guns came to be represented by an elephant has become part of the mythology of English gun lore, yet no one has seen any actual press clippings or other hard evidence of its authenticity. The perhaps apocryphal tale tells of an escaped circus elephant, uncontrollable and restive, outside Charing Cross Railway Station in London and of how Charles Greener, whose family retail business was just around the corner at 68 Haymarket, was asked by the police to shoot the potentially dangerous animal. Greener, aware of the publicity coup, subsequently dispatched the animal with one of the firm's big-game rifles and was awarded the head and trunk for his trouble. In an effort to keep the incident fresh in the sportsman's mind, the company adopted the elephant as a trademark. In an amusing aside, I was once shown this trademark by an American gun dealer keen to make a sale. He pointed to the elephant on the barrel of a Greener gun and whispered, "Indian proof marks." I attempted to explain, but it was in vain—he was adamant: "Indian proof marks."

No company in the history of the Birmingham gun trade was more aware of the power of publicity than Greener. The company appeared at all of the international exhibitions, which were a feature of the late Victorian world, winning a grand prize at the Great Exhibition held at the Crystal Palace in London in 1851. For the Chicago Exhibition of 1893 the firm constructed a special pavilion and stocked it with enough high-grade guns to fill a thirty-two-page illustrated catalog. No doubt many of these guns were sold in Chicago, which perhaps inspired Greener to build the greatest show gun of them all, the Saint George gun.

According to an unpublished manuscript dated 11 August 1972 and signed by Leyton Greener, Harry Greener's son, the legend of the Saint George gun started about 1880:

> Greener gun No. 52227, according to the story handed down, stemmed from [a] minor misfortune during 1880, when one of a pair of best Damascus barrel tubes was accidentally damaged and rejected because it could not be finished with full choke. At the time, only five years after W. W. Greener introduced choke boring, there was difficulty in coping with the flood of orders for guns with full choke and no market for a gun to provide more widely spread shot pattern.

About ten years later, when Smokeless gunpowder and driven game had come into favour the beautiful but also hitherto unwanted tubes appeared ideal for a 'Show gun' that would be suitable for fast shooting and an example of the finest materials and workmanship that could be offered by W. W. Greener and his team of craftsmen. In addition, it was decided that this exhibition piece should be designed and built for practical demonstrations of its advantages by Harry Greener, who was already in partnership with his father and was an exceptionally good performer with gun, rifle and pistol.

Leyton Greener goes on to say that Harry Greener not only oversaw the building of the gun but also fashioned and finished the stock himself and designed its "inertia weight" single trigger:

> My father chose for the show gun a beautifully figured piece of Circassian walnut

A W. W. Greener .577 (three-inch) Treble Wedge Fast boxlock non-ejector double rifle. Greener employed a special machine to decorate the frame of this model gun. (Sotheby's)

that had previously been rejected on grounds that mending its many faults would be uneconomical. I forget the precise number of inserts needed but am sure it exceeded one hundred; that none of those has fallen out, or even become obvious by wear and tear of service, seems all the more remarkable because the only suitable adhesive for securing them was glue, made from horse hoof, which is soluble in water.

He contended that well mended stocks were as good as sound ones of similar quality provided that their natural faults did not create serious weakness. Acceptable faults are generally knot holes and cavities formed by inclusion of stone, etc., during growth of timber. Mending such faults means repairing by fitting one or more inserts so that they are unobtrusive and durable; that requires a flair for selecting good matching colour, texture and grain of insert, plus a good fitting. Experience is necessary because the final appearance of a mend cannot be judged until the job has been finished.

The stock was left uncheckered—a Greener preference—and was shaped to a pattern designed by William Wellington Greener known as the "Rational." The Rational stock has a rounded semi-pistol hand and a high-arched comb and, like many of W. W.'s inspirations, appears to have had its origins in continental Europe, in this case Belgium. Leyton Greener claimed it prevented bruising of the cheekbone when the gun was improperly mounted, while the only person I know who shoots one—Mike Newland of the Birmingham Science Museum—thinks it was designed especially for shooting ground game. Leyton Greener wrote:

Harry Greener also designed the engraving, but the formidable task of copying his pen sketches while carving the forged steel, with hammer and chisels only, was accomplished by Harry Tomlinson. He was a first class engraver and inlayer of precious metals who, like most of his fellow craftsmen, spent all his working career at St. Mary's Row. He maintained that only those who have become proficient in carving steel can really appreciate the difficulty of achieving symmetry, correct depth of cut, good form and finish on concave flowing to convex surfaces with intricate design that must not offend the hand or entangle fibres of clothing.

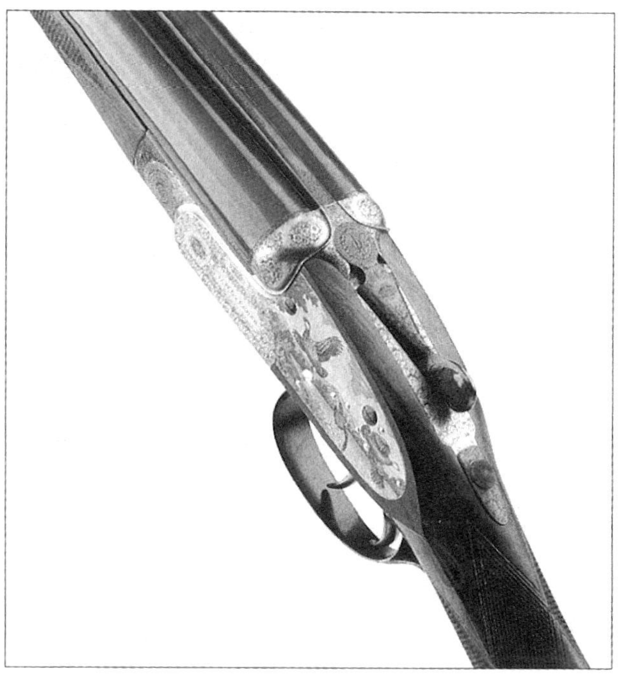

A W. W. Greener sidelock ejector engraved with French partridge by Alan Brown. (David Grant)

To reduce the risk of undue eye stress and anxiety neurosis, he was instructed only to work on the show gun when he felt inclined. Even so, on two occasions during the twelve months required to complete the task, Tomlinson was overtaxed, with results that surprised everyone who knew him well. He then screamed, scattered his well ordered and treasured tools, rushed from his workshop uttering a torrent of invective until he was served with alcohol in the Public House (The Bulls Head) opposite the factory gates; there he remained for several days, unconscious for most of the time. After recovery, he had no knowledge of the lapses and complained bitterly that someone had interfered with his tools. Those setbacks did not appear to have any permanent effect and he was justly proud of, perhaps, the finest example of his skill; shortly before he died, he told me that my father's approval of it still appeared the best reward he ever earned; a silver tankard was involved.

Tomlinson's work was splendid. The action body, furniture, and barrel breeches were chased in deep relief with a theme of St. George—the patron saint of England—slaying the dragon. Each side of the action body shows St. George in armor facing a winged dragon within acanthus scrolls, while the hinge pin features that most enduring of English symbols, a wild rose. Both fences are engraved with a shield bearing the cross of St. George, which is also the flag of England, upon a trophy of arms. The trigger guard bow shows St. George in fluted armor standing victorious on the neck of the dragon, which has a snout in the form of a *fleur-de-lis*, the symbol of France. When viewed from above, another view of the dragon stands out in bas-relief, with its head and snout extending forward down a broad, tapering rib, its wings shrouding the standing breech, and its body and tail making up the top lever. Panels of deep foliate scrollwork straddle the breech ends of the barrels while the trigger, furniture, and exposed ends of the through lumps are chiseled with foliate and shell motifs.

The action chosen was the "Unique," a boxlock modified by W. W. Greener after a design by Joseph Needham. Today, no show gun would be built on a boxlock action, but at the onset of the present century, boxlocks were thought to be a coming idea. It was assumed that the new compact gun would eventually replace the sidelock, which was thought of as the final evolutionary stage of the obsolete hammer gun. Which is not to say that Greener did not offer sidelock guns: In its Fine Guns catalog for this period, L grade best London pattern sidelocks, stocked to the fences, are priced at £94, ten shillings while the "ST. GEORGE GRADE GUNS" are priced at £125.

Throughout its history, Greener built over 4,000 sidelocks but made more than 28,000 guns on the Unique action. They were a reliable workhorse but could be problematic when serviced by those unfamiliar with their intricacies, as Leyton Greener explains:

> . . . in general, they gave many years of trouble free service. However, when fracture of components or lack of normal attention led to attempts to repair by those who did not understand the mechanism, trouble sometimes arose for all concerned. Maladjustment due to faulty workmanship generally resulted in more widespread breakdown of lock and ejecting mechanisms, followed by a bill for corrections from Greener's that often appeared excessive to the unfortunate gun owner. Analysis of the causes of complaints during half a century indicated that mistakes by trade repairers had become progressively more frequent—particularly after World War II—and in 1929, mainly to obviate dissatisfaction they created, Greener's abandoned their Unique system in favor of one that was more widely understood and easier to service and repair.

Leyton Greener also claimed that "the non selective single trigger" of the show gun "was designed by H. Greener in 1882 employing the well known inertia weight principle." A search of the patent records shows no designs at all registered by Harry Greener in 1882, but two other patents (Numbers 4,156 of 1898 and 7,930 of 1899) are for single triggers.

The show gun was not fitted with a safety, and once again Leyton Greener explains:

> The absence of a trigger locking device (so called safety catch) is unusual; I believe it was intended to invite comment and thus create [the] opportunity to stress that such devices do not render loaded weapons safe. The very efficient intercepting catches built into the lock mechanism of all high grade

Greener guns are designed to guard against accidental discharge if, due to falling or other severe shock, the main sears are jarred out of bent; but no such mechanism can be made utterly reliable and therefore an unloaded gun is the only safe gun. The absence of a trigger lock encourages caution and in practice does not appear to increase accident rate in the field.

When William Wellington Greener retired, he gave a speech in which he emphasized advertising and credited the show gun with helping promote the firm. Leyton Greener recalled:

> On that long remembered occasion he also offered advice for the future, based on his outstanding success in business which he attributed partly to good advertising of his products. He finished by declaring that the Show gun in the hands of his son Harry has been the best advertisement so far tried and presented it to its handler.

Harry renamed it "The Saint George" and took it to shoots, where it continued to attract attention. On one such occasion, a Persian nobleman offered to buy the gun and when Harry declined, the gentleman ordered a near duplicate. The scalloped backed action and engraving were identical to the original gun, but the copy was made with double triggers, a Greener side safety, and checkered stock. It can be seen in W. W. Greener's *The Gun and Its Development* (the classic ninth edition of 1910) facing page 278 and is captioned "The Highest Development of the Sporting Gun." With its crocodile-hide case fitted with silverplated, horn-handled tools, the gun was ready for shipping in 1913, but Leyton Greener writes, "It was lost in transit to the customer when the Empress Class luxury liner carrying it sank in the Mediterranean on her maiden voyage." Exhaustive research by Geoffrey Boothroyd has failed to find any record of an Empress Class liner

sinking in the Mediterranean during 1913—maiden voyage or otherwise.

Two World Wars later, Greener's fortunes began to decline in ways scarcely suggested by Charles Greener in *The Causes of Decay in a British Industry*. In 1965 Greener's was sold to Webley & Scott, which finished much of the stock it acquired at that time, mostly Empire and Blue Rock models in the 67,000 to 79,000 serial number range. The only gun W. & S. appears to have continued to produce was the G. P. or general-purpose model, a single-barreled Martini-action gun offered as the Webley/Greener Trap Gun.

In 1985, a fifth generation of the W. W. Greener family, Graham Greener, together with David Dryhurst, Richard Tandy, and Ken Richardson, repurchased the company and began once again offering the finest quality sidelocks, over-and-under and side-by-side shotguns, including double-barrel rifles built with the treble wedge-fast system.

Two years later, in a move that would have been appreciated by previous generations of Greeners, the company began work on a new show gun. Once again the gun would represent the finest in British gunmaking, and once again it would be chiseled in high relief with the theme of St. George and the dragon. The original gun was made on a Facile Princeps system that is no longer economical to build; therefore, the new gun would be built on the sidelock system.

In the tradition of the older Greener gun, the straight hand stock was left uncheckered while the lockwork was designed (Number 5090 of 1914) by Harry Greener. Alan and Paul Brown designed and executed the engraving. Each lockplate has a helmeted but otherwise naked St. George astride a rampant horse, about to plunge his lance into the dragon. Once again the hinge-pin terminals are engraved with a wild English rose and the fences are chased with the cross of St. George upon a trophy of arms. The trigger guard bow features the coat of arms from the cover of *The Gun and its Development*, while the top lever is engraved with the disembodied head of the Dragon. On the underside of the action, the winged Phoenix, looking a little like the American eagle, rises not from the ashes but from the fire, representing the return of the Greener name after an absence of twenty years. The gun was built by David Dryhurst who is a director of the present company. He was one of the last fully trained apprentices of the original Greener Company.

JOHN HARPER

Like most Birmingham gunmakers, most of John Harper's production ended up with someone else's name on it. This firm, which spanned several generations, specialized in building guns for the provincial and London trade, and, as a result, relatively few guns remain with the Harper name on them. This plus the lack of extant records has meant that little is known about this particular company.

What we do know comes almost entirely from business directories, and this source seems to suggest a dynasty in two parts: a succession of John Harpers working in the Black Country town of Darlaston as lockmakers and a second branch of the family situated in the Birmingham gun quarter building guns.

The earliest John Harper is recorded making gunlocks at The Green, Darlaston, Staffordshire, in 1849. The next entry is for a

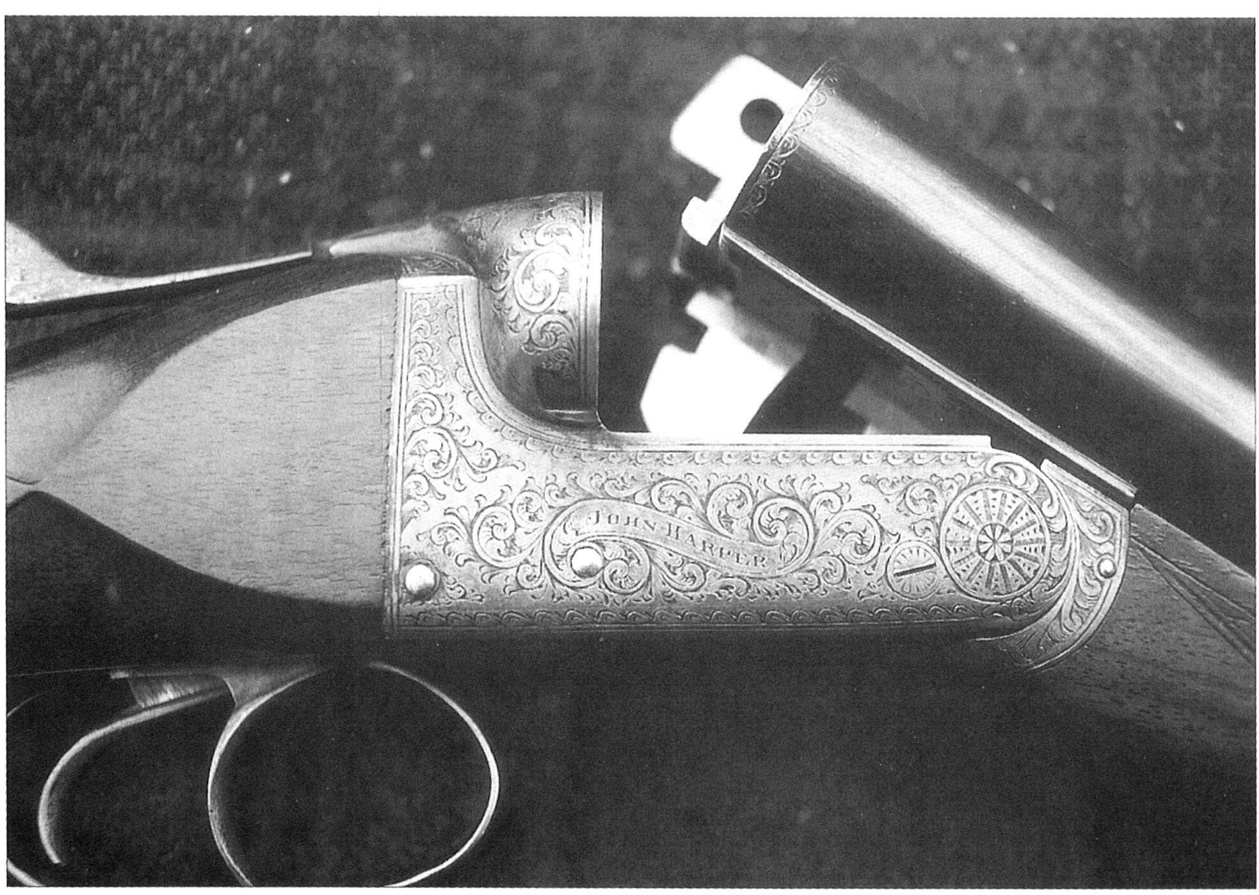

A John Harper boxlock ejector with Greener crossbolt. (Dr. Paul Brown)

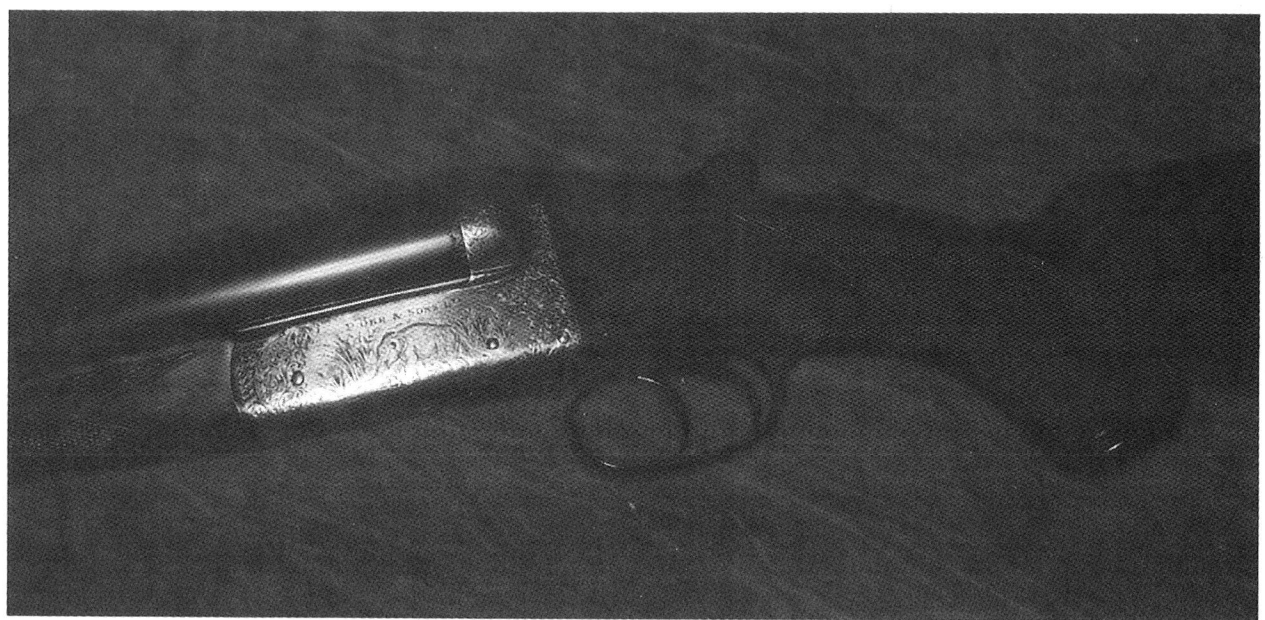

This John Harper .577 Nitro Express double rifle was made for P. Orr & Sons Ltd. of Madras and Rangoon. It was carried by professional hunter Bryan Coleman during his tenure in East Africa and saved his skin on at least one occasion when he was run over by a Cape buffalo. (Mims Reed)

John Harper at 10 Bush Street, Darlaston, from 1878 to 1879. There was also a John Harper at Eldon Street in 1887, at Court No. 8 Bell Street in 1881, and at 27 Eldon Street from 1895 to at least 1900. In Victorian England it was common to give firstborn sons their father's Christian name and surname, especially when it was anticipated that they would one day inherit the family firm. This may well be the case with the lockmaking John Harpers of Darlaston. On the other hand, perhaps all of these entries refer to a single individual whose long career spanned half a century and the various addresses simply represent changes of premises.

Darlaston, along with Wolverhampton and Wednesbury, supplied the Birmingham makers with gunlocks, and trade directories for that town reveal a number of other Harpers making locks there throughout the nineteenth century: Joseph Harper in 1827, who may have been the founder of the Harper dynasty; William Harper in 1867; and William Watson Harper on Willenhall Street

in 1864 to 1865 and at The Leys from at least 1871 to 1880. These last two may be the same man.

The Birmingham directories, too, contain a succession of entries in the name of Harper, but here also, only the bare bones of knowledge exist. James Harper was at 85 Weaman Street from 1842 to 1847, Theodore Harper at 71 Weaman Street in 1846, and Richard Harper at 13 Great Hampton Street in 1849. From 1847 to 1854, Samuel Harper was at work at Numbers 1 and 2 Newton Street and at 88 Steelhouse Lane in 1853, from 1855 to 1861 he was at 123 Steelhouse Lane, and at 126 of the same street from 1862 to 1895. From 1897 until at least 1910, Albert J. Harper was in business at the same address, and for this reason we are almost certain he was the son of the previous occupant. The first of the Birmingham John Harpers made his appearance at 124½ Steelhouse Lane from 1908 to 1910 and was at 28 Whittall Street from 1915 until 1935.

A second John Harper was at Tiger Works, 3 Price Street, from 1941 until at least

John Harper. (Dr. Paul Brown)

his own name. The exception is Model 110, a single-barrel "Anson & Deeley pattern trap gun" with "Beaver-tail fore-end" and "Made for 2¾ and 3 inch cases." Because of its design and specifications, this particular gun may have been intended for the American market and is consequently engraved with the maker's name on both the barrel and the action.

I once owned a superb little .410 boxlock engraved with the name of W. R. Pape of Newcastle upon Tyne. I looked it up in Pape's records, only to find it was by Harper. David Trevallion, the ex-Purdey craftsman who now works in Maine, was sent a delightful 28-bore James Woodward that was unusual in that it did not have arcaded fences, and when he looked it up in

1950, and Mike Newland, curator of the gun collection at the Birmingham Science Museum, is certain that this is the son of the John Harper mentioned above. He moved to 63 Price Street in 1955 and remained until 1968, and here at last we can begin to put a little flesh on our admittedly skeletal knowledge. I was given a photocopy of the front cover of a catalog for John Harper, Tiger Works, Whittall Street that shows a handwritten inscription, May 8th 1976, John Harper. So Harper was still in business in 1976, and he served as Birmingham Gun Barrel Proof House Guardian as recently as 1980.

Typical for a maker who specialized in building guns for others, the catalog is filled with guns covering the spectrum of qualities and all but one of them have vacant banners or cartouches in which the eventual provincial retailer could engrave

New Buildings, Price Street.

the Woodward records, it too had been made by Harper.

JOHN HARRIS

On a windy morning in April I walked down Queensway with Robert Siceloff, an American interested in Birmingham's gun-making heritage. Empty beer cans followed us down the street, and clouds the color of bruises scraped the roof of St. Chads Cathedral. Opposite the Black Bull tavern, a plastic Marks and Spencers bag fluttered in the wind like a cavalry standard. I had come to visit the remnants of the Birmingham trade, but Bob's attention was divided among box-locks and bitter, so after seating him in The Bull I crossed Price Street to an ancient edifice laughingly called "New Buildings."

I entered Unit GF2 first and stepped into a Dickensian workshop. Ray St. Ledger is Britain's best color-hardener, and he and his son were case-hardening gun actions in a space that wouldn't stand much cat swing-ing. Neither was in a mood to see me. The elder St. Ledger said he had not spoken to any writers in twenty years—since he had been misquoted in Britain's premier shoot-ing magazine. It seems he had gone to a great deal of trouble to explain that actions were hardened after gold was inlaid and the trick was to get the colors right without melt-ing the gold. The journalist, it seems, had written that, owing to the high temperatures needed during hardening, gold could be in-laid only after the hardening was complete.

Ray had felt betrayed. The retelling of this two-decades-old story angered him, and he was soon pointing out the door. He soft-ened a bit when I told him he was currently doing some work for me, and he suggested I try upstairs at Unit FF1.

Barry King, who owns the Thomas Wild and Rowland Watson names, was just leaving his workshop, a model of the one downstairs, and we collided. I knew I was doing little to endear myself to the craftsmen of Price Street, but I asked for a moment of his time anyway. Reluctantly he fielded a few questions: Yes, he owned the Thomas Wild and Rowland Watson names and records, but no, he hadn't built a gun in a decade—it was all repair work now. No, of course he had no apprentices. Yes, it was all over for those two famous names when he retired.

He stood on the threshold of his work-shop, coat on, one hand on the door knob, the other jangling his keys. He had a dental appointment, and I suspected he was eager to get it over with. I stepped aside, and he was gone.

I'm not really your persevering type—a couple of refusals to dance at the old Club Agogo were enough to retire me to the bar feeling sorry for myself. I was thinking about this and wondering how the London gunmak-ers might like to be written about when I entered Unit SF2.

"Hello! Come in," accompanied a friendly handshake, a broad smile, and the offer of a mug of tea, all from a man with a powerful build but no longer young. "Come on in; find a place to stand." There was cer-tainly nowhere to sit. Although this garret was identical to the two others, it seemed smaller because every available space was taken up by gun barrels, stocks, and actions. Shortage of work was not a problem here.

John Harris is generous by nature, and he spent more time than was good for busi-ness reminiscing about his initiation into the trade, his apprenticeship as a stocker, and his eventual acquisition of the name, good-will, and records of the well-known firm of G. E. Lewis after the last George Lewis died in the late 1970s.

He arranged for me to interview a retired craftsman from Skimin & Wood, the firm fa-mous for its two-inch guns, showed me some old G. E. Lewis catalogs—which he eventually gave me—and in his own affable and accommodating way broadened my understanding of the Birmingham gun trade. He even offered to take me home to show me some guns he had built under the G. E. Lewis name, which he jokingly referred to as the "John Harris retirement fund."

I told him of my American pal sitting in The Bull, and he said, "Bring him along." What we saw at John's home would have gladdened any lover of fine guns, but it also saddened me. Though the guns were of high quality, with the best imaginable wood-to-metal fit, we could not escape the impression that we were seeing the last of the Birmingham guns. All of the craftsmen we met in Brum [Birmingham] are John's age, and none are training younger men.

Perhaps it was this knowledge, or maybe the quality of the work, but Bob was soon asking about prices. To his credit, he didn't attempt to deal but paid what was asked for a game gun and a wildfowling weapon. The first was a boxlock built to commemorate the death of the last George Lewis. It has case colors ranging from straw to aquamarine that subtly contrast with the maker's name inlaid in gold. The fences were chased by John in a manner similar to the work of the first George Edward Lewis, himself a gun engraver. The second piece was inspired by line illustrations of G. E. Lewis guns in old catalogs John acquired when he bought the company. It was a traditional heavy fowler with a broad fore-arm and full pistol hand. The base plate and side of the action are

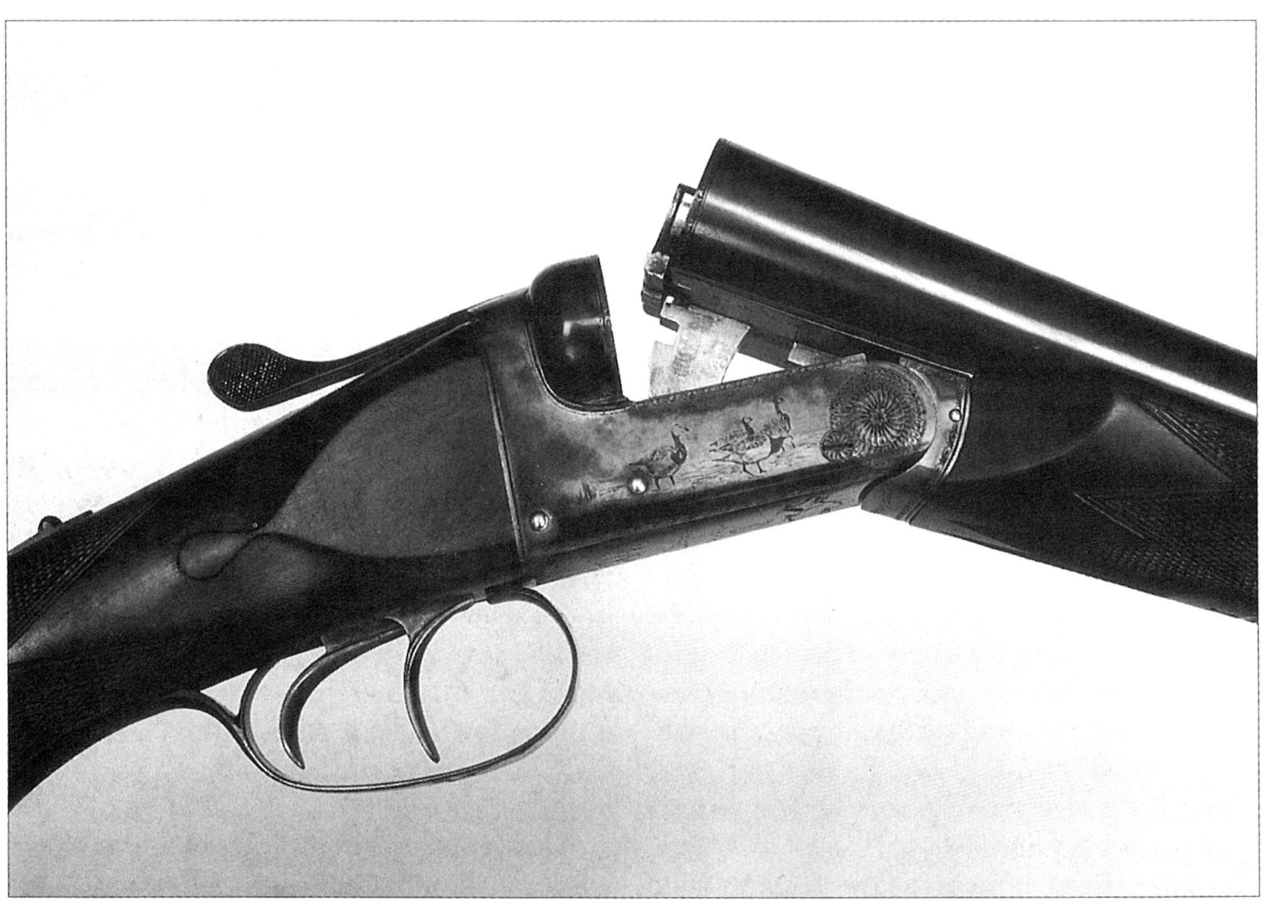

The right side of this new G. E. Lewis gun by John Harris features brant engraved by Malcolm Hicken. (Keith Flannery)

engraved with geese and ducks taken from the pen-and-ink studies Hugh Monahan did for Aylmer Tryon's 1952 minor classic *The Wildfowling Year*. The animated and realistic engraving is by Malcolm Hicken.

The beavertail fore-end is inlaid with marquetry brant from the same book. More than any other aspect of the gun's craftsmanship, the woodwork left the deepest impression. Both guns featured perfectly fitted and finished stocks of walnut marbled like the endplates of rare books. John Harris is a master gunmaker whose carved fences prove he is capable in many areas of gunmaking, but it is the woodwork that is clearly his greatest source of pride.

Work of this quality has not escaped the attention of the trade, and John is often called on to stock the guns of other makers. One of these, arguably Britain's best and a notorious perfectionist, once sent John work on a regular basis. A few years ago John was sent a pair of identical London-pattern sidelock ejectors and a fletch of the finest Circassian walnut with which to stock them. He divided the wood and stocked both so that the grains matched. He then sent them to an outworker who does all his checkering. The outworker removed the wood from the metal and began working on a wrist with the stock in one hand and the checkering tool in the other. The phone rang, and as he spun round to answer it, he shattered the two fingers of wood that reach to the fences against his vise.

The fellow was contrite, but the damage was done. Both guns might now have to be restocked with a very expensive replacement fletch. Instead, however, John restored the broken wood, making the joints invisible with a series of knots he fashioned, and fitted to both guns so they would match. After the guns were delivered, the owner called to congratulate the gunmaker, who in turn phoned John to pass on the pleased owner's compli-

ments about the woodwork. John told the gunmaker about the repair.

The maker was less than happy. He has never sent John work since. I suspect he was more annoyed at his own inability to detect the repair than at anything else. John bears him no grudge and with characteristic generosity of spirit offered him his hand when the two chanced to meet at a recent game fair. Our perfectionist was slightly nonplused.

Stocking at John's level is sometimes compared to wood sculpture, and in the last few years he has sculpted the handles of walking sticks in the shape of gamebirds and gundog heads. Not to everyone's taste, perhaps, but there can't be many stockers willing or even capable of this level of craft.

The last time I was in Unit SF2, John Harris was reshaping the stock on someone's Japanese claybuster. I remember thinking, as I crossed Price Street to meet Bob in The Bull, that it was a bit like having Fabergé decorate Easter eggs.

HOLLOWAY & NAUGHTON

One of the most recurring characterizations in all of Charles Dickens's novels is the orphaned boy, poor but industrious, who, despite all circumstance and with the help of an older benefactor, becomes a successful Victorian gentleman. His biographers claim these characters were based on Dickens himself, but they could just as easily have been based on the Birmingham gunmaker Thomas Naughton.

Left fatherless at age six, employed at age ten, Thomas must have been an intelligent and enterprising young fellow. His first job was with Charles or Joseph Mayberry of St. Mary's Row, probably pushing an old pram filled with gun parts from barrel maker to jointer and from jointer to stocker in a ritual familiar to generations of young men trying to gain entry into the mysteries of the trade. He accumulated experience quickly and by the age of fifteen occupied a man's position at the bench. A few years later he gained employment with Christopher George Bonehill at his Belmont factory in an effort to learn about the new machine methods of gun manufacture. Shortly after that and still chasing experience—this time of the high-quality handmade gun—Naughton found work with James Carr & Sons, where he stayed for five years until he emerged as a master craftsman.

At this juncture in his life Naughton was fortunate enough to meet G. O'Connor Holloway, a hardware merchant and a Birmingham city councilor. Like most hardware dealers in the age before shotgun certificates and home security cabinets, Holloway sold shotguns from his Lionel Street premises and was interested in investing in their manufacture. Having sold Naughton-made guns, Holloway was familiar with them, and the two entered into an agreement that saw the former renting property from the latter at a rate of £16 a year for the purpose of making and selling guns. Birmingham street directories record Holloway as a gunmaker as early as 1887, but this is not necessarily the date he entered into business with Naughton, since the term "gunmaker" was liberally used at the time to include those who retailed guns with their own name on them.

Customers pronounced the pair's guns "some of the finest they had ever seen," and they also won "highest possible awards" at a Paris exhibition. Holloway's salesmen took so many new orders that a new factory had to be built at 10, 12, and

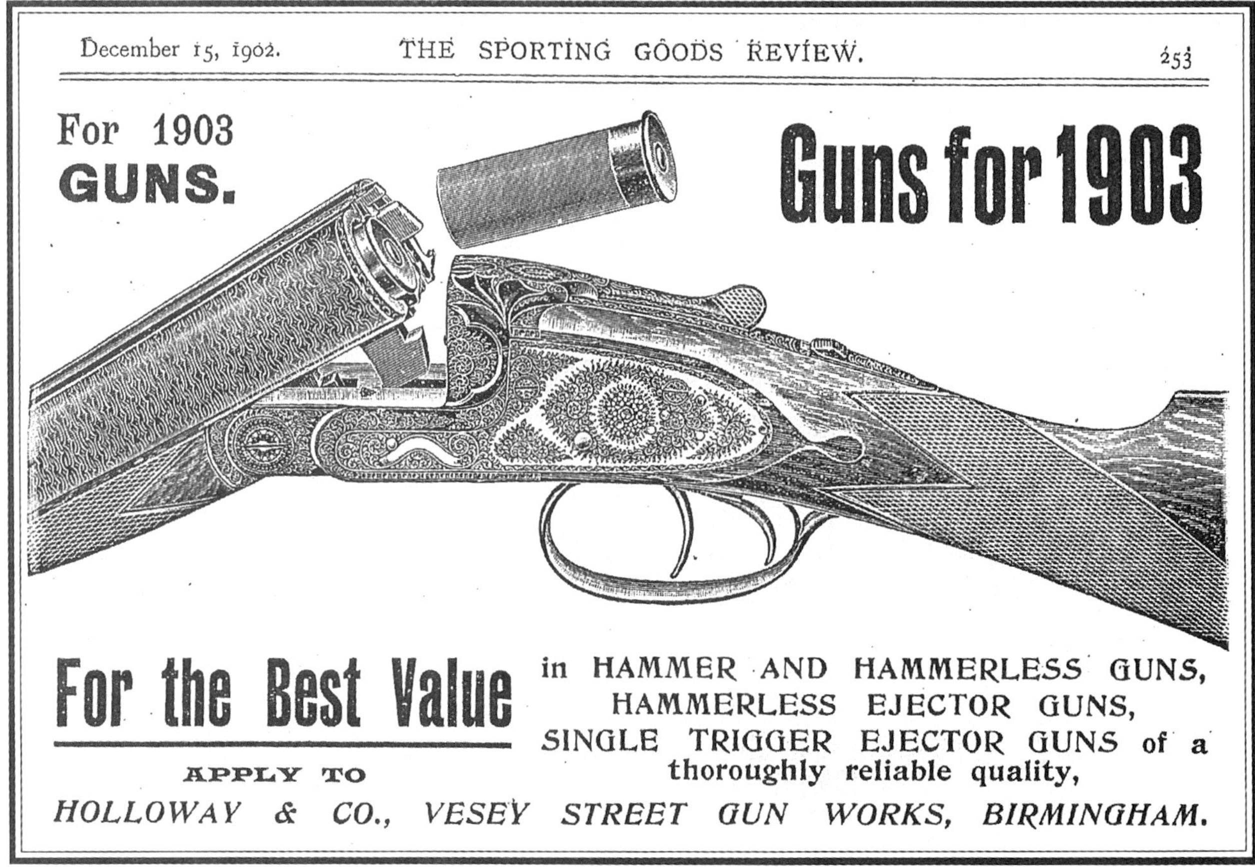

14 Vesey Street. Thomas Naughton managed Holloway & Co. for fifteen years and was eventually offered a partnership—which for unknown reasons he declined. Holloway finally sold his business to H. Ludlow England, owner of the Midland Gun Company, whose Demon Gun Works was just around the corner in Price Street. In 1907, Ludlow England patented an improvement for Anson & Deeley-action guns (Number 27,065 of 1907) in which the "lifter" on the knuckle "is made as an integral part of the gun." The patent is interesting because it was lodged by H. L. England "trading as Holloway & Co."

Naughton stayed on as manager and eventually acquired the company in the early months of 1909, changing the name to Holloway & Naughton. The following year, *The Sporting Guns Review* published an article titled "A Birmingham Gun Factory" that included the following description:

> The premises in Vesey street are not only extensive, but also admirably equipped. While capable of dealing with military and other orders on a large scale the firm also is careful to maintain its reputation for work of specially high class, in which most skillful handicraft and most minute scientific precision are required.

Apparently, Naughton's time with both Bonehill and Carr had not been wasted. During the time the firm was known as Holloway & Co., it had been company policy to advertise each winter using an engraving of a high-quality gun and a short catch phrase. In December 1902, the engraving, was of a sidelock 12-bore with bouquet and scroll engraving, carved fences ribanded in a trefoil motif, and the slogan read, "Guns for 1903."

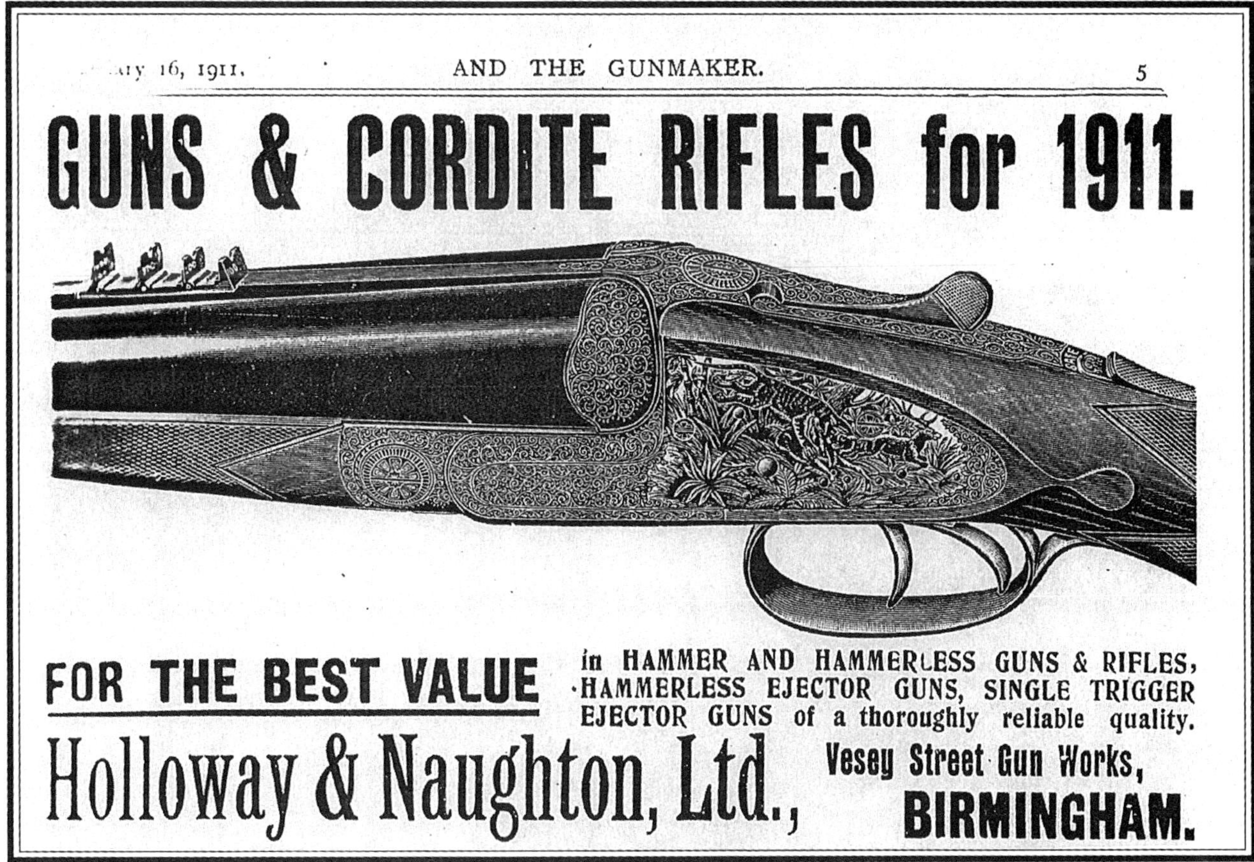

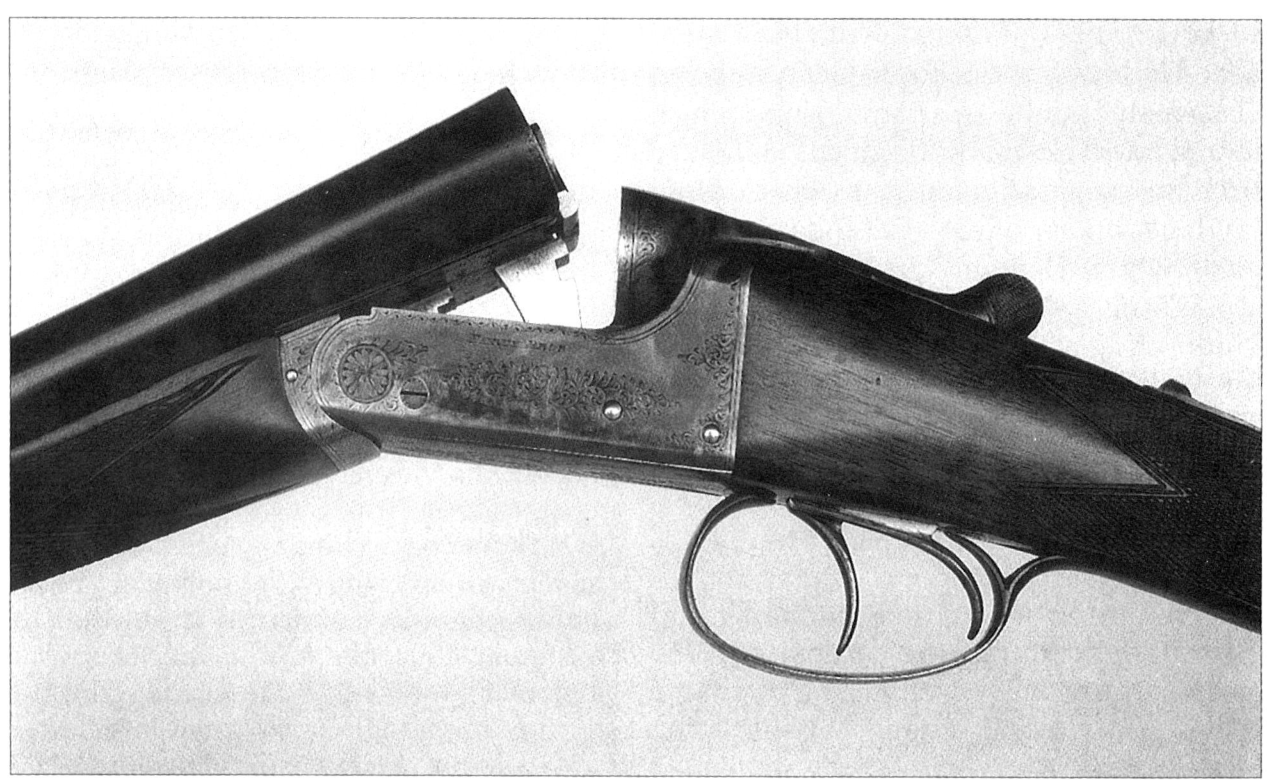

This Hardy Brothers of Alnwick piece was made by Holloway & Naughton. (Keith Flannery)

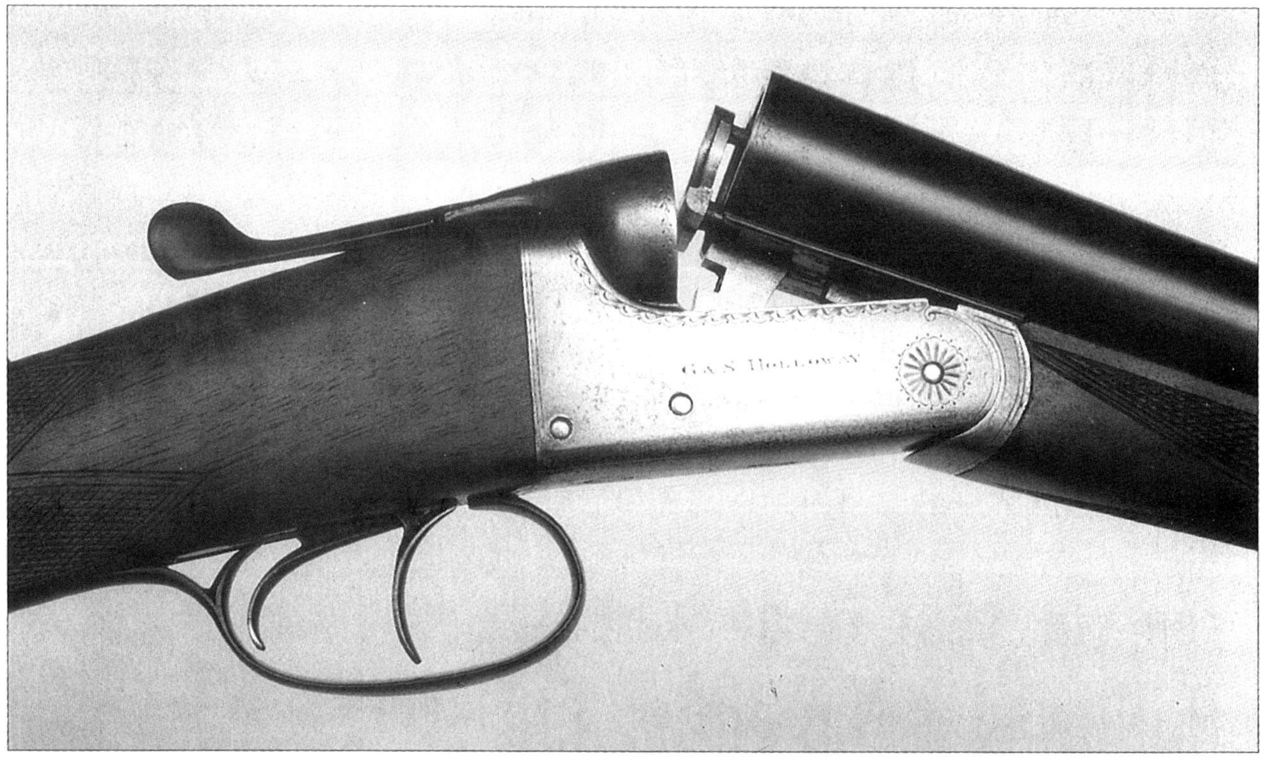

A basic boxlock non-ejector by G. & S. Holloway. (Keith Flannery)

It was a tradition Thomas Naughton continued. In his first full winter the engraving was of a massive double rifle with clipped fences and sidelocks depicting a tiger slaying a deer among jungle foliage, and the slogan read, "Guns and Cordite Rifles for 1911."

Many of Naughton's advertisements at this time feature live-pigeon and trap guns, but so did everyone else's. What Naughton did that his competitors did not do was to employ W. Ellicot, who had been the English clay-pigeon champion several times, to act as a traveling salesman for his guns. It appears that target shooting was very popular in the period just before World War I, and Naughton sold many guns of this type, particularly in the colonies.

At about this time, a second company appeared in Vesey Street calling itself G. & S. Holloway. This was George and Sidney Holloway, who may have been descendants of the original G. O'Connor Holloway. They had a strong Hibernian connection and were represented in the "Irish Free State" by both Thomas H. Henshaw & Co. of Dublin and the junior partner, "Sid." Their catalogs are quick to distance themselves from Thomas Naughton:

WARNING: G. & S. HOLLOWAY are our real names. We have been in the Gun Trade over 25 years, and have no connection whatever with any other firm using the name of Holloway as a Trade name. Insist on the Initials G. & S.—the "Hall Mark" of good work.

As managing director of Holloway & Naughton, Ltd., Thomas Naughton could hardly let this stand, and he responded in his own catalog:

IMPORTANT NOTICE: We understand that a certain amount of confusion has been caused amongst our customers by the fact that there is now another firm in the gun business trading in the same street as ourselves under the name of Holloway. We therefore take this opportunity of stating that we have no connection with any other firm. Ours is the old-established gun manufacturing business which has been carried on under the name of HOLLOWAY & CO. in this street for upward of twenty-five years. We would therefore respectfully ask our friends to carefully address all letters, parcels, or packages intended for us:

HOLLOWAY & NAUGHTON, LTD.,
Vesey Street Gun Works,
BIRMINGHAM.

Sidney Holloway died late in 1916, but his company continued to supply barrel actions throughout the '20s and '30s to Robert Jenkinson of 762 2nd Avenue in the Murray Hill section of New York City. In the mid '70s, G. & S. Holloway diversified into copper tanks, and it disappeared in the late '80s when Graham Holloway, last of the gunmaking Holloways, died.

Thomas Naughton died 6 September 1921 and was buried three days later at St. Michael's Church, Boldmere. He was mourned by the luminaries of the Birmingham trade, including Leslie B. Taylor of Westley Richards, Charles Ellis of Charles Osbourne, and Samuel Skimin of Skimin and Wood, who had at one time managed Holloway & Naughton. The company was carried on by a son T. J. Naughton, and was acquired in the early 1950s by F. J. Wiseman, whose father, J. H. Wiseman, had at one time rented bench space from Holloway & Naughton. The firm of F. J. Wiseman is still in business in Cannock, Staffordshire, and is once again planning to make guns using the Holloway & Naughton name.

The first will be an over-and-under sidelock designed by John Wiseman, currently F. J. Wiseman's managing director, and former British Open Sporting Champion Andrew Harvison. The gun, a 12-bore, has

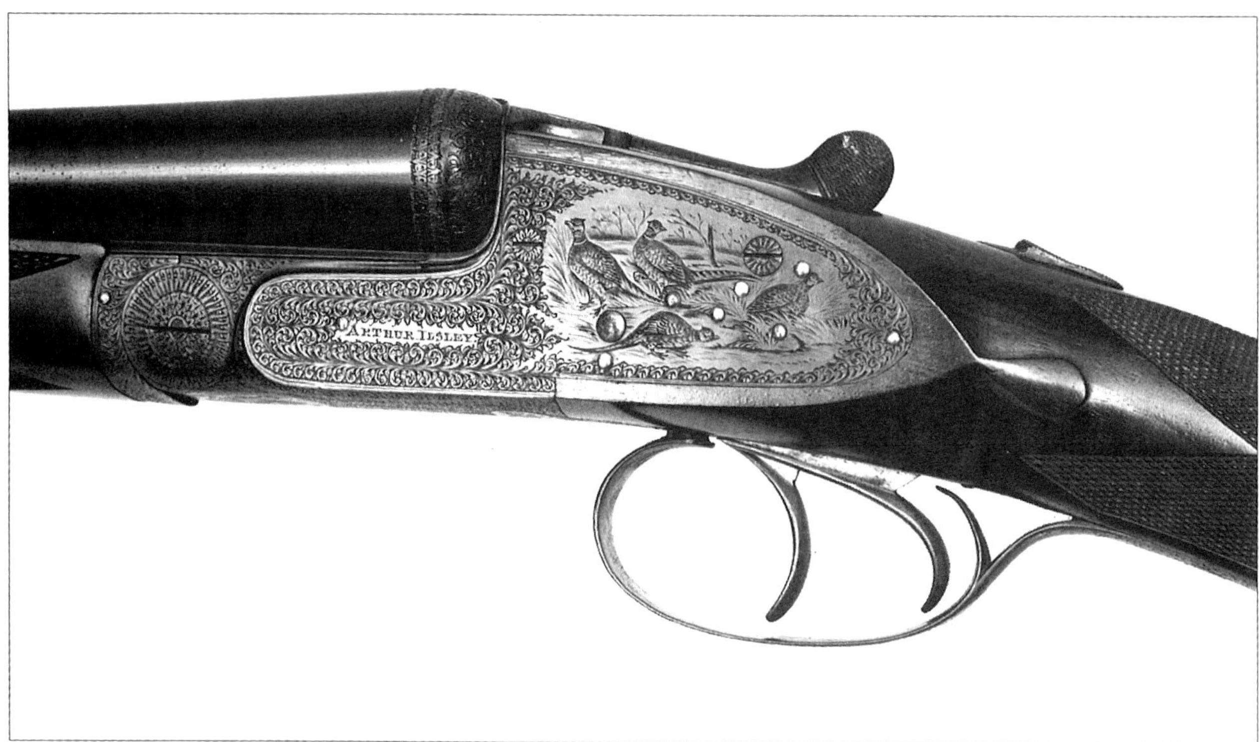

This best London-pattern Arthur Ilsley gun has an engraved nye of pheasants on the left lockplate identical to one shown in Harry Kell's pattern book and may well be the work of the master engraver. (Weller & Dufty)

28-inch barrels and has been designed so the barrels hinge on side projections and bolt midway down the action face. The action is therefore only marginally deeper than the barrels, making for a shallow, elegant gun that weighs only 7¼ pounds. The gun will be engraved in Italy and sold by Bonhams, the Kensington auctioneer. Thomas Naughton would no doubt approve.

ARTHUR ILSLEY

Birmingham's gun trade is synonymous with certain gun actions, the ubiquitous Anson & Deeley and also the flat-back sidelock, the latter a style of bar-action sidelock in which the stock does not reach to the fences. The flat-back is not as a rule associated with the best London-pattern sidelock in which the stock does reach the fences and in which a hidden third fastener strengthens the action without impeding loading.

But best guns were made in Birmingham, and one maker who appears to have made a specialty of them was Arthur Ilsley. Born in 1885, he was probably the second son of Thomas Ilsley, grandson of an earlier Thomas Ilsley, and great grandson of William Ilsley. The Ilsley family were specialist stockers and finishers to the Birmingham trade, and W. W. Greener's records show that an Ilsley was employed by or at least contracted to them in this capacity. Unfortunately, the records are unclear exactly which Ilsley this was.

Street directories are no more revealing and frequently compound the researcher's difficulties by misspelling the name, which sometimes becomes "Illsley" or even "Hilsley" even though it is clear from other evidence that the same individual is being addressed.

All we know about Ilsley is that he started work at age thirteen, working initially for Armstrong Stevens & Son of 15 Whittall Street, and then for Arthur Henry Ward at either

65 Weaman Street or 27 Loveday Street or possibly Ward & Sons of 24-27 Bath Street. About 1906, Ilsley established his own business as a stocker and finisher, and accounts vary as to whether this was at 131 Steelhouse Lane or 2 St. Mary's Row.

If accounts of Ilsley's early years conflict, the consensus on the quality of his work is complete: Every writer who has ever mentioned his name agrees that Arthur Ilsley was a maker of best guns. Mike Newland, curator of firearms at the Birmingham Museum of Science & Industry and a researcher who has compiled files on most of Birmingham's gunmakers, records Ilsley as a maker of "Best Quality Hammerless, Sidelock Ejector Shotguns around the turn of the century."

Arthur Ilsley died in 1976, but his legacy gets a new breath of life every time one of his creations comes to auction. In the spring of 1994, Weller & Dufty, the Birmingham auction house, offered a small collection of Ilsley sidelock ejectors, and its catalog had this to say: "Arthur Ilsley made best quality guns for the Birmingham and London trade." No one who had the opportunity to see these wonderful guns exhibited at the West London Arms Fair would disagree. Most had chopper lump barrels and Anson fore-ends, were exquisitely engraved, and all realized good prices.

In 1995, too, an Ilsley best gun came to auction. In its Billingshurst sale of 14 December, Sotheby's offered a single-trigger model with Woodward-type arcaded fences, Purdey-style bouquet and scroll engraving, and with the action bar signed in gold. The gun shared a page in the catalog with a Holland & Holland "Royal," and both guns commanded the same pre-sale estimate of £3,000 to £4,000.

The evidence of an Ilsley sales catalog, undated but with an address of 8 Whittall Street, also supports the contention that Ilsley made fine guns. The cover claimed "High class gun & rifle makers," and though some of the guns featured are the prosaic products of the Birmingham trade, a "Presentation Gun" for 100 guineas certainly is not. With fleur-de-lis checkering and gold inlays, it is priced ten times higher than a .318 Mauser rifle by the same maker. Lest we miss the point, the catalog tells us, "The ornamentation and finish of this gun, are of the highest art obtainable."

Featured in the same catalog is a "Side Lock Ejector, grade 8" with Southgate ejectors, a hidden third fastener, and a double bar to the action. It is by any standard a superb London-pattern best gun of a type not usually associated with the Birmingham gun trade, and it makes an observer wonder how many other fine guns with London names were actually made in Birmingham by Arthur Ilsley and his contemporaries.

WILLIAM PALMER JONES

G. T. Teasdale-Buckell called him "the principal inventor to the (Birmingham) trade" and "an inventor who has tried most things." These praises may give the impression that William Palmer Jones was a prolific gun mechanic in the style of William Baker or William Wellington Greener, but he has a mere seven patents to his name and appears to have been more interested in shooting than in gun design.

Born in 1845 to a family of gunmakers, he was given his father's Christian name; his middle name, Palmer, is believed to be his mother's maiden name. The family firm was started by his grandfather, who was born in 1778. William Jones I began making guns and pistols at 86 Lichfield Street, Birmingham, in 1811 after serving an apprenticeship with a gun engraver, Charles Rayner. In 1820 James moved to Number 2 Newton Street, and in 1826 his son, also named William, took over the business when the old man retired.

William Palmer Jones, who eventually inherited the firm, considered this the date of its inception and proudly proclaimed "established 1826" in his advertisements. William Jones I died on 22 April 1828 at age fifty.

The second William Jones moved to 23 Lench Street in 1834 and to 75 Bath Street in 1852. In the early 1880s the firm was handed over to the third-generation Jones, William Palmer, and the second William Jones died a few years later, in 1886. Before entering into his family's business, the young William Palmer had attended Moseley school with Henry Webley, who would become an even greater giant in Birmingham gunmaking circles.

W. P. Jones made his first foray into patent protection in February of 1875 with a provisional patent (Number 510 of 1875) for an action with a third bite. The abridgement doesn't show a drawing, and the description is couched in nebulous terms. It is hardly surprising then that the idea never achieved full patent status. In 1886 Jones, together with Harry Alfred Smith of Whittall Street, was granted coverage (Patent 2,725 of 1886) for a hammerless gun action, and in 1888 Jones patented a "firing appliance" (Number 17,732 of 1888) that would "enable three or four barreled guns to be fired by two hammers." The idea was simply to have a movable nose on a conventional hammer; in concept and execution it was so similar to A. A. Thorn's idea of six years previous that an observer wonders how it achieved patent status.

Sometime in the late 1880s, Jones's interest seems to have shifted subtly from guns to shooting, and in 1889 he took out the first of two patents (Number 1,157 of 1889) for a try gun. In his obituary, *The Sporting Goods Review* made much of this:

> One of the inventions by which Mr. Jones is best known is that of his "Try Gun," patented in 1889. Before its introduction customers were "measured" for their guns by means of a set of dummy weapons. The "Try Gun" is now in universal use by the Trade.

There were try guns before Jones, but few, if any, measured for cast, drop, and length of pull, and none were as successful. Jones licensed the use of his in the capitals of England and Ireland—Holland & Holland was allowed its use in London while Truelock & Harris had the permit in Dublin. Jones retained for himself the exclusive right to use the try gun in Birmingham. Some indication of the importance Jones attached to his try gun can be gleaned from his naming his premises at 25 Whittle Street "Try Gun" works.

Later in '89 Jones changed his try gun (Number 5,372 of 1889) to include a joint high in the head of the stock. Conventional lockwork would have interfered with the joint, and the patent drawing shows a needle-fire action by Needham that, though while obsolete, allows the necessary modification.

It is claimed that W. P. Jones developed *The Field* force gauge for measuring penetration and *The Field* mechanical gun rest used in *The Field* rifle trials of 1883, but there appears to be no record of either device ever having been patented.

Over the years, Jones designed and built shooting ranges at Ward End and at the rear of his premises in Whittal Street, developed a steel bird he called the "Collapso" (Patent 17,833 of 1896), and invented a target-throwing machine he designated the "Prfektr." The "Prfektr" was capable of throwing conventional clay targets or "Collapso" steel birds, which had the decided disadvantage that they had to be whitewashed after every use.

He also developed two cartridge-loading machines. The first of these, the "Accuratus," was designed for loading on a small scale while the second, the "Multiplex Accuratus," filled ten cartridges at a time.

G. E. Lewis III in the gun room just before World War II. (John Harris)

on the involuntary pull system, which they then modified (Number 5,543 of 1895) later the same year. The single trigger based on the three-pull system seems to have been something of a Holy Grail with William Baker, who had been pursuing the idea since 1882, when he filed his first patent on these lines.

From 1894 until 1914, Jones served as a guardian of the Birmingham Proof House, laying out a range at Small Heath for the use of registered members of the trade. He also laid out a covered range at the same location that remained in the hands of the guardians long after B.S.A. took over most of the surrounding ground for its factory.

William Palmer Jones died on 19 October 1920, aged seventy-five, just eleven days before his old school chum Henry Webley. The business was carried on by his son, William Jones, and appears to have traded as recently as the 1970s.

G. E. LEWIS

George Edward Lewis was born in Birmingham on 23 January 1829. He apprenticed in "all branches" of the gun trade and at the same time studied art at evening school. After completing his apprenticeship, he started out in his own business. His obituary, written in 1917, claimed that in 1850 he erected the building—still occupied by the firm at that time—located at 32-33 Lower Loveday Street. But the question of where a twenty-one-year-old journeyman gunmaker would have

It was claimed that the larger of the two had "an average accuracy of charge within one eighth of a grain." Jones also invented a shot-counting trowel called the "Perfection," which was credited with improving the accuracy of loading cartridges.

In 1895, Jones was back at the patent office. Together with William Baker, he patented a single trigger (Number\ 1,844 of 1895) based

G. E. LEWIS,
MANUFACTURER OF AIR GUNS AND CANES,
ALSO OF
EVERY DESCRIPTION OF POWDER WALKING STICK GUNS, ETC.,
ON MOST IMPROVED PRINCIPLES,
WORKS: 32 & 33, LOWER LOVEDAY STREET,
BIRMINGHAM.

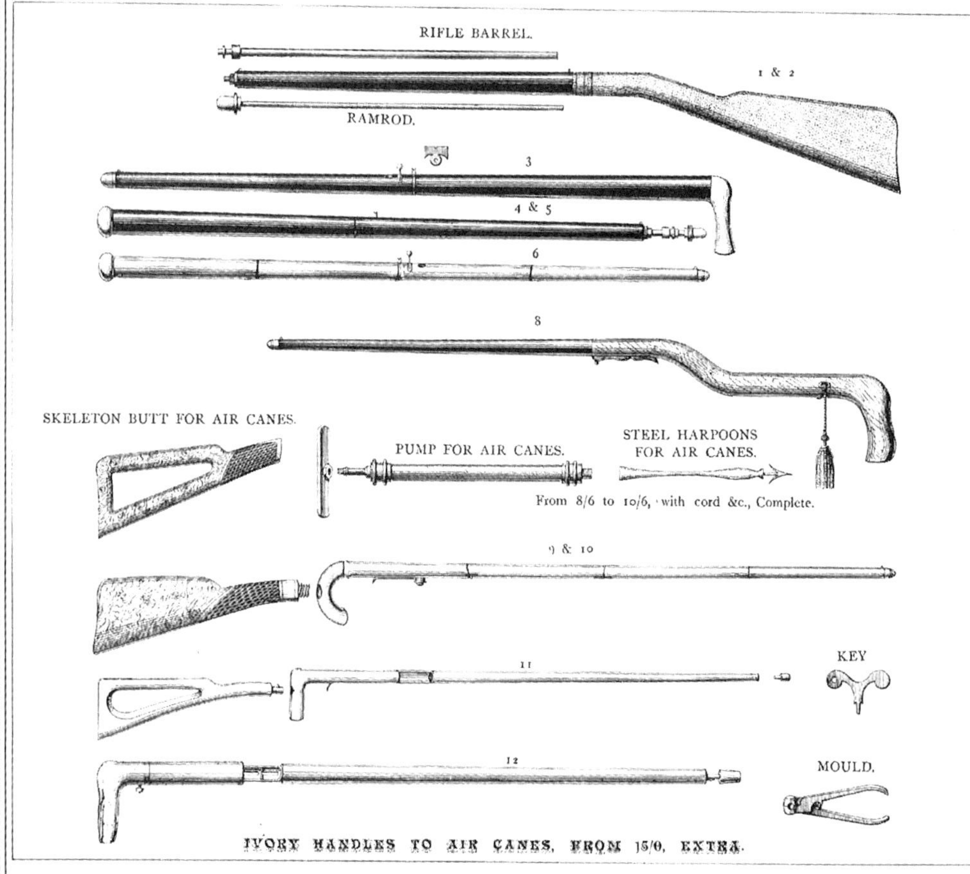

LIST OF PRICES.

		Best Quality.	Second Quality.	Third Quality.
1	Butt Air Gun, with Rifle and Shot Barrels, Pump &c., complete, … … …	140/0	135/0	130/0
2	Ditto only Rifle Barrel is Breech-loading,	10/0	extra	
3	Improved Air Cane, to load at the breech, with Stub twist Rifle Barrel, two leaf sight, Ivory handle, Pump &c., complete,	300/0	290/0	280/0
4	Air Cane Gun with Rifle and Shot Barrels, Pump &c., complete, … … …	75/0	70/0	65/0
5	Air Cane Gun with Rifled Barrel, or Smooth Bore Barrel for Shot, with Pump &c., complete, … … … …	70/0	64/0	58/0
6	Air Cane Gun with Rifled Barrel, to load at the breech, with Pump &c., complete,	78/0	73/0	68/0
7	Crooked Air Cane Gun, same shape as No. 8, to fire from the shoulder, with Pump &c., complete, … … …	88/0	83/0	78/0

		Best Quality.	Second Quality.	Third Quality.
8	Crooked M. L. Walking Stick Powder Gun, to fire from the shoulder, …	50/0	47/0	44/0
9	Muzzle-loading Walking Stick Powder Gun, with Butt. … … … …	60/0	55/0	50/0
10	Ditto without Butt 13/0 less,			
11	G. E. Lewis's Breech-loading Walking Stick Gun, with Attachable Butt, 410 bore, 63/0, 28 bore 84/0, 20 bore 105/0, Choke bores 10/6 extra, Safety Bolt to trigger, 3/6 and 5/0, extra.			
12	Breech-loading C. F. Walking Stick Gun, Covered with Bamboo Cane, with Buck Horn Handle, 320 bore 30/0, 380 bore 32/0, 410 bore 40/0.			

CARTRIDGES FOR NO. 12,   320 BORE,   BALL. 3/6,   SHOT 4/6 PER 100.

    „   „   „   380 BORE,   BALL. 4/6,   SHOT 6/0   „

    „   „   „   410 BORE,   BALL. 4/9,   SHOT 6/6   „

SHOT CARTRIDGES FOR AIR CANES 7/0, PER GROSS.

Prices to any Quality or sizes of Air Guns or Canes not quoted in this List, can be had on application.

TERMS :—NETT.

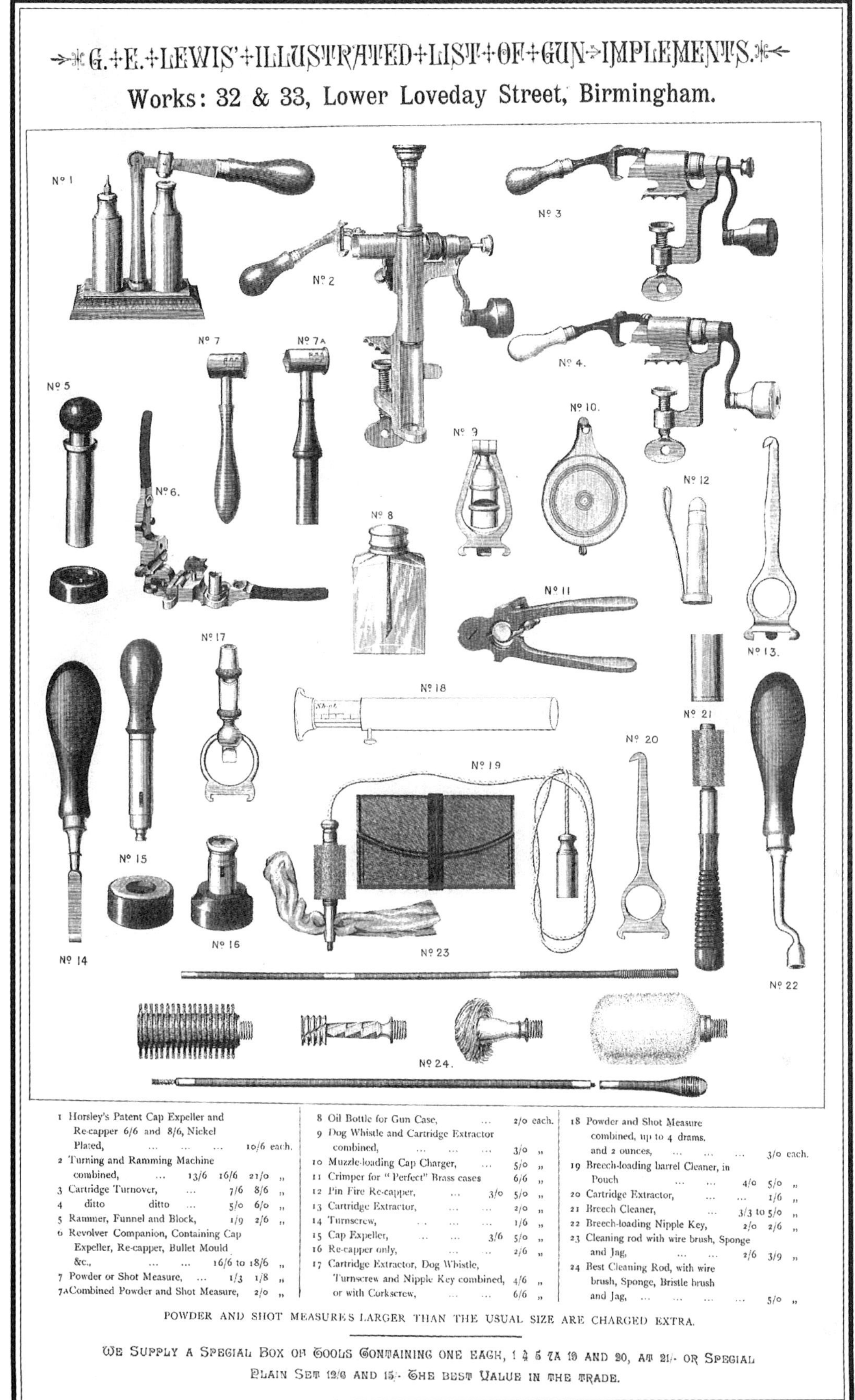

1 Horsley's Patent Cap Expeller and Re-capper 6/6 and 8/6, Nickel Plated, ... 10/6 each.

2 Turning and Ramming Machine combined, ... 13/6 16/6 21/0 „

3 Cartridge Turnover, ... 7/6 8/6 „

4 ditto ditto ... 5/0 6/0 „

5 Rammer, Funnel and Block, 1/9 2/6 „

6 Revolver Companion, Containing Cap Expeller, Re-capper, Bullet Mould &c., ... 16/6 to 18/6 „

7 Powder or Shot Measure, ... 1/3 1/8 „

7A Combined Powder and Shot Measure, 2/0 „

8 Oil Bottle for Gun Case, ... 2/0 each.

9 Dog Whistle and Cartridge Extractor combined, ... 3/0 „

10 Muzzle-loading Cap Charger, ... 5/0 „

11 Crimper for " Perfect" Brass cases 6/6 „

12 Pin Fire Re-capper, ... 3/0 5/0 „

13 Cartridge Extractor, ... 2/0 „

14 Turnscrew, ... 1/6 „

15 Cap Expeller, ... 3/6 5/0 „

16 Re-capper only, ... 2/6 „

17 Cartridge Extractor, Dog Whistle, Turnscrew and Nipple Key combined, 4/6 „ or with Corkscrew, ... 6/6 „

18 Powder and Shot Measure combined, up to 4 drams. and 2 ounces, ... 3/0 each.

19 Breech-loading barrel Cleaner, in Pouch ... ... 4/0 5/0 „

20 Cartridge Extractor, ... 1/6 „

21 Breech Cleaner, ... 3/3 to 5/0 „

22 Breech-loading Nipple Key, 2/0 2/6 „

23 Cleaning rod with wire brush, Sponge and Jag, ... 2/6 3/9 „

24 Best Cleaning Rod, with wire brush, Sponge, Bristle brush and Jag, ... 5/0 „

POWDER AND SHOT MEASURES LARGER THAN THE USUAL SIZE ARE CHARGED EXTRA.

WE SUPPLY A SPECIAL BOX OF TOOLS CONTAINING ONE EACH, 1 4 5 7A 19 AND 20, AT 21/- OR SPECIAL PLAIN SET 12/6 AND 15/- THE BEST VALUE IN THE TRADE.

found the resources to erect a factory is not addressed. Other sources maintain that Lewis did not occupy the Lower Loveday premises until 1859, and this explanation seems more likely.

There can be little doubt that he was a success, having shown guns at most of the international exhibits that were a feature of commerce in the second half of the nineteenth century. Like so many Birmingham makers, Lewis was a generalist who built heavy guns when the demand was for heavy guns and light ones when the fashion changed. He built sporting guns for India and Australia and military rifles for the French during the Franco-Prussian War and the Southern States during the American Civil War. It is likely that much of his early success was due to his ability to get rifles through the Yankee blockade. The Confederate government paid him in cotton, which was delivered to the Manchester Exchange in the same ships that had delivered the guns. After the war Lewis sold sporting guns through the pages of such American magazines as *Turf, Field & Stream* and *The Spirit of the Times* until the introduction of the punitive McKinley tariff of 1890 effectively closed the door to British guns.

In 1863, together with Henry Walker and Joseph Blout Wayne, who may have been employees of Lewis's, he patented a dropdown-action breechloader. Judging from the patent drawings, the mechanism was similar to the Dougall Lockfast, and

since no examples have survived, it is unlikely that it was a success. British Patent 2,100 of 25 August 1863 was George Lewis's sole venture into the area of new gun development, and when he died on 17 January 1917, *The Sporting Gun Review* wrote, "Mr. Lewis was not known as the author of any notable new development. He strove to produce a gun which should be perfect in detail and finish." In this regard he must have been abetted by his broad apprenticeship and perhaps even more so by the time he spent in art school. Lewis guns are characterized by fine quality and game-scene engraving, and even five years after his death, the more expensive guns featured in the Lewis sales catalog for

1922 all have good-quality engraved game scenes. Indeed, we know he was an accomplished engraver who used his talents to reduce hunting scenes from the canvases of that great Victorian wildlife artist Sir Edwin Landseer to a size appropriate for gunlocks.

In 1878, George Lewis introduced "The Gun of the Period," a phrase he registered like a trademark. Characteristically, these guns are beautifully finished but embody no new mechanical improvements. They were offered in hammer and hammerless forms and even as a cape gun with one barrel rifled on the Henry system and the second smooth for shot. The only feature that unifies them, apart from the title, was the use of a treble grip that operated between the ejectors, and

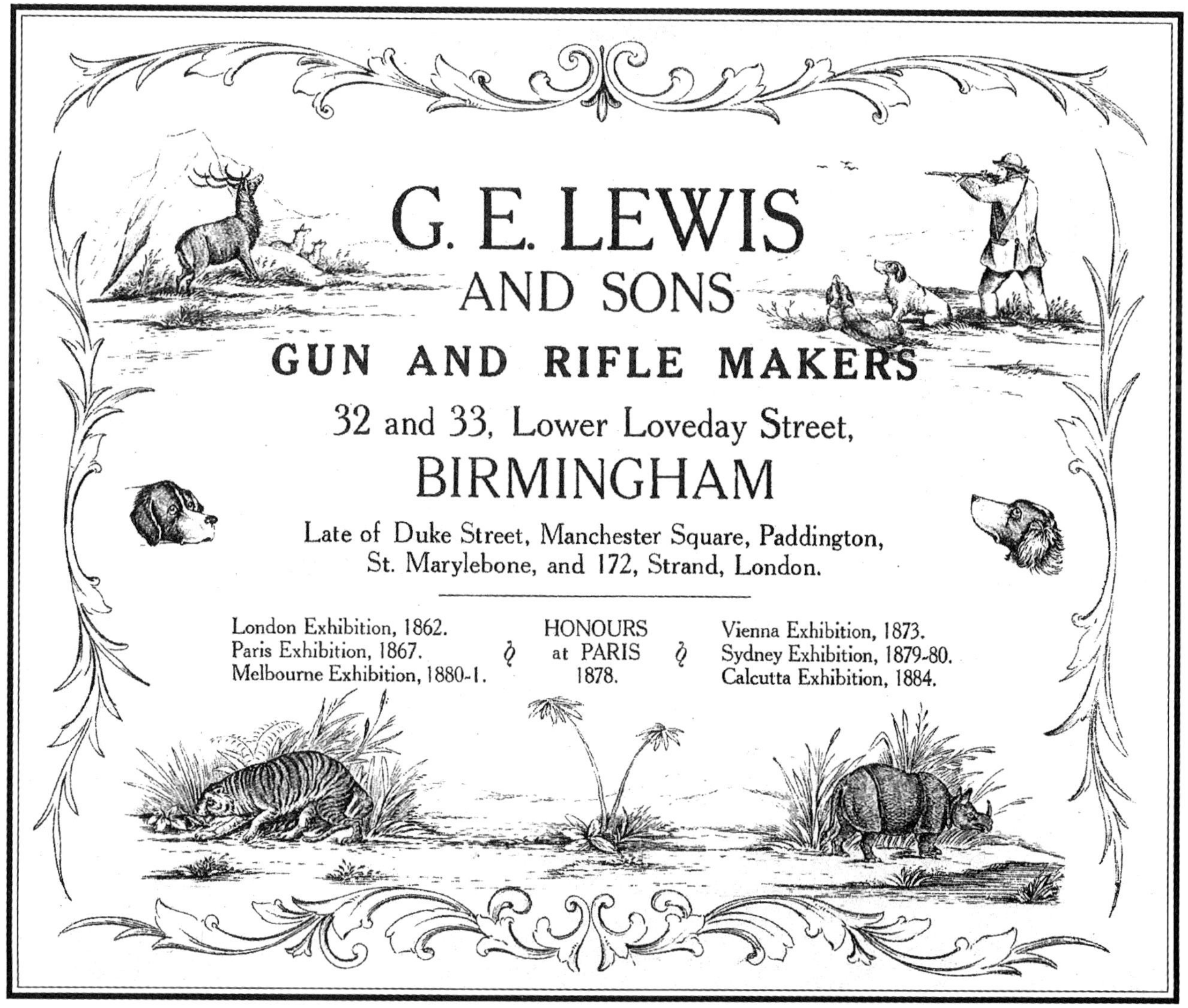

even this feature could be replaced by a Greener type or square cross bolt. This model was well received, winning honors at exhibitions in Paris in 1878, Sydney in 1879 and 1880, Melbourne in 1880 and 1881, and Calcutta in 1883 and 1884.

When George Lewis died, his two sons took over. The elder, also G. E. Lewis, was responsible for day-to-day company operations while the younger, E. C. Lewis, personally shot and regulated every gun the firm made. E. C. had a regional reputation as a rifle shot, winning the Birmingham rifle club championship six times and the 25 Guinea Gunmakers Association challenge cup for five successive years. The Lewis company took a special pride in the patterns produced by its guns: In the nineteenth century, the founder had developed a recessed choke that he claimed gave patterns "equal to the average of the six best guns at the late *Field* trials." During the twentieth century, when E. C. Lewis tested every gun, the company advertised that "probably no firm in the gun trade pays as much attention to the shooting and regulating of guns as we do."

In an age when all 20- and 16-bore guns made in England had 2½-inch chambers, the Lewis company introduced guns in both gauges chambered for 2¾-inch cartridges, which it called "magnum small bores." They were tested by W. Baden-Powell, K.C., under the auspices of *The Field* magazine, and Lewis afterward advertised "that excellent results can be obtained with these guns when properly bored and regulated."

In the 1920s, when Robert Churchill developed and promoted his XXV (a lightweight gun with 25-inch barrels), the Lewis firm was quick to recognize an opportunity and began marketing its own lightweight gun known as the "Ariel." It weighed 5¾ pounds and had 28-inch barrels as standard, though barrels could be "supplied shorter if preferred." The gun was advertised as suitable for sportsmen "in a hot climate" and having the advantage of "a larger killing circle than a smaller bore of the same weight." In some examples, every effort was made to give the appearance of an A & D Churchill with flattened ball fences, Churchill-style bouquet and scroll engraving, and a scalloped-back action body.

Sometime in the 1930s, a third-generation G. E. Lewis took over the firm. Second son of E. C. Lewis (the elder son, E. V. Lewis, was, like his father, a crack shot and led a sniper team of sixteen through the First World War), this G. E. served as guardian of the Birmingham Proof House in 1951 and died in 1988.

In 1988, the last of the gunmaking Lewises died, and the company was purchased by John Harris, a man who had stocked many of the Lewis guns. Like the original G. E. Lewis, he was a master gunmaker who had studied the trade "in all its branches." John built a commemorative gun to mark the passing of the last Lewis and, in a gesture that would certainly have been appreciated by the founder, did much of the engraving himself.

I would like to thank John Harris, without whom this chapter could not have been written. For further information on G. E. Lewis guns, contact John at 6 Haden Hill Rd., Halesowen, West Midlands, B63 3NQ.

DANIEL LEONARD

One of the most contentious aspects of the British gun trade is the relationship between the London and Birmingham makers. At its most polarized, the argument is represented by those who insist that the London makers are in every way superior and have always existed in total isolation from their Midland cousins. On the other hand, there are those who think that all London guns, including best guns, were made in Birmingham. Somewhere between these two extremes lies the truth.

On the best evidence, it appears that the top echelon of West End makers had occasional recourse to the Birmingham trade. The boxlock guns retailed by James Woodward & Sons are clearly Webley products, and in the collection of H.R.H. the Queen at Sandringham are a pair of Purdey pistols with Birmingham black-powder proofs. But among the top tier of London makers, Birmingham guns are the exception, not the rule.

With the second tier, the story is very different. Many London gunmakers in this second group appear not to have made guns at all; Army & Navy, for example, seems to have had all its guns made by W. & C. Scott. And throughout its history, E. J. Churchill used a host of Birmingham makers, including William Baker, A. A. Brown and, in the post-war years, S. Wright & Sons of Bath Street.

Churchill began by making its own guns, but as costs rose and profits diminished, the firm learned that quality guns could be had in Birmingham at reasonable prices. This also seems to have been the case with William Jackman Jeffrey. Originally from southwest England, Jeffrey was established in London by the 1880s, and, based on the devices he patented—which are almost entirely improvements for rifle sights—he appears to have been more interested in rifles than shotguns. Jeffrey's advertising catalogs feature many more rifles than do those of his contemporaries.

Today, the Jeffrey name is synonymous with certain big-game calibers used in Africa

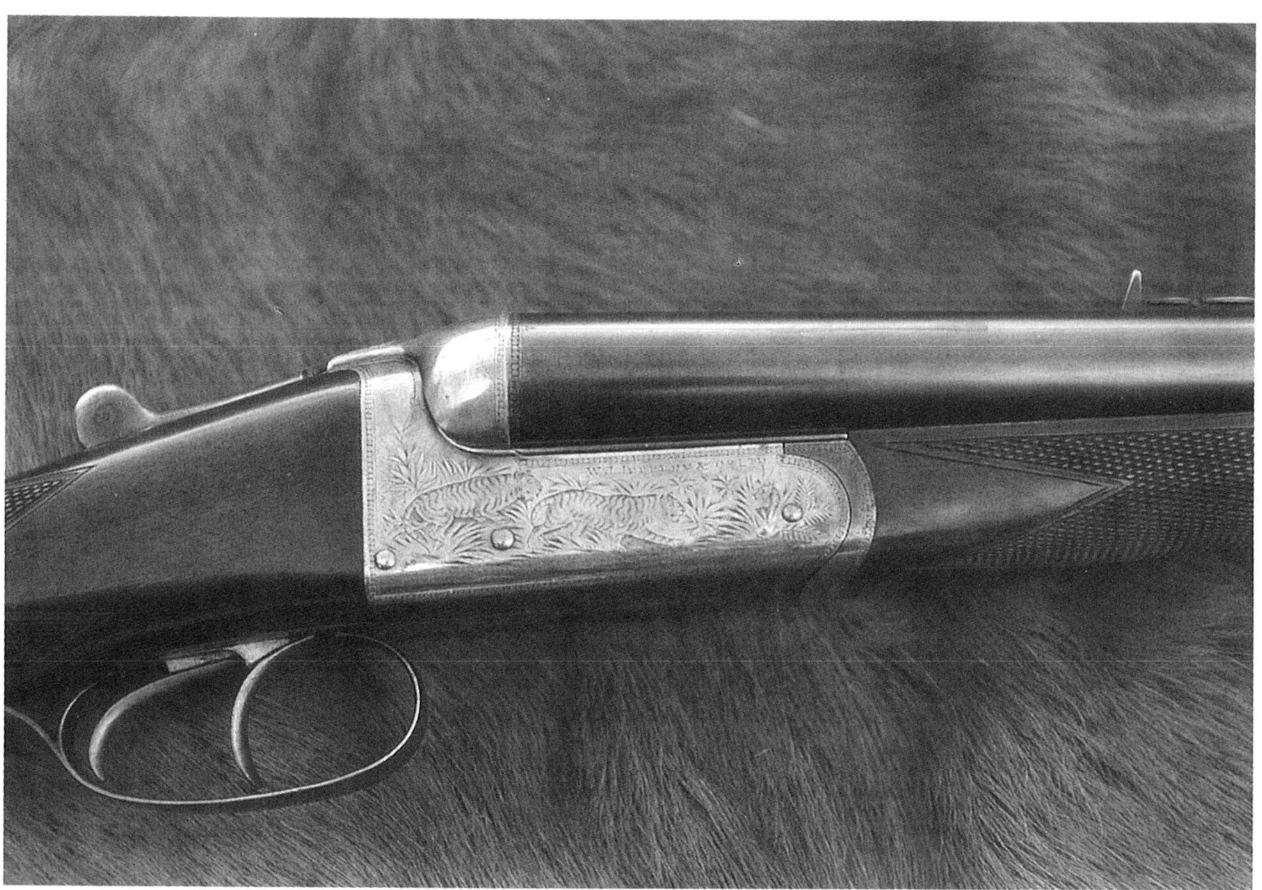

This .450-400 double rifle, built by Leonard for W. J. Jeffery in 1913 and sold by Walter Locke of Calcutta, Delhi, and Lahore, is engraved with stalking tigers. (Tim Crawford)

Most of the Leonard family's output was for the trade, so this gun signed by Leonard is rare. The asymmetrical bow or shaped action was a feature of many of the guns the Leonard family built for W. J. Jeffery. (A. A. Brown & Sons)

and India, including .404 Jeffrey, .333 flanged Nitro Express, and .600 Nitro. Of these, the .600 Nitro is the most famous. The most powerful sporting cartridge produced until the recent development of the H & H .700, the .600 Nitro was described by John "Pondoro" Taylor as "primarily designed and intended as an elephant STOPPER." Very few .600 doubles were ever made, and it has long been rumored that W. J. Jeffrey built the most in the trade—a total of six. The irony is that most, if not all, were made in Birmingham by D. Leonard & Sons.

Daniel Leonard appears to have been established as a gun and pistol maker in the Birmingham gun quarter as early as 1832.

In about 1859, his address changes from 89 to 90 Aston Street, as a consequence of street renumbering. In 1866, the firm became Daniel Leonard and Sons. The company acquired additional premises at Whittal Street in 1874 and moved to 131 Steelhouse Lane early in 1885. Another street renumbering changed Leonard's address to 133 Steelhouse Lane, where the firm remained until at least 1895.

In 1895, D. Leonard & Sons advertised itself in *The Sporting Goods Review* as "practical gun and rifle manufacturers." This periodical was the organ of the British and particularly the Birmingham gun trade at the time, and Leonard's presence in the magazine seems to suggest that he was so-liciting the trade, rather than the public at large, for business. The ad offers "wild fowl, pigeon & keepers' guns always in stock." At about this time Leonard, supplied the pro-vincial gunmaker W. R. Pape of Newcastle upon Tyne with a small number of 16-bore back-action non-ejectors with Damascus bar-rels. The guns are of middling quality and certainly qualify as keeper's guns. The same ad went on: "Specialty: double express rifles & rifle shot guns, from 10 guineas to £40."

By the late 1880s, both Jeffrey and Leonard had outlets on Queen Victoria Street in London, Jeffrey at Number 60 and Leonard at 147. Shortly thereafter, the Jeffrey records show that many of its double rifles were being built by "H. Leonard." (Another Birmingham gunmaker John Saunders, of Anderton Square, Whittal Street, appears to have built many of the Jeffrey shotguns.) Harry Leonard was the son of Daniel Leonard and brother to Daniel and Samuel. He had a workshop at 19 Lench Street in Birmingham's gun quarter, and a signature feature of many of his guns and rifles was a bow back to the action that Jeffrey called a "shaped action" in his catalog.

George Ellis, who worked for the Leonard brothers as an actioner and jointer, remembered that the Leonards also built guns and rifles for Daniel Fraser, then of Edinburgh. Significantly, many Fraser guns also feature bow backs. In another near coincidence, the Jeffrey books also record the name of Ellis as a builder of guns and rook and rabbit rifles.

Ellis also recalled how Sam Leonard went out to the U.S. and would advertise when he would be in various cities to carry out repairs, so that guns could be sent to an address and await his arrival. Since the Leonard name by itself couldn't have carried much clout, these trips may have been organized by Jeffrey.

The patent record has two entries in the name of Samuel Arthur Leonard. One (Num-ber 14,159 of 3 July 1908) describes a single-trigger, double-barreled gun "of the type in which the sears are lifted by a swinging blade mounted on the trigger." The second (Num-ber 172,066 of 30 July 1920) is for an action with a solid body in which the "hammers and sears are operated by helical springs." Both single triggers and coil-spring guns were thought to be coming ideas in the early twen-tieth century gun trade and are a recurring feature of contemporary gun patents. Time has proven that both were passing fads, though some American riflemen still insist on single triggers for their double guns.

Between the dates these patents were taken out, the Leonard business was inter-rupted by the Great War (1914-1918). John "Jack" Rowe, a Birmingham gunmaker now living in Enid, Oklahoma, remembers that Harry, Daniel, and Samuel Leonard served as armorers, all with the rank of Sergeant.

Neither Jeffrey nor Leonard survives today; Jeffrey was absorbed by Holland & Holland in 1960, and Leonard disappeared about the time Birmingham's gun quarter was gutted to make way for the inner-ring road a few years later. Although both firms have gone, it is fascinating to speculate on just how many other London and Birmingham gunmakers enjoyed similar symbiotic relationships during the golden era of English gunmaking.

JOSEPH NEEDHAM

The history of Joseph Needham is a his-tory of firsts—the first hammerless gun, the first ejector, and the first barrel-cocked ham-merless gun.

The Needham company was started in Birmingham in the early 1840s, then moved to London, where it traded as William Needham at 26 Piccadilly. In 1851, the name was changed to William & Joseph Needham, presumably to accommodate Joseph, who was perhaps a brother or more likely the son of the founder.

Whatever the relationship, the newcomer was an inventive individual who patented (Number 184 of 1852) Britain's first double-barreled hammerless shotgun. Unlike a later generation of guns with dropdown barrels, the Needham was rigid in construction and was similar to two Dreyse bolt-action needle guns joined together with an upper and lower rib. Despite requiring its own special cartridge, the design was a success and may even have been shown at the Great Exhibition of 1851. The catalog records that Needham exhibited "double and single guns to load at the breech." Both double- and single-barreled guns built on the Needham patent have survived, so it is possible that this design is the subject of the catalog's reference. Most of the extant examples are engraved with the W. & J. Rigby name, and in 1860 John Rigby and Joseph Needham patented (Number 3,140 of 1860) an improvement to the basic design.

Two years later, Joseph Needham patented (Number 1,544 of 1862) another classic design. The specifications describe yet another improvement to his needle gun and at least four separate gun designs, but only one was destined to be a classic. This was a single-bite snap-action hammer gun with a horizontal spindle lying transversely through the breakoff that engaged a rearward-projecting lump attached beneath the barrels. The spindle was rotated, and the gun opened, by pushing down on a slim lever that ran alongside the right-hand action bar. The lever also withdrew the strikers and brought the hammers to half-cock—which, in the years before Stanton's rebounding lock, was a safety feature. Needham exploited this feature in his advertising: "By this arrangement a premature explosion of the cartridges is a moral impossibility, and Messrs. Needham guar-

antee its mechanical efficiency for seven years." The method of locking the gun was favorably compared with the Purdey underbolt in the contemporary press, and the design was adopted by such famous makers as Henry Holland in London and Westley Richards in Birmingham. None of this is surprising to anyone who has seen one of these guns, as they are most elegant. The long, slightly down-curved lockplates, which are of vestigial muzzleloader design, are set in a bar of fine walnut. The pin-fire hammers and fences are sensuously curved, and the lack of a top or bottom lever gives the gun a streamlined profile unequaled in the age before the hammerless gun evolved.

Over the next decade Needham patented a series of designs for sliding, hinged, and revolving breechblocks, together with a dagger handle. All are forgettable. Then on 7 April 1874 he registered (Number 1,205 of 1874) yet another classic design, the first practical barrel-cocked hammerless ejector shotgun. While it is true that John Henry Walsh, editor of *The Field* magazine, had earlier designed a gun in which the lockwork was cocked by the fall of the barrels, it was an obscure, awkward design that never got far beyond the prototype stage, whereas the Needham was widely adopted. The rise in popularity of driven shooting encouraged the development of speedy reloading, and therefore ejectors, but Walsh was loath to acknowledge this, writing, "I confess I cannot see the gain resulting from this arrangement, if a loader is employed he almost always has plenty of time for extraction by the fingers."

The shooting public and rival gunmakers thought otherwise. The gun was widely licensed, and the split-stem ejector, which had two semicircular rods sliding in one hole, was thought of as a great innovation. Not only did it kick fired cartridges free from the gun, but it also slightly withdrew live rounds so they could be removed more easily by hand. Looking back with the advantage of hindsight, two things are striking about the gun: just how mechanically advanced it was for its day and just how aesthetically defective it looks by modern standards. The three major progressive features of the design—the lack of external hammers, the locks that are cocked by the fall of the barrels, and the ejectors—were individual innovations worthy of the ultimate compliment—emulation. Taken together, they produced a revolutionary design, and Needham received the royalties and remunerations that are the rewards of a registered design widely reproduced. However, to modern eyes at least, the gun looks like a transitional design, a hammer gun without hammers, and the box beneath that action that houses the ejectors is an ugly protrusion.

The ejectors, however, when redesigned by no less an authority than William Wellington Greener, were accommodated in the body of a modern gun, initially the "Facile Princeps" and later the Anson & Deeley. It seems that W. W. Greener, seeing the success of the Anson & Deeley action, wanted to be able to offer it himself, but because he had publicly championed his own very similar design and denigrated the A. & D., he was, initially at least, sheepish about doing so. Greener therefore acquired Joseph Needham's company in the early 1880s and, operating from "Damascus Works" in Loveday Street, used the firm to sell conventional, medium-quality, A. & D.-actioned guns fitted, at least in the beginning, with modified Needham ejectors as a token gesture to Needham's reputation.

Three models were eventually offered, all called "The Challenger" and numbered 1, 2, and 3. Number 1 was a basic, border-engraved, non-ejector; Number 2 was banner-and-scroll engraved with a Greener Treble Wedge-Fast cross bolt; and Number 3 was fitted with the "undoubted luxury" of "automatic" ejectors. Ironically, the later models were fitted with an ejecting system other than Needham's. Today, the tokenism continues: The resuscitated W. W. Greener company continues to offer the "Needham No. 5," a basic A. & D.-actioned gun in 12-, 16-, and 20-bores or as a .410.

CHARLES OSBOURNE

The history of the Birmingham gun trade abounds with Osbournes: John Osborne was in Russell Street in 1770; Robert Osbourne (the various spellings seem to have meant little in an era when most people could not write), a "gun worm maker" [a spiral tool for unloading muzzleloaders] in 1767, was listed as a musician by 1777; and Thomas Osborn worked as a gun and pistol maker at Newton Row from 1807 until his death in 1811. Thomas's son, Henry, assumed control on his father's death and, together with a certain Mr. Gunby, was granted contracts with the Board of Ordnance and the East India Company, seemingly for military rifles.

In 1812, Osborn precipitated a riot by 1,200 striking Birmingham barrelmakers when he introduced a welding machine that threatened to replace them. They marched on his home on Stratford Road armed with their forge hammers, and disaster was averted only when troops were assigned to guard both Henry's home and his new invention. All of this occurred when the British army was desperately trying to rearm against Napoleon—and three years before Waterloo and just one year after a similar but more famous riot gave the language the word "Luddite."

Charles Osbourne, who some believe was related to Thomas Osborn II, a nephew of the barrel-machine inventor, claimed to have established his business in 1838, but is not mentioned in Birmingham street directories until 1845. The catalog of the Great Exhibition of 1851 lists him at 1 Lichfield Street,

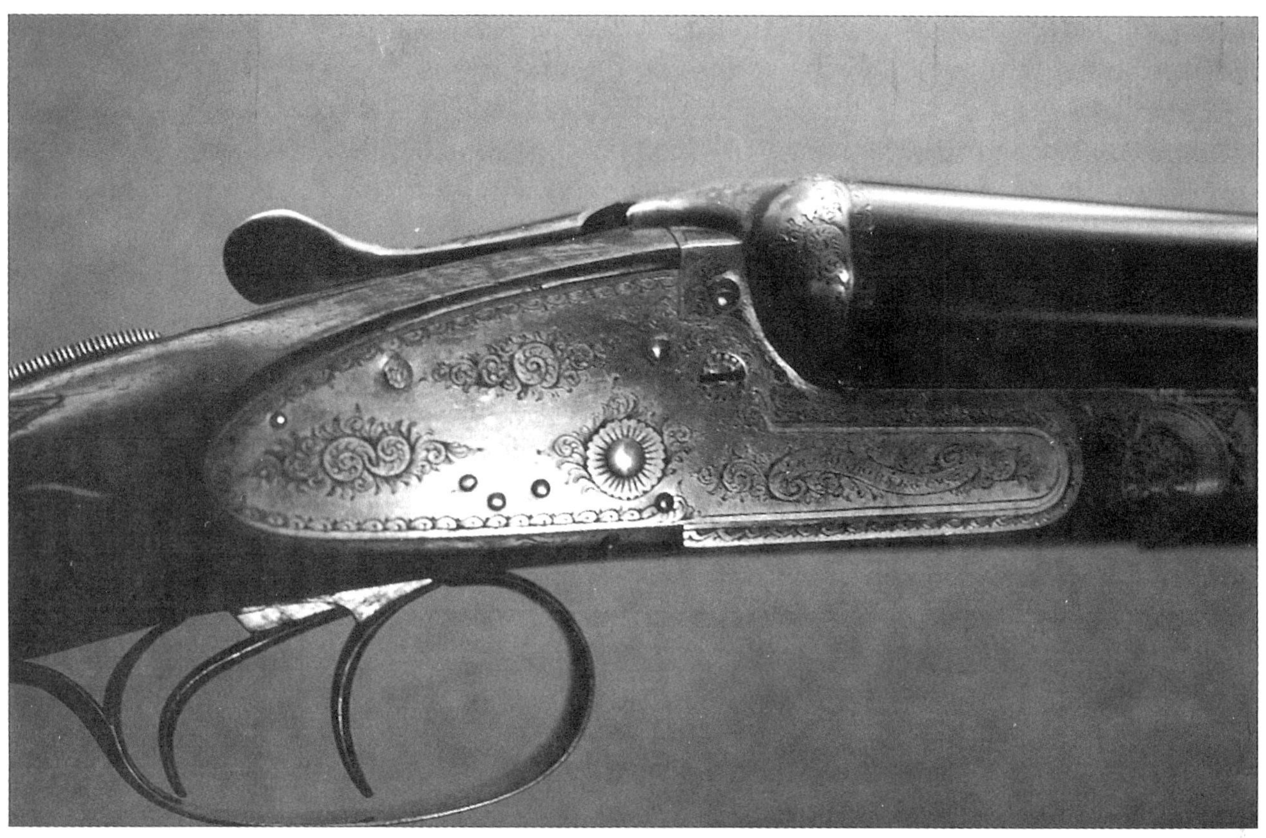

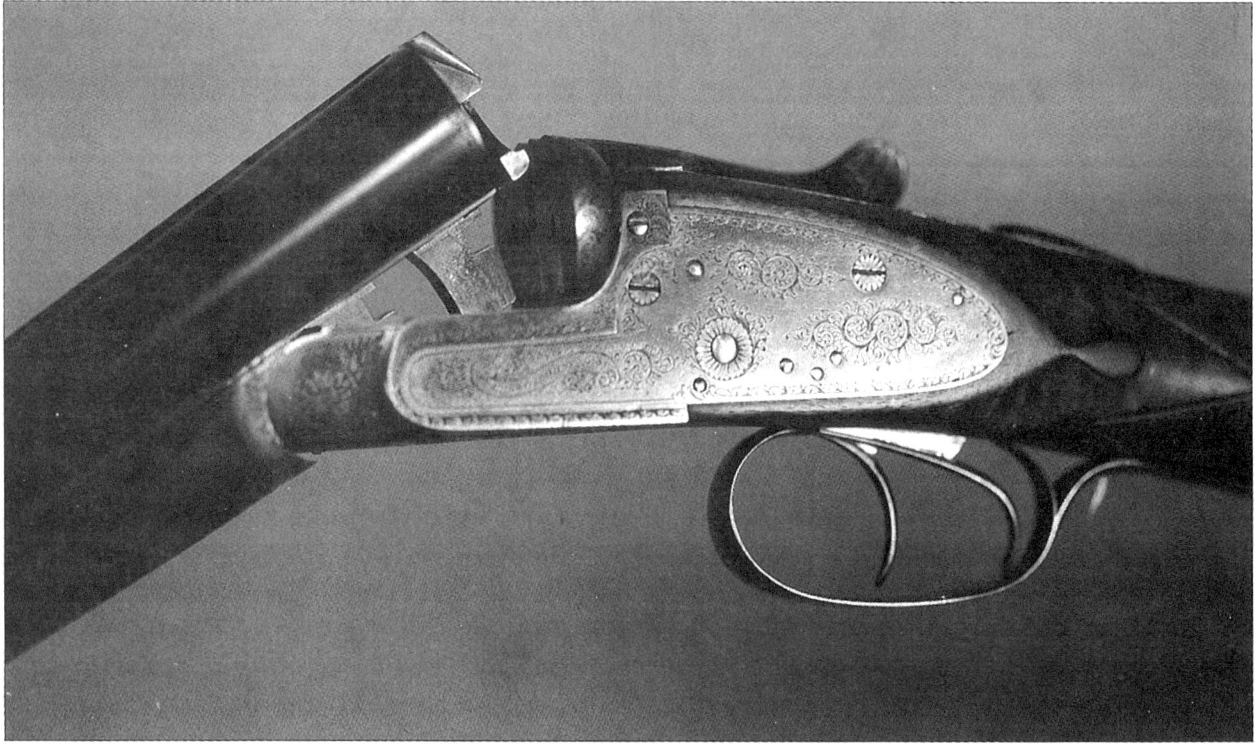

A flat-back-action 12-bore by Charles Osbourne. (Jeff Bird)

Birmingham. Among the items he exhibited are "improved central fire double guns with chain twist barrels" and "tube single gun, large single gun with Colonel Hawker's improved ignition." The use of the term "central fire" is a reference not to a breechloader but rather to a percussion gun in which the flash of the cap is directed to the center—rather than to the side—of the loaded powder. The "chain twist barrels" are a type of fancy Damascus in which the pattern closely resembles a chain. The "large single gun" is thought to be a single-barreled wildfowling gun built on an improved version of Colonel Peter Hawker's ignition system.

By 1877 Charles Osbourne Ellis, grandson of the founder, had succeeded to the head of the firm. He took as his partner Edward William Wilkinson, who had apprenticed with Charles Osbourne. The two men continued to trade as Charles Osbourne & Co. while embarking on a series of patents they hoped would make their fortunes. The first was for a fore-end fastener (Number 292 of 1877) that was both complex and already obsolete by the time it appeared in 1877. The simpler Deeley & Edge and Anson fore-ends of a few years earlier were both destined to gain much wider acceptance.

The two men then patented a system of rebounding strikers (Number 8,402 of 1884) for hammerless guns and a system of ejectors (Number 7,222 of 1887), both of which appear to have been no more successful than their fore-end fastener. Next came a sliding breech-block mechanism (Number 11,879 of 1888) for a punt gun, then an extractor (Number 5,151 of 1896) for a revolver.

In the last ten years of the nineteenth century, Britain's—and especially Birmingham's—gunmakers vied with each other to develop a reliable single-trigger that would fire the barrels of a double gun one at a time. As the old century ended and the new one began, Osbourne and

Wilkinson patented single-trigger systems three times: Numbers 12,050 of 1898, 26,493 of the same year with W. Jerman, and 3,088 of 1900. If the number of guns produced on a given patent is an indicator of success, Osbourne and Wilkinson's single triggers were outright failures.

The final patent (Number 2,576 of 1909) in the Osbourne story is one taken out by Charles Ryland, who appears to have apprenticed with Osbourne & Co. Ryland would go on to develop perhaps the most successful of the actions that utilized helical springs—the Ward "Target" gun, which must have brought him financial rewards because he is recorded as living in Barnt Green, Worcestershire, at that time a prestigious suburb of Birmingham. However, the design he produced for Osbourne & Co. in the early months of 1909 appears to have been something of an anomaly. The specification reads, "The action body has open sides, and the hammer, cocking rod and cocking lever are assembled before being placed in position." Perhaps it was an attempt to build a boxlock with detachable locks in the manner of Westley Richards but with the locks coming through the sides rather than the bottom of the action. Since no specimens have survived, we may never know.

In the previous year, Osbourne introduced a machine-made single-barreled shotgun. It was a concept that would prove successful for Webley, who introduced a similar gun, the Model 100, six years later, but the Osbourne appears not to have taken off.

After the First World War, Osbourne attempted to rebuild after "completion of important War Work upon which they were engaged." Apparently this war work "called for their utmost endeavors in the requirement and interests of the nation." Both quotes are from an "emergency catalog" Osbourne & Co. published in 1920 to accompany its display of guns at an arms fair. The catalog is revealing for a number of reasons. First, it is in English, French, and Spanish; is "wholesale only;" and is filled with hammer and boxlock guns and big-bore double rifles. This fact, together with street and cable addresses in Birmingham and London, seems to suggest that Osbourne was competing for the colonial markets of Latin America and Africa.

The London street address was 10 York Buildings, Adelphi, and the cable address "pivotgun, London." The front page of the catalog features a trademark of a pivot harpoon whaling gun, and the exhibit the catalog was intended to accompany also had as its centerpiece the whaling gun with which Osbourne had won a gold medal at the international exhibition of 1883. During World War I, seventeen of these muzzleloaders had been sold for use on the whaling stations of the East African coast. An earlier catalog had described this same model "for shooting bottle nose whales."

Charles Osbourne & Co. was purchased in the spring of 1928 by Skimin & Wood, which announced that Charles Osbourne would "continue to trade in this name at their new premises at 10/14 Vesey Street, Birmingham." This was, of course, the address of Skimin & Wood at the time. It appears the Skimin-controlled Osbourne firm continued to supply the more remote corners of the world with muzzleloaders and hammer guns well into the 1940s, finally dropping from sight sometime in the early 1950s.

WILLIAM POWELL & SON

In Victorian Britain, every town and city had its high-street gunmaker whose clientele were the rural gentry of the immediate vicinity. In Birmingham, the High Street gunmaker was William Powell.

Birmingham's gun quarter, located just north of the city center, may have provided guns for some of the London and most of the provincial trade, but when a local gentleman wanted a gun, he bypassed the gun quarter and went to William Powell on High Street. Powell appears to have distinguished itself by the simple expedient of establishing a retail business in the heart of Birmingham's shopping district, thus soliciting the shooting man directly.

The first William Powell established his business with Joseph Simmons on Birmingham's High Street in 1802 and became the sole proprietor when Simmons died in 1812. In 1823, Powell had a son whom he christened William Powell. In the same year he moved to 3 Bartholomew Road but was back on High Street on the corner of Carrs Lane by 1830. The premises at this time had doors that opened onto both streets, 49 High Street and 9½ Carrs Lane. William Powell purchased land in Carrs Lane, and a factory and warehouse were erected. Five generations and 194 years later, his descendants are still making guns on Carrs Lane. One of the fine examples of the gunmaker's craft a visitor can see at the Powell premises is a single-barreled flintlock built by the first William Powell during the 1830s. Less than nine inches long and only a few ounces in weight, it is inlaid with silver wire and the lock still functions: Peter Powell can remember his father breaking a window demonstrating the gun to local prep school kids!

The firm moved to 11 Carrs Lane in 1846, just three years after the twenty-year-old William Powell joined his father. In the following year, the younger Powell became a father himself and named his son William Leith Powell. The catalog of the Great Exhibition held at the Crystal Palace in 1851 shows that Powell displayed a "double barreled rifle and gun; pistols, improved safety

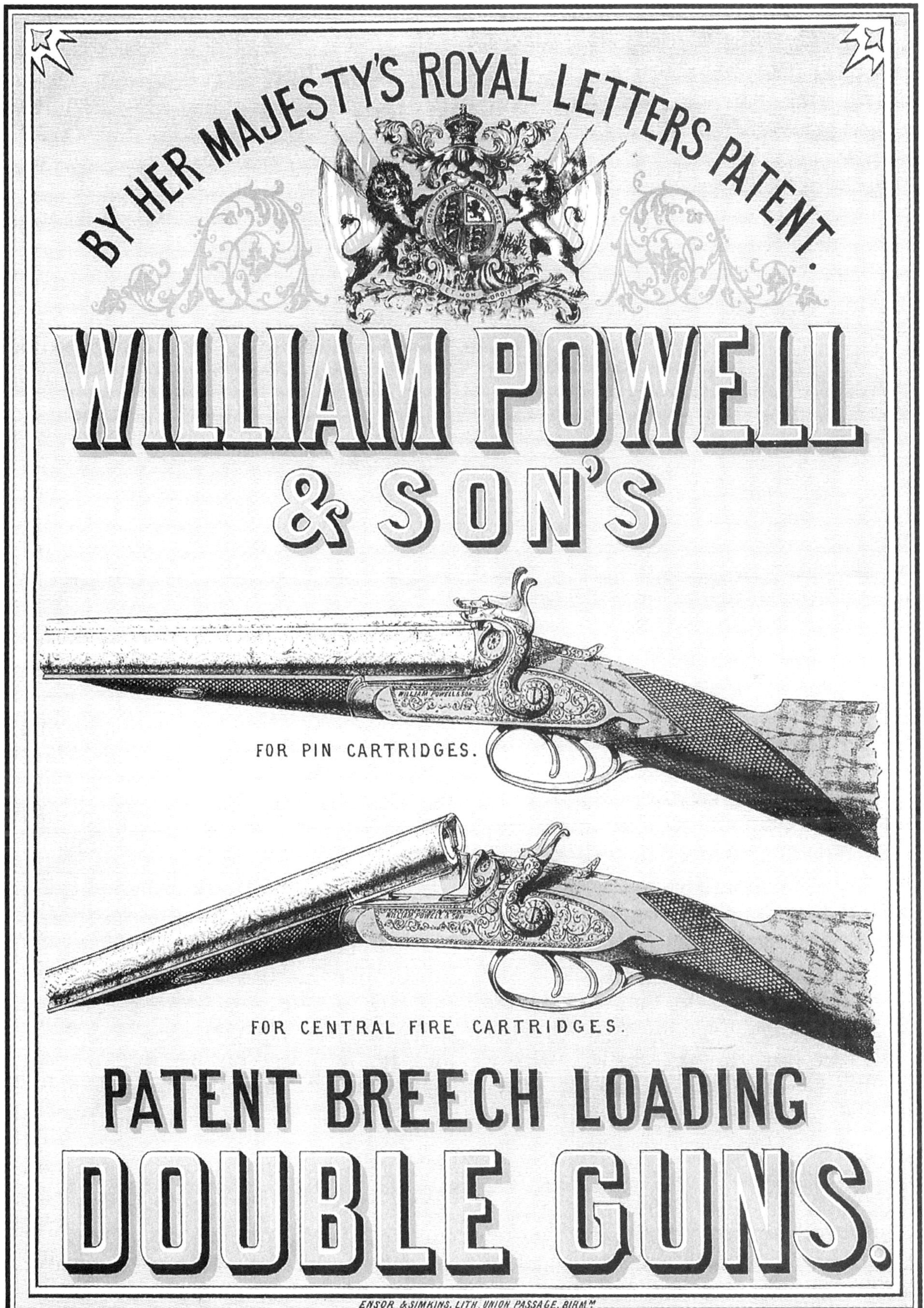
BY HER MAJESTY'S ROYAL LETTERS PATENT.
WILLIAM POWELL & SON'S
FOR PIN CARTRIDGES.
FOR CENTRAL FIRE CARTRIDGES.
PATENT BREECH LOADING
DOUBLE GUNS.
ENSOR & SIMKINS, LITH. UNION PASSAGE, BIRM.

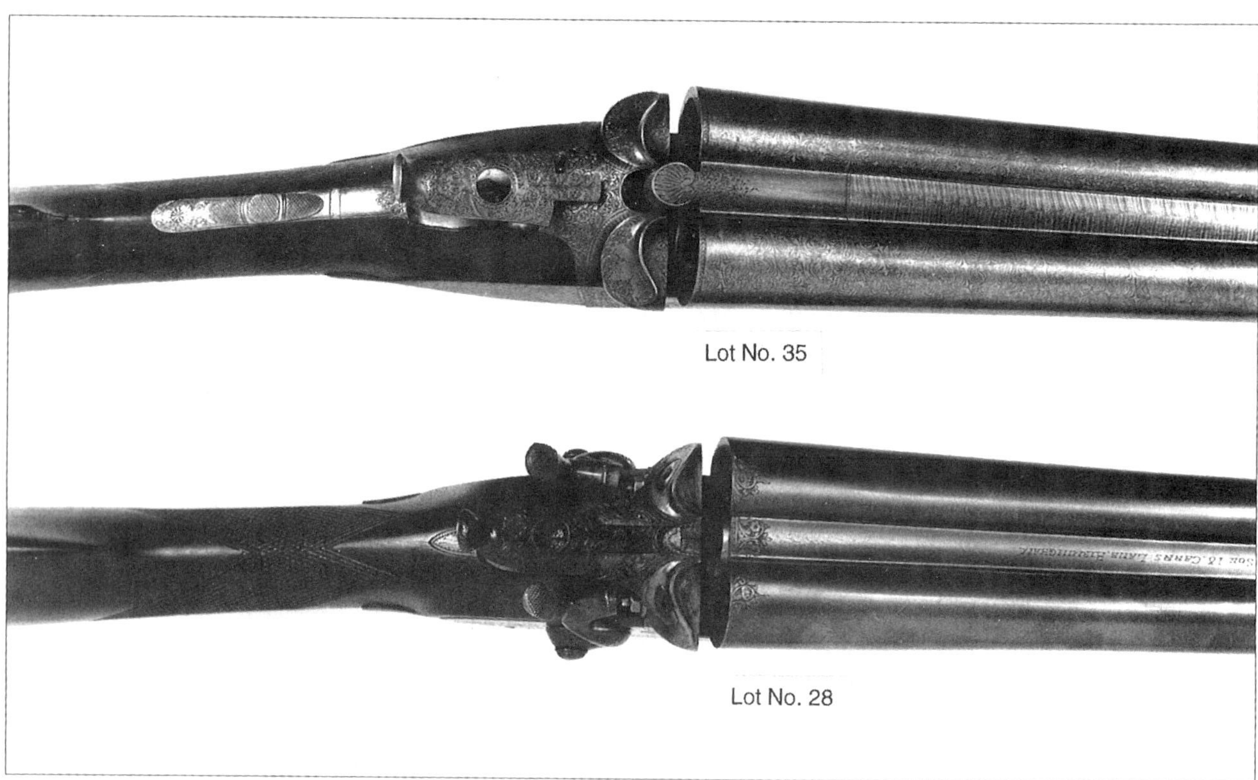

Two guns that feature Powell's patent "Lift Uplever." The top gun, a boxlock, was retailed by W. B. Barratt of Burton on Trent while the gun at bottom is a bar-in-wood hammer gun signed by William Powell. Both feature signature Powell fences. (Weller & Dufty)

trigger guard, pair of lock actions, etc." In 1862, the third William Powell entered the firm at age fifteen.

In 1864, William Powell patented (Number 1,163 of 1864) a gun action with a top lever that lifted up to open the gun. It was a considerable success, and today guns built on the patent are still frequently encountered—hardly surprising since over 5,000 were made. Although many bear the names of provincial gunmakers, they are identifiable as Powell products by the distinctive Powell fence, which is a stylistic vestige of the pin-fire era and looks almost as if someone impressed a thumbprint onto the still-molten metal. Although it is unclear when Powell stopped making "Lift Uplever" guns—which were of snap-action design—they were made well into the hammerless era, and Powell could, if requested, incorporate the patent into a new bespoke gun.

The Lift Uplever gun was, of course, conceived as a hammer gun, and one of the problems with early hammer guns was that they could accidentally discharge if the gun was closed with cartridges in the chambers and the hammers uncocked. In 1866, together with a gun finisher named William Poole Bardell, Powell patented (Number 2,287) a rebounding lock that addressed this problem. Unfortunately, John Stanton, the famous Wolverhampton lockmaker, patented his own version of a rebounding lock the very next year, and it was the Stanton lock, rather than Powell's, which found universal acceptance with the trade. Nevertheless, Powell's rebounding locks continue to be recalled by the legend "Patentees 1866," which appears on the firm's current letterhead and trade labels.

When center-fire guns began to replace pin-fire guns at about this same time, one

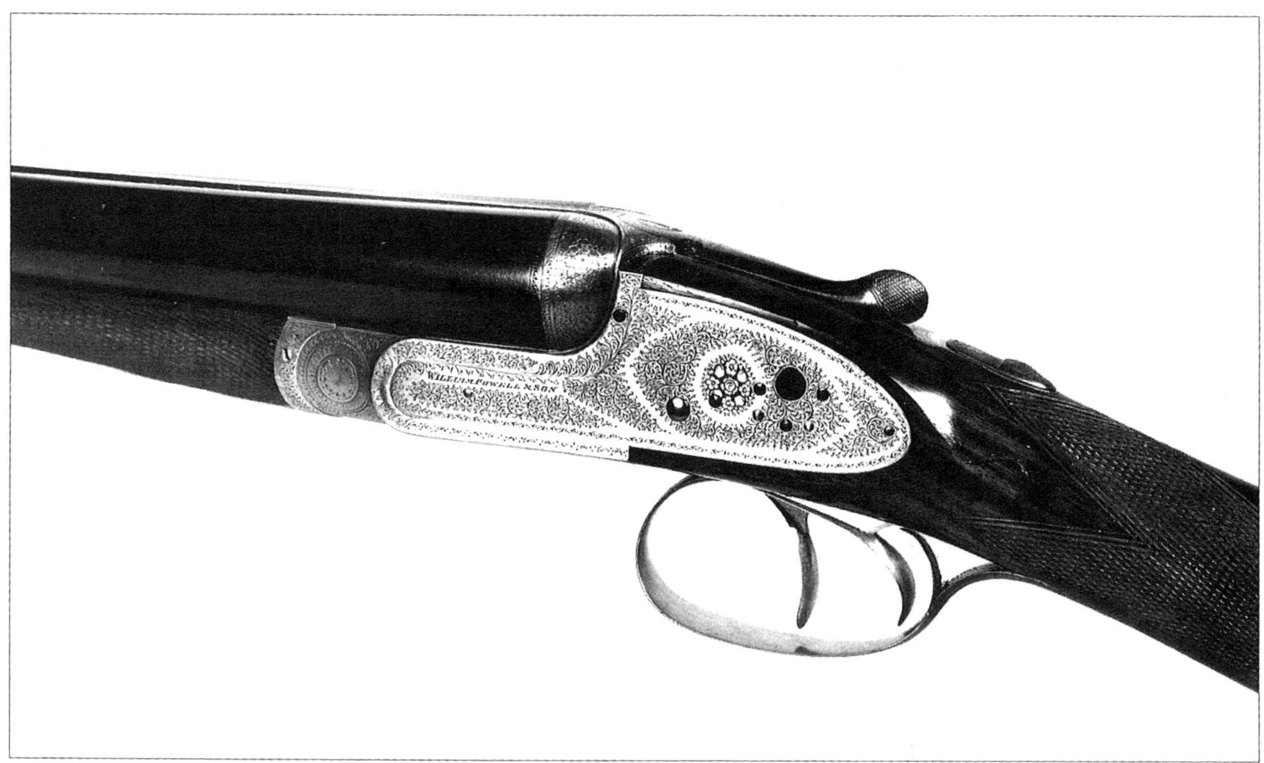

A sidelock ejector by William Powell & Son. (Elderkin & Son)

of the recurring criticisms of the new ignition system was that it was impossible to tell when a gun was loaded. With the old system, the pins of the cartridges were visible protruding through small holes in the top rear of the barrels, and sportsmen complained that the new guns must be constantly opened to determine if they held cartridges. In 1869, William Powell patented (Number 1,055) an improvement to his Lift Uplever gun in which the rear end of the strikers were gold inlaid with the word "loaded."

In 1873, he provisionally patented (Number 2,193) a fore-end fastener, followed three years later by a spindle and bolting system (Number 493), neither of which appears to have enjoyed wide acceptance. In addition to his efforts to improve the British shotgun, William Powell, like his father before him, also served the trade by acting as a Proof House guardian between 1862 and 1902. He died in '02 at age seventy-nine, having served the last eleven years of his life as Proof House treasurer.

On his death, his son, William Leith Powell, became the senior partner. In the previous year, he and A. Dean had patented a single trigger (Number 6,584 of 1901) on the involuntary pull system, but it does not appear to have found wide acceptance. Indeed, it may be significant that the only single-trigger Powell that I have seen was fitted with the Boss single trigger. Like his father, William Leith Powell also served as a guardian of the Birmingham Proof House.

William Leith Powell was head of his family's firm for only fourteen years. When he died in 1916, his obituary ran to two pages in both *Arms and Explosives* and *The Sporting Goods Review*. His services to the community at large and the gun trade in particular were

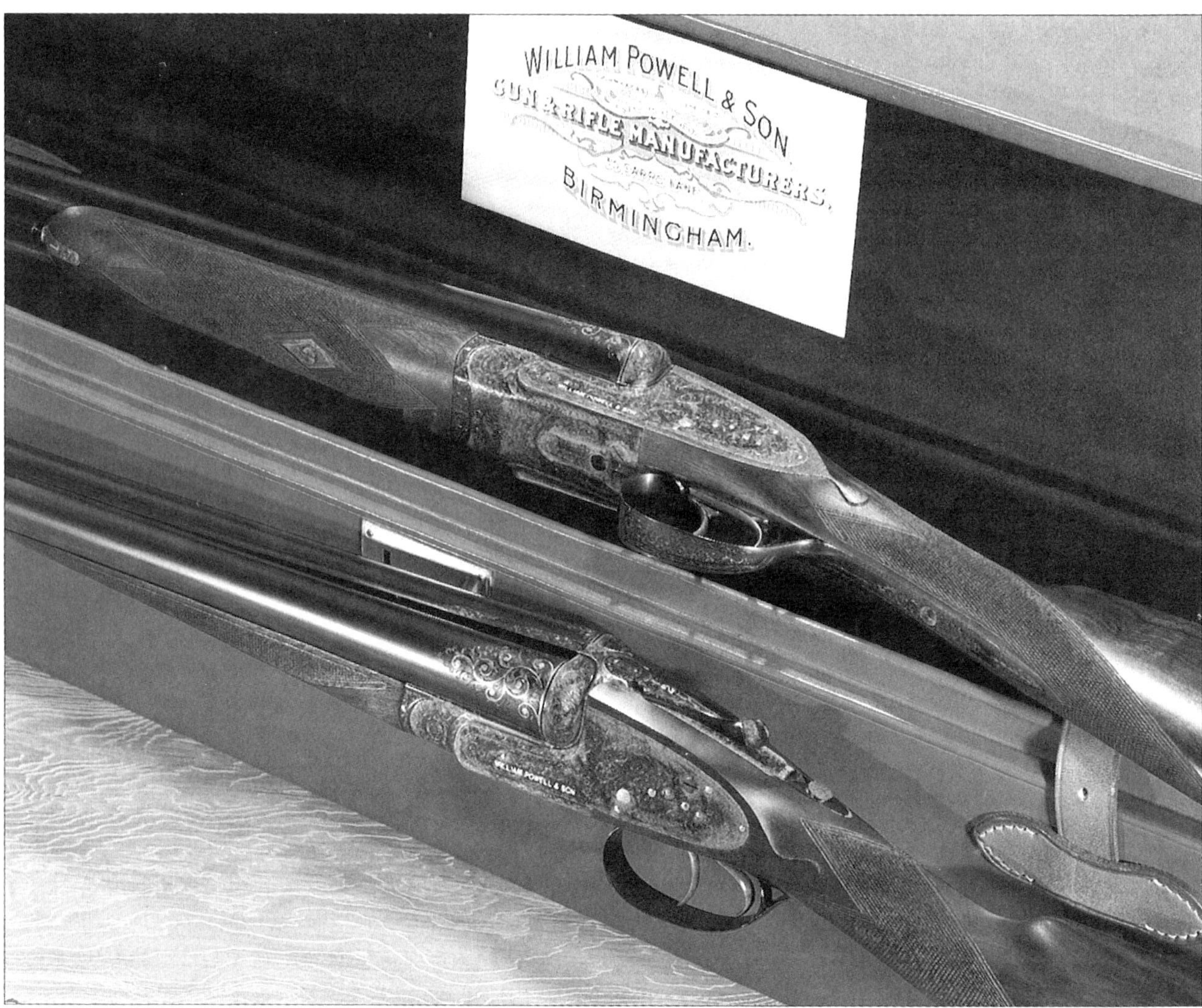

A pair of William Powell No. 1 sidelocks with gold-inlayed triangular motifs to the barrels. (William Powell)

enumerated with the generosity of the genre, but only *The Sporting Goods Review* mentioned the firm's output:

> The fame of the Powells was made chiefly by the supply to order of sporting guns and rifles of the highest class.

It continued,

> Mr. W. L. Powell had for many years the assistance of two younger brothers, Mr. Ernest Powell, and Mr. G. Victor Powell, the former dealing more especially in the ammunition department, and the latter assisting in the making and fitting of guns. The business will be continued under the joint charge of these two gentlemen.

Both had sons: Ernest was succeeded by his son Conrad and George Victor by his son Bernard Victor.

Sometime in 1920, a trade fair was held in Birmingham, and the Powell firm exhibited, among other things, the miniature flintlock made by the first William Powell, which one correspondent claimed had been shown at the Great Exhibition of 1851. The firm also showed a number of its Lift Uplever guns, one of which sold, and the same correspondent wrote, "It is rather interesting to note that Mr. G. Victor Powell, who now carries on the business, (1916) sold during the period of the Fair, a snap action (Lift Uplever) gun which was made by the firm in 1865."

George Victor Powell was the current owner's grandfather, and he worked until the day he died—Christmas Day 1952. His son, Bernard Victor, who was born in 1907 and joined the firm on 16 August 1923, retired on the same day fifty years later. At that time, David Michael Powell, who had joined the firm in 1955 and is the son of Bernard Victor Powell, was voted in as managing director. David continues to run the firm with his brother Peter, who is works director.

In the 1950s, Powell opened its magnificent retail showroom on the ground floor of the factory on Carrs Lane. Apart from guns and shooting accessories, it opened fishing tackle and country clothing departments. In following years the company expanded into mail order, and its catalog is distributed throughout the world. The United States has become its largest export market, and in 1992, the firm opened a New York office.

It is significant that Powell continued to prosper throughout the 1950s, '60s, and '70s when other British gunmakers were falling faster than pheasants to Lord Ripon's gun. The brothers' vision for the future of the firm now seems prescient, and the decision to diversify into accessories, country clothing, and mail order seems particularly progressive. The mail-order catalog, which has a circulation of 140,000 worldwide, has proven a most satisfactory strategy and has quadrupled in size during the last few years, with Powell expanding its markets to almost every country in the world.

Of course, it is gunmaking that remains the heart and soul of William Powell & Son. "It is who we are," says Peter. "It defines us as a family and as a company." Today Powell continues to supply quality shotguns worldwide as it has for almost 200 years. The quality of Powell guns is legendary, the sidelock and high-grade boxlocks being true best-quality guns in every sense of the word. Peter Powell estimates that in the last century—roughly the period of the modern hammerless side-by-side shotgun—the company has built about 12,000 sporting arms, ranging from A & D boxlocks of all grades to sidelocks with all the subtle refinements we associate with a best gun.

At present, Powell still has four gunmakers on the bench at its Carrs Lane shop, while two other craftsmen work almost exclusively for the firm. Other jobs, such as barrel filing and engraving, are contracted to outworkers in the best traditions of the Birmingham trade, except that today, outworkers are as likely to live in the rural areas of England, Scotland, or Wales as they are to be found in the almost-deserted gun quarter. "With the exception of barrel work and engraving, we can still start and finish a gun completely at Carrs Lane," Peter said. "However, depending on how busy we are at one time or another with orders, we will have some craftsmen on the trade working on our guns."

Powell builds about eighteen to twenty shotguns a year, and the firm currently offers seven models. The standardbearers of the Powell line are its Number 1 best-quality sidelock and its Number 3 best-quality Anson and Deeley boxlock. Both are handcrafted using all British materials (with the exception of the walnut, which comes from either France or Turkey) and British workmanship. They feature chopperlump barrels, solid forged actions, and exhibition-grade walnut, and a self-opening action based on the Holland & Holland system is available as an option. The Number 1 sidelock begins at £27,037 and the Number 3 boxlock at £16,537. There is also the Number 4 boxlock, which is all British built, using dovetail lump barrels and slightly less expensive walnut, which begins at £14,385.

Less expensive and consequently more popular are the "Heritage" series guns, which have actions, locks, and barrels made in Italy and Spain. Two sidelocks are offered, one of which is an easy opener. It starts at £8,580. Two boxlocks in the same series start at £10,250 for a round-bodied gun that resembles an Edinburgh round action and £13,950 for a droplock-style gun. All four are stocked, engraved, and finished in Birmingham to British standards and tastes. Secondhand buyers should be aware that one unscrupulous American was ordering Heritage-series guns, removing the engraved legend that reveals their true origin, then having the barrels reblacked and offering them as English-made! Of course, when Peter and David Powell found out, they refused to sell him another gun.

Integrity is just one reason Powell has been in business for almost 200 years. Even by English standards, a firm that remains in the hands of the founding family for five generations is a rarity. The only other gunmaking firm that comes close is the London company established by John Wilkes in 1830, some twenty-eight years after Powell. Because Powell adopted a survival strategy that acknowledges a changing world and avoids the stagnation and complacency so common in any business with strong links to conservative and traditional values, it deserves to succeed where others have failed.

Both David and Peter Powell have followed their ancestors in serving the gun trade. David has been on the Council of The Gun Trade Association since 1974 and is a past chairman. He also served on The British Shooting Sports Council. Peter was secretary of the Gun and Allied Trade Benevolent Society for eighteen years. He was elected as a guardian of the Birmingham Gun Barrel Proof House in 1974 and has been chairman since 1993.

Today, Peter Powell continues to sit as chairman of the Proof House Guardians on a board that has been served by four previous generations of Powells. He is also regarded as a de facto spokesman for the Birmingham gun trade, and, as of this writing, he is singlehandedly managing William Powell & Son due to the ill health of his brother. Few men are better suited by birth to shoulder such responsibility.

The last time I visited Carrs Lane, a gentleman had just ordered a pair of guns for his teenage son. They would take two years to build and would be a twenty-first-birthday present. The man was ordering from Powell because his father bought him a pair of Powell sidelock ejectors when he was twenty-one. It seemed appropriate that a third generation of shooters would benefit from five generations of Powell experience.

CHARLES ROSSON

The Rosson dynasty is representative of the way in which several Birmingham firms developed: The company name, assets, and clientele were passed from generation to generation until sufficient capital was generated to allow expansion into the provinces. Each successive Rosson attempted to make some innovative contribution to gunmaking that would give the company a competitive edge.

The first Charles Rosson is listed in Bailey & Nye's directory of English gunmakers as a gun and pistol maker at 56 Hatchett Street, Birmingham, from 1840 until 1856. An earlier Rosson, Thomas, was making guns at 22 Lancaster Street in 1838, and Mike Newland, curator of the gun collection at the Birmingham Science Museum, is convinced that Thomas was Charles's father. In 1857, Charles moved to 19 Livery Street in the Snowhill section of Birmingham.

In 1841, Charles had a son of his own, also named Charles, who inherited the business in 1872 when the old man retired. In *Experts on Guns and Shooting,* published in 1900, G. T. Teasdale-Buckell tells us that Charles Rosson (junior) apprenticed to John Frazier and then worked under Hollis & Sheath, which advertised itself as being at "11, 10, 9, 8, 7, 6, & 5, Weaman Row, St. Mary's Square, Birmingham." Mike Newland disputes this:

> Having studied the dates relating to John Frazier's and Hollis & Sheath's businesses I suspect that the opposite may be the case, Rosson having been apprenticed to Hollis & Sheath and afterwards working for a period with John Frazier & Co.

The question now arises as to why a man whose father was an established gunmaker should apprentice with another gunmaker and then work for a third before taking over the family concern? The likely answer is that Rosson Junior was trying to acquire the broadest possible experience of the trade before ascending to his father's mantle. This is borne out to some extent by the nature of the two firms he worked for: On the one hand, John Frazier was a one-man concern that was instrumental in the development of an early breechloader, and on the other, Hollis & Sheath was a large company of jobbing gunmakers:

> Manufacturers of every description of Double and Single Barrel Fowling Pieces, Rifles and Pistols, including every variety of Revolving, repeating and Breech loading Arms . . . as supplied to Her Majesty's Troops at home and abroad.

Clearly, the experience served Rosson well because over the next few years his name was associated with a cartridge-loading machine "capable of filling 2,000 per hour," a try gun, a fore-end fastener, and a patented (Number 15,313 of 1889) ejector mechanism. He also left Birmingham and lived at Mona Villa in Derby, where he established a business at Market Head and a second branch of the same business in the East Anglian town of Norwich. The guns from this period all have Birmingham proof marks, so presumably Rosson was supplied by his contacts in the Birmingham trade. Charles Rosson died on Tuesday, 8 August 1914:

> He had been in indifferent health for several years, but was at business as usual so lately as Saturday, 5 August, so that almost literally he died in harness, continuing his occupation as a gunmaker to the end.
>
> *[Sporting Goods Review]*

Both legs of the business were initially carried on by his two sons, Percy James Rosson and Charles Stanley Rosson. The Derby end of things soon went under, but the Norwich business continued to prosper at 13 Rampant Horse Street.

In the late '20s or early '30s, Rosson introduced its "Norfolk" gun with 27-inch barrels. The barrels were an attempt to introduce a signature feature to a gun that was already distinctive. Today, we still associate Churchill guns with 25-inch barrels and Woodward comes to mind when 29-inch barrels are mentioned, but the 27-inch Rosson seems not to have been a success. Perhaps the reason is the radical nature of the other options on this particular model. In 1930, Rosson applied for a patent—which does not appear to have been granted—for a slide-opening gun in which a second projection on the top strap in front of the safety opened the gun. Similar to a Horsley action but moving forward instead of backward, the design was a drastic departure from the norm. Reviewing the gun in 1931, a thinly disguised Major Burrard, under the *nom de plume* of "Argus," wrote that the "slide opener deserves serious consideration, and Messrs. Rosson deserve every credit for their ingenious invention." Faint praise indeed. Another option available on this model was that it could be had as a self-opener. Once again, instead of the tried and

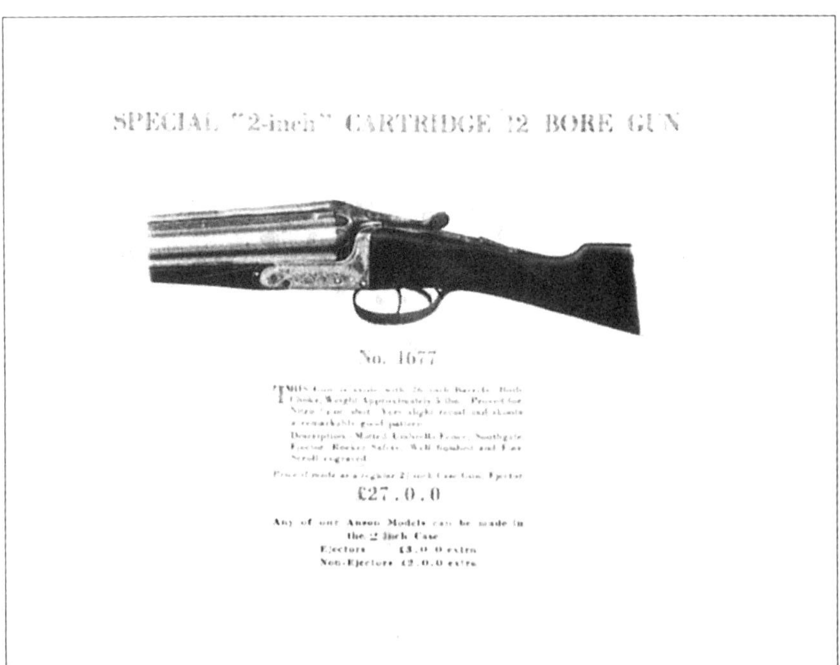

A page from a Holloway & Naughton catalogue featuring a two-inch 12-bore with arcaded fences. (Kirk Merrington)

tested Beesley action or the familiar Holland and Mansfield system, Rosson went with the unusual. Using a mechanism devised by a Birmingham gunmaker named Edwin Smith (Patent Number 372,035 of 1932) in which the closing of the barrels compressed the main-springs, ejector springs, and cocking springs, Rosson built a gun that Burrard claimed was "stiff to close." The only person I know who has owned one of these self-openers disputes this criticism and called it "easy to open, easy to close."

Shortly after the Second World War, Rosson went into a joint venture with the London gunmaking firm of Charles Hellis to manufacture cartridges. The business was housed in a new factory, and both partners had the highest of hopes for the new concern, buoyed to some extent by the reputation enjoyed by Hellis's Hyde Park outlet as the largest seller of cartridges in Britain. But social change after the war meant that fewer people were shooting, and the business failed in 1957.

With the failure of Hellis-Rosson Ltd., the Rosson name just disappears from the pages of shooting magazines and gunmaker directories. An ignominious end to a proud dynasty.

SKIMIN & WOOD

One of the fascinating ways in which the Birmingham gun trade differed from other traditional gunmaking centers was the way in which the craftsmen were organized. In London or Edinburgh, the famous firms generally trained and employed their own workforce and all aspects of manufacture were supervised and conducted under one roof. Birmingham's gun quarter, on the other hand, was a labyrinth of self-employed specialists. An entrepreneurial "gunmaker"—who was often not a gunmaker at all but simply a businessman—would buy the basic material and market the finished product, engaging outworkers to perform the various tasks in the gun's construction. Such a man was Samuel Skimin.

Samuel Skimin started in business for himself at 1920 at 31 Loveday Street, St. Mary's Square, after having managed Holloway & Naughton. I have been unable to discover anything at all about Mr. Wood, whom I suspect was a silent partner who may have come up with the capital to start the company. Holloway & Naughton had built a lot of heavy pigeon guns, and not surprisingly, Skimin's earliest models were pigeon guns, too. He also made a number of over-and-under trap guns for the Colonial Ammunition Company in Auckland, New Zealand. But times were changing: Just before the First World War, live-pigeon shooting had been banned in Britain and overseas demand was down.

The fashion in the '20s was for lightweight game guns. Perhaps it was because so many emancipated young women took up shooting, or possibly it was a demand created by Robert Churchill to sell his new 25-inch-barreled guns. For whatever reason, the 6 pound (or less) 12-bore was the gun to own.

Today, when we think of lightweight 12-bore guns, the 2 inch 12 comes immediately to mind. In order to understand why they are appreciably different from their near relatives, it is important to consider their history. Short cartridges first made their appearance in Britain as the result of the development of nitro powders in Germany. It was found that an equivalent charge of the new powders occupied less space than the old black powder, and, consequently, short cartridges could be made. A. A. Thorn loaded the new shells with "Walsrode" powder

and sold them under the brand name "Pygmies" through his company, Charles Lancaster.

He promoted them by arguing that the sportsman could carry more of them than of the standard 2½-inch case. He also stated that they could be used "for any length of chambering." As a promotional device, this made perfect sense as the true 2-inch 12-bore-chambered gun had yet to be developed. (It is an interesting aside that "Pygmies," at least according to the Eley price list for 1910-1911, were also 2¼ inches long!) Thorn first offered the new shells at the beginning of the 1897 shooting season, but by November of the following year, they had begun to be heavily criticized in the sporting press. The problem was balling (the fusing together of some part of the shot charge), and one abstract from contemporary correspondence is worth quoting:

Surely there are enough dangers in covert shooting without this new terror

A George Bate two-inch 12-bore. (Jeff Bird)

stalking in our midst, and putting a further fear of death into us. The beater is worthy of his hire; why, then, drive a hole through him that would stop a rhinoceros? The ordinary host has no particular craving to turn his covert shoot into an Omdurman; and he has enough luxuries to provide, without being obliged to add an ambulance and staff to the already lengthy list.

H. Cumberland Bentley
The Field Nov. 1898

Apparently, in some cases, shot charges were expanding upon leaving the short case and were then welded together when they met the end of the chamber, causing balling. Clearly, what was needed was to make cartridge and chamber the same length. A small number of 2-inch guns may have been built at this time, but, more likely, the sensationally bad press brought the short-cartridge concept to a premature though temporary halt.

By the early 1930s the short-cartridge idea was back with a vengeance, and, this time, gun and cartridge were in accord. Sam Skimin was a great proponent of the 2-inch 12-bore, and in 1930 he built a boxlock that weighed less than five pounds! The gun was given serial number S3512 and had its stock inset with a silver oval inscribed "Presented to R. R. Kellend as a memento of the first '20th Century Gun' made by Skimin & Wood 1-7-30." Indeed, the two-inch gun appears to have been a '30s phenomenon: Every Holland & Holland, Purdey, and Stephen Grant I have seen with two-inch chambers was built in the late '30s.

The advantage of this new generation of short-chambered guns was that they were significantly lighter than their conventionally chambered contemporaries.

As early as the sixth edition of *The Gun and its Development*, which appeared in 1897, W. W. Greener recognized that if a gun were not to "recoil unpleasantly," it should weigh ninety-six times heavier than its shot load— which meant a six-pound gun for an ounce of shot, a 6¾-pounds for 1⅛ ounces, and a 7½-pound gun for 1¼ ounces. Using this rule of thumb, builders of the new two-inch gun, which was originally intended to shoot ¾ ounces and later ⅞ ounces of shot, could construct a gun that weighed considerably less than the standard 12.

This was done in a number of ways. First, Skimin in his role as expediter had Joseph Asbury, a gun-action machinist then in Lench Street, make up a number of 20-bore actions with 12-bore faces. Then a specialist barrel worker named Chaplin would take conventional barrels and lighten them, using hacksaw and file. It was even rumored that the barrels were further lightened when the guns were returned from proof. Mitchell Bosly of Bath Lane would provide the lightest walnut available.

Skimin & Wood, by this time located in Vesey Street, offered the finished gun to the trade "wholesale only" in August of 1930. Provincial gunmakers seem to have been the best customers, and Graham of Inverness bought some, as did Macphersons, also of Inverness. Indeed, Hamish Macpherson worked in Vesey Street for Skimin & Wood and lodged with Skimin during his stay in Birmingham. The Twentieth Century gun was also marketed in the U.S. by The Kimball Arms Company. Another buyer was Linsley Brothers of Leeds, and Alastair Kissack, who worked with Linsley, recalls patterning the guns:

> We had never before seen patterns so consistent and even. They were quite superior to the 16-bore gun. I think it was agreed that the short and nearly square column of the two-inch was the secret.

Today, the most frequently encountered twentieth century guns bear the Macpherson and Linsley names, but C. S. Rosson's catalog also offered them. In 1934, Holland & Holland introduced a model it designated the "Twelve Two," designed for use with the two-inch cartridge. It was made in three grades: the Royal, Badminton, and Dominion. In the Christmas issue of the *Shooting Times* for 1936, Westley Richards advertised a side-lever single-barreled hammerless gun chambered "For the NEW 2-inch 12-BORE," which they called the "XXth Century Cartridge."

One difficulty with the two-inch 12 was the insistence of the London and Birmingham proof houses to prove the gun with standard 2½-inch cartridge load pressures. In November 1935, a petition protesting this decision was presented to the Proof House guardians:

> We, the undersigned, being members of the Birmingham gun trade and gun manufacturers, express our concern at the decision of the authorities to alter the proof charge for the 12-bore two-inch gun as published in the circular letter dated 1 October 1935.
>
> At the present time there is an increasing demand for a special light weight 12-bore which demand is being met by the adoption of a 12-bore two-inch chamber gun. This gun adequately meets the demand of many of the present day sportsmen and is found to be not only light in handling but regular in execution and is specially built for an English cartridge which gives a considerably lower pressure than the ordinary 12-bore 2½-inch cartridge and for the Proof Authorities to submit such a gun to the ordinary 12-bore 2½-inch chamber pressure is not only damaging to the gun but negates all its advantages and frustrates the one great object of the designers. Such action by the Proof Authorities is most detrimental and is calculated to destroy the whole of the trade, which is now attained to considerable proportions. We therefore, respectfully ask that the whole matter may be reviewed by the two proof houses and that some special arrangement may be made which would allow for the sale of this particular light gun

for which there is a considerable demand and which demand, if destroyed, will cause considerable loss of trade.

The petition was proposed by a W. Skimin, perhaps a son of Sam Skimin—or perhaps the minute keeper at the Birmingham Proof House was guilty of a typographical error. It was seconded by William Bourne and signed by thirteen other Birmingham gunmakers. A joint meeting of the representatives of both Proof Houses was held to evaluate the proposal. F. W. Jones headed the Birmingham delegation while James Purdey (the fourth), Tom Purdey, and Major Burrard represented the London committee.

Mr. Skimin's proposal was rejected, and the committee minutes tell us only that the "proof of the two-inch chamber gun should be identical with the 2½-inch chamber gun" but offers no explanation for the decision. Fortunately, the Purdey brothers published a book three years later called *The Shotgun*, which sheds some light on the subject. Though their language is discreet and their manner diplomatic, it is clear that they were concerned by the pressures generated in the Belgian two-inch zinc-cased cartridges available at that time. A Parker-Hale catalog from the same year as the Purdey book offered the Belgian zinc cartridges but warned that they "must not be used in a 12-bore two-inch chambered gun if they have been proved for a lighter load of powder and shot."

By the time the rules of proof were revised in 1954, Skimin had got his way and the highest service pressure for the two-inch 12 gun was 2¾ tons per square inch, as opposed to three tons f or the standard 2½-inch 12.

The lack of flexibility inherent in the two-inch cartridge eventually led to its fall from popularity, but the few surviving examples of twentieth century guns today have a cult following among those who appreciate a lightweight gun.

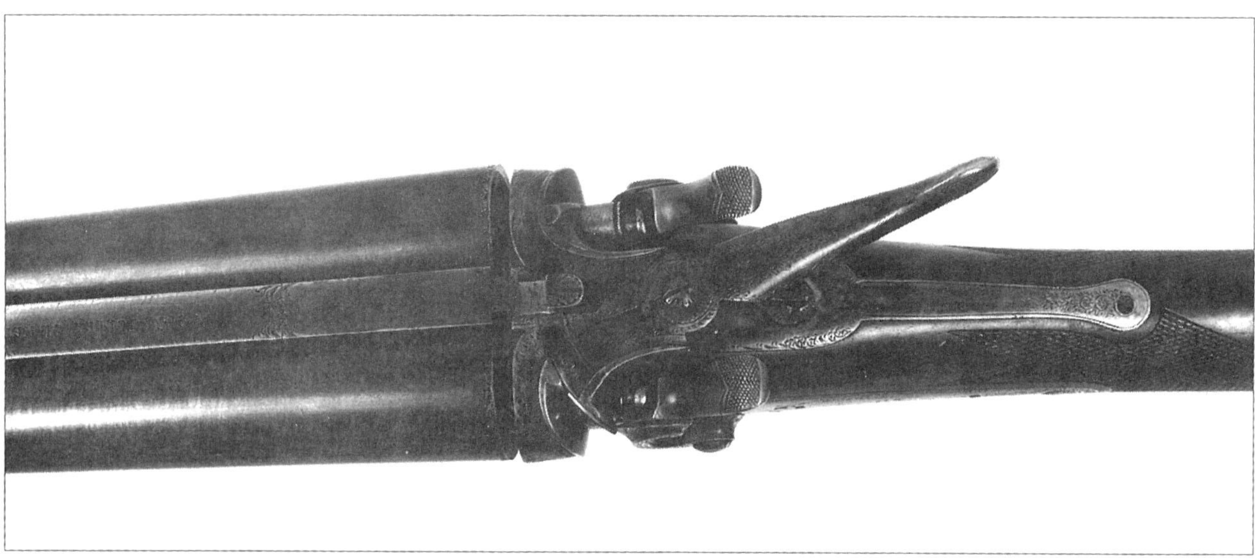

An example of the Henry Tolley "Giant Grip" action of 1877. (Weller & Dufty)

Today, the firm of Skimin & Wood exists in name only as one of a group of names owned by the umbrella company of F. J. Wiseman—a victim of the high cost of making guns in Birmingham since the Second World War. It is slightly ironic that the only new two-inch 12-bore currently available is made by A.Y.A. of Spain.

HENRY TOLLEY

Henry Tolley makes his first appearance in street directories at 65 and 66 Weaman Street in 1880, but the patent record shows him active three years earlier. Patent 461 of 1877 is for a cocking mechanism and a breech fastener that would become famous as the "Giant Grip" when it was strenuously marketed by J. & W. Tolley, established at 22 St. Mary's Row in 1859.

Based on the information above, some authorities have speculated that Henry Tolley was the younger, more inventive brother of James and William who started his own business only after serving time with his more established siblings.

All very well, but the only thing that can be proven is that Henry was the most creative of three Tolleys who worked in the Birmingham gun quarter at approximately the same time. The sole evidence for this theory are the six patents issued to Henry Tolley between 1877 and 1886. Of these, just the first, for the Giant Grip, and the last two, dating from 1886 for "The Times Hammerless Gun," appear to have made any lasting impression.

The Giant Grip was a large hook attached to the top lever that engaged an enormous slot cut into an oversize rib extension, but the patent specifications also describe the earliest design in which the energy stored in the mainspring is used to cock the hammers. An alternative method of cocking the gun is offered in the same patent whereby the drop of the barrels pulls forward a link that cocks the hammers. All of the examples I have seen—whether backlock, barlock, hammer, or hammerless—have been signed by J. W. Tolley, which seems to lend credence to the theory of a relationship between the two Tolley firms.

In 1879 Henry Tolley was back at the patent office with a rod-cocking gun action and a safety that bolted the fall of the hammers. Both ideas were the subject of numer-

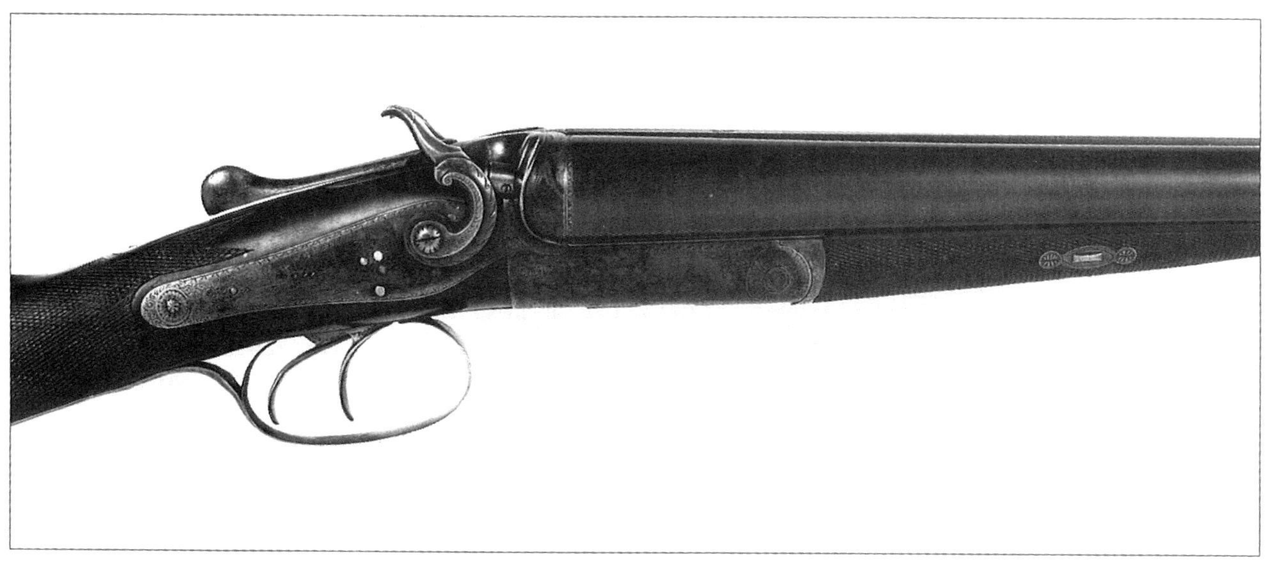

A "Giant Grip" gun signed J. & W. Tolley. (Weller & Dufty)

ous contemporary patents, which is perhaps why Tolley's (Number 649 of 1879) never went beyond provisional protection.

Tolley's next effort (Patent 1,515 of 1883) used the mainsprings "for giving the snapping action to the bolts for locking the barrels." The specifications also describe a safety that slides forward and engages a rib extension to provide a third fastener moments before the gun is discharged. The basic idea of a lever-cocked hammerless gun enjoyed such wide currency at this date that Tolley's action was lost among a plethora of similar designs.

Undeterred, Henry Tolley was again back at the patent office the next year with another spring-cocked hammerless gun. In this design (Patent 10,101 of 1884), a U-shaped mainspring was employed in the bar of the action, its longer, lower limb engaging the tumbler while the shorter, upper limb protruded through the action flats to be compressed by the fall of the barrels.

Two Henry Tolley patents (Numbers 2,663 of 1886 and 10,303 of 1886) provide the basis of what was perhaps his most successful gun. It was called "The Times" and is perhaps the Henry Tolley design most frequently encountered in our own age. It

sold for eight guineas, and Tolley thought it important enough to print special trade labels announcing that Henry Tolley & Co. was the "Inventors, Patentees & Manufacturers of The Times Hammerless Gun." As with G. E. Lewis's "The Gun of the Period," the title was intended to leave no doubts about the modernity of the piece. Henry Tolley was so enamored of the name that he also called his workshop at 65-66 Weaman Street the "Times" gun works. The gun embodied the improvements outlined in the patents, including a blocking safety attached directly to the external tang safety, a variation on the Scott spindle that was canted instead of perpendicular, and cocking slides activated by the movement of the fore-end iron. The gun was a flat-back action with back-acting mainsprings and was of middle quality, though it nevertheless found a market.

Henry Tolley disappeared from the Birmingham gun scene in 1892. His modest company was almost certainly absorbed by a larger firm, and at least one authority has suggested James & William Tolley as the likely culprit. However, it is unlikely that this theory will ever be substantiated.

J. & W. TOLLEY

Birmingham's specialist gunmakers are rare; B.S.A. may have attempted to build a business solely with machine-made guns, and the Leonard brothers certainly made more big-bore double rifles than most, but Birmingham's gunmakers were generalists that built whatever they could sell.

Among a handful of exceptions were the brothers James and William Tolley, who first appear in 1859 at 22 St. Mary's Row as "gun, pistol and rifle makers." Their earliest advertisements feature guns "suitable for the African markets," which was a reference to an inexpensive type of trade gun. However, over the years the company eventually developed a reputation as builders of excellent wildfowling guns.

When *The Field* magazine organized a trial in 1866 to compare breechloading pin-fire and center-fire guns, J. & W. Tolley entered one of the latter, built on a Lefaucheux action. When the results appeared, the makers probably wished they hadn't. Of thirty-two guns entered in the 12-bore class, the Tolley gun finished thirty-first.

In 1879, a couple of years after moving to Loveday Street, the brothers provisionally patented a gun action (Patent 5,002 of 1879) described in the abridgments as:

> Breech actions, drop down barrel. The bolt which locks the barrels of drop down guns is prolonged so that when the lever withdraws the locking bolt the prolongation actuates a cam which cocks the hammers. A safety bolt consists of a lever which fits into the back of the trigger guard. The lever acts on a dog under the trigger plate and locks either the sears or the hammers.

Judging by the description, the design was too nebulous even to gain full patent coverage, let alone become a successful design. Nevertheless, some may have been built and may be found engraved with the name "Perfection." Patent Number 5,002 was James and William Tolley's first and final attempt at shotgun design, at least as far as the patent record is concerned. From that day on the brothers would employ the designs of others and in the process establish themselves as the wildfowler's gunmaker.

In 1882, when Dr. John Henry Walsh, editor of *The Field* magazine, published his two-volume set *The Modern Sportsman's Gun and Rifle,* he credited James and William Tolley with the "Tolley Giant Grip." This was a third fastener consisting of a huge hook attached to the top lever and engaging a monster rib extension which, when used to supplement an ordinary Purdey underbolt, was well suited for use on big-bore fowlers. However, Dr. Walsh was wrong. Though James and William undoubtedly made many Giant Grip guns, the design was the work of Henry Tolley, who worked one block away at 65-66 Weaman Street. The patent (Number 461 of 1877) also used the movement of the barrels opening to cock the tumblers. Most Giant Grip guns that show up today are signed by J. & W. Tolley.

Even though the Tolley brothers made a range of guns, they became particularly famous for their big-bore wildfowling guns and only slightly less so for their double rifles, which included a number of huge double 4-bores. They may be even better known for their "Handy" punt guns, built on the Snider action and offered with bores of $1^3/_{32}$-inch, 1¼-inch, 1½-inch, 1¾-inch, and 2-inch.

Their success, by 1882, was sufficiently broad that they opened a retail outlet in London. Many Birmingham makers had shops in London, but most were in or around Victoria Street in an area close to Wellington Barracks, the Horse Guards, and the War Office—all the better to supply officers on their way out to India. James and William

Tolley chose a more prestigious location on Conduit Street, just off Regent Street in the fashionable West End, and were soon able to advertise that they were "Makers by Special Appointment to the Persian Royal Family."

Sometime late in the century, the Tolley brothers moved from their Pioneer Works in Loveday Street to a new workshop at 10, 12, and 14 Vesey Street, which they also named Pioneer Works. From this address the firm launched a new model known as the Altro. This heavy (7½-pound) gun with three-inch chambers, side clips and a half pistol hand was intended as an all-around gun. Advertisements claimed, "This new weapon is equally suitable for ordinary game as well as duck or pigeon shooting" and went on to say, "This gun will be most useful to those sportsmen who do not wish to keep more than one gun for all purposes."

To add to the Altro's appeal as an all-around gun, the Tolley's also offered a pair of "Ubique" ball barrels:

> Shooting thirty-four grains Cordite or Axite smokeless powder (equal to 4 drs. of black), and 750 grains heavy metal based conical bullet, makes a complete, efficient, and inexpensive battery suitable for all shooting in any part of the world.

The name reflects the Victorian and Edwardian fondness for Latin nomenclature, intended to convey a certain urbanity but also to give the impression that Britain's Empire was a great civilizing influence in the tradition of Greece or Rome. The name Ubique is particularly appropriate for an all-around gun as the word means "everywhere" in Latin. The Altro probably enjoyed some success as a fowling and pigeon gun, but it was clearly on the heavy side for rough and game shooting. Few are encountered today, suggesting perhaps that the gun was not sold in great numbers.

In 1910, J. & W. Tolley was registered as a private company, and at least one au-thority, Mike Newland of the Birmingham Science Museum, thinks it was taken over by Holloway & Naughton at about this time. If this is the case, guns bearing the J. & W. Tolley name may once again be built because Holloway & Naughton was acquired by F. J. Wiseman in the early '50s and continues to trade from its premises in Cannock, Staffordshire.

THOMAS TURNER

Few of Birmingham's gunmakers were specialists; most simply made whatever was in demand at any given time. Thomas Turner, whose output appears to reflect his reputation as a generalist, would, I think, like to be remembered as a builder of fine rifles.

Although Thomas Turner claimed on his trade label "established 1805," most sources agree that 1805 was actually the year of his birth. It was characteristic of Victorian gunmakers to overstate the years they had been in business, but they usually found some way to justify their exaggerations by claiming direct lineage to a father or master who was established at some earlier date.

This may have been the case with Turner, who is thought to have served his apprenticeship with John Field of Newton Row, Birmingham. John Field was succeeded by Charles Phillips Swinburn, and the firm subsequently became John Field Swinburn, leading some authorities to conclude that John Field Swinburn was the son of Charles Phillips Swinburn—although it is just as likely that Swinburn adopted John Field's more established name, just as A. A. Thorn would do with the Charles Lancaster name in a later era.

In 1853, Thomas Turner and John Field Swinburn were granted patents for a breech plug and a rifle sight, beginning a career, at least for Turner, that would be defined by a professional interest in gun barrels and a passion for rifles.

Turner most likely apprenticed as a barrelmaker; certainly the first mention of him in street directories is as "a gun-barrelmaker" at Court 5, Aston Road, Birmingham. Few barrelmakers became successful gunmakers, due to the nature of the work. Before the development of machine tools, the outside of gun barrels was shaped by a huge spinning stone wheel located in the floor of the barrelmaker's workshop. The craftsman would sit on an old chair with the legs cut down and contour the barrel against the grinding stone. The amount of iron and stone dust suspended in the air must have been considerable, and most barrel workers succumbed to lung disorders at about the time they became proficient barrelmakers. Turner may have understood the dangers; by 1838 he had relocated to 8 Fisher Street and directories record him as a "gun and pistol maker."

In 1860 Turner patented a system of barrel boring (Number 958 of 1860) in which "fouling is prevented by gradually decreasing the depth of a portion of the rifling towards the muzzle." Two years later, together with W. Taylor, he provisionally patented a breechloader of the "drop down barrel" type in which the end of the barrel was formed as a segment of a circle struck from the joint pin. By 1864 Turner was back with rifles, patenting one (Number 2,458 of 1864) with a sliding breechblock.

None of the above appear to have been widely adopted by the trade, but in 1864 Thomas Turner patented a breechloader (Patent 2,585 of 1864) that, judging by the frequency with which it is encountered today, enjoyed some degree of popularity. (This was not the Thomas of the chair with the cutdown legs but rather his son Thomas Jr., who would eventually run the firm with his brother, James.) It was for a breechloading snap-action opened by a lever immediately behind the trigger guard. Contemporary advertisements extol its "Handiness, Neatness,

Simplicity and Durability," but Turner seems to hedge his bets by offering a wide variety of rifles in a footnote to the same ad. Other ads for the same action have rifles as a secondary theme:

> Turner's double barrel rifles are acknowledged to be the most accurate for match shooting, and, with shell, the most destructive for sporting purposes ever sent to India. The Sportsman's Prize, for double barrel rifles of any bore, open to all India, has in each case been won with one of these rifles.

Two years after Thomas Turner Jr. introduced his breechloader, he and a lockmaker named William Siddon Jr. developed an extractor (Patent 2,227 of 1866), which does not appear to have been widely copied, probably because it was obsolete before it was registered. The next Thomas Turner patent (Number 898 of 1876) provided provisional protection only for a cylindrical chamber in front of the cartridge chamber in a rifle and was intended to prevent fouling of the lands.

For *The Field* trial of 1875, which pitted choke-bored guns against cylinder bores, Turner entered a gun with .005 of an inch constriction in the muzzles. Though not strictly a cylinder-bore gun, it did win the category for cylinders and even shot tighter patterns than some entries in the choke-bore category. Five years later, Turner was still interested in choke-bore guns. He acquired the rights to a detachable-choked muzzle from John Sidney Heath (Patent 984 of 1880) and advertised it widely as his own patent, claiming it could be "converted from cylinder to choke in one minute while in the field."

A short time later, Turner was again interested in barrels. In 1885, he and G. Allen patented a Damascus barrel material (Number 12,616 of 1885) formed by casting steel around iron bars. It may appear odd that gunmakers were still developing types of twist barrels twenty years after Sir Joseph

Whitworth patented his fluid steel process. However, in tests conducted by the Birmingham Proof House during 1888 and published in 1891, Whitworth steel placed second for "merit of endurance" to machine-forged, three-rod, laminated steel. Appropriately, Thomas Turner Jr. acted as secretary of the committee that oversaw the tests.

During the late 1880s, there was a fad for lightweight guns, and Turner, like most of his colleagues, offered a featherweight 12-bore. Turner's, which he called the "Levissimus" from the Latin word *levis,* meaning light, weighed a mere 4¾ pounds with 24-inch barrels or five pounds with 27-inch barrels. No special action was developed to solve the weight problem. A conventional gun was simply reduced to the minimum safety allowed, using saw, file, and rasp.

In 1887, Turner patented a vernier sight (Number 7,155 of 1887), again reflecting the lifelong interest in rifles he inherited from his father. The younger Turner was a lifelong member of the National Rifle Club who won numerous trophies at Wimbledon, then the home of competitive English rifle shooting. Among the prizes won by Turner were:

Earl de Grey Cup– 600 yards–1864

Prize for the Secretary of State for War–1879

Dudley Trophy–1,000 yards –1879

Any Rifle Wimbledon Cup–1886

The Bass–1886

Obviously, Turner's expertise with the rifle had prime public-relations value and must have won numerous new customers to an already successful firm.

In 1899, when Samuel Blakemore Allport died, Thomas Turner Jr. became Proof Master of the Birmingham Proof House. His first job in office was to oversee the revision of proof testing to accommodate the nitro powders

that were then beginning to enjoy general acceptance. To do this, he established a laboratory, still in use today, where cartridges could be tested and pressures measured. The work started by Turner in 1899 eventually resulted in a revised proof test and new proof marks, adopted in 1904.

During the spring of 1914, Thomas Turner Jr. retired and moved to Sutton Coldfield. He died in January 1931 at the age of eighty-six. *The Sporting Goods Review and Gunmaker* of January 31 noted his many contributions to gunmaking. The obituary also acknowledges that the Turner firm "was a very old one and specialized in the production of first class rifles for which they became justly famous."

Some idea of just how successful the Thomas Turner company was can be gained by its having operated retail branches in

Barry King is listed at UNIT FF1 at 63 Price Street. (Douglas Tate)

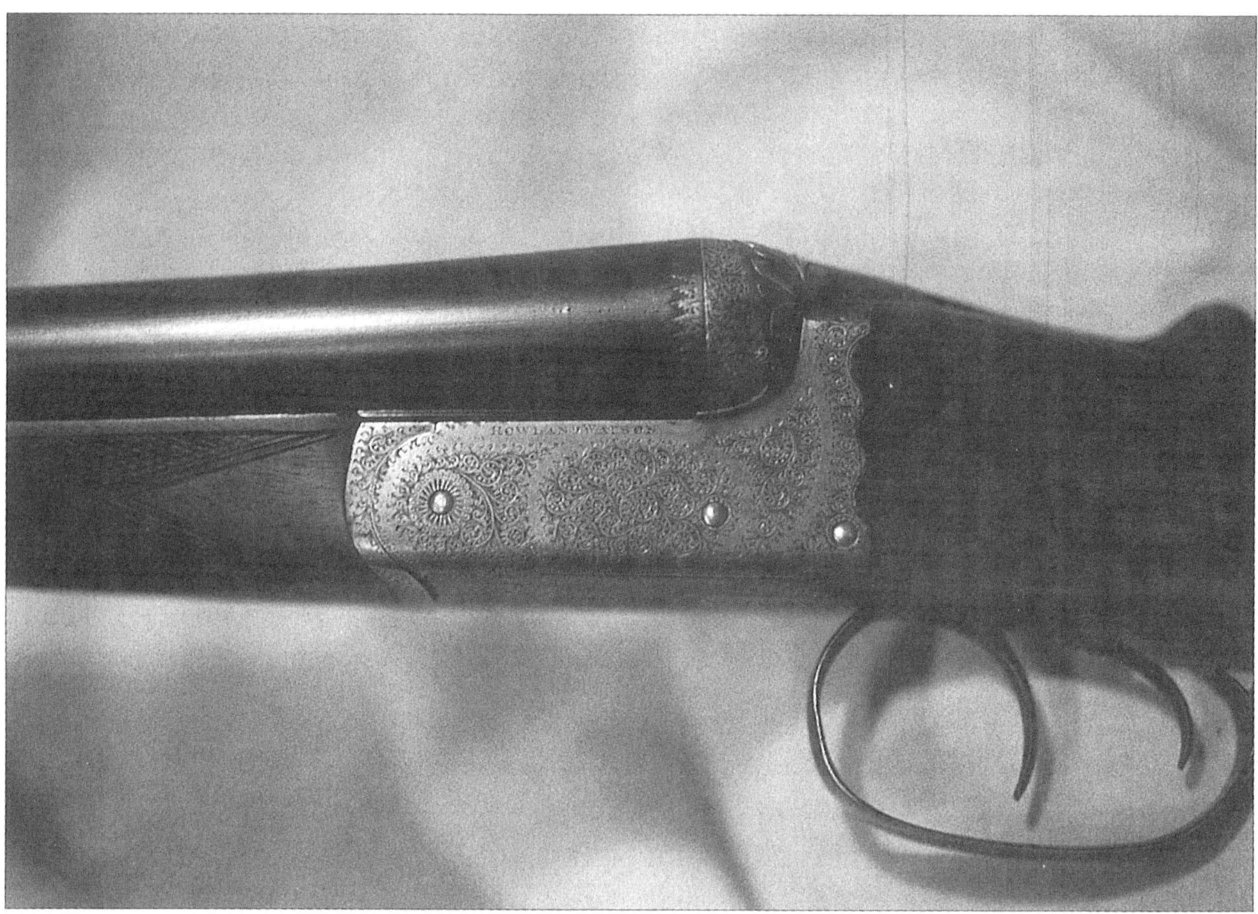

A Rowland Watson boxlock with scalloped action and carved fences. (Dave Jones)

Reading, Newbury, Basingstoke, and London at the height of the British Empire. The firm's fortunes appear to have faded after Thomas Turner Jr. retired, and today the company no longer exists.

ROWLAND WATSON & THOMAS WILD

On an unassuming doorway in a building on Birmingham's Price Street, a sign reads "Unit F/F1." Behind that door, however, lies the story of almost 275 years of toil, invention, and entrepreneurial spirit that began with lockmaking and spans almost 2¾ centuries of one firm's history.

The Watson firm was founded by Benjamin Watson, a gunlock maker from Darlaston who established a gunmaking business on Whittall Street (then named Catherine Street) in Birmingham in 1723. By 1777, Watson entered into partnership with William Ryan, and the two were trading as Watson and Ryan at 27 Whittall Street in 1799.

Ryan set up a separate business with his son in 1820 when Benjamin Watson II died, although he maintained his interest in the Ryan and Watson firm until 1830, making "guns, rifles, air guns and pistols of every description." When the Birmingham Proof House was established in 1813, Ryan and Watson were among the original subscribers to the fund to raise money for the erection of the building. They subscribed £100 Proof House stock, which was redeemed in 1855, and William Ryan sat on the original governing body of the Proof House and became one of its guardians, retiring about 1830. Benjamin Watson II died in May 1820, and the company's £100 share was transferred to gunmaker John Clive in partial payment of a debt.

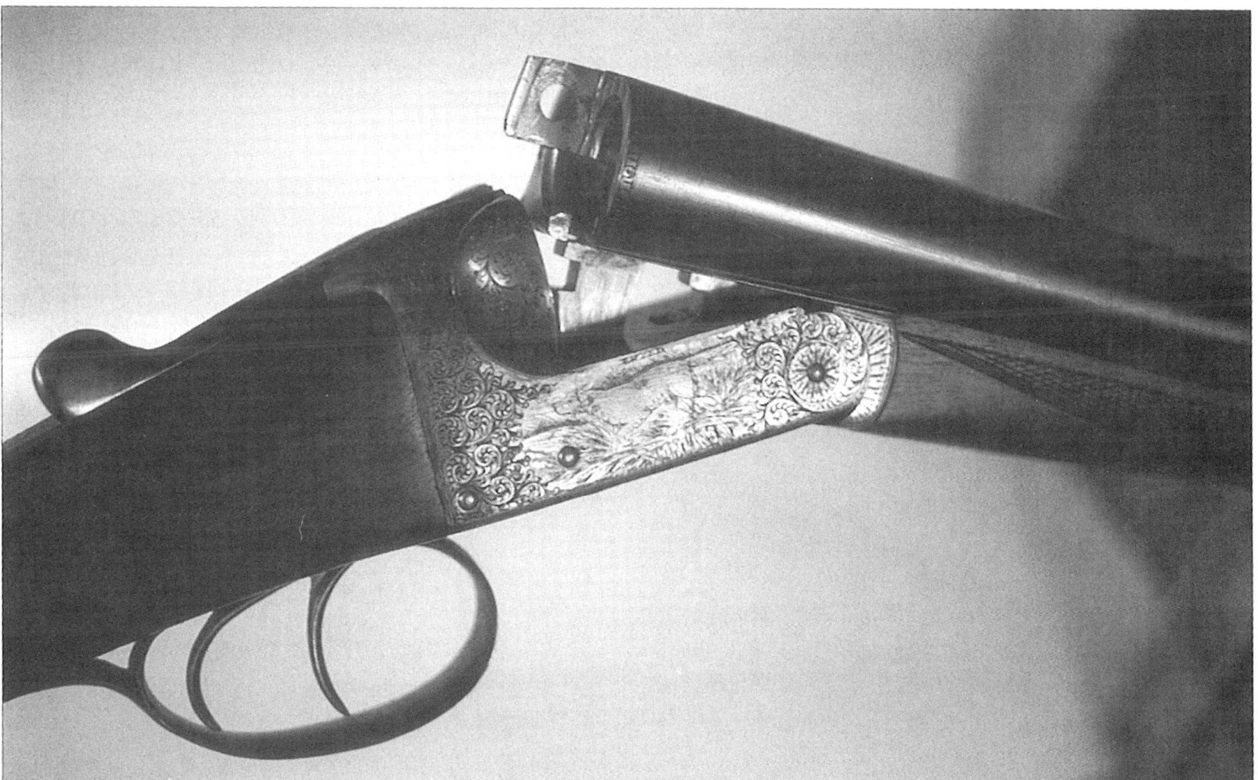

A Thomas Wild boxlock with game-scene engraving. (Douglas Tate)

By 1857, the business was taken over by Thomas Wild, who was Benjamin Watson III's son-in-law. He changed the firm's name to Thomas Wild, under which name it traded until his death in 1893, when it reverted to Rowland Watson. Ironically, many more guns are encountered with the Wild than the Watson name, suggesting that Wild guns were produced long after the title had reverted to Rowland Watson. Rowland Watson was the nephew of Thomas Wild and grandson of the second Benjamin Watson. When he died in 1941, Gilbert Watson took over the firm and in 1946 was succeeded by a second Rowland Watson, who, like his ancestor, served as a Proof House guardian. In 1987, Rowland Watson retired, and the firm is now run by Barry King. Barry began working for Rowland Watson when he was twelve, almost forty years ago. He is the first person outside the Watson family to own the two names. In the best traditions of the Watson family, Barry is a Proof House guardian, having served since 1988.

An indication of the quality of the company's guns can be gleaned from the following quote, abstracted from *The Sporting Goods Review and the Gun Maker,* organ of the Birmingham gunmakers for the first half of this century. It appeared in 1920, just as the trade was recovering after World War I:

A gratifying sign with regard to the future of the trade is the manner in which some of the older firms are bestirring themselves to take advantage of the opportunities which are opening. For instance, Mr. Rowland Watson, of Whittall Street, Birmingham, is the inheritor of the business which was founded by Mr. Benjamin Watson in the same street in 1723, and which, therefore, in three years will be celebrating its bicentenary. . . . The firm is laying itself out for the production of hammerless guns of medium price on a larger scale than formerly. These guns, especially one selling at £35 are meeting with much success.

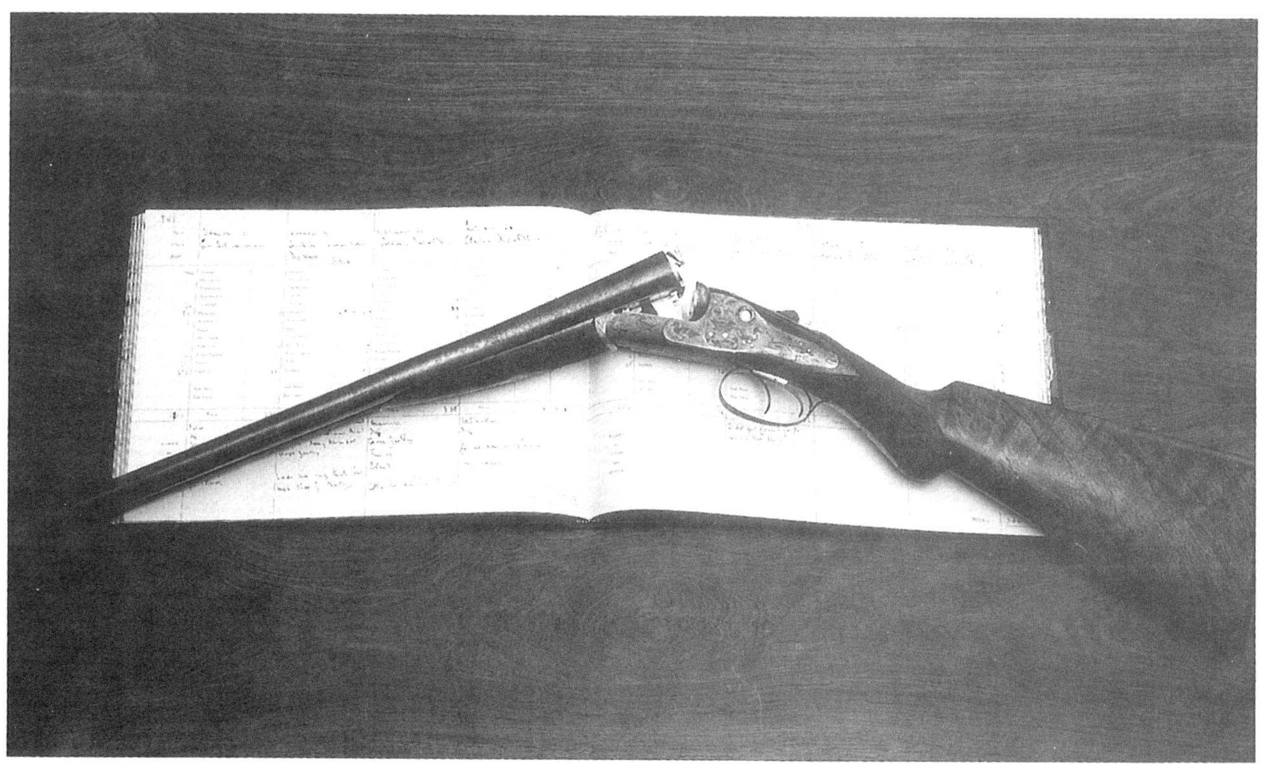

The Excellentia B with a game book for a background. (Larry Barnes)

Even in 1920, £35 was not a lot to pay for a new gun. About this same time, W. W. Greener was advertising his best boxlocks at three times the price of a Rowland Watson.

WEBLEY & SCOTT

If there was ever a need to show how Birmingham gunmakers supplied a worldwide trade, it would be difficult to find a better example than Webley & Scott. Most of the sporting shotguns made by the Birmingham gun trade were engraved with the retailer's name, not the maker's. It was the nature of the trade to make the best gun possible at a given price and then let some distant seller take the credit simply by signing the gun. Every gunmaker in Birmingham played the game, but none better than Webley & Scott.

Famous London makers with West End locations, like William Evans, sold Webley & Scott guns as their own. Provincial makers, like William Rochester Pape of Newcastle upon Tyne—sometimes called the "Purdey of the North"—did the same. Nowotny of Prague in eastern Europe and William Read & Sons of Boston, Massachusetts, also sold Webley & Scott guns. Today, students of fine gunmaking know them by their Webley and Brain-patent top fasteners, their Rogers lockwork, and distinctive engraving patterns like the ribanded trefoil motif chased to the fences of both best boxlocks and sidelocks. Only a few of these pieces are found stamped with a Webley & Scott trademark.

Webley & Scott was capable of supplying the huge demand created by a large international market because of a significant merger. The amalgamation of P. Webley & Son and W. & C. Scott & Son in 1897 created the most prodigious maker of quality double guns in Britain. In its first decade, Webley & Scott Revolver and Arms Co., as the firm was called, built 2,500 doubles every year—not a lot for an armaments manufacturer, then or now, but an unrepeatably high number when

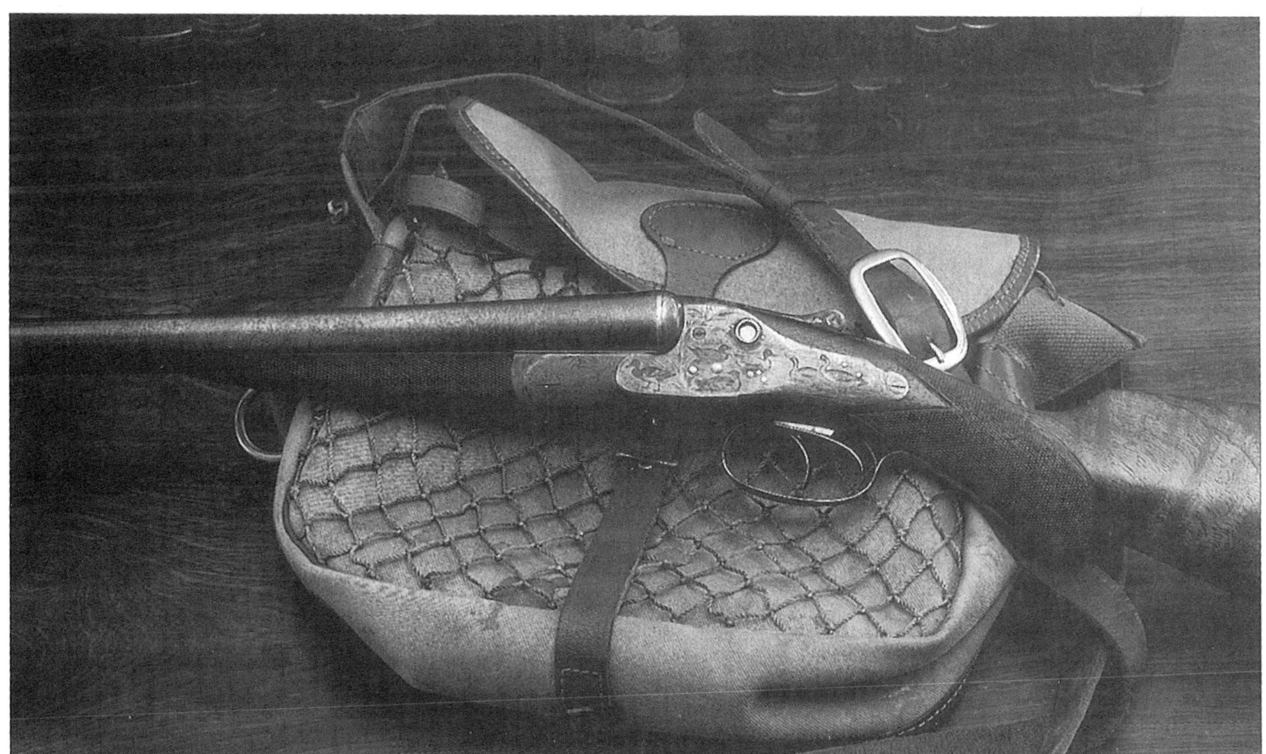

An Excellentia B with patent crystal cocking indicators. (Larry Barnes)

one stops to consider that every action was created from a machined forging by a man with a file, every barrel was struck up by hand, and every stock was created individually.

To understand how a world-class crafter of fine arms could hand-build 2,500 guns a year, it is necessary to go back almost to the turn of the previous century, when the individuals who started P. Webley & Son and W. & C. Scott & Son became active in the gun business.

P. WEBLEY & SON

Philip Webley began his apprenticeship as a lockmaker in 1827 at the age of fourteen, probably with the firm of Ryan and Watson. On becoming a journeyman, he and his brother, James, went into business. Within a few years the partnership was dissolved, and Philip married the daughter of William Davis, a "bullet mould and gun implement manufacturer" of 84 Weaman St. When Davis died, his wife ran the firm but was eventually succeeded by Philip Webley in 1845. During the 1860s, Philip was joined by his sons, Thomas William and Henry, and the firm changed its name to Philip Webley and Son.

In the hands of Philip Webley the old company known for its bullet molds, gun implements, and gunmakers' tools was transformed into a modern manufacturing concern. Webley's older son, Thomas William, was put in charge of making sporting shotguns while the younger, Henry, was responsible for revolvers. The company also made muzzle-loading and breechloading military rifles, handcuffs, and boarding pikes, plus the original bullet molds.

A search of the patent records reveals four in the name of Henry Webley. Perhaps not surprisingly, three are for revolvers while one is for a falling-block rifle. Thomas William, on the other hand, has ten patents to his name. Many are concerned with rifles, but others are for sporting shotguns and

worth mentioning. The first (Patent 2,030 of 1865) is of provisional status only and reads, "The hammer or tumbler for firing pin fire cartridges is provided with a projection for striking a firing pin when using centre fire cartridges." Superficially similar to a Westley Richards design (Patent 1,960 of 1866) for a center-fire gun with pin-fire hammers, Thomas Webley's design was clearly an attempt at a gun capable of digesting both pin-fire and center-fire ammunition.

The second (Patent 2,040 of 1859) is for an improvement to one of Birmingham's most famous gun actions, the double-screw grip operated by an underlever, invented by Henry Jones. Though the design was widely adopted, Jones never fully benefited because he didn't keep the patent current by paying a stamp duty. One of the strongest gun actions made, it is often found on big-bore fowlers and the heaviest of double rifles. Its sole weakness was that it was an inert rather than a snap action, meaning that it had to be physically closed rather than just snapping shut when the gun was closed. Thomas William Webley's improvement (Patent 3,022 of 1866) was to attach a spring so the gun would function as a snap action.

T. W. Webley later patented a trigger-plate action (Number 1,860 of 1880) and then an extractor (Number 5,143 of 1881) in conjunction with his younger brother. The most significant of his shotgun patents was also filed in 1882. This comprehensive patent covers several mechanical innovations, but only one of them was adopted on a large scale. Taken out in conjunction with a gun-action filer, Thomas Brain of Weaman Street, the patent's relevant passage describes a screw grip machined into the top of a Scott spindle. The spindle and top lever operate a conventional sliding Purdey bolt in the ordinary way, with the addition that the screw at the top of the spindle engages a barrel-rib extension to form a third fastener. When the

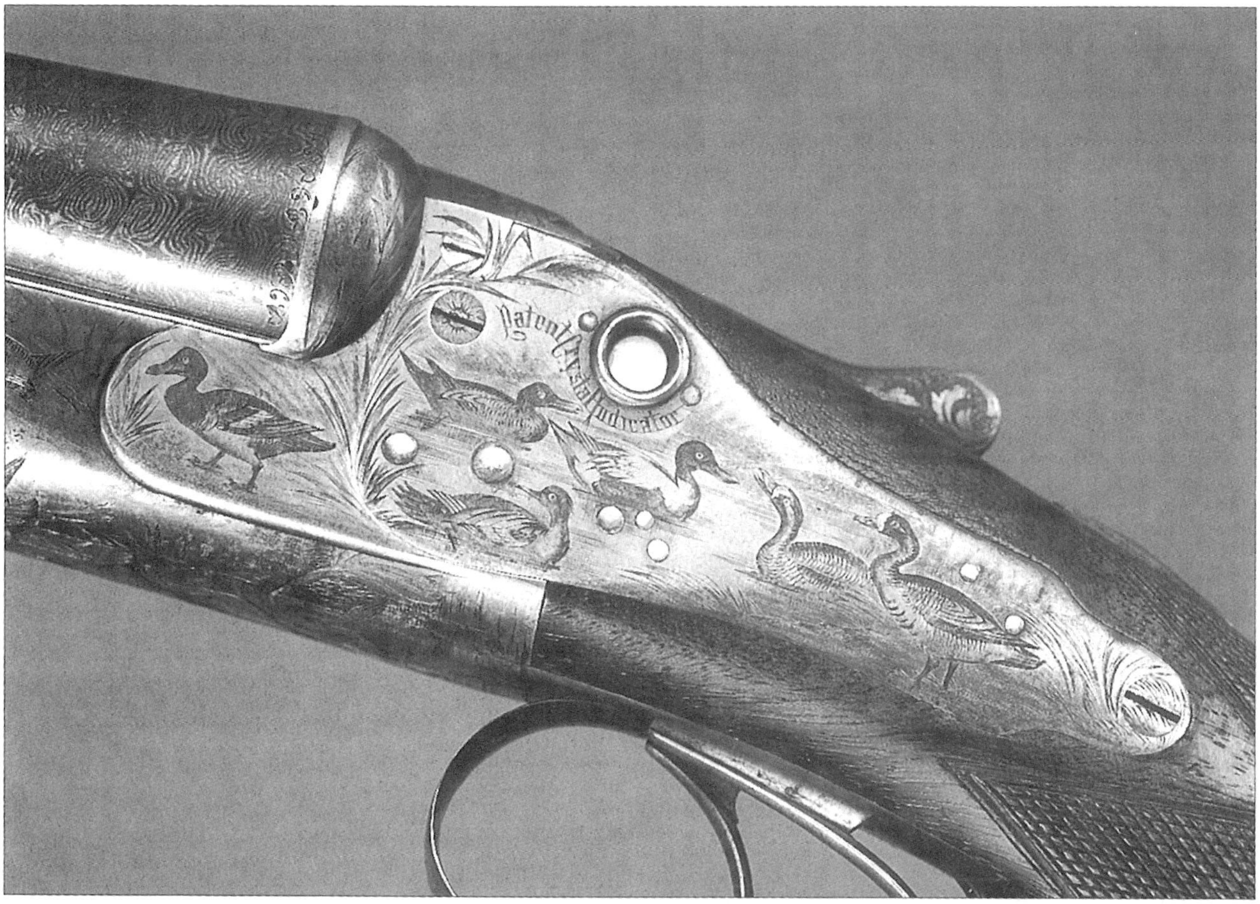

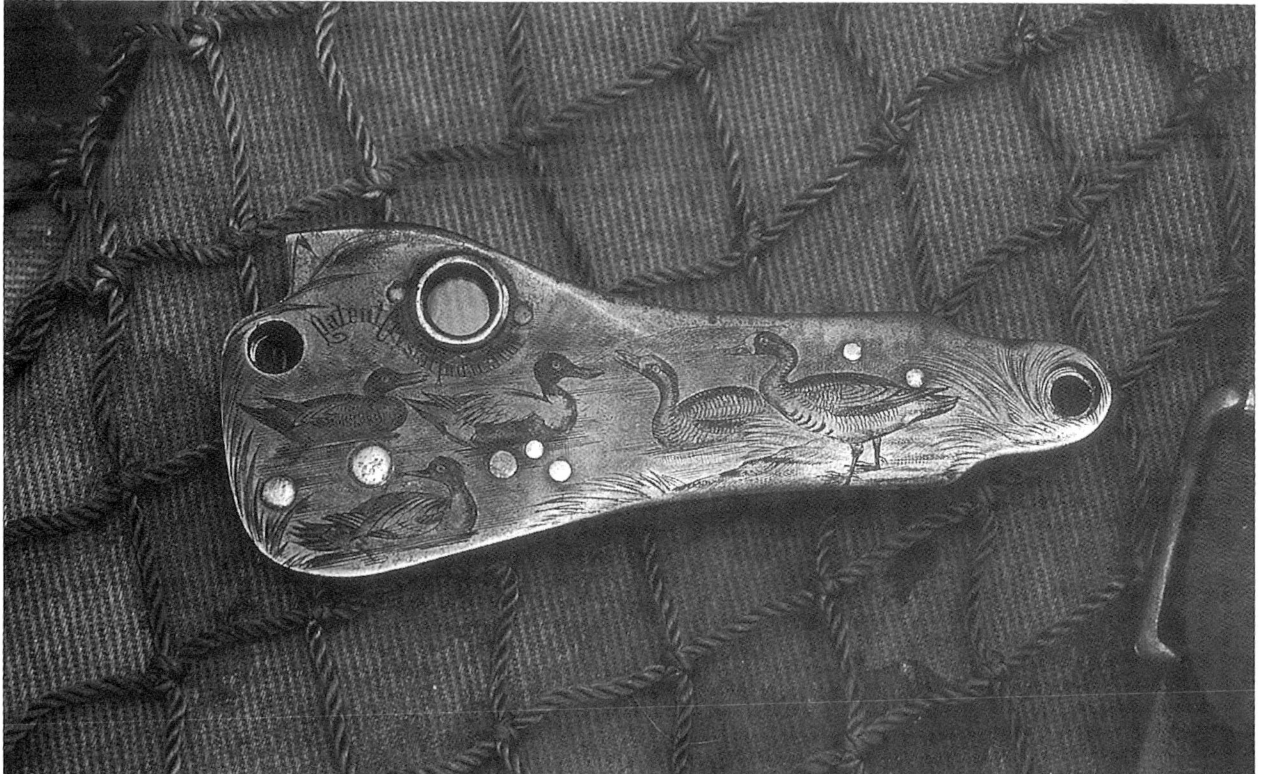

Detail of the lock on the Excellentia B showing the superbly engraved wildfowl. (Larry Barnes)

barrel is closed, the sprung lever returns and the threaded spindle bears down on the extension to provide a secure bolt.

The patent (Number 3,053 of 1882) was made with a straight rib extension for inexpensive models and a doll's head for better-quality guns. Today its presence on a provincial or foreign gun is one indication that Webley or Webley & Scott may have made it. Three more shotgun patents were registered by T. W. Webley that deal broadly with safeties, but none was as significant as the screw grip. One of these (Patent 1,463 of 1883) deserves passing mention because it was taken out with George Bouckley and Edwin Charles Hodges. Hodges was an action filer from London with strong ties to Henry Atkin, but the patent seems never to have gone beyond provisional protection.

Although Webley built many fine shotguns for the provincial and foreign trade and even opened a London showroom in Shaftesbury Avenue during 1893, the major part of its business was always revolvers. Even after 1897, when it merged with W. & C. Scott, this tradition continued.

W. & C. SCOTT & SON

In 1806, when William Scott was born, Britain was in a state of revolution. The Industrial Revolution had created burgeoning urban centers with large populations, while the Agricultural Revolution had introduced intensive cultivation that led to the enclosure of common lands. Poor farmers were driven from the soil and flocked to the towns, where they provided the labor force for the new industries. Most walked to the nearest industrialized center, which is why Welsh names like the previously mentioned Davis and Jones are common among the Birmingham gunmakers. Few of these victims of rural flight had marketable skills.

One of those who did was William Scott. Before he found his fortune in Birmingham, he had served an apprenticeship with a small gunmaker in the market town of Bury St. Edmunds in Suffolk, and this must have given him an enormous advantage.

William Scott left the family farm at Bradfield Combust at age twenty-one and signed indentures with a local gunmaker. The only gunmakers listed in directories for Bury St. Edmunds at the time of Scott's apprenticeship were Benjamin Parker, Charles Parker and William Young, but we don't know which one he worked for. Neither do we know who he worked for when he arrived in Birmingham in 1834, though several Parkers and a Young were listed at the time. Scott eventually set up in his own right as a gunfinisher at 11 Lench Street.

In 1840, William's brother Charles joined him and the firm became known as W. & C. Scott. Working from a succession of locations in the heart of the gun quarter, the brothers established a reputation as builders of high-quality "birding" guns. In the 1850s two of William's sons, William Middleditch and James Charles, joined the firm. When Queen Victoria paid Birmingham the compliment of an official visit in 1858 to open Aston Park, the brothers constructed a triumphal arch on behalf of the gun trade and decorated it with arms and standards. A contemporary engraving in the collection of the Birmingham Public Library shows the young monarch passing beneath the arch while Prince Albert acknowledges the crowd by waving his hat, watched by an escort of hussars.

Within the confines of the gun quarter, the arch must have created celebrities of the two brothers, but William Middleditch Scott would experience more enduring fame as the patentee of a series of improvements that would define his generation of Scott guns. The first of these, for a top lever and spindle with which to operate the Purdey underbolt,

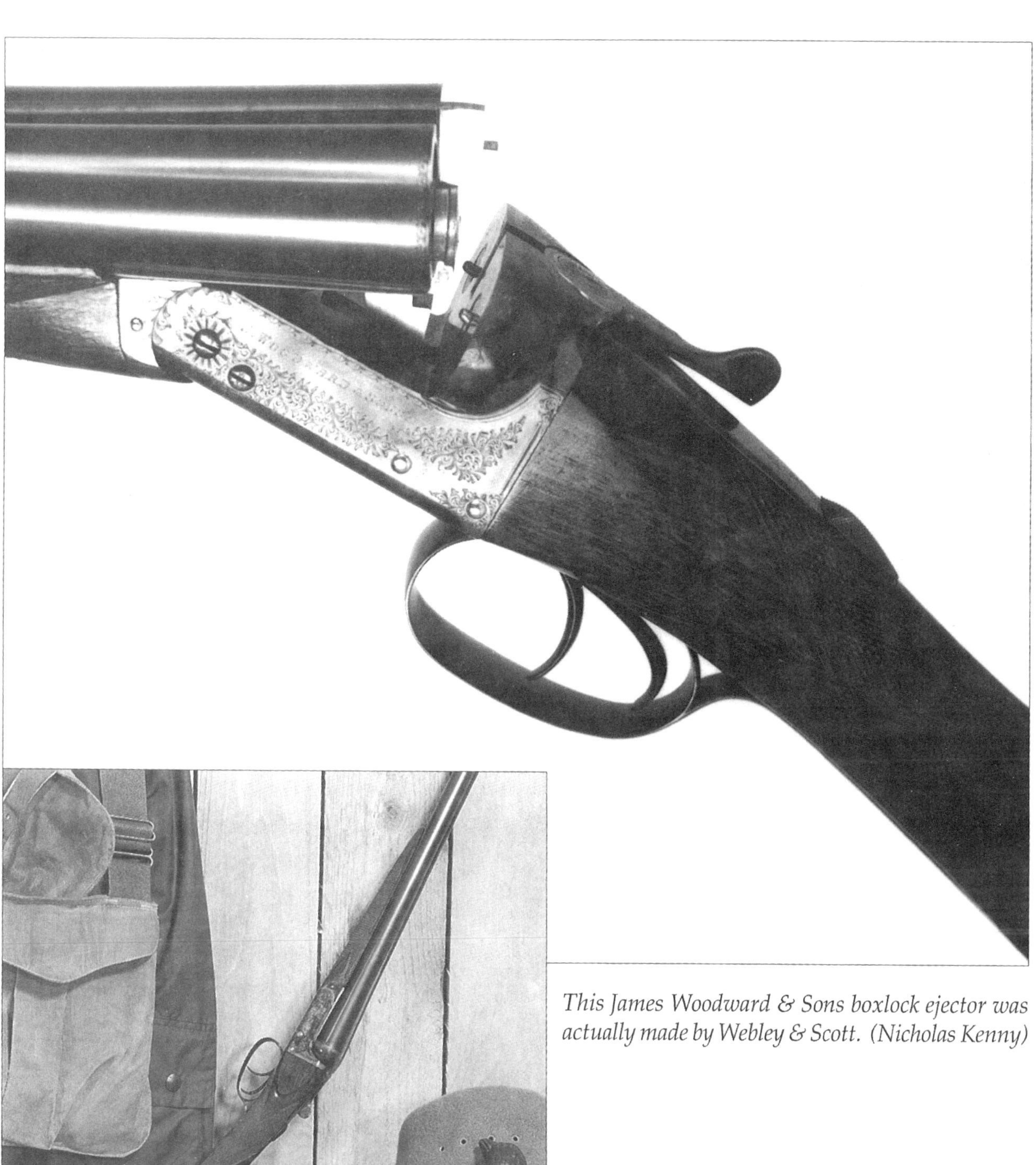

This James Woodward & Sons boxlock ejector was actually made by Webley & Scott. (Nicholas Kenny)

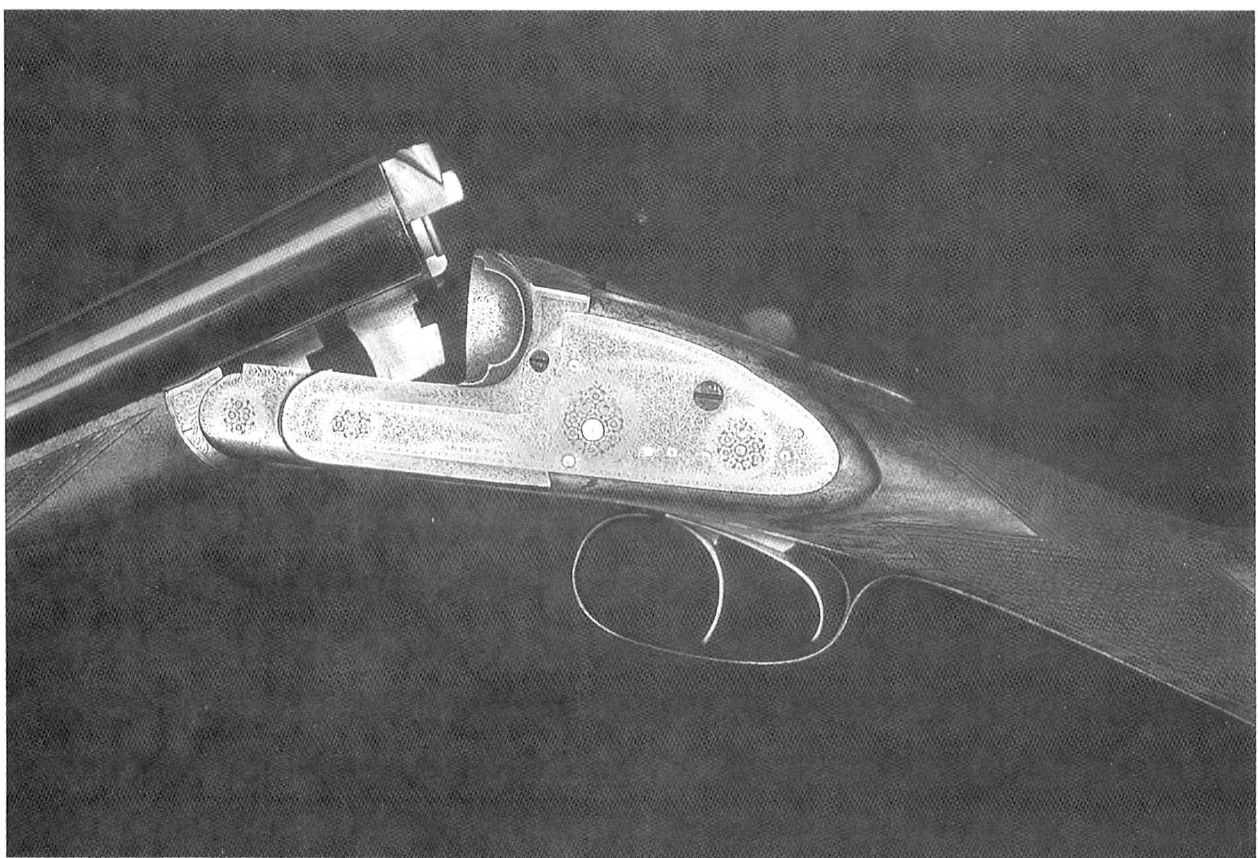

This Webley & Scott Model W & R first quality (the W & R stands for Webley and Rogers) was retailed by Army & Navy. (Keith Flannery)

is, along with the Anson & Deeley action, among the most significant of all the Birmingham gun patents. Of Scott's more than twenty patents, it is certainly the most enduring and is the standard means of opening a double gun used in Britain to this day. Previous to Scott's invention (Patent 2,752 of 1865), the Purdey underbolt was operated by a lever terminating in a broad thumb lever built into the front of the trigger guard. Scott's spindle provided a means of connecting the underbolt with a toplever. The strength of the design lies in its simplicity; it made the gun more aesthetically elegant and at the same time easier to use. With the Purdey thumbhole system, the right hand had to be physically removed from the grip to open the gun. With the Scott design, the gun could be quickly reloaded while the index finger remained close to the trigger and the thumb remained close to the hammers.

Other gunmakers such as Pape of Newcastle and Westley Richards patented top levers, but it is William Middleditch Scott's design that has endured.

The 1860s were a decade of great prosperity for the Birmingham gun quarter. The American Civil War created a boom in the military branch of the trade, and capable workers were able to earn upwards of £20 a week. (To put this into context, when I started my apprenticeship exactly 100 years later, I earned £4 a week!) During 1862 Birmingham sent 388,462 guns to the United States, and in the period 1861-1864 a total of 733,403 were sent. Birmingham in general and W. & C. Scott in particular became rich. In 1865, Scott expanded dramatically, building a new factory—the Premier Gun Works—on Lancaster Street and extending the gun quarter in the process. The firm also opened a showroom at 7 Dorset Place, just off Pall Mall in a fash-

An over-and-under built by William Baker from his own design but retailed by Robert Lisle of Derby and engraved in the Celtic style. (Matched Pairs)

A. A. BROWN & SONS

A pair of Supreme Deluxe guns, circa 1996, in their oak-and-leather, London tan case. (A. A. Brown & Sons)

A. A. BROWN & SONS

A pair of new Supreme Deluxe single-trigger sidelock ejectors with black-and-gold stocks and gunmetal finish. The cutaway scroll engraving is by Keith Thomas. (A. A. Brown & Sons)

A double-trigger Supreme Deluxe, circa 1991, with standard shape, and a single-trigger Supreme Deluxe, circa 1993, with semi-rounded body. Both guns were engraved by Charles Lee. (A. A. Brown & Sons)

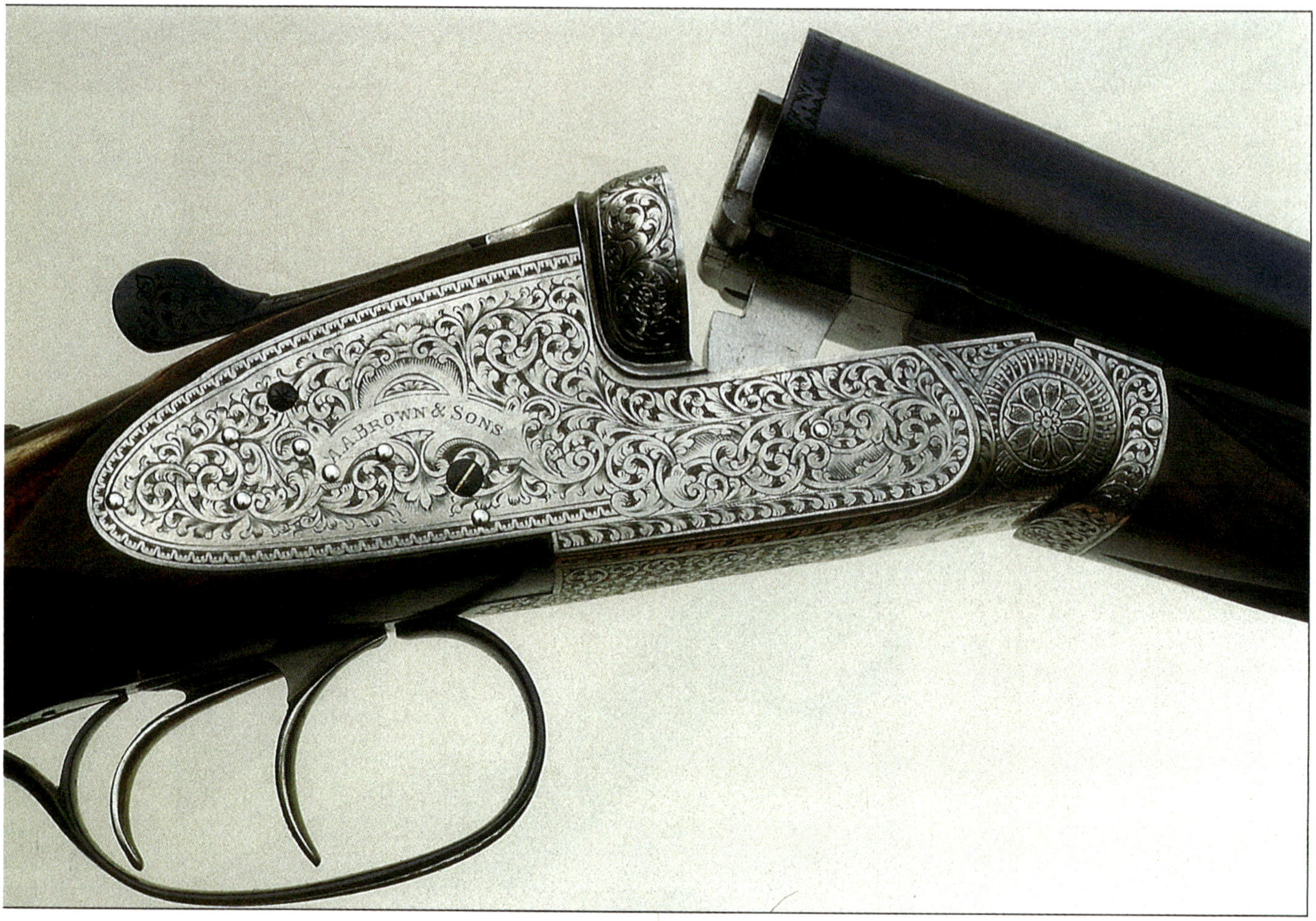

One of a pair of Supreme sidelock ejectors with cutaway scroll engraving by Les Jones, built in 1970. (Keith Flannery)

A. A. BROWN & SONS

The rounded undersides of this pair of Supreme Deluxe guns are engraved with English gray partridges and Scottish red grouse by Keith Thomas. (A. A. Brown & Sons)

B.S.A.

The machine-made B.S.A. was the precursor of the Winchester Model 21. Both guns shared the dovetailed lumps patented by B.S.A. employer G. Norman in 1911, and both guns have simple lines and finish. (Keith Flannery)

A 16-bore Cashmore with sideclips and Greener crossbolt. (Keith Flannery)

WILLIAM CASHMORE

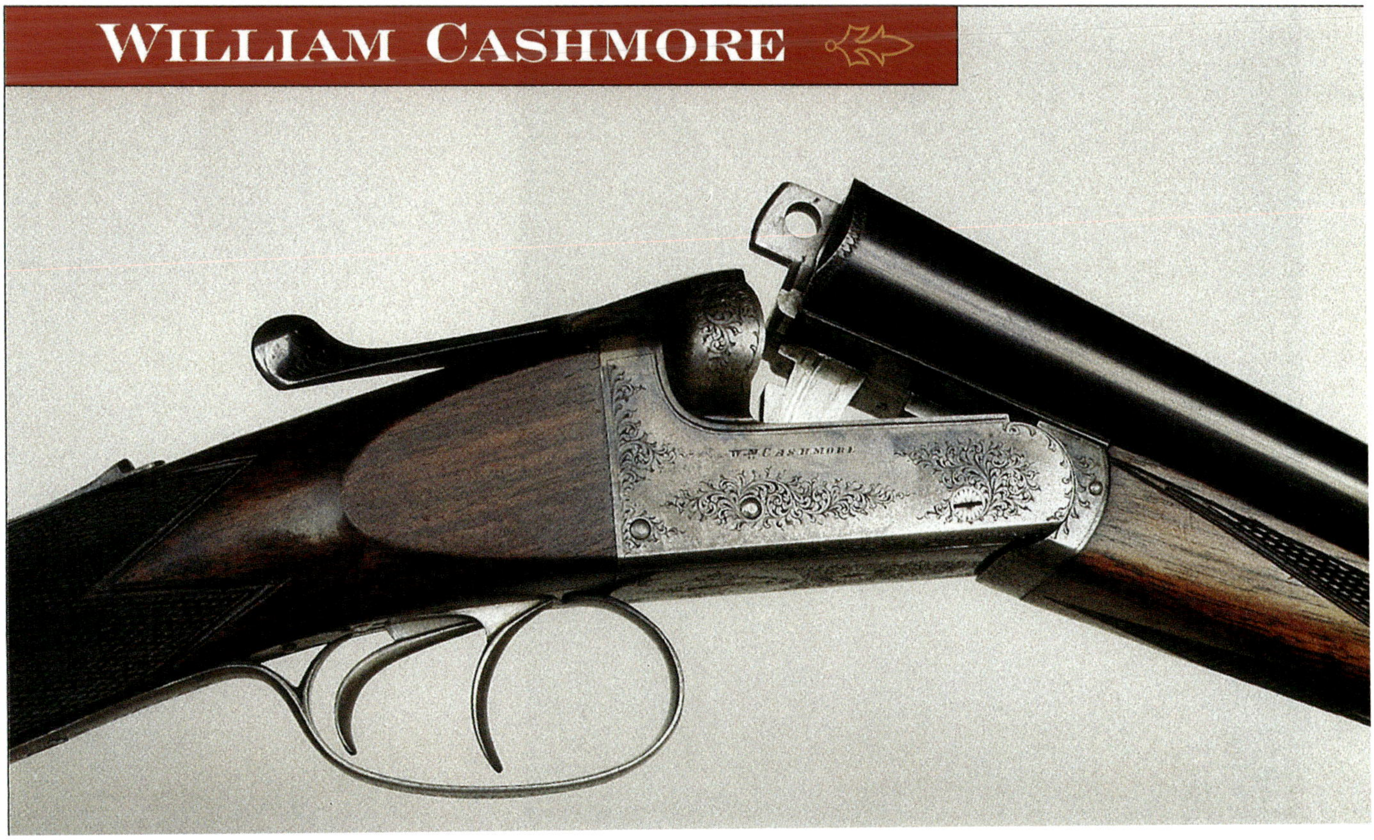

WILLIAM FORD

A best sidelock ejector game gun by William Ford. (Sotheby's)

A three-inch-chambered boxlock ejector pigeon gun with beaded fences and scalloped back-action by William Ford. (Christie's)

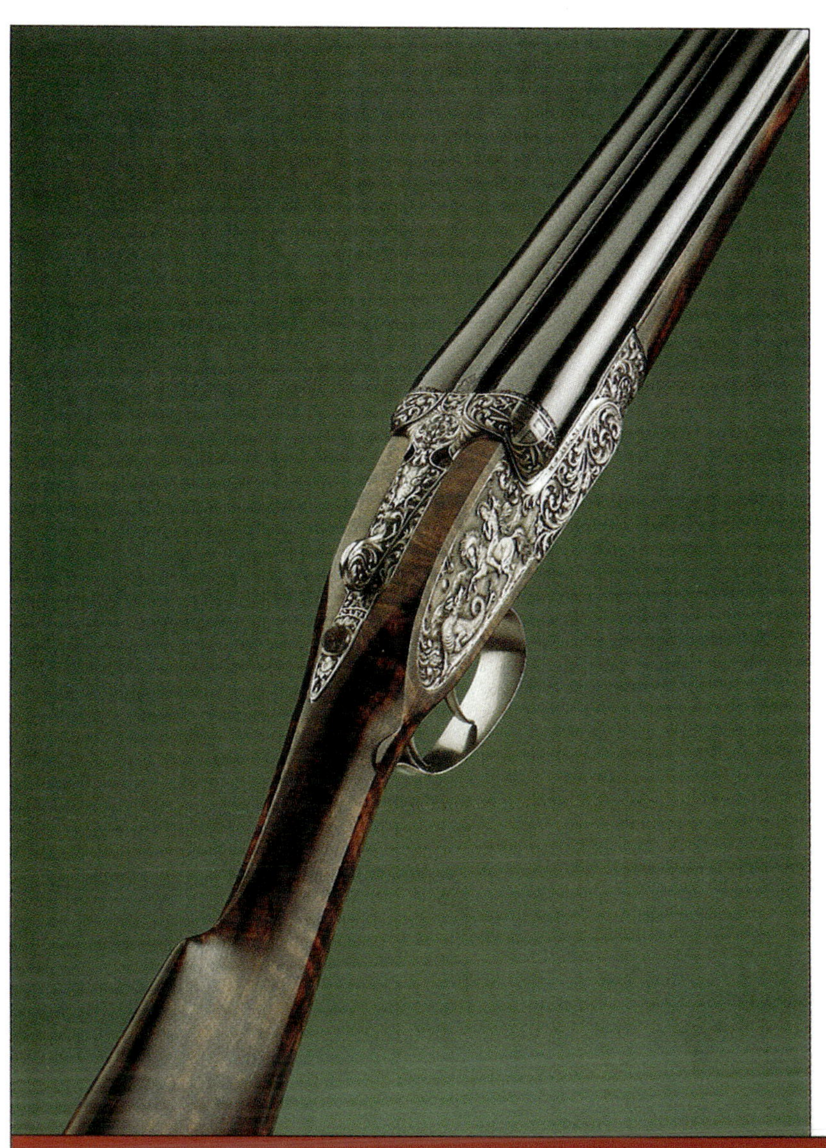

Two views of the modern Greener Saint George gun. (David Grant)

W. W. GREENER

A set of three hammer guns by W. W. Greener consisting of a consecutively numbered pair of 28-bores and a single 12-bore, stocked and finished by John Wilkes. (Christie's)

W. W. GREENER

A pair of 32-bore sideplated-boxlock ejector guns by W. W. Greener. They feature scroll-back, action bodies, rolled-edge trigger guards, best foliate-scroll engraving with added gold-encrusted bouquets, the maker's name and serial number gold inlaid, with full color-hardened and blued finish, and well-figured stocks. The barrels have game ribs and gold-encrusted breech ends. The guns were originally completed circa 1937. (Christie's)

W. W. GREENER

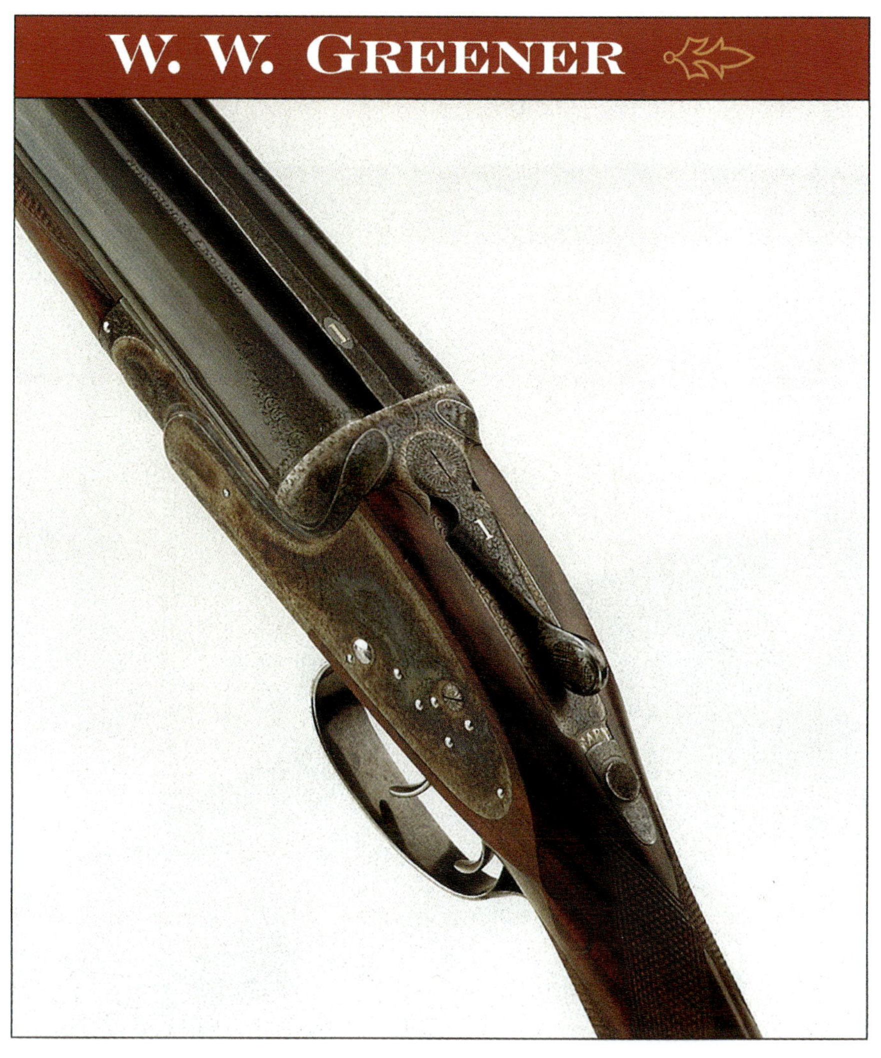

A new lightweight W. W. Greener best London-pattern sidelock ejector. (David Grant)

A "G 60"-grade hammerless boxlock ejector by W. W. Greener features arcaded fences and Harry Greener's patent trigger of 1899. (Sotheby's)

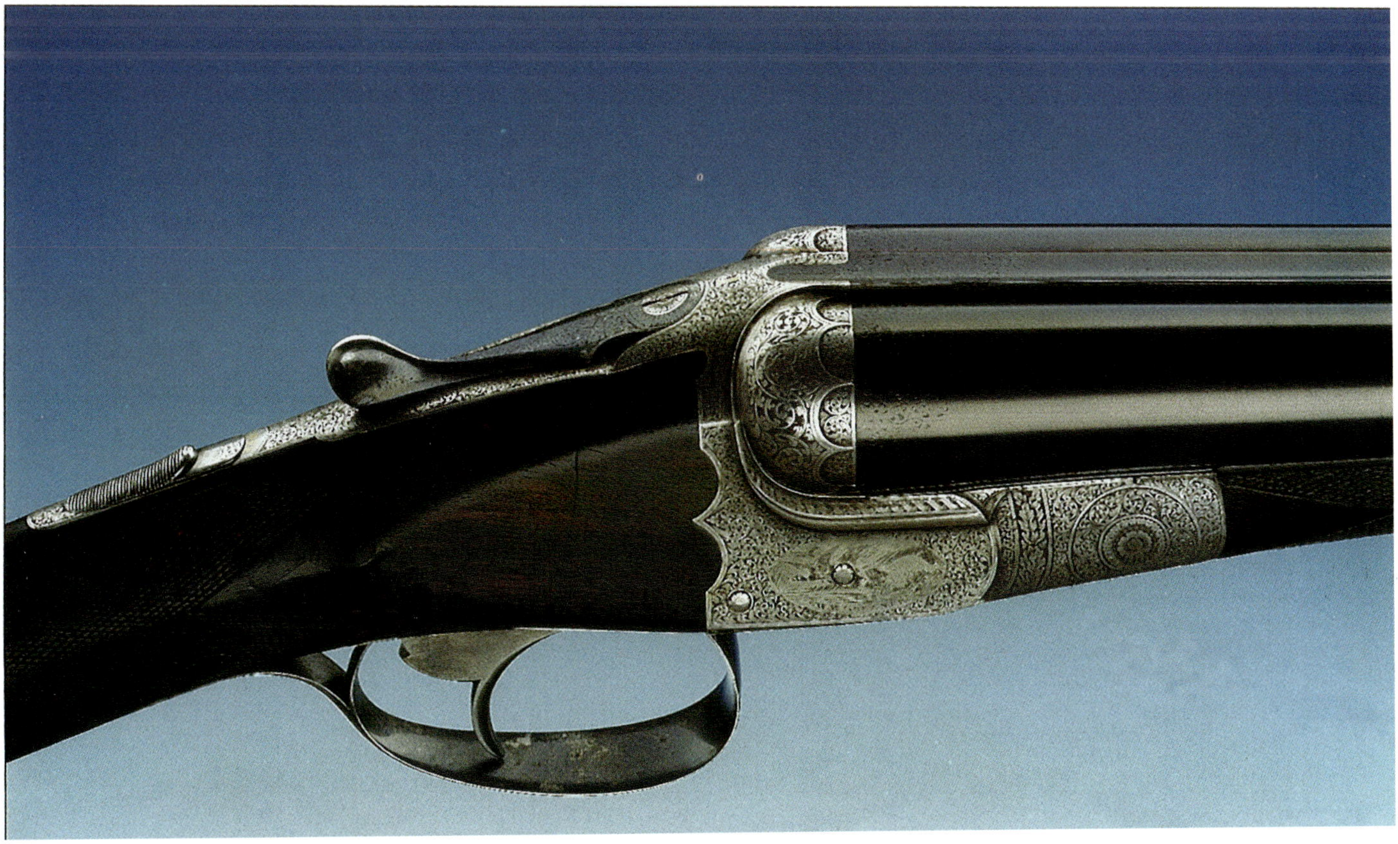

HOLLOWAY & NAUGHTON

This Hardy Brothers of Alnwick piece was made by Holloway & Naughton. (Keith Flannery)

This William Palmer Jones 12-bore hammer gun with a rifle barrel in .360 is activated by what Jones called his "firing appliance" of 1888, which enabled a three-barreled gun to be fired by two hammers. (David Grant)

WILLIAM PALMER JONES

A best sidelock ejector by William Palmer Jones, engraved with a nye of pheasants. (Sotheby's)

DANIEL LEONARD

CHARLES OSBOURNE

This .450-400 double rifle, built by Leonard for W. J. Jeffery in 1913 and sold by Walter Locke of Calcutta, Delhi, and Lahore is engraved with stalking tigers. (Tim Crawford)

This .360 double rifle with Celtic engraving was retailed by W. R. Pape of Newcastle upon Tyne. Pape's records reveal that the gun was actually built by Charles Osbourne. (Michael Howarth)

WILLIAM POWELL

A single bouquet of roses was a signature engraving feature of older Powell sidelocks. (Sotheby's)

Number 1 of a pair of William Powell sidelock ejector game guns. (Sotheby's)

A pair of new, best-quality Model No. 1s with game-scene engraving. (William Powell)

WILLIAM POWELL

A William Powell No. 1 with oak-leaf fences and gold-washed pins and triggers. (William Powell)

A miniature flintlock made by William Powell in the 1830s and inlaid with silver wire. Less than nine inches long, its small size is apparent from the 12-bore cartridges. (William Powell)

A Skimin & Wood two-inch 12-bore retailed by J. Graham of Inverness. (David Williams III)

A W. & C. Scott hammer gun.

A high-quality Monte Carlo B pigeon gun engraved with blue-rock pigeons. (Larry Barnes)

A Premier Grade hammer gun by W. & C. Scott. (Larry Barnes)

WEBLEY & SCOTT

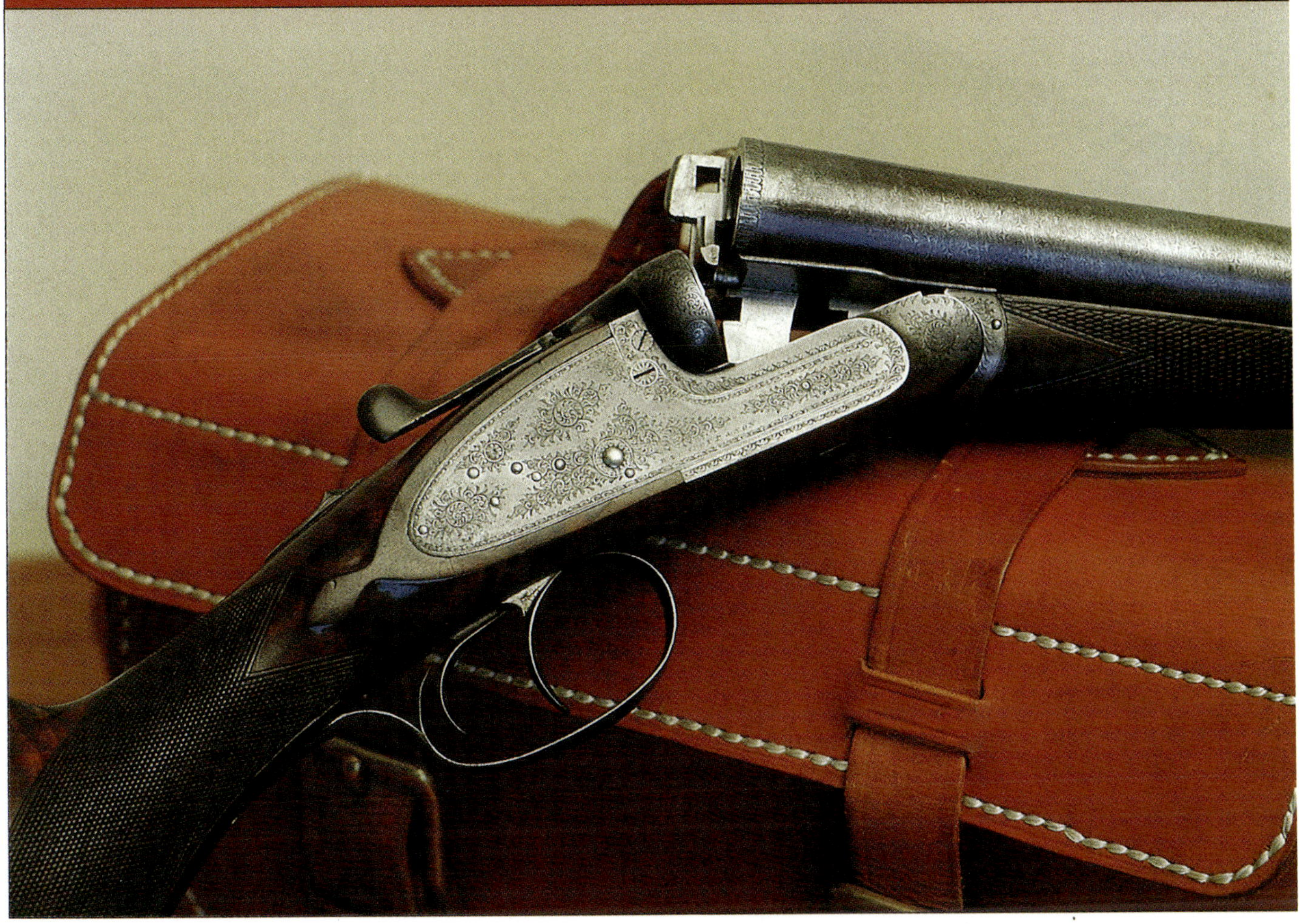

This hammerless sidelock features the distinctive Scott square crossbolt and removable block safety bar locks. (Larry Barnes)

This Scott back-action lock was patented by J. Needham and G. Hinton in 1879 and assigned to W. M. and J. C. Scott. (Larry Barnes)

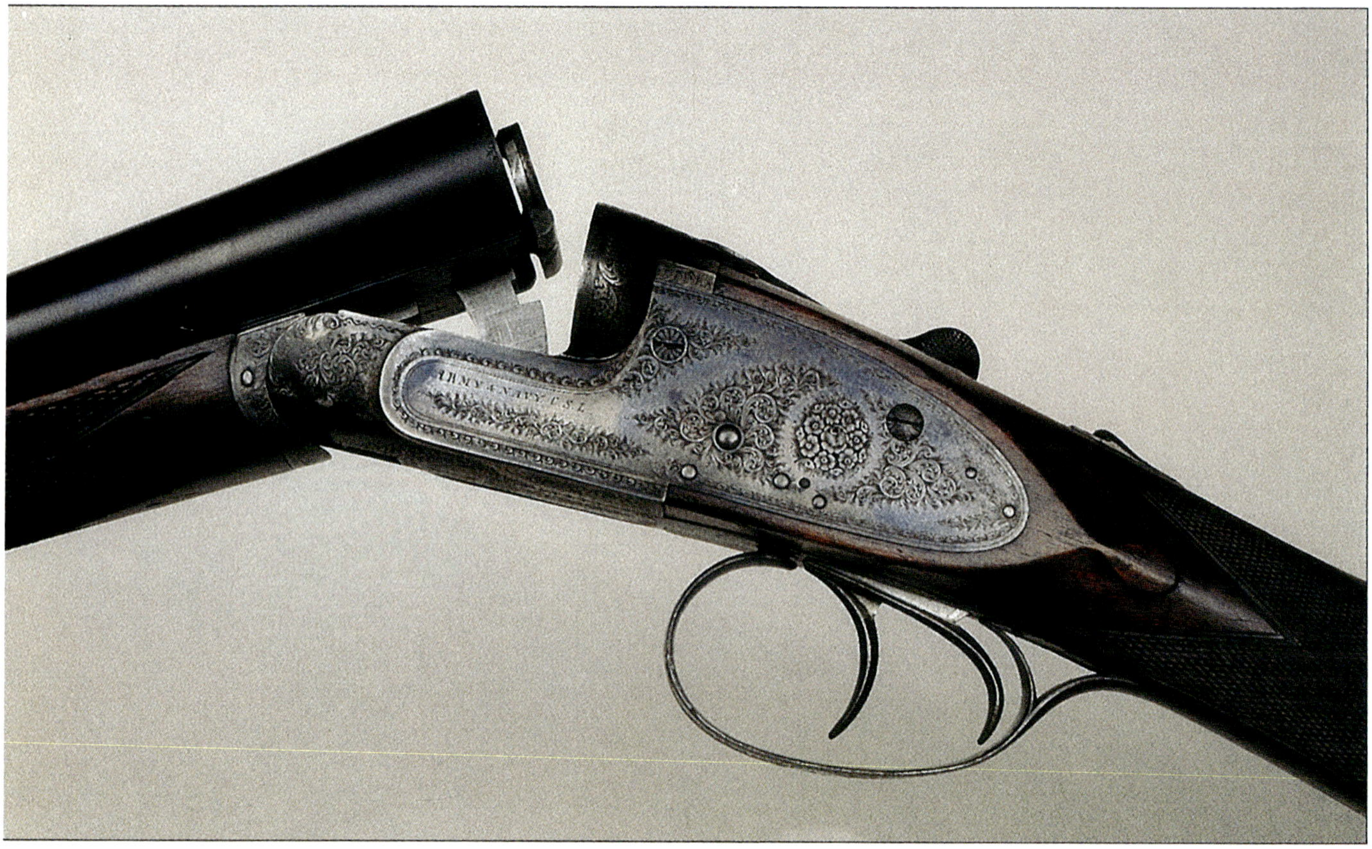

This Webley & Scott Model W & R first quality (the W & R stands for Webley and Rogers) was retailed by Army & Navy. (Keith Flannery)

WEBLEY & SCOTT

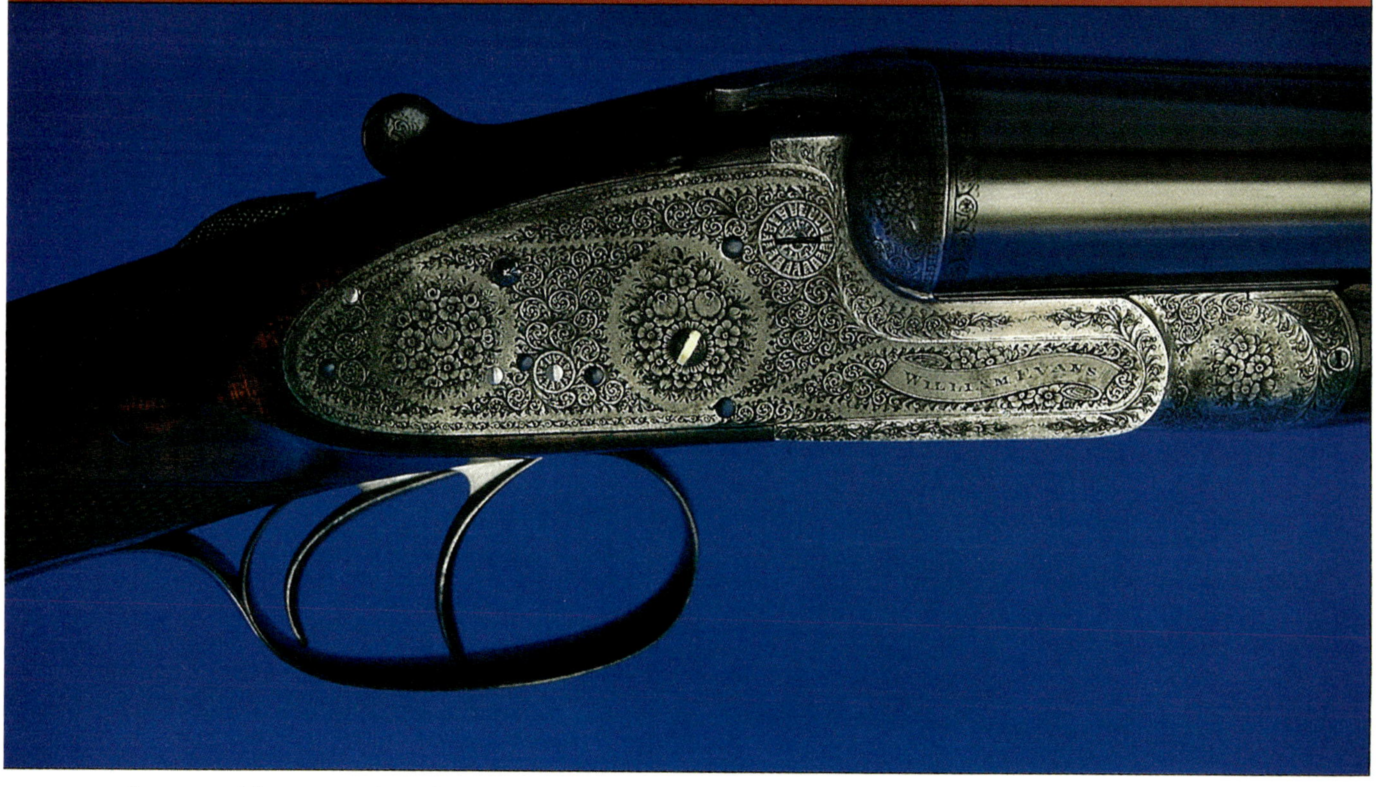

Exceptional bouquet and scroll engraving marks this Webley & Scott built for William Evans. (Keith Flannery)

WESTLEY RICHARDS

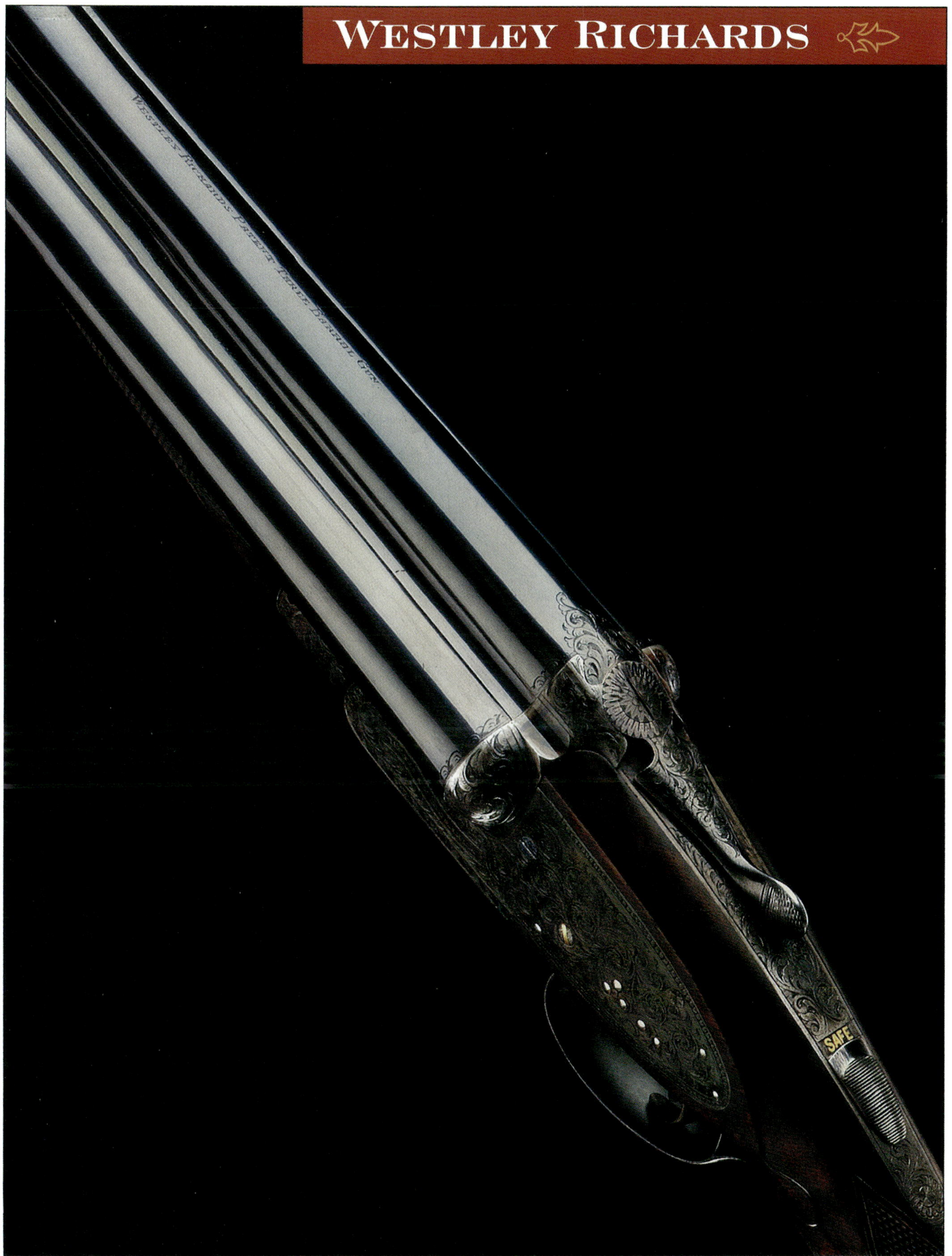

A rare Westley Richards three-barreled gun patented by Edwinson Green and shown at the Turin exhibition of 1911. (Christie's)

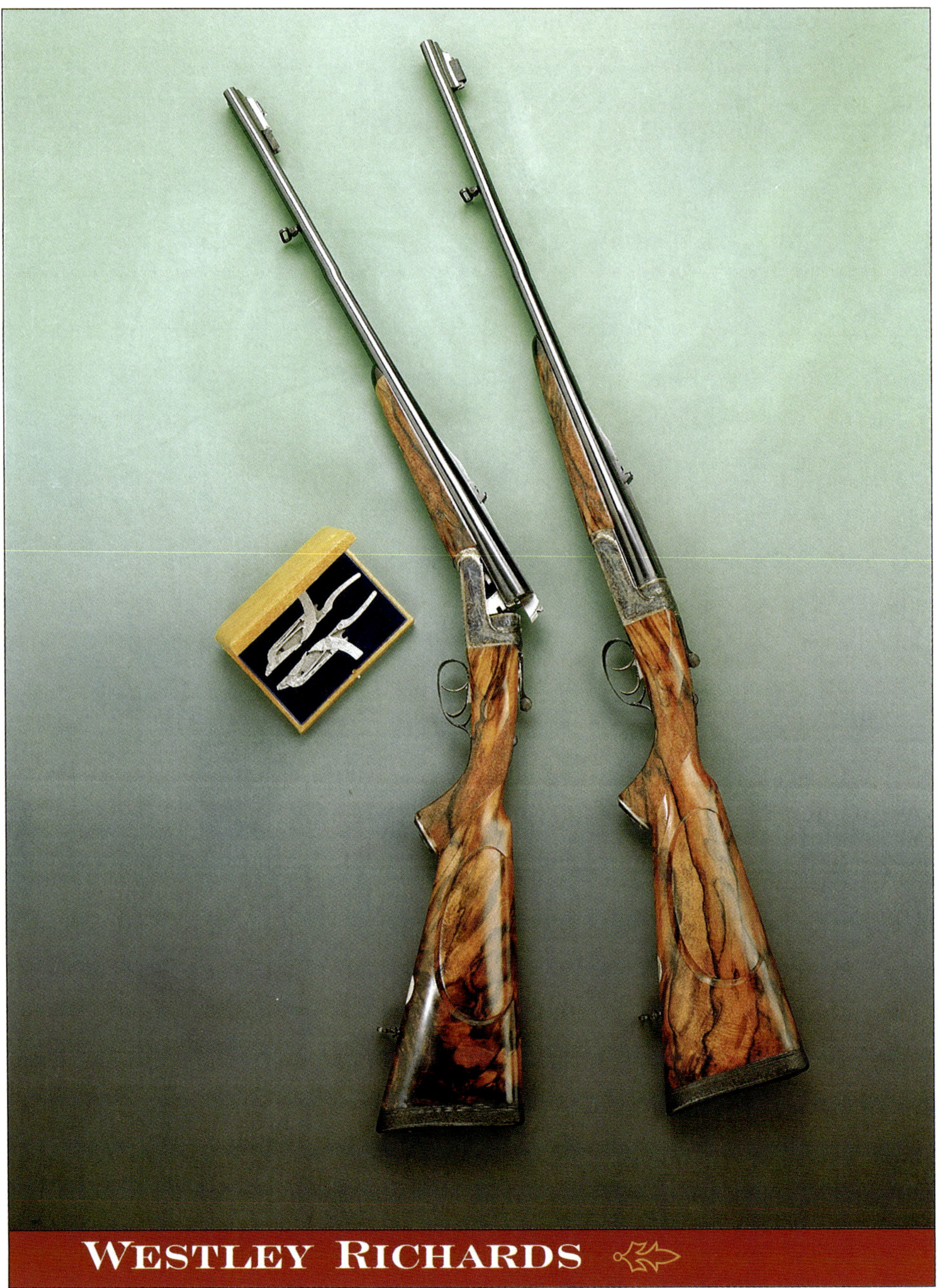

WESTLEY RICHARDS

A pair of detachable-lock double rifles in .375 H & H, shown with an optional set of interchangeable locks.

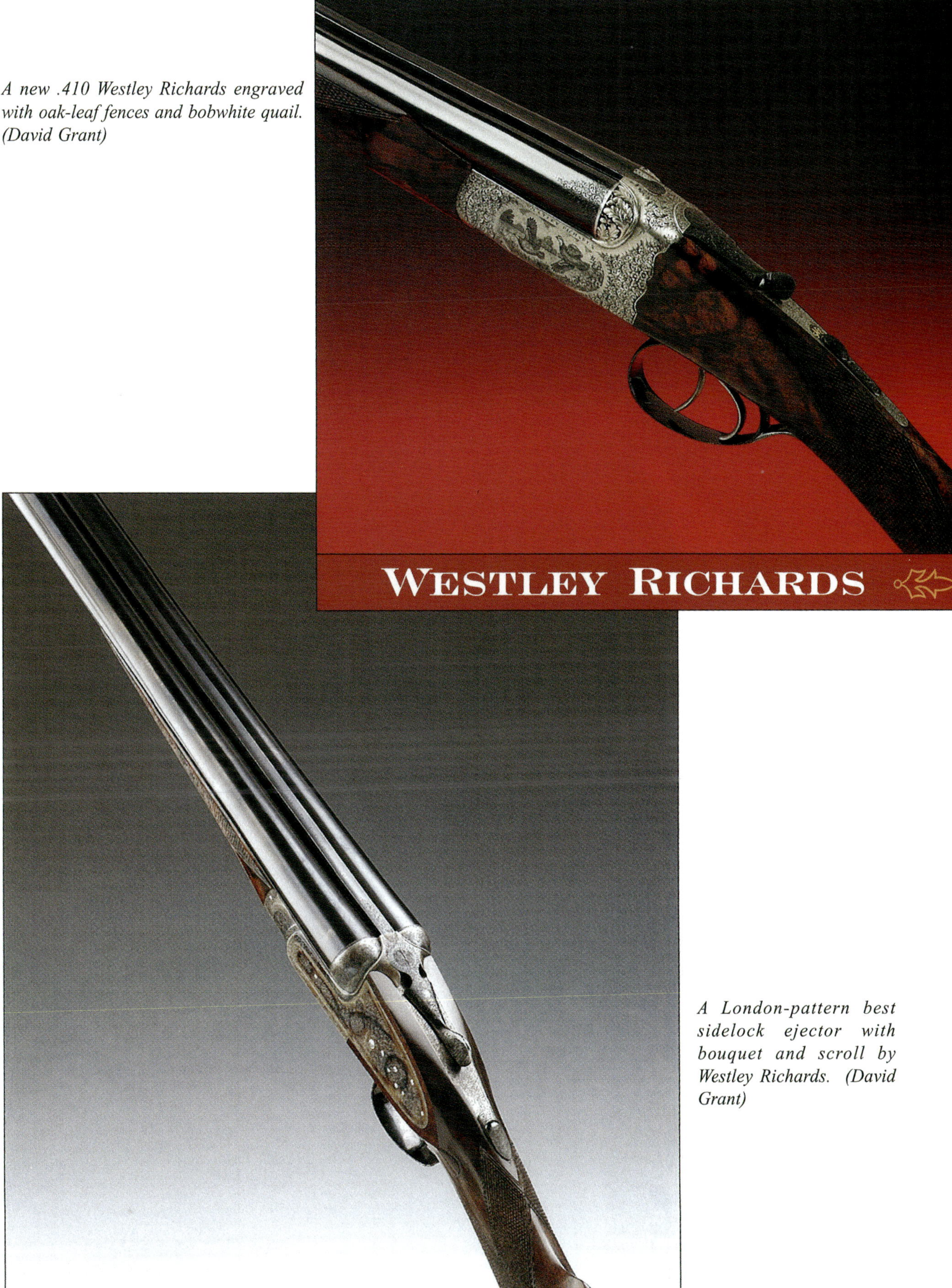

A new .410 Westley Richards engraved with oak-leaf fences and bobwhite quail. (David Grant)

A London-pattern best sidelock ejector with bouquet and scroll by Westley Richards. (David Grant)

WESTLEY RICHARDS

This sidelock ejector is gold inlaid with the symbols of England, Scotland, and Wales. (Westley Richards)

The ruffed grouse on this Westley sidelock appears to be flying through a window of stylized acanthus scroll. (Westley Richards)

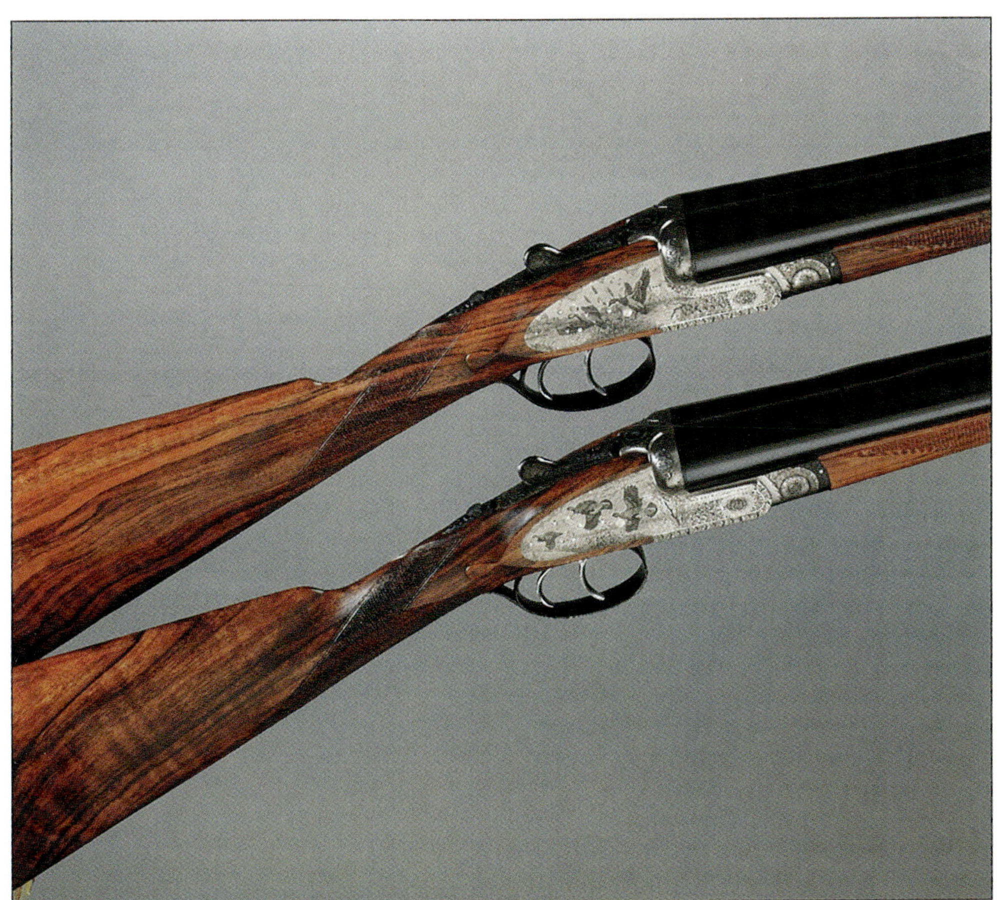

A pair of "William Bishop" 20-bore sidelock ejectors engraved with mallards and English gray partridge. (Westley Richards)

Westley Richards still offers a broad range of guns. (Westley Richards)

WESTLEY RICHARDS

Number 3 of a trio of heavy double rifles. (Westley Richards)

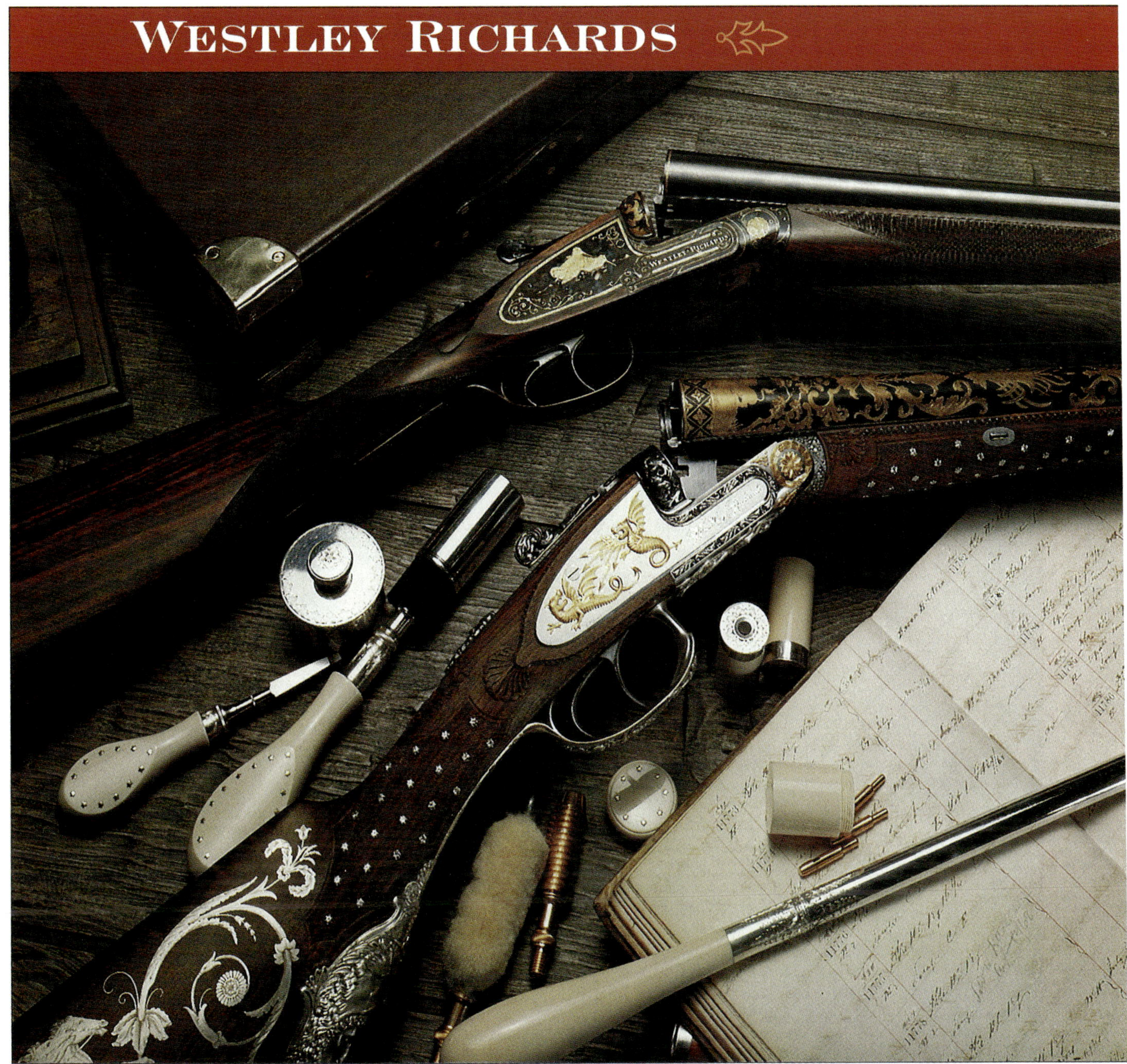

Two Westley Richards sidelocks. On top is a gold-inlaid presentation gun while the gun on the bottom is inlaid with diamonds, silver, and gold in the style of Boutet, Napoleon's gunmaker. (Westley Richards)

WESTLEY RICHARDS

A deluxe 12-bore Westley Richards sidelock ejector built in 1984 and gold inlaid by Keith Thomas. (Christie's)

WESTLEY RICHARDS

A new 12-bore Westley Richards sidelock engraved with mallards. (Westley Richards)

A single-trigger double rifle built by Westley Richards in 1906 in .256 Mannlicher and later converted to .300 Winchester Magnum. (Christie's)

A .303 single-trigger droplock with dummy sideplates and enamel of a Bactrian tribal leader in uniform and with orders on the top lever, built in 1910. (Sotheby's)

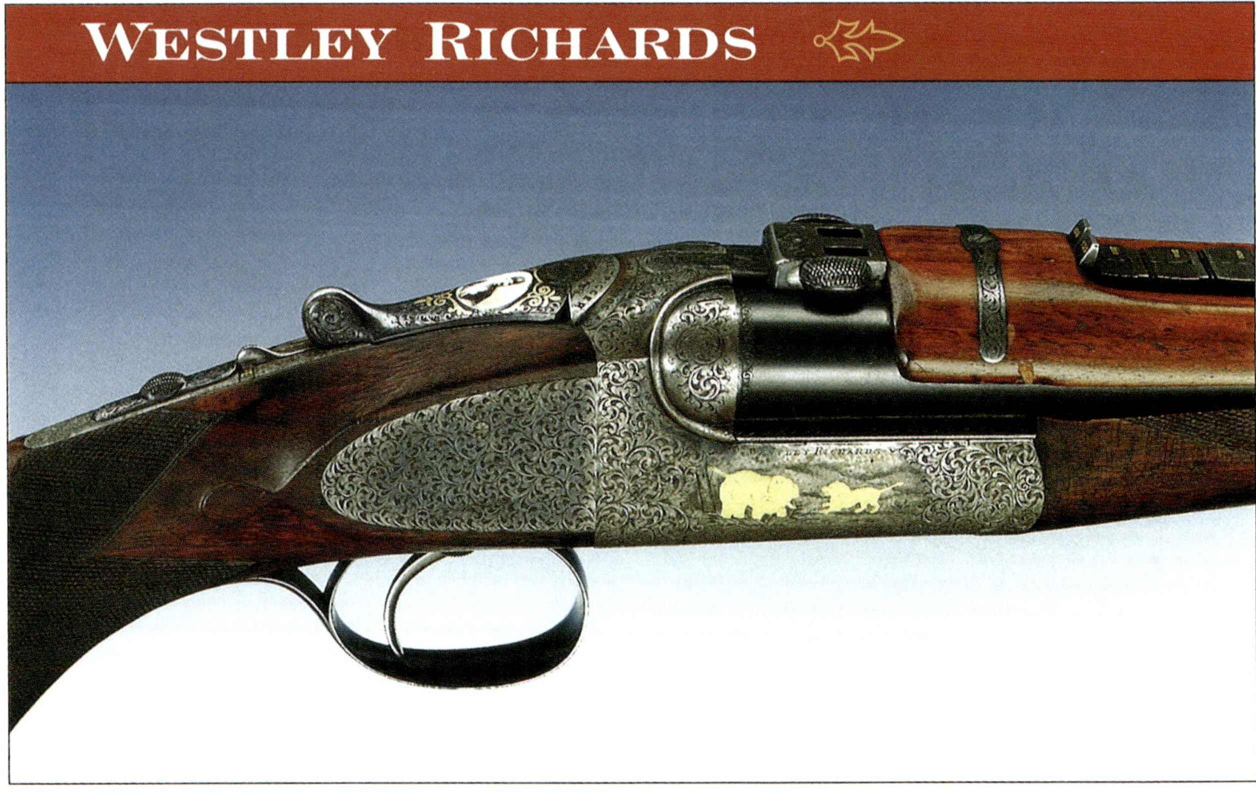

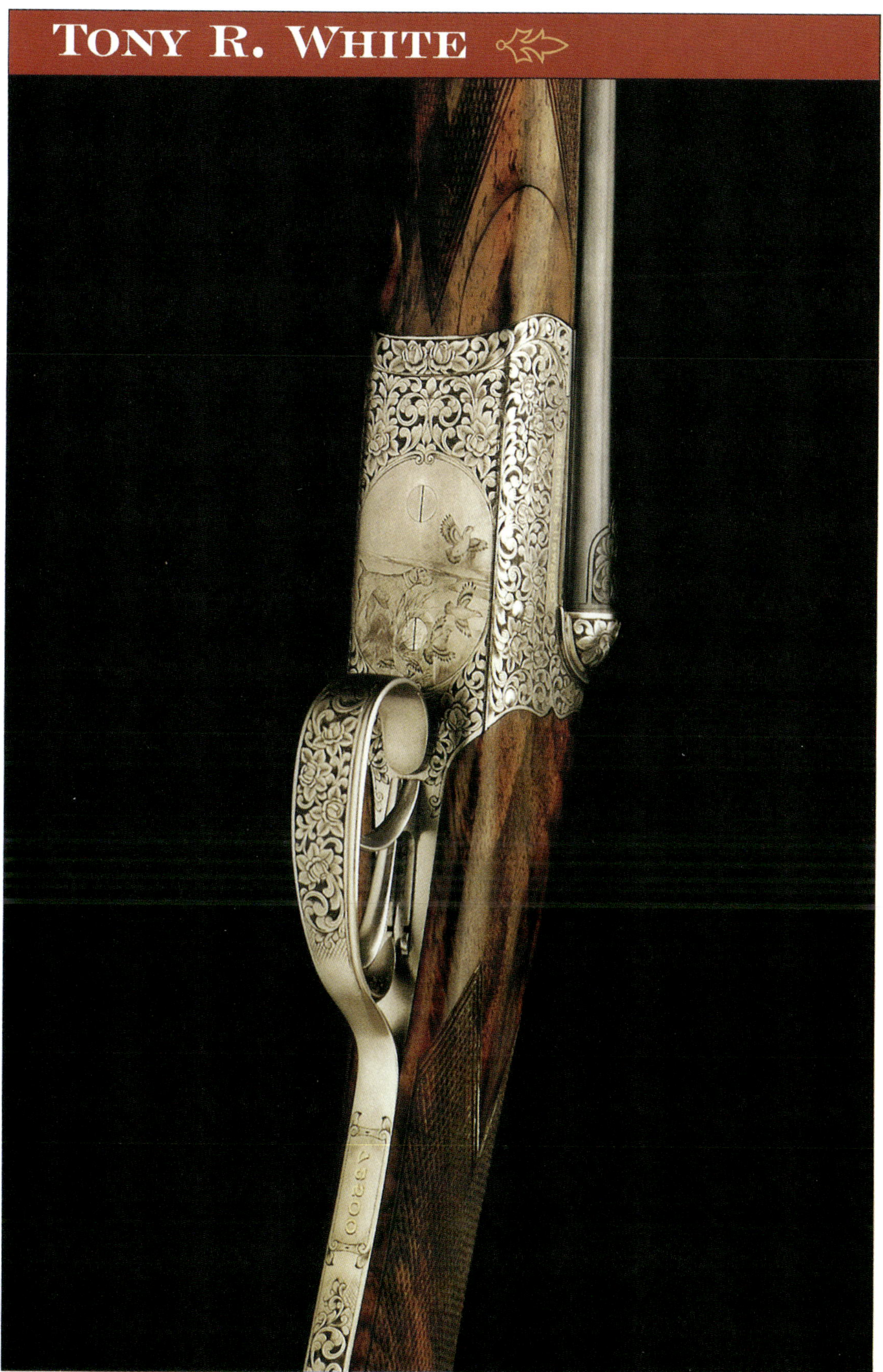

A 20-bore round-bodied gun built for Cogswell & Harrison by Tony R. White. (Cogswell & Harrison)

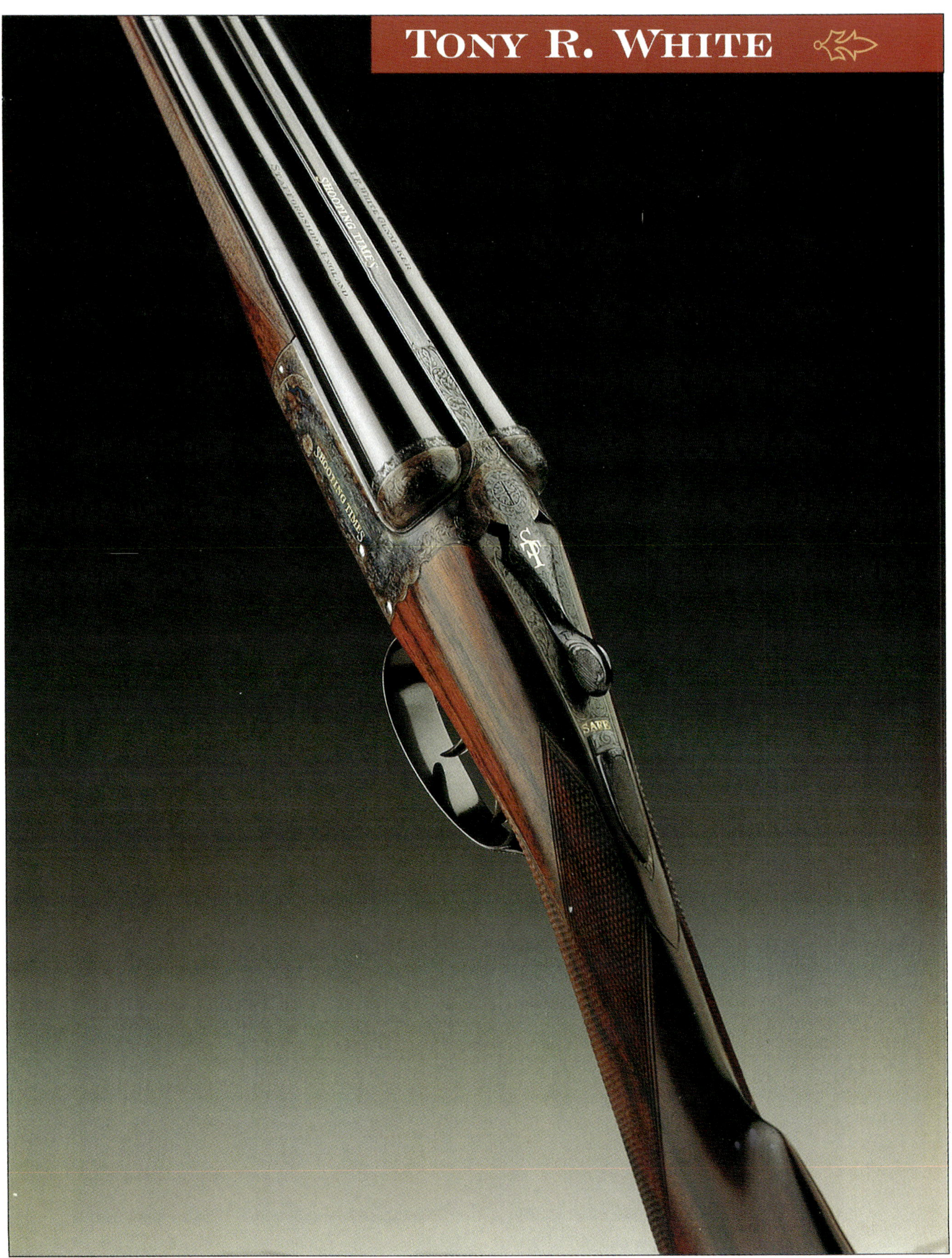

A 20-bore round-bodied boxlock built for and raffled by The Shooting Times & Country *magazine.* (Tony White)

ionable part of London, and an office in Turin run by Frederick Moore Scott, who held an interest in the firm. Furthermore, it acquired the business of Moore & Harris, whose Great Western Gun Works on Constitution Hill at the opposite end of the gun quarter had sold at auction the previous year. Moore & Harris had strong links to the U.S., and Scott used this connection to sell guns in America.

Much of Scott's trade was with North America, where break-action shotguns were often distrusted because early models had a propensity to shoot loose. In 1870 W. M. Scott developed a gun with a sliding front lump that could be adjusted, with only a screw-driver, to compensate for any looseness that might develop (Patent 452 of 1870). The advantage was that a gun could be put back on face under frontier conditions far from the nearest gunsmith's workshop.

In 1872, W. M. Scott proposed a modification (Patent 452 of 1872) to his spindle that increased the leverwork and probably the mechanical efficiency. The design appears to have been a complication rather than an improvement, and it never saw the wide application of the original.

The following year he patented two methods of retracting firing pins by linking them to the top opening lever (Patent 1,268 of 1873) and a rib extension (Patent 3,756 of 1873) that was held down during discharge by a pair of diametrically opposed spring bolts. Incidentally, both patents also describe fore-end fasteners.

During 1874, W. M. Scott was again active at the patent office, registering Patent 712 for yet another fore-end fastener, Patent 2,052 for a gun that employed no less than five bolts to secure the barrels to the action, and Patent 3,424 for a top or underlever cocking hammerless action similar to the Gibbs & Pitt.

It was typical of the Birmingham gun trade that a master took credit for the inventions of the men he employed. In the larger factories where men were employed by the hour, all of a man's gun designs became the property of his boss. Consequently, it is difficult to know at this late date who the actual inventor of a particular mechanism was, especially when the name on the patent is one of the famous family firms of Birmingham. Many of the larger gunmakers registered designs but were not capable of the improvements they claimed as their own. William Middleditch Scott, on the other hand, probably designed the patents he registered. His obituary in *Arms and Explosives* claimed he left school "at thirteen and a half years of age" and became "an expert in the use of file and chisel and at the age of twenty one was a thoroughly practical workman."

W. M. Scott registered two patents in 1873, three in 1874, and four in 1875. He would never be this prolific again. His efforts for 1875 were for twin bolts that engage top extensions on the outsides of the barrels (Patent 186), choke bores for cylinder guns (Patent 312) with John Rigby of Dublin, a rib extension that mates with the classic Scott spindle (Patent 1902), and the famous crystal cocking indicators (Patent 3,223). These last two would become distinctive aesthetic features that helped define a Scott gun. The rib extension had at least three variants and became known as the "Triplex Top Lever Grip," and crystal cocking indicators were employed on almost all Scott hammerless sidelock guns from the date they were introduced until 1892.

During the 1870s, the new hammerless guns were widely regarded as unsafe by a generation that had grown up shooting hammer guns. These gentlemen objected to the lack of a visible means of determining whether a gun was cocked or not. Scott's crystal cocking indicator was an attempt to reassure them. It consisted of the simple expedient of a half-inch hole drilled in the side of a lockplate and situated so the tumbler was visible when cocked. To prevent the elements from fouling the lockwork, the hole was provided with a window of "glass or other transparent substance."

During 1876, W. M. Scott registered a patent (Number 615) with his nephew, Martin Scott, whose occupation is given as "Gun Works Manager," for three methods of bolting guns. The ideas are for hooks that engage rib extensions, but as John A. Crawford and Pat G. Whatley point out in their well-researched book about W. & C. Scott, "None was commonly applied to Scott guns."

In 1878, W. M. Scott patented (Number 761) a hammerless design with a gun-action maker named Thomas Baker. Whatley and Crawford tell us the design became "the mainstay of Scott's production of hammerless guns from 1878 to 1892." Hooks on the barrel flats draw forward a cocking rod, which runs diagonally through the action body. The mainsprings are helical and surround the cocking rod. The fall of the barrels draws forward the rods, which have collars attached that compress the springs, cocking the gun. Scott built guns on this patent for prestigious London firms and for American retailers. In London, Holland & Holland and Cogswell & Harrison were not ashamed to put their own names on these pieces, but in the United States Scott sold them as its own, enhancing a reputation that one correspondent compared to Purdey's!

In the following year W. M. Scott filed a patent (Number 3,883 of 1879) with John Tonks for a lever-cocking hammerless gun that never went beyond provisional protection. Also in 1879, Joseph Vernon Needham and George Hinton patented (Number 706) an intercepting safety that—judging by the patent drawings—was developed with the Scott sidelock in mind. The invention was assigned to W. M. and J. C. Scott and the company thought so much of it that it occupied a full page in Scott catalogs as late as 1891.

The following page of the same catalog advertised a gas check for hammerless guns:

The essence of this patent consists in establishing a communication between the recess in which the cap is placed and the outer air, allowing the fumes to pass off without entering the striker hole.

The design (Patent 617 of 1882) was the work of W. M. Scott and Thomas Baker and was, as the description suggests, a method of preventing escaping gases from the primer getting into and corroding the lockwork by way of the striker holes. It consisted simply of channels cut into the breech face around the striker holes, which then vent to the sides. To promote the idea, Scott built a gun in which his gas check was cut on the right side only. He fired 200 rounds through each barrel and then showed the locks to a correspondent of *The Field*, who reported, ". . . one of which is quite rusty, while the other is perfectly bright."

Also in 1882, W. M. Scott registered another patent (Number 1,209) for a cocking mechanism for a hammerless gun that didn't go beyond provisional protection. The same year he also improved the mechanism he had patented in 1878 with Thomas Baker so that it became an assisted opener (Patent 1,320 of 1882). The next year, W. M. Scott proposed an improvement (Patent 727 of 1883) to a Thomas Perkes patent (Number 1,968 of 1878) that Scott had purchased in which it too became a spring opener. Also in 1883, W. M. Scott patented yet another barrel-cocking hammerless gun (Number 3,859) together with Charles Proctor. The design does not appear to have been widely adopted.

In 1884, W. M. Scott patented a gun (Number 5,564) in which the fall of the barrels cocked one lock while the other was cocked as the gun was closed. This ingenious concept attracted the attention of numerous British gunmakers before the introduction of the ejector—with its second pair of springs to compress—consigned it to obscurity.

Today, because of his twenty-one patents taken out over a nineteen-year period, William Middleditch Scott enjoys a reputation as one of Birmingham's greatest gunmakers, and rightly so. Students of firearms, particularly those of a mechanical bent, will point to his improvements and especially the continuing use of his spindle and top lever as a measure of his genius. But what of his younger brother and partner, James Charles Scott?

James Charles Scott was two years younger than his brother and joined the firm in 1858 at age twenty-one. Unlike W. M. Scott, he showed no aptitude for mechanical skill; instead, he concentrated on the aesthetic aspects of firearms. His obituary in *The Sporting Goods Review* provides a few clues:

> During his early youth he was an earnest student at the School of Design, and proved an apt pupil. He produced as a student a number of very fine designs, including some for the decoration of guns and revolvers. On the conclusion of his apprenticeship he devoted his time as an improver to gun engraving, and in this art he showed conspicuous ability. It was as an engraver that he worked for the firm as a journeyman until he became a partner.

Scott guns from the period when William and James ran the company are characterized by crystal cocking indicators, the gas check venting system, and numerous other W. M. Scott patents. They are also conspicuous for their engraving. At a time when game-scene engraving on even London guns was at its best, Scott guns were decorated with shore birds, ducks, and geese that are fluid and realistic. Throughout its history, game-scene engraving has tended to shadow popular mainstream art, and the birds engraved on Scott guns are reminiscent of the works of the great ornithological illustrators such as Wolf, Smit, and Keulemans. The

engraving is highly naturalistic, as if executed by a keen observer of live birds, and it would be decades before other British gunmakers would produce engraving as good. Engraving of this quality must have gone a long way in enhancing Scott's reputation for fine guns.

It's possible that J. C. Scott engraved these guns, and it's tempting to speculate that he did. However, it's impossible to know for certain. All we can be sure of is that his aesthetic sensibility somehow influenced the way these guns look and the way they look helped to sell them. J. C. Scott started a tradition for quality engraving that was continued by Joe Brown after the amalgamation with Webley and with Walter Howe in the post World War II years.

When W. M. Scott retired in 1887, J. C. Scott became head of the family firm and remained there until its merger with P. Webley & Son a decade later. The amalgamation with Webley occurred when he was 60, and he took the opportunity to retire. He had three sons. The eldest, W. J. Scott, had previously worked in the family business but left at the time of the merger and went to live in America. The youngest, Harry E. Scott, also moved to America, while the third son, F. C. Scott, still in school at the time, eventually started his own gunmaking business in Princip Street.

In October 1897, W. & C. Scott & Son merged with P. Webley & Son to form the Webley & Scott Revolver and Arms Co., Ltd. The trade magazine *Arms & Explosives* had this to say:

> The new concern will include the business of Messrs. P. Webley & Son, also two other businesses which it has absorbed, viz., that of Messrs. W. & C. Scott & Son, and Messrs. Richard Ellis & Sons, all of the same city. The managing director of the company will be Mr. T. W. Webley, and the secretary Mr. Murray. Mr. Henry Webley will not be actively connected with the management, as his state of health and other reasons suggest the advisability of his retiring.

The article continued:

The name of Webley is very well known in connection with the service and other models of revolvers made by them. In a lesser degree, it is known to the public of the rifles and shot guns which it has supplied in a wholesale way. Much the same methods as are adopted for the manufacture of pistols have been utilized in the work of [shot] gunmaking, machine processes carrying the manufacture up to a very advanced stage. The effects of a careful system of viewing, and the method of making as many parts as possible on the interchangeable system, have shown themselves in the excellent workmanship turned out.

The correspondent then turned his attention to Scott:

Messrs. W. & C. Scott have, in the same way, been noted for a very high class of work, in fact, many of the very best guns turned out within the last few decades have been built by them. The characteristic feature of their work has always been the perfect line of their weapons, which have given to them an unmistakable artistic finish. Like the firm of Webley, their guns are chiefly sold in this country in a wholesale way, and consequently they have not laid themselves out for making a reputation among sportsmen. This, however, they have done in America, where they have catered for the sportsman direct.

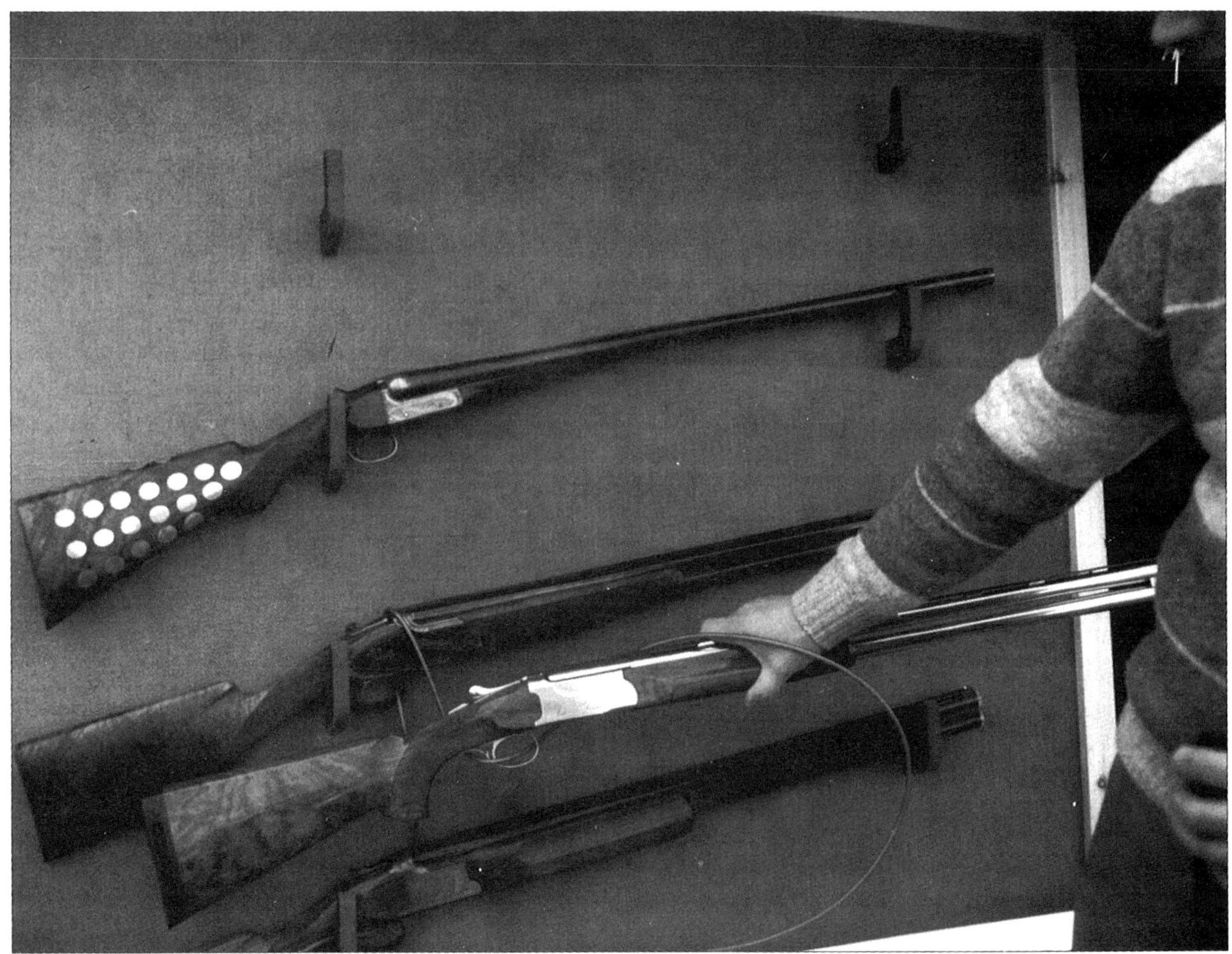

Legendary wingshot & shooting instructor Percy Stanbury inlaid the stock of his gun with inscribed silver ovals to record his successes at competitive shoots. Here some of the forty-five ovals are clearly visible. (Tony Jackson)

He also made this point: "It will be quite the largest gun manufacturing concern in Birmingham, excluding the Birmingham Small Arms Co., which goes in for quite a different class of trade."

Like shrewd politicians who maintain the status quo in the wake of a *coup d'état*, Webley & Scott's management continued to operate the two companies as independent businesses. The Premier Works remained at 123 Lancaster Street, and gun production was unchanged. After two years of this, Scott's London showrooms were closed and all of the company's guns were sold through the Webley showroom. Frank T. Murray became managing director when Thomas William Webley died in 1904, and the name of the company was shortened to Webley & Scott in 1906. Webley's old factory continued to produce revolvers, and the company took out numerous patents for improvements to handguns, including modifications to the Forsby automatic revolver in 1900 and a series of patents between 1903 and 1908 that culminated in the Webley automatic pistol. Meanwhile, the Lancaster Street factory continued to turn out an estimated 2,000 double guns each year from 1909 to 1913.

During World War I, Webley & Scott manufactured upwards of 310,000 revolvers and 290,000 automatic and flare pistols, while sporting-gun production was substantially reduced and stopped altogether between August 1917 and March 1919. Henry Webley came out of retirement to serve on the board of directors during the war and died shortly after the armistice was signed.

Early in 1920, the Birmingham gun trade held an exhibition to celebrate the end of the war and display its new wares to the wholesale trade. The event was covered by *The Sporting Goods Review,* which had this to say:

WEBLEY AND SCOTT, LTD.— A display full of points of special interest was made by Webley and Scott, Limited. At this time of day a new gun for home and export capable of being made in large quantities by economical methods of pro-

Percy Stanbury with his Championship Webley & Scott. (Tony Jackson)

duction, without sacrifice of efficiency or style, naturally claims the attention of trade buyers. This is furnished by the new Webley and Scott hammerless gun with treble bolt. Its parts are standardized and interchangeable, and have been designed to facilitate manufacture by means of machine tools. One special feature is the soundness of the head. Among other novelties which received approval were the lever spring and the safeties. The exhibit of the firm comprised sporting guns of all grades and types and samples of the highest art in engraving, both on specimen plates and on finished guns. . . . Parts of guns and rifles in various stages of manufacture were exhibited to demonstrate the perfection of the work done by the tamping machines, also tubes for barrels, in various stages of manufacture up to the filed barrel. The collection of parts included drop forgings for body, fore ends, and many small limbs. Some of the smaller limbs are machined out of the bar.

The Sporting Goods Review was a trade magazine, and what was revealed here was never intended to be read by the sportsman. Webley & Scott was capable of building 2,500 guns a year for the wholesale market because its gun parts were "standardized and interchangeable" and were "designed to facilitate manufacture by means of machine tools." They were no longer exclusively using the craft methods of W. & C. Scott, but were instead employing the methods for making of revolvers, as noted by the correspondent for *Arms & Explosives* at the time of the merger: "Much the same methods as are adopted for the manufacture of pistols have been utilised in the work of [shot] gunmaking, machine processes carrying the manufacture up to a very advanced stage."

In the immediate post-World War I period, Webley & Scott catalogs featured models identical to the ones from just before World War I, even going so far as to reuse old illustrations. One significant difference is in the description of the "latest 1922 Model Webley 'Proprietary' Hammerless Ejector Gun," which is described, for the first time, as being "made on the interchangeable principle, every part being viewed before assembling, in the same manner as our Revolvers and Automatic Pistols."

Higher-quality guns featured in the same catalog included the popular "A & W" and the "W & R" models. The first was a boxlock sold in five grades: 1, 2, 54, 52, and 51. The A & W stood for Anson and Webley, Anson for the Anson and Deeley action and Webley for the Webley and Brain top fastener. "Carved leaf fences" were offered as an extra, and the catalog shows these to be ribbons chased in a trefoil motif. Most William Evans, Harrod's, and Army & Navy boxlocks encountered today are A & W models. This is particularly true of those built as pairs.

The second quality piece was a sidelock called the "W & R" after Webley and Rogers. The W stood for the Webley and Brain patent while the R stood for Rogers. John Thomas Rogers and John Rogers were action filers with a workshop at 78 Lower Tower Street at the northern limit of Birmingham's gun quarter. In 1881, they patented (Number 397) a cocking system for double guns whereby a pair of levers in the action bar cock the tumblers when acted upon by the fore-end as the gun opens.

The W & R was offered in five grades: 1st, 2nd, 4th, 7th and 10th. The postwar catalog showed a 4th grade, which was a flat-back-actioned gun, open with the Webley and Brain doll's head visible, while the prewar catalog featured a 1st grade—a high-quality gun with fine Purdey spectacle-style bouquet and scroll engraving and ribanded fences. Contemporary William Evans and Army & Navy catalogs, not surprisingly, featured an identical gun.

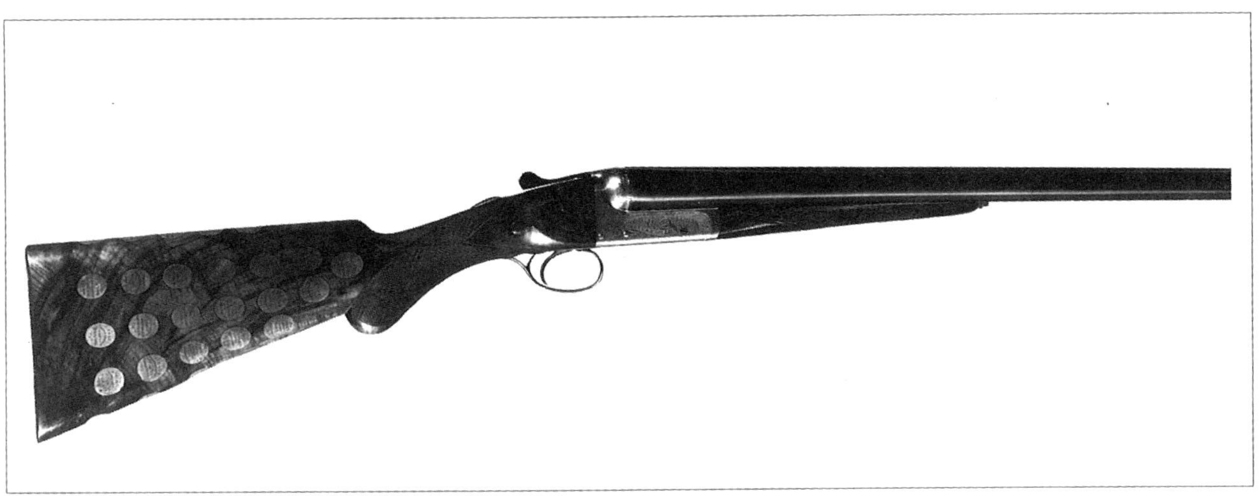

The Percy Stanbury Championship single-trigger live-pigeon gun is a 12-bore Model 500 Webley & Scott. (Christie's)

Another significant difference between the prewar and postwar catalogs was in the variety of live-pigeon guns offered. Pigeon guns were still available in 1922, but at a much reduced level. Whereas five models were so designated in 1914, only one was listed in 1922. W. & C. Scott had long enjoyed a reputation for competition guns of all types and even had a model named "The Monte Carlo" after the world's most prestigious live-pigeon venue. But in the aftermath of World War I, competitive live-bird shooting had lost some of its luster. One story, perhaps apocryphal, tells of Princess Alexandra visiting a shoot before the war and being misfortunate enough to have a wounded, flapping pigeon land in her lap. When the bloody bird was removed and the Princess of Wales regained her composure, she expressed her negative opinion of the sport. It is difficult to imagine today, but in an age before film stars and sports celebrities, the royal family were the ultimate arbiters of style and taste. What they did and did not do was emulated by a fawning public. After the wounded-pigeon incident, competitive pigeon shooting became less fashionable and the famous Hurlingham club banned it altogether. It became illegal in England with the passing of the Captive Birds Act of 1922, but continued in Monte Carlo

until another princess, Grace, petitioned for its cessation on the grounds of cruelty.

Clay-pigeon shooting, on the other hand, was becoming more popular. Sometime in the 1920s, Percy Stanbury bought a Model 500 boxlock ejector pigeon gun, Serial Number 95188, by Webley & Scott, and had it converted to a single trigger. With it, he won almost fifty major clay tournaments between 1926 and 1953, including eighteen British titles.

In 1922, Douglas Vaughan Johnstone replaced F. T. Murray as the firm's managing director. Under his direction, Webley & Scott made more than 1,000 double guns every year until 1925. However, for Webley & Scott, the '20s didn't roar; a shrinking demand for rifles and shotguns forced the company to explore the market for pneumatic guns. Between 1923 and 1929, D. V. Johnstone, F. Clarke, and John William Fearn took out a series of patents that would culminate in the classic Webley air pistol. Although the gun, so familiar to every English schoolboy, has undergone sporadic facelifts and name changes, it is a measure of the soundness of its design that it continued to be built as recently as the 1970s.

With the Wall Street crash, the company's plight worsened. Webley & Scott closed its

London showroom in 1929 and made only about 100 guns in 1932. The problems of the Great Depression ended with Hitler's invasion of Poland in September 1939. During the war, Webley & Scott once again made service revolvers and filled other essential War Department needs. It built no shotguns at all between July 1940 and December 1945.

In the austere period after the war, Webley & Scott introduced two new models, the Standard and the Special, which were made for only a couple of years. By 1947, the raw material for making quality guns was once more becoming available, and Webley & Scott introduced its 700 Model. It was promoted as reliable and affordable: "This model can be confidently recommended to sportsmen requiring a hard hitting gun of sound construction at a moderate price." And it became a great success; more than 25,000 were made between 1947 and 1979.

The company prospered throughout the 1950s, selling approximately 1,000 guns every year. Many of these were sold within the British gun trade and were eventually retailed with other makers' names on them. Geoff R. Worrall, gun sales manager at Webley & Scott for a couple of years in the late '50s, recalled that at the time the company made the Holland & Holland "shot & regulated," the Churchill "Crown" grade, the Westley Richards "Gold Name," the Cogswell and Harrison "Konor," and the Thomas Bland Model "B." Webley & Scott charged the ultimate seller a premium of 25 percent for "loss of advertising."

In 1958, Webley & Scott was acquired by the Windsor Group of Companies, which issued a catalog featuring only four break-open shotguns, all boxlocks. Three of these were variants on the Model 700—the basic 700, a slightly better gun called the Model 702, and the top-of-the-line 701. All were available in 12-, 16-, or 20-bore, and the two higher grades could be had with barrels of any length between 25 and 30 inches.

The other gun, also a boxlock, was the Model 100, a "Single Barrel Semi Hammerless Ejector." The Model 100 had first appeared in Webley & Scott catalogs in 1914. In its earliest incarnation, it was based on the design of William Baker (Patent 6,223 of 1910), but the postwar Model 100, although externally similar to the Baker gun, was the work of D. V. Johnstone and John William Fearn. Based on a series of patents taken out by Johnstone and Fearn between 1922 and 1924, the gun was cheap and machine-made, and it found favor with a new generation of rough shooters born after World War II.

In 1959, Arusha Industries took over Webley & Scott and six years later absorbed W. W. Greener. In 1973 the company was sold again, this time to the Harris & Sheldon Group of Companies, which terminated shotgun production in 1979. The following year a splinter group broke away and began trading under the old name of W. & C. Scott. Twenty-six craftsmen were installed in a small workshop on Tame Road in Witton, nostalgically named "Premier Works." In a sense the reborn company had come full circle: Tame Road was not in the traditional gun quarter but in suburban Birmingham, just north of Aston Park. It was the opening of Aston Park by Queen Victoria 122 years earlier that had introduced William and Charles Scott to the gun trade.

Catalogs from this period feature a best London-pattern sidelock and three grades of boxlock. All are named after "famous sporting estates." The sidelock was "Blenheim," the palace built by John Churchill, the first Duke of Marlborough, to celebrate his victory over the French in 1704 during the War of the Spanish Succession. The boxlocks are named the "Chatsworth," the "Bowood," and the "Kinmount" after the estates owned by, respectively, The Duke of Devonshire, The

Earl of Shelburne, and E. H. Birbeck. Photographs of the guns are accompanied by line drawings of the great houses.

In 1985, W. & C. Scott was acquired by Holland & Holland, which refined the Scott boxlock action by introducing a detachable hinge pin and reshaping the action body. The improved action became the basis of the Holland & Holland "Cavalier," a high-quality shotgun with chopperlump barrels that first appeared in 1987. A less-expensive boxlock named the "Northwood" after the Holland & Holland shooting grounds was also built at the Premier Works.

Holland & Holland was itself acquired by the luxury goods company Chanel in 1989, and two years later, W. & C. Scott ceased operations. "The decision to close Scott was based largely on worldwide economic conditions, which have resulted in decreased demand for fine double guns." This is how John A. Crawford described the end in the addendum to his and Pat G. Whatley's book on W. & C. Scott. After 157 years and more than 150,000 guns, many of which were made for the trade, no new Webley & Scott pieces would be available. Perhaps because so many were made, or perhaps because machines assisted in their manufacture, Webley & Scott guns continue to be undervalued.

WESTLEY RICHARDS

Birmingham was once known as the "workshop of the world" and "the city of a thousand trades." Silverware, jewelry, and guns were all made here, and the jewelry and gunmaking quarters to this day lie adjacent to one another. The gun quarter's famed elasticity is due in part to workers from other metal trades switching to gunmaking in times of boom, then returning to

Inside the gun room at Westley Richards. (Martin Westley)

their native craft when things became quiet. This was true of jewelry engravers, who could be called upon to engrave guns, often with the result that guns were decorated with motifs, like bouquets of roses, that had previously been seen only on the backs of lockets and pocket watches. Old street directories list gunmakers who also worked in silver; one of these was Thomas Richards, who was at 53 High Street from 1747-1784.

When Thomas Richards died in 1779, Theophilus Richards took over the business and was listed as a "gun and pistol maker." He was also a silver gun/furniture maker [a trigger guard is an example of gun furniture], cutler, and jeweler who passed his skills to his sons, Theophilus II and William Westley. The elder Theophilus died in 1828 and his second son, Theophilus II, just five years later, ending the firm of Theophilus Richards, though there was an elder brother named Bingham who could have continued the firm had he not gone into law and moved to London. This would have been the end of the Richards dynasty were it not for William Westley Richards, youngest of the three sons, who in 1812 founded his own company at 82 High Street, Birmingham.

William Westley Richards once explained to one of his brothers that he intended "to be the maker of as good a gun as can be made." To what extent he succeeded can be gauged by Colonel Peter Hawker's comment that Richards was fast becoming known as:

> Joe Manton the second . . . and deservedly so from what I have seen of him and his work. Mr. Richards is really a scientific man, instead of having more tongue than brains like many of our Charlatans. His barrels are as good as any in the world, being made of pure Holland stubbs, and twisted in a manner best suited for service and safety. Within these last few years Mr. Richards has run some of the best London Gunmakers so hard that they

began to wish him and his prime minister Bishop in—'another and better world!'

The man Colonel Hawker called "prime minister Bishop" was William Bishop, William Westley Richards's appointed London agent. In 1815 Richards opened a retail establishment at 170 New Bond Street, as prestigious an address in Regency London then as it is now. The shop was divided in two, one half offering jewelry, the other guns. Presiding over both halves was a "large roomy man . . . a right reverend and episcopal figure" who, on account of his always being dressed in black, was known as the Bishop of Bond Street.

The Birmingham businessman and his West End representative were very different people. William Westley Richards was by birth and education a member of the merchant class, someone who rode to hounds and a man who had taken the grand tour. William Bishop was "a rough cut gem from Ealing." Westley Richards was respectable, a warden of the Birmingham Assay Office, who acknowledged his position in society by distributing charity to the poor. Bishop was a gambler who organized cock fights and bare-knuckled boxing matches. Richards was a devout Christian who was churchwarden at St. Philip's, the predecessor of Birmingham Cathedral. The closest the Bishop of Bond Street came to committing a Christian act was the time his railway carriage was raided by the Bow Street runners on the way to one of his prize fights. Hiding the pugilists beneath the seats seconds before the police arrived, he affected a demeanor appropriate to his nickname and appearance and exclaimed, "Prizefighters?" turning up the whites of his eyes and lifting his hands in pious horror. "Good gracious, what do you mean? We are going to the consecration of a new church."

Though William Westley Richards was much different than his London associate, the two men dovetailed together to form a relationship that was greater than the sum of its parts. Some idea of just how well they worked can be gleaned from G. T. Teasdale-Buckell's tome, *Experts on Guns and Shooting,* published in 1900:

It is unquestionable that Westley Richards' guns owe much of their success to the personal skills and management of Westley Richards' famous lieutenant, Wm. Bishop; under his regime the house in Bond Street became quite an Institution.

Teasdale-Buckell gave Westley Richards guns a similar review:

The old guns of this make had always much to recommend them. Although essentially Birmingham built, they were totally distinct from the class of Birmingham guns. Why this should have been the case we are unable to explain. Colonel Peter Hawker himself, when passing his strictures on Birmingham guns as being in general coarse and ill-designed, entered the saving clause that he made an exception in the case of the work turned out by Westley Richards. A Westley Richards gun of forty years ago [1849] was invariably a thorough sportsman's tool, and had all the appearance of being what it was. There was nothing to distinguish it from the best London gun as made by one or two firms at that day. It was neat and elegant in outline, and balanced and handled to perfection. The parts fitted closely and accurately, and the general tout ensemble exhibited correct taste.

Westley Richards made his guns in Birmingham, and William Bishop sold them in London, where they competed with the best bespoke makers. The guns were off-the-shelf and in no way tailor-made to a customer's requirements. Sir Ralph Payne-Gallwey referred to this type of gun as a horrible monster, ". . . a ready-made, reach-me-down Birmingham gun, is fit for neither man, nor bird, nor beast, and is a mere unwieldy log of iron and wood when compared to the perfect article produced in London." However, Teasdale-Buckell saw things differently:

. . . and here comes in the speciality of Westley Richards, that whereas for a gun by any other first-rate

A Westley Richards trade label with the 178 New Bond Street address. (Douglas Tate)

maker it would be necessary to wait several months for the completion of the order, here a sportsman may be suited immediately, and in most cases as well as if he had waited four or five months, and even then, perhaps, might not like the gun when he sees it.

One reason a young sport might buy a Westley Richards over a bespoke London best was that Richards and the firm he founded were always at the technological forefront, while the capital's gunmakers were intrinsically a conservative lot. While most of his competitors were still building flintlocks, William Westley Richards freely adapted the percussion system patented by the Reverend Alexander Forsyth in 1807 to his own series of designs that featured pills, patches, and tubes. Of the three, the tubelock was probably the most successful. It was based on the idea of a tube filled with compound that exploded when struck a heavy blow. It sat in a specially adapted nipple, which could also accommodate a conventional percussion cap. The claim made for the design (Patent 6,071 of 1831) was that it could be used in "hard driving rain" and could, with the addition of a little beeswax, "be fired under water." Not surprisingly, the invention was popular with wildfowlers, and one of these, the indefatigable Colonel Peter Hawker, who had criticized earlier efforts at a "detonating system," had this to say:

> Of all the inventions that have been brought out since the flourishing days of Joseph [Manton], this, in my humble opinion, is the best, I have tried it repeatedly and never yet knew it to fail; and my son shot with it for a whole season, and never once had a miss fire. The next season he accompanied me to the coast, where we had heavy seas and much wet weather; and while my copper caps were missing about two shots out of ten his primer never failed once.

Although the system appears to have been superior to early percussion-cap guns, the primer tubes were expensive and Westley Richards never made them available on the scale of the common copper cap. The result was that a better, if slightly more expensive, mousetrap was ignored while the world beat a path to another door. Undeterred, William Westley Richards continued to patent a series of improvements to firearms that included the first flip-up tangent sight to be used in the British Army (1834) and a revolver (1855) that utilized an ordinary shotgun sidelock with the mainspring extending down inside the grip. By the time he died in 1865, Richards had nine gun-related patents to his name.

When William Westley Richards retired in 1840, he was succeeded by his son Westley, born 8 August 1814. Where the old man was charitable and well liked by his workforce, the son was feared and regarded as "harsh" and "hard." To some degree both men embodied the spirit of their times: William's attitude toward his men was a sort of Georgian *noblesse oblige*, illustrated by the story of a certain workman who, through no fault of his own, was down on his luck. He owned some modest property but had borrowed on it until he was deeply in debt and would have to forfeit. He asked the old man's advice. To his surprise, William Westley Richards, a day or two later, made him a present of his mortgage.

Westley Richards, on the other hand, was a product of the Victorian age, an inflexible martinet who adhered to Old Testament values. He could easily have been the inspiration for some of Dickens's more draconian despots in novels like *Hard Times* and *Bleak House*. Once again, a story involving an employee offers insight into the way Westley differed from his father: Apparently, a workman had refused to obey some command, lost his temper, and become abusive. Westley Richards fired him immediately. Several weeks passed, and a small contingent of employees petitioned Westley Richards for the man's reinstatement, explaining that he had found no other work and that his family was suffering. Richards was unyielding. "He is starving, Sir," they finally explained. "Then let him go to the workhouse" were the boss's final words.

Westley Richards lost his wife in a riding accident when she was only twenty-four, and he never remarried. Perhaps the loss hardened an already steely heart, but if that is the

to the Chassepot needle-fire rifle (Number 3,195 of 1872), and a whole series of patents beginning in 1868 and culminating in 1871 in a falling-block rifle patronized by the Prince of Wales. Others were for features familiar to anyone who has ever owned a Westley Richards breechloading hammer gun: the doll's-head extension and crab joint (Patent 2,506 of 1862) and the triangular top lever (Patent 2,623 of 1864), which were built into a 16-bore shotgun Queen Victoria gave her son Prince Arthur, Duke of Connaught, during Christmas 1870. Yet other patents covered

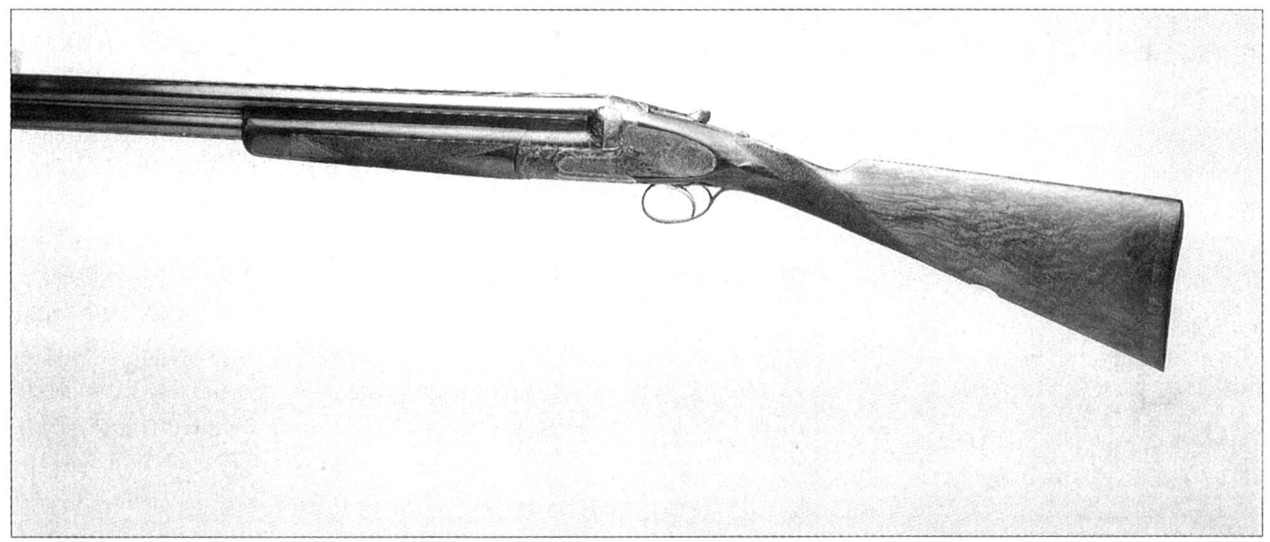

A Westley Richards "Ovundo." (Sotheby's)

case, he never showed any malice to horses, seeming to prefer them over some people—those people he considered his social inferiors. Despite a rigid disposition, Westley Richards was even more inventive than his father, filing over twenty firearms-related patents during his life. Writing in 1913, Leslie B. Taylor acknowledged his qualities: "We should say that the son was the father multiplied to many powers."

Many of the patents were for rifles: a capping breechloader (Number 2,718 of 1855) with J. R. Cooper, the famous monkey-tailed carbine (Number 688 of 1866), improvements

obscure and unrelated devices like the one (Patent 3,478 of 1862) for rifle sights, an adapter for converting a breechloader to a muzzleloader, and a gun rest with a tripod base. Multiple ideas on one specification, like this one, inspired Leslie B. Taylor to write:

> Even twenty two new and original conceptions expressed in mechanical construction is a goodly number to have emanated from one brain, but it should be remembered that, at the period of time they covered, the law allowed as many new ideas and principles of construction as the inventor could manage to include in one

specification; so that one patent grant might include four or five different inventions so broadly separated that they never would have been coupled or set together in any man's mind but for the purpose of gaining legal protection at the most economical outlay. Consequently the actual number of separate and distinct inventions represented by the specifications of letters patent granted to Westley Richards is more than doubled, if computed from the description and claims set forth in each document.

Other developments for which Westley Richards should be given credit are the drawn-brass cartridge case, his work with Lord Hardinge on the development of the Enfield rifle, and his efforts with the hexagonal-bore rifle. His work on six-sided rifle bores is notable because of the collaboration of two of the Victorian age's great engineers, Sir Joseph Whitworth and Isambard Kingdom Brunel. After Richards's death, a correspondent for *The Birmingham Magazine* said:

> Every military rifle adopted by the Government since 1852 has been improved at the hands of Westley Richards and Co. To Westley Richards the Government were indebted for the solid drawn metallic rifle cartridge, adapted for the small Gatling gun, and also for the production of the Enfield rifle. Mr. Richards was also associated with Sir John [sic] Whitworth in the production of the Whitworth rifling.

Westley Richards retired from business in 1872 and died at eighty-three on 27 May 1897. At the time of his retirement, he entrusted John Deeley with the practical management of the firm. Deeley, half of the

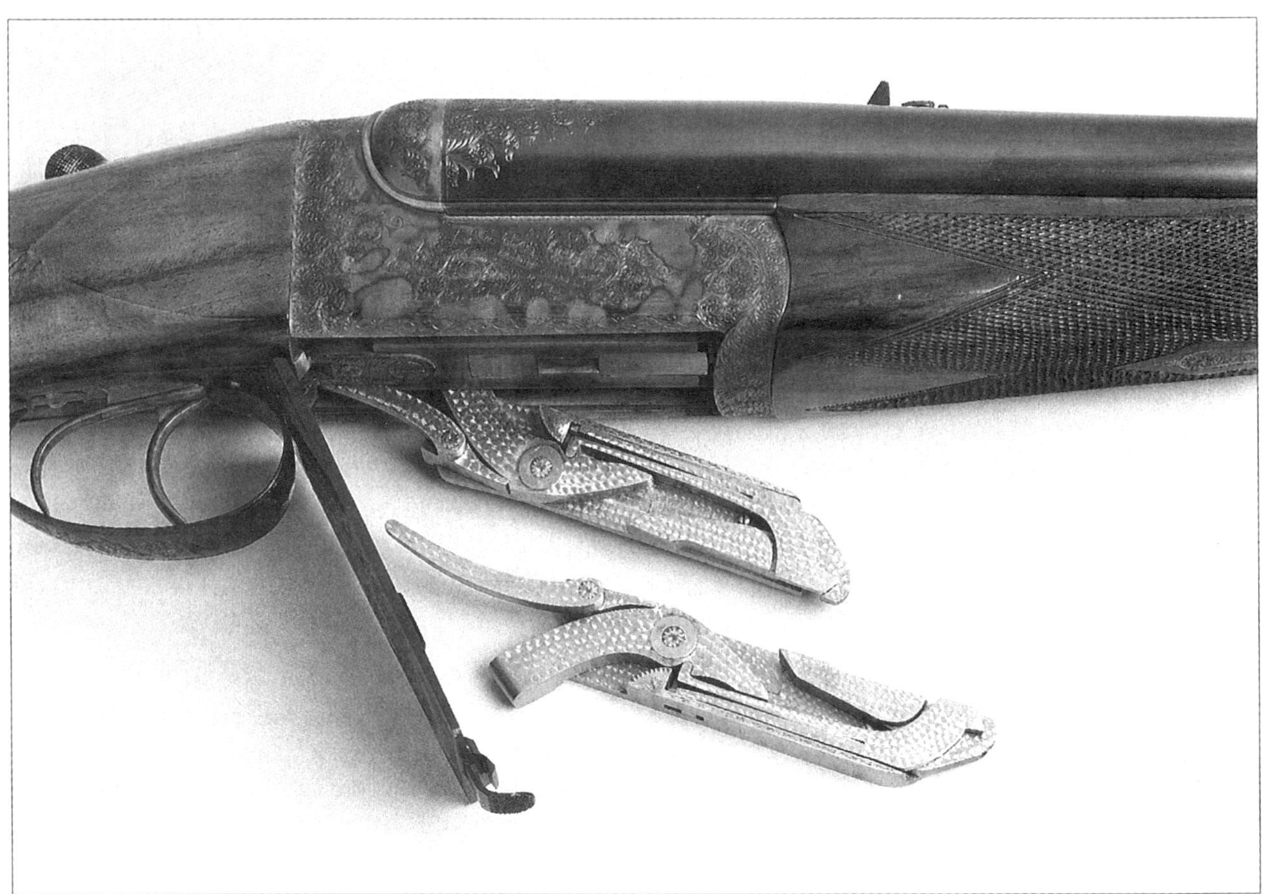

The famous hand-detachable droplocks patented by John Deeley and Leslie Taylor in 1897. (Westley Richards)

team instrumental in developing the quint-essential Birmingham gun, was born in 1825, the son of a steel toy polisher. Back at the beginning of the Victorian era, toys were not the children's models and dolls of to-day but rather buckles, the purse mounts, the chatelaines, the brooches, the bracelets, and the endless varieties of steel watch chains, sword hilts and other small wares of iron, or iron and steel. John Deeley may have apprenticed as a toymaker with his father—we know he started work at the age of nine. Like many metalworkers in Birmingham, he probably gravitated to the gun trade during one of its periodic booms.

In Birmingham, he also worked as a silk mercer's clerk, a shopman, and as an accountant. It was as an accountant that Deeley initially proved his worth to Westley Richards, balancing the books, which had not been looked at for the previous three years. Although Deeley came from humble origins, he was ambitious and naturally curious. He was self-educated, had learned French, and had used his time with Westley Richards to study gunmaking. As Leslie B. Taylor said of the man and his ambitions:

> Every detail in each branch and process of construction was studiously investigated and mastered, and soon he came to know the place and need of each technical item in a gun's economy, as he knew the debit and credit values in accounts. In due time he became a gun expert.

Once Deeley had mastered gunmaking, he worked with James Simeon Edge, who was foreman of Westley Richards's sporting and military rifle department. The two men were

Inside the workshop at Westley Richards. (Martin Westley)

granted joint patents on several gun-related designs. The most famous of these are the fore-end fastener (Patent 1,422 of 1873) and, on the same specification, a sliding-block rifle. The Deeley-Edge rifle has the striker and tumbler built as a single unit, which is cocked by a lever that forms the trigger guard. It was a compact design and may have had its origins in a variant of Westley Richards's falling-block rifle (Patent 2,427 of 1869), which employed a similar firing mechanism. The design appears to have been the inspiration for Birmingham's most famous gun action and the world's most famous sporting shotgun design.

At least H. John Blanch thought so. In his 1909 book, *A Century of Guns,* he said:

> The Westley Richards falling block rifle, 1868 [sic], had the tumbler which also formed the striker, pivotted directly under the breech end of the barrel, and in front and above the tumbler under the barrel was placed the mainspring. This arrangement

adapted to a double gun, with the novel feature of connecting the tumblers, by means of the forward extension of them, underneath the mainsprings, with levers operated by the forepart, re-cocking the locks, was patented by Anson and Deeley and introduced by Westley Richards in 1875.

The action was patented on 11 May 1875 (Number 1,756) and credited to William Anson, foreman of Westley Richards's shotgun action department, and John Deeley, who was by then managing director and major shareholder of the company. In *A Brief History of the Westley Richards Firm 1812-1913,* Leslie B. Taylor, himself a managing director, wrote that "Mr. John Deeley conceived the principle of the gun" while "Anson worked out the design."

It was an enormous success. True, there were rival hammerless guns, but most were simply hammer guns with the hammers tucked inside the action: "spaniels without ears," as one wag defined them. The A & D

Guns and rifles by Westley Richards. (Westley Richards)

was recognized as a great improvement over its predecessors, and many makers sought to build it for a fee while others attempted to adapt the design to the point where they could claim it as their own and thus avoid paying the licensing costs.

Besides being the world's first enormously successful hammerless design, the Anson & Deeley was also one of the earliest designs in which the fall of the barrels cocked the locks. There had been hammerless guns before, and there had been guns in which the fall of the barrels cocked the locks, but few designs incorporated both improvements and none was this simple. And simplicity is the key to the gun's success. Where previous hammerless designs were merely hammer guns with the hammers reduced in size and incorporated into the body of the action, the Anson & Deeley was a revolution in design. It incorporated tumbler, hammer, and striker into a single limb, which was cocked as the barrels fell by a pivoting lever. Together with mainspring and sear, the combined tumbler/hammer/striker and cocking limb made for only four components to the lockwork, as opposed to almost four times that many in a hammer gun. Writing in 1900, G. T. Teasdale-Buckell in his book *Experts on Guns and Shooting* made the point that:

> Nobody before 1875 . . . had succeeded in making an action with so few parts . . . and the limbs are, consequently, enabled to be made much broader and stronger . . . the tumbler possesses great strength and solidity, the bent being nearly twice the breadth of that in the ordinary tumblers.

Strong, simple, and efficient, the Anson & Deeley became the quintessential Birmingham gun action. Later, when coupled with a Scott spindle and toplever and the Purdey underbolt, it would become the world standard. Hundreds of thousands were sold, and the system's strength and simplicity made it a favorite in far-flung corners of the globe.

This .577-500 Number 2 black-powder double express rifle exhibits many signature features of Westley Richards hammer guns such as the doll's-head extension, crab joint, and triangular top lever. (Christie's)

Many were taken to Africa, many more were sold in India.

In 1897, John Deeley, together with Leslie B. Taylor, patented (Number 17,791 of 1897) a variation on the A & D system in which the lockwork was built onto plates that could be removed through the bottom of the action. Westley Richards' "droplock" has enjoyed a cult following ever since. Its benefits were praised by Major Sir Gerald Burrard in his three volumes on *The Modern Shotgun*. He noted the design's simplicity, "a sure token of the efficiency of the invention" and added:

> The workmanship of these locks is really beautiful and this action cannot help but appeal to those who like to be able to inspect and clean their locks regularly; while the system also admits to having

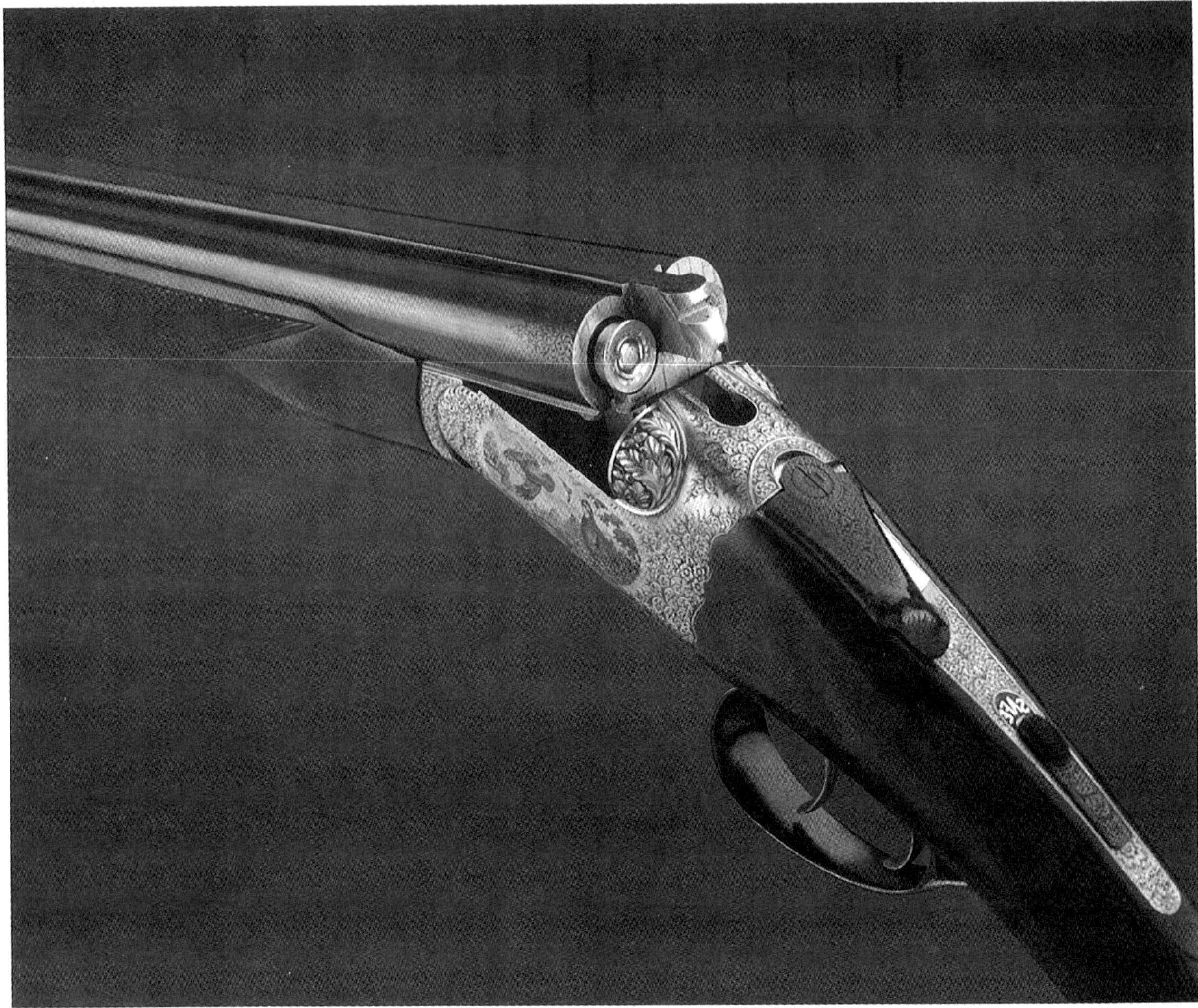

A new .410 Westley Richards engraved with oak-leaf fences and bobwhite quail. (David Grant)

duplicate locks, a decidedly useful safe-guard in out of the way countries.

High praise indeed for one who con-sidered hand-detachable sidelocks "unnecessary." Burrard also thought that the Anson & Deeley action lacked the beauty of the bar-action sidelock. In the area of aesthetics, he had many allies. Writing half a century before Burrard, Teasdale-Buckell noted:

We found the present Westley Richards gun to retain many features in common with its predecessors, although, being made on the Anson & Deeley principle, it is not quite so elegant in its outline. They used to be peculiarly 'snakelike,' rakish, and elegant. The gun is now more 'cobby.' This stumpiness of appearance is due to a width and thickness in the neighbourhood of the lock. If this part could be lightened some-what, and lessened in circumference, with-out curtailing necessary lock space, it would add much to the elegance of the gun.

Not until the present day and the intro-duction of the round-bodied boxlock by William Powell and Tony R. White was the British Anson & Deeley improved aestheti-cally. However, one last improvement was made before the design calcified mechani-cally. The slide safety on Anson & Deeley guns bolts the triggers so that if the sear and bent are jarred out of engagement, the gun will discharge. Better-quality Westley Richards boxlocks have intercepting safeties patented (Number 4,089 of 1882) by William Anson that are recognizable by a small screw visible in the angle between the top strap and the rear of the standing breech. Even if the sear is jarred out of the bent, the fall of the tumblers will be blocked and the gun will not discharge.

John Deeley had the original Anson & Deeley gun specially engraved "The First Anson & Deeley Hammerless Gun, Patented 11th May 1875" and used it as a display piece at shows and expositions. He bequeathed it to Mr. Haines, sanother Westley Richards director, and it held pride of place on the gunmaker's stand at exhibitions as recently as the 1920s. However, after the first quarter-century of displaying the Anson & Deeley gun, the firm was looking for another extraordinary example of gunmaking to show off its skills to best advantage. Ironically, for a company that prided itself on its design team, this gun would be the work of a gunmaker from beyond the firm and would be a novelty with three barrels!

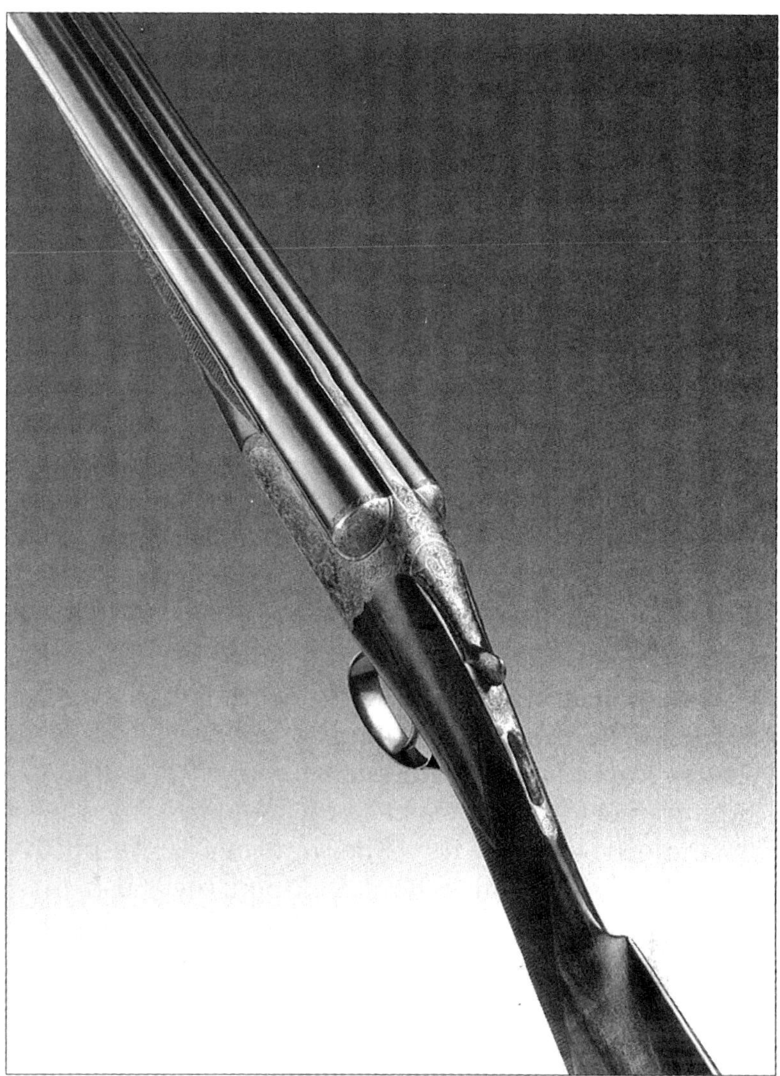

A fine quality Anson & Deeley gun with doll's-head extension and triangular top lever. (David Grant)

Late in the last century, during the golden age of the shooting party and before our prejudice for the standard game gun had quite congealed, gunmakers experimented with several ideas for getting more shot into the air. Prime among them was Henry Alfred Alexander Thorn. Thorn, who had a penchant for repeaters and multi-barreled guns, imported a number of Spencer-Roper pump-action shotguns from the United States and fitted them with tubular magazines and barrels of finest Damascus. Thorn had acquired the name and goodwill of the Charles Lancaster firm, which had enjoyed a reputation as Joseph Manton's barrelmaker, and he no doubt intended to capitalize on this reputation when he offered these multi-shot repeaters under the Lancaster name.

No contemporary account of driven-game shooting with pumps has come down to us, suggesting that they never found wide acceptance. However, Thorn was undeterred.

Concurrent to his efforts with repeaters, he experimented with a series of four-barreled guns, patenting four variations throughout the 1880s. These found no more favor than the infamous Spencer-Roper pumps.

In Edinburgh, John Dickson and A.G. Murray patented a three-barreled gun in 1882, but their intention seems to have been to show the adaptability of the round-action design, rather than to build a true multi-shot weapon. Dickson's records show that the gun was built for Murray, who was then managing director of the firm, perhaps suggesting that its *raison d'être* was as a show-piece of the company's skills.

Other three-barreled guns followed: the Boss of 1898, a design by Allen E. Lard in the same year, and the Edwinson C. Green of 1902. All of these appear to have been vehicles to publicize the respective maker's single triggers. There was a great demand for single triggers at the time, and every gunmaker knew that if he developed the single trigger that became the trade standard, he could license the result to his competitors and make his fortune. The difficulty was that most single triggers did not work very well and often discharged both barrels of a double gun at once. The triple-barrel, single-trigger concept was an attempt to win over a skeptical public with reasoning that if a single trigger can work effectively in a triple-barrel gun, then it should have no problems with the lesser complexities of a double-barreled gun.

Westley Richards, then one of Birmingham's preeminent gunmaker, must have watched all these developments closely. In 1895, the company had introduced its own single trigger (Patent 21,346), which was the work of F. J. Penn and J. D. Deeley. This was the same John Deeley who was famous as half the team that had developed the Anson & Deeley action, but the single trigger he designed with Penn was apparently not a

success. We know this because Leslie B. Taylor, who succeeded John Deeley as managing director of Westley Richards in 1899, patented (Number 11,062) another single trigger in 1901. Although Taylor was a prolific inventor, this new trigger was not his own work but rather the brainchild of an American named Allen E. Lard, who had patented a triple-barreled gun three years before in 1898. It seems reasonable to assume that if the Penn/Deeley single trigger had been successful, there would be no reason for Westley Richards' managing director to patent a design by an American.

Leslie B. Taylor was a renaissance figure who was to Westley Richards what H. A. A. Thorn was to Charles Lancaster & Co. Like Thorn, he held numerous patents in his own right and was a tireless, and some might say shameless, self-promoter. Both men wrote books waxing lyrical about their respective firms, but unlike Thorn, Taylor was also an urbane and articulate individual who spoke French and had a working knowledge of Greek and Latin.

In 1900, the only English entry to win a gold medal at the *fin de siècle* exhibition in Paris was a double-barreled gun fitted with hand-detachable lockwork. It was patented by Leslie B. Taylor and John Deeley (Number 17,731 of 1897) and fitted with a single trigger designed by the American Allen E. Lard and patented in England by Leslie B. Taylor (Number 11,062 of 1901). Huge exhibitions of art and industry were frequent events in the Victorian and Edwardian world and were not restricted to Europe. Westley Richards won similar awards at Philadelphia in 1876 and Calcutta in 1884, exhibitions for which it specially commissioned lavish show guns. Prestigious international fairs were a rich source of public relations for gunmakers, and the medals won at them frequently found their way onto the makers' trade label, where they provided additional advertising.

In 1911, an exhibition was held in Turin, and Westley Richards built a special gun to compete for the gold. Once again a single trigger was chosen, and once again it was of a new design, the difference being that the gun would have three barrels. The single-trigger, triple-barreled design was the work of Edwinson C. Green, an independent gunmaker who had worked in the Birmingham trade before moving to Cheltenham, a resort town in rural Gloucestershire, where he hoped to find a well-heeled clientele with the abundant leisure time to enjoy country sports. On 9 July 1902, Green patented (Number 15,307) his design in which the right and left tumblers are cocked in the normal way by cocking rods while the central tumbler is cocked by a pin protruding from the right-hand hammer. The single trigger is a sophisticated design and, like the well-known Boss, works on the involuntary pull system. By 1904, Green had built at least two versions, one a 16-bore and the other a 12. Both received a brief mention in *The Sporting Goods Review,* then the chief organ of the Birmingham gun trade, and this is perhaps where Leslie B. Taylor became aware of their existence.

The Westley Richards three-barrel built on the E. C. Green patent (Number 15,307 of 1902) was given serial number 17272 and finished on 30 April 1911. It was built with the third barrel above the two others and was consequently more elegant than the previously mentioned Boss, which was side-by-side-by-side—a configuration that gave it the strange appearance of a beautiful woman with three buttocks. The Westley Richards three-barrel design won a gold medal later that year in Turin. On 2 October 1911, Frederick Courteney Selous, Britain's

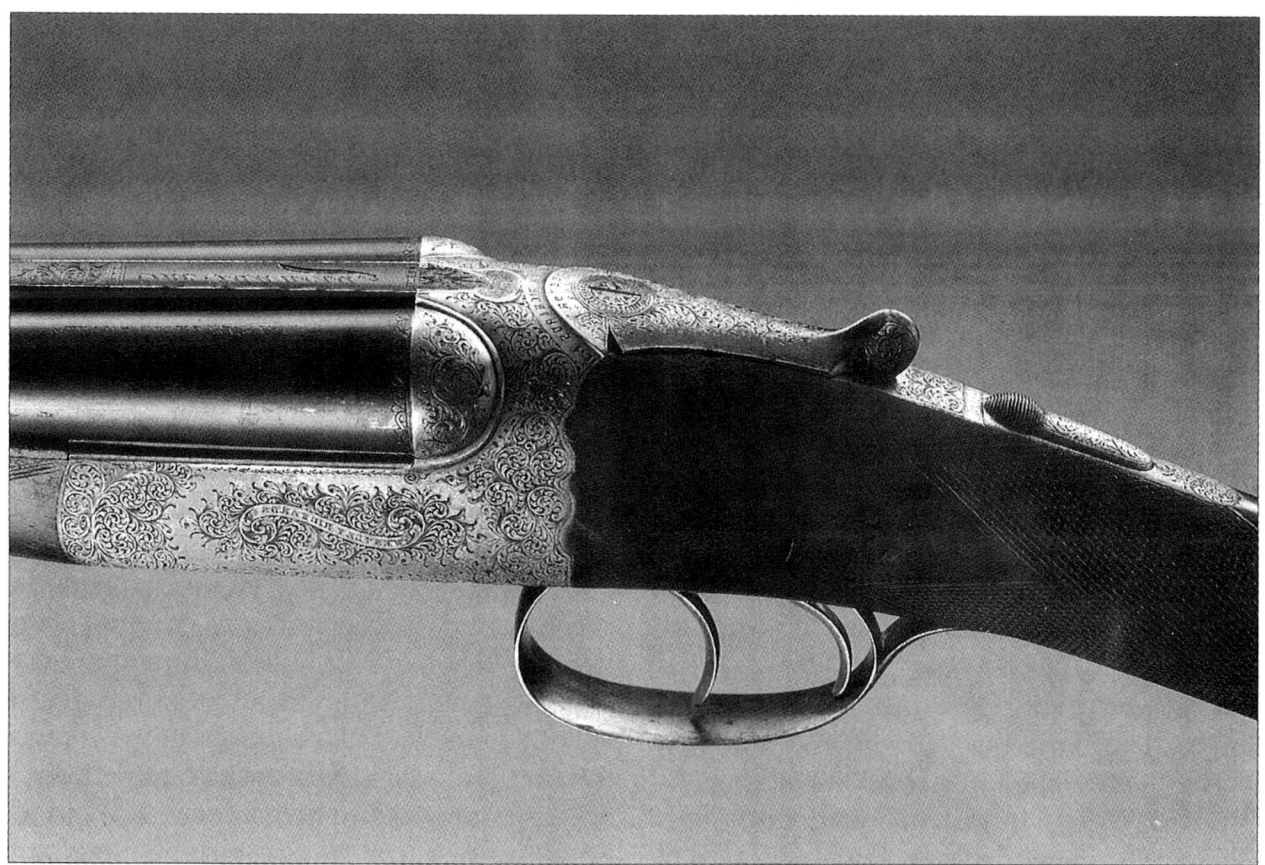

"The Fauneta" ball-and-shot gun. (Sotheby's)

best-known African hand and the model for Allan Quatermain in "King Solomon's Mines," wrote to Westley Richards after a visit to Turin: "Yours was far and away the best exhibit of Sporting Guns and Rifles (British and Foreign) in the whole exhibition." Later that same month Selous ordered a .425 Mauser-actioned Westley Richards rifle, Serial Number 20149.

Westley Richards also won two Grand Prix awards, one of which, appropriately enough, went to Leslie B. Taylor. Writing in *A Brief History of the Westley Richards Firm 1812-1913* published in 1913, Henry Sharp had this to say:

> In recognition of his many achievements Mr. Leslie B. Taylor was awarded a Diploma of Honour at the Industrial Exhibition of Turin, 1911; and of the many notices in the Press referring to the same, I give the following extract from *The Field* newspaper of 4th May, 1912: Mr. Leslie B. Taylor, the Managing Director of Messrs. Westley Richards & Co., whose activity as an inventor of rifle bullets, sights, etc., has frequently been brought to the notice of readers of this paper during the past ten or fifteen years. A man of virile and energetic personality, he has kept the firm in the fore during an epoch when invention was proceeding at a rapid rate, and improvements turned more than at any time in the past on the practical application of science and mathematics.

The continuity of talent at Westley Richards was perhaps the biggest reason for the company's success in its 100 years of existence. When the founder stepped down, he was succeeded by a son who was the "father multiplied by many powers." When the son retired, he was replaced by a man who designed the gun the Birmingham trade designated "our most saleable gun." In 1899, when John Deeley, at the age of seventy-four, handed over the practical management of his firm, he did so to Leslie B.

Taylor, a man who at that time had ten patents to his name and who would eventually accumulate thirty-one more.

Twelve of Taylor's forty-one patents were for rifle sights, many shared with a prodigious designer named E. H. Parson. One of particular importance was for a hinged floor plate (Patent 23,008 of 1908) by which Westley Richards "droplocks" are removed from the body of an Anson & Deeley action. Another, shared with a Mr. F. Hughes (Patent 11,681 of 1913) was for hinged lockplates. Leslie B. Taylor even patented his own single trigger (Patent 26,659 of 1909), and it was this design that became the classic Westley Richards single trigger. If you order a Westley Richards today and opt for a single trigger, this is the design you will get. The single trigger was perhaps Taylor's most successful design, after the hand-detachable lock he shared with John Deeley. However, what was needed at the beginning of the new century were not improvements to established designs but an entirely new gun. In 1914, Leslie B. Taylor lodged two patents that would eventually culminate in a twentieth century design. Like the three-barreled gun, it would be a novelty, but this was no "one off" show gun but an over-and-under that would create a new market for itself, particularly in America.

At the beginning of the twentieth century, Westley Richards, as well as most other British gunmakers, was offering guns that had undergone no dramatic design developments in twenty-five years. It was a quarter-century since Anson & Deeley had perfected its boxlock, and the problems of a gun that never became obsolete were becoming apparent— the sportsman never needed to replace it. What was needed was a design novel enough to stimulate sales. The answer came from a Scottish gunmaker who had once worked for Westley Richards before buying Boss and Company in London. In 1909 John Robertson patented an over-and-under gun he called his "superposed." He marketed it by claiming the narrow sighting plane turned "expert rifle shots into expert game shots in a remarkably short space of time." The gun was a success, particularly in America, a nation of riflemen and a market every British gunmaker longed to conquer.

All of London's gunmakers followed suit, building over-and-unders with a view to capturing their share of U.S. sales. Some designed their own guns while others bought designs— but all built sidelocks. In Birmingham, Leslie B. Taylor responded by registering two patents that would eventually be built into Britain's first boxlock over-and-under. The first of these (Number 8,853 of 1914) was for a system that bolted the gun closed. Hooks extended from the sides of the barrels and fitted into the face of the standing breech. Bolts controlled by the top lever locked down these extensions when the gun was closed. It was a neat arrangement that would have made for a shallow action were it not for a vestigial lump beneath the barrels that provided a hook for the hinge. Robertson had solved the problem by attaching barrels to action with a bifurcated joint pin that mated with slots machined into the sides of the lower barrel. The Boss was an expensive gun whereas the first "Under & Over," as Taylor called it, could be had for as little as thirty guineas.

One of the major problems with all over-and-under designs is that the strikers are at acute angles to the cartridge primers—which does not always result in positive ignition. In the same year Taylor patented his barrel-bolting system, he also patented strikers (Number 9,410 of 1914) that "Consist in providing under and over guns with pivoted firing pins or supplementary hammers adapted to be struck by the hammers proper." In the previous year, while presumably working out design problems, Westley Richards registered the trade name

"Ovundo" (Registration Number 354045 of 1913), and the gun was marketed as the:

> Westley Richards Patent 'OVUNDO' Gun, toplever action, embodying all the well- known Westley Richards features: new quadruple grip, top safety bolt, Westley Richards well-known ejector mechanism, hand detachable locks and hinged cover plate, and reliable one-trigger system.

This last sentence, which appeared in Westley Richards catalogs in the period immediately after World War I, is a remarkable piece of advertising copy and justifies closer scrutiny because each of the features mentioned was patented by an employee of Westley Richards:

> "top lever action" Patent 2,623 of 1864
> –Westley Richards
>
> "new quadruple grip" Patent 4,853 of 1914
> –Leslie B. Taylor
>
> "top safety bolt" Patent 12,324 of 1892
> –Deeley & F. J. Penn
>
> "well-known ejector" Patent 4,289 of 1886
> –John Deeley Jr.
>
> "detachable locks" Patent 17,791 of 1897
> –Taylor & Deeley
>
> "hinged cover plate" Patent 23,008 of 1908
> –Leslie B. Taylor
>
> "one trigger system" Patent 26,659 of 1909
> –Leslie B. Taylor

The Ovundo also had a hinged trap on the dummy side plates "which enables the One Trigger mechanism to be oiled with a feather," which was also a patent (Number 170,703) Taylor had taken out with D. J. P. Haines, another Westley Richards director. The idea was thought to be essential in hot climates like California, where it was hoped the gun would sell. Add to this the Anson & Deeley firing mechanism, and you can see that the Ovundo was an all Westley Richards gun with a total of nine in-works patents embodied in the design.

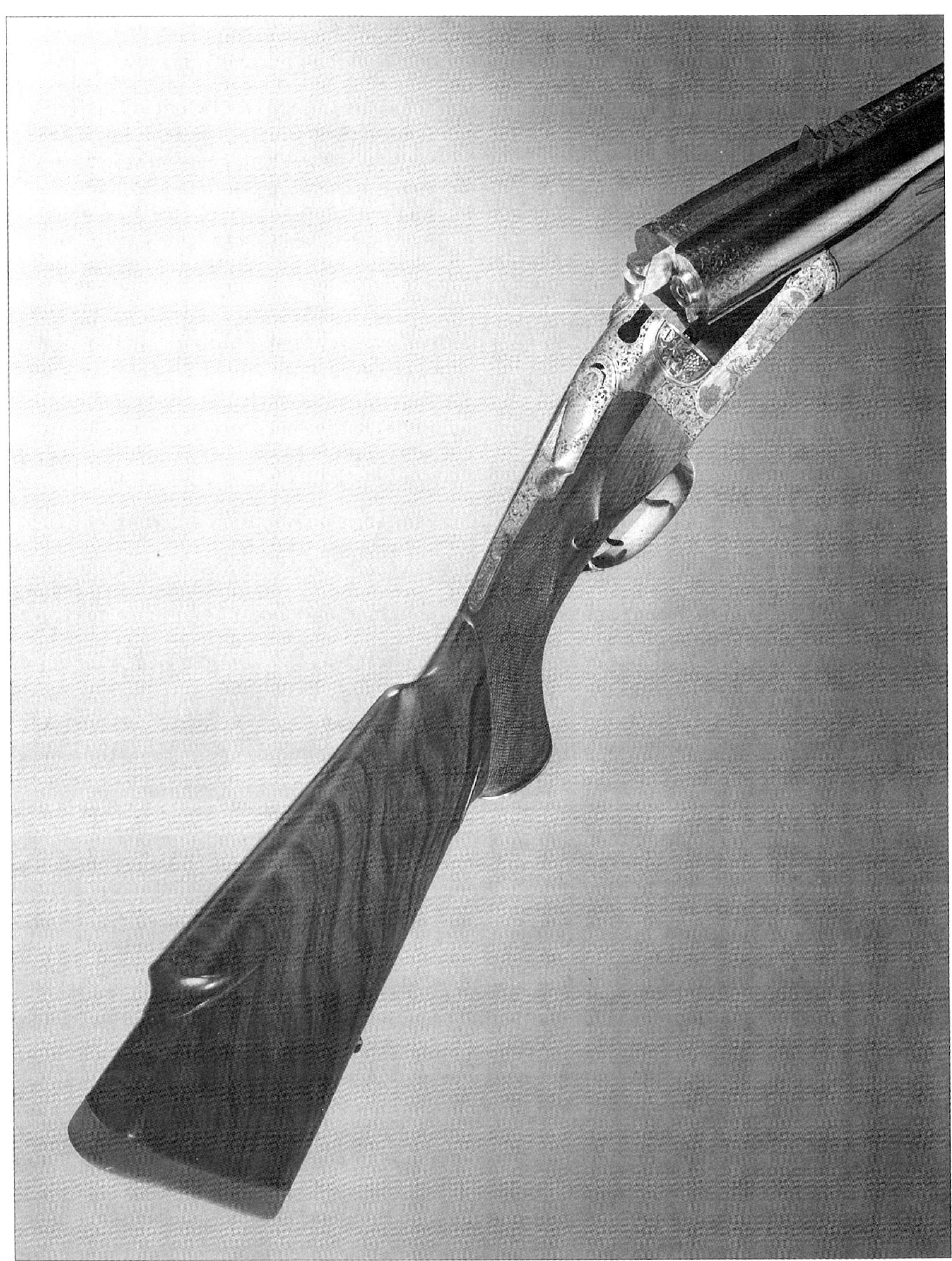

A .458 double rifle showing Westley Richards distinctive top lever and doll's head. The game scenes are appropriate to the caliber, and the fences are carved with fruiting vine. (Westley Richards)

The Ovundo was a boxlock with a hook beneath the barrels that made it a deeper, less elegant design than the sidelock Boss. It was nevertheless a modest success, especially in the U.S., where Henry Ford bought one. It was particularly popular as a target gun and was used by Henry Quersin, the editor of *Chasse et Peche* and a noted live-pigeon shot, when he won the Championship of Brussels Club in 1925. It was also made as a ball-and-shot gun in 20-bore and called the Fauneta. Built with a "mild form of rifling," its shotgun pattern was claimed to be a 33 percent improvement over previous ball-and-shot guns. A special bullet called the "L.T.," presumably for Leslie Taylor, was recommended with the Fauneta, and one contemporary claimed it was an improvement over Holland & Holland's Paradox bullet.

Like the Boss, the Westley Richards over-and-under was also built as a double rifle. Although it could be had in every cartridge from .22 Hi-power to .425, the most popular caliber appears to have been Westley Richards's .318 accelerated express, one of several proprietary cartridges popular with big-game hunters in India and Africa. John "Pondoro" Taylor, in his classic *African Rifles and Cartridges,* claimed the .318 was "undoubtedly the most popular and most widely used British medium bore." He also made the point that the .318 was underpowered for dangerous game and then tells how "Karamojo" Bell discarded his .318 after the base of a cartridge separated, leaving the body of the shell sticking in the chamber. Many of "Pondoro" Taylor's comments on Westley Richards continue in the same vein: Of the .375 Rimless Westley Richards, he said, "It's one of life's little mysteries to me how this cartridge ever came into existence." The .360 Westley Richards "failed to satisfy," and even though the .425 Westley Richards was an:

. . . excellent cartridge and a real killer . . . the makers, who patented the cartridge, made the mistake of fitting absurdly long 28 inch barrels to their rifles for stock and also of building a cheap model for the colonial trade. The result was that the weapons got themselves a bad name; the most usual complaints being the unnecessary length which made them very clumsy and ungainly in thick cover, and the fact that the magazine springs were not always up to their work. Five shot magazines were customary, and it was found that the springs had a habit of weakening and were unable to press up the last shell sufficiently for the bolt to get hold of it. They were also known to kick like mules, because they were really too light for their power.

Faint praise indeed!

Taylor approved of the Ovundo concept, though he did say he had been asked by Westley Richards (sic) "not to say a great deal about these weapons because he does not expect to be able to make any more for some considerable time." This certainly is in accord with a letter I received in 1992 from Walter A. Clode, the current chairman of Westley Richards, who wrote that the Ovundo was "a discontinued model . . . not pursued because of some weakness encountered at proof." Today, the Ovundo is a prized collectors' item, occasionally seen at auction, and though it does not command anything like the prices obtained for the Boss over-and-under, it is still a high-priced gun.

After the Ovundo, Westley Richards introduced no new innovations and few new guns of any kind. In his book *Best Guns,* Michael McIntosh makes the point that the history of Westley Richards in the twentieth century reflects how the English gun trade in general has been "savaged." Certainly the English trade is only a shadow of its former self, but in the "workshop of the world" and "the city of one thousand trades," Westley Richards is a survivor and will still be making its droplock guns in the next century.

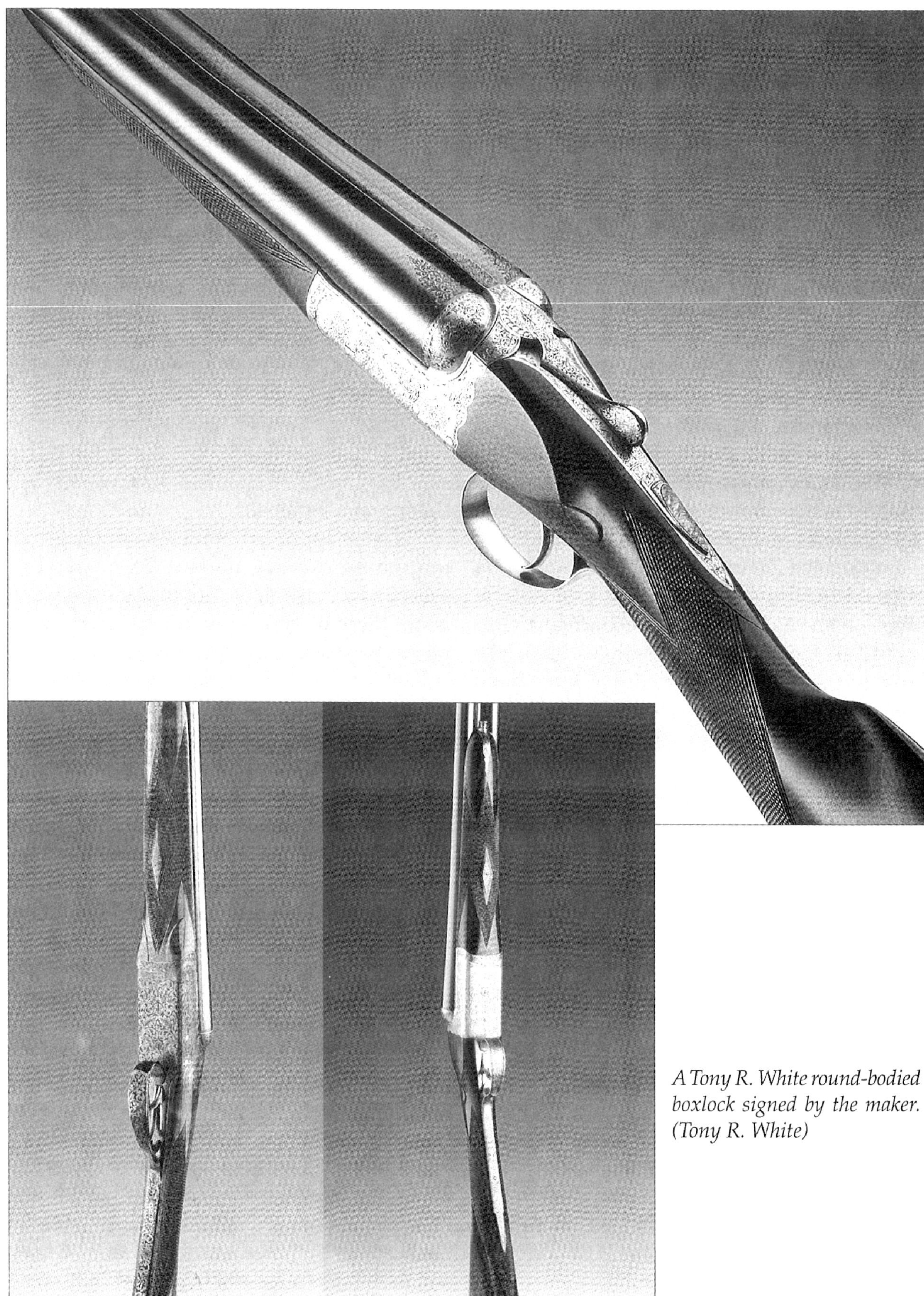

A Tony R. White round-bodied boxlock signed by the maker. (Tony R. White)

TONY R. WHITE

Of all the world's shotgun designs, none is more imitated than the Anson & Deeley. If you buy a boxlock in Brazil, Turkey, Japan, or anywhere in Europe, it will be built on the A & D system. The action was patented on 11 May 1875 (Number 1,756) and credited to William Anson, foreman of Westley Richards's gun-action department, and John Deeley, the company's managing director and major shareholder.

As mentioned earlier, the Anson & Deeley became the quintessential Birmingham gun action and, later, when coupled with a Scott spindle and toplever and the Purdey underbolt, the world standard. The protectionism therein was intended to encourage a nascent American shotgun industry, and it was effective with regard to cheap machine-made repeaters. In the mid to upper price range, too, the effects were felt for a while. Certainly, turn-of-the-century America produced many boxlocks designs that were in direct competition with the Anson & Deeley. It is significant, however, that except for the A. H. Fox reproduction, the A & D has outlasted them all. Indeed, the only new double to be built in the U.S. recently—the Hatfield Uplander—acknowledged A & D superiority by the sincerest form of flattery.

In Birmingham today, the A & D has become something of a wallflower. Because its comely cousin, the more esteemed sidelock, doesn't cost that much more to make, the boxlock is always available but rarely seen. The few remaining gunmaking firms in Birmingham all offer new boxlocks but sell few. W. W. Greener's most recent catalog shows three boxlocks—the "New Imperial DH 75," the "New Easy Opener DOH 90," and the "Needham No. 5"—of which only the DOH 90 claims Anson & Deeley lineage. The two others are descended from rivals of the A & D. The New Imperial is the latest in a family of "Facile Princeps" guns initially developed by Greener in 1880 to circumvent the A & D patents. When first introduced, it was so similar to the A & D that Robert Edward Couchman, then a director with Westley Richards, cried foul. But in the ensuing court case, which was taken to the House of Lords, Greener prevailed. The Needham, too, was once a unique hammerless design, but today it is a "Needham" in name only: Internally it has A & D lockwork. Ironically, none of the above have proven big sellers for the recently resuscitated Greener company, while sidelocks continue to sell. William Powell of Carrs Lane, Birmingham, also offers an A & D gun, which is built on the continent. Known as the Heritage, it sells less well than Powell's sidelocks. Of all the traditional Birmingham gunmakers associated with boxlock guns, only the originator of the design, Westley Richards, has a solid clientele for the design.

Today, one new firm specializes in building boxlocks—though it will also build a sidelock to order. Tony R. White, who served his apprenticeship as a stocker, finisher, and freer with W. & C. Scott, has set up in an old barn within earshot of the Shugborough shooting school. Situated on Lord Lichfield's estate on the edge of Cannock Chase in Staffordshire, Tony is a long way from Birmingham's traditional gun quarter. South Staffordshire is nevertheless an area with strong gunmaking connections and traditionally supplied the Birmingham trade with many of its components. Here, beyond the suburbs in rural parkland, Tony employs two journeymen to build the next generation of Anson & Deeley guns. These have intercepting safeties of Tony's own design built onto the trigger plate. Tony has applied for patents on his design, and, if they are granted, they will be the first tangible improvements to the A & D design in 100 years.

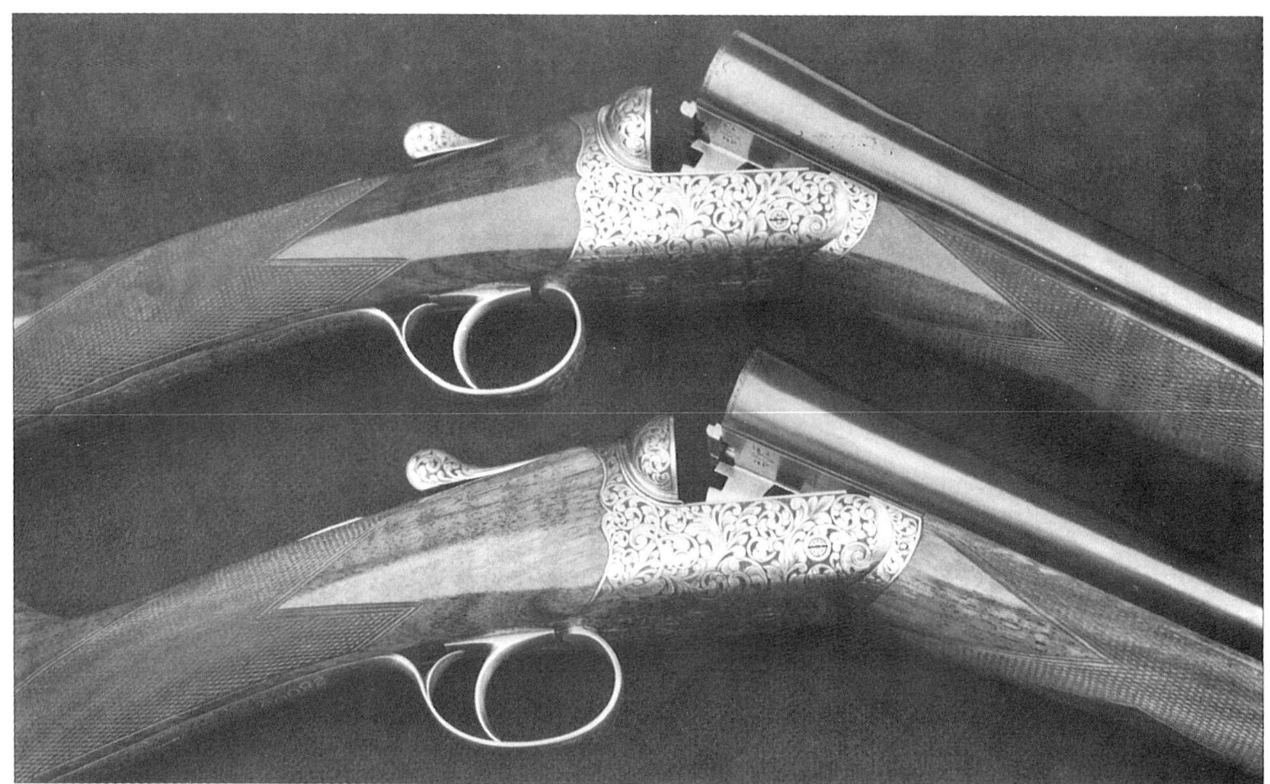

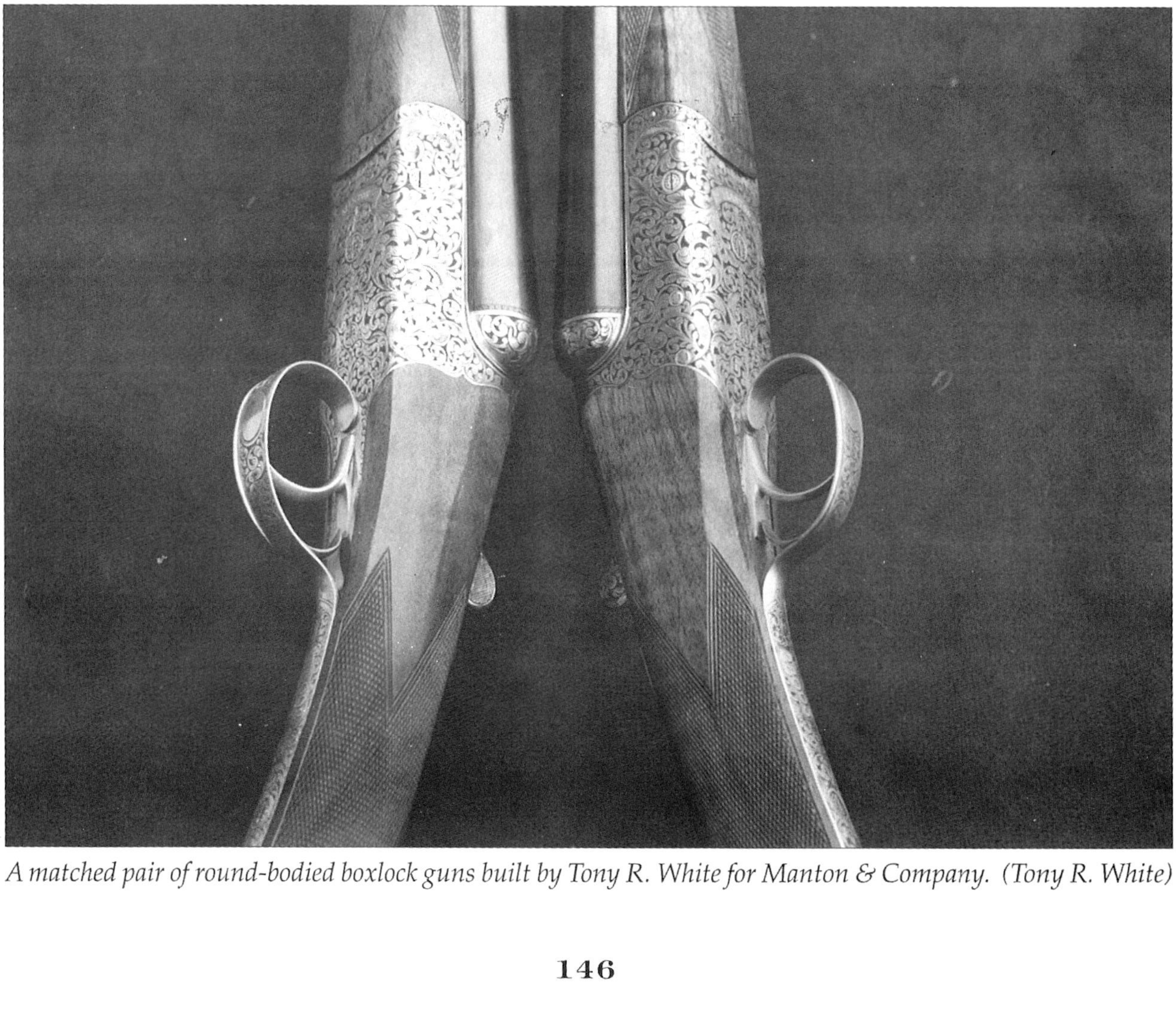

A matched pair of round-bodied boxlock guns built by Tony R. White for Manton & Company. (Tony R. White)

Tony worked for fifteen years with W. & C. Scott, between signing his indentures in 1974 and striking out on his own in 1989. He was one of the few craftsmen kept on after the takeover by Holland & Holland. He met his workforce, John Chandler and Ted Atkinson, during this period: John strikes up the barrels, does restoration work, and starts the process of making intricate gun parts from solid steel. Ted joints barrels to actions, connects the inside work to the ejectors, and also cold-chisels the fences to enhance the action. Tony stocks each gun in best-quality French walnut to the customer's requirements, frees and regulates new guns, and makes sure the trigger pulls are crisp. But his greatest responsibility is to oversee the gun from start to finish and make sure "our bespoke guns leave the workshop

having been built to the highest possible standard." I looked at a 28-bore with a scalloped frame and close bouquet and scroll engraving similar to that found on Churchill boxlocks, which is hardly surprising since the work was done by Philip Duffill, who learned his technique at Churchill's. This lovely little toy was destined for the collection of an American who limits himself to guns made by people who put their own names on them. Next I looked at a very similar 20-bore, this one commissioned by the British weekly shooting magazine—*The Shooting Times*—and inlaid in gold with the periodical's name. The magazine's editor, John Gregson, who had the gun built as a prize for a raffle, had wisely left the specifications to Tony. In a reflection of recent trends, Tony chose 20 for the gauge and short

A 20-bore round-bodied boxlock built for and raffled by The Shooting Times & Country *magazine. (Tony White)*

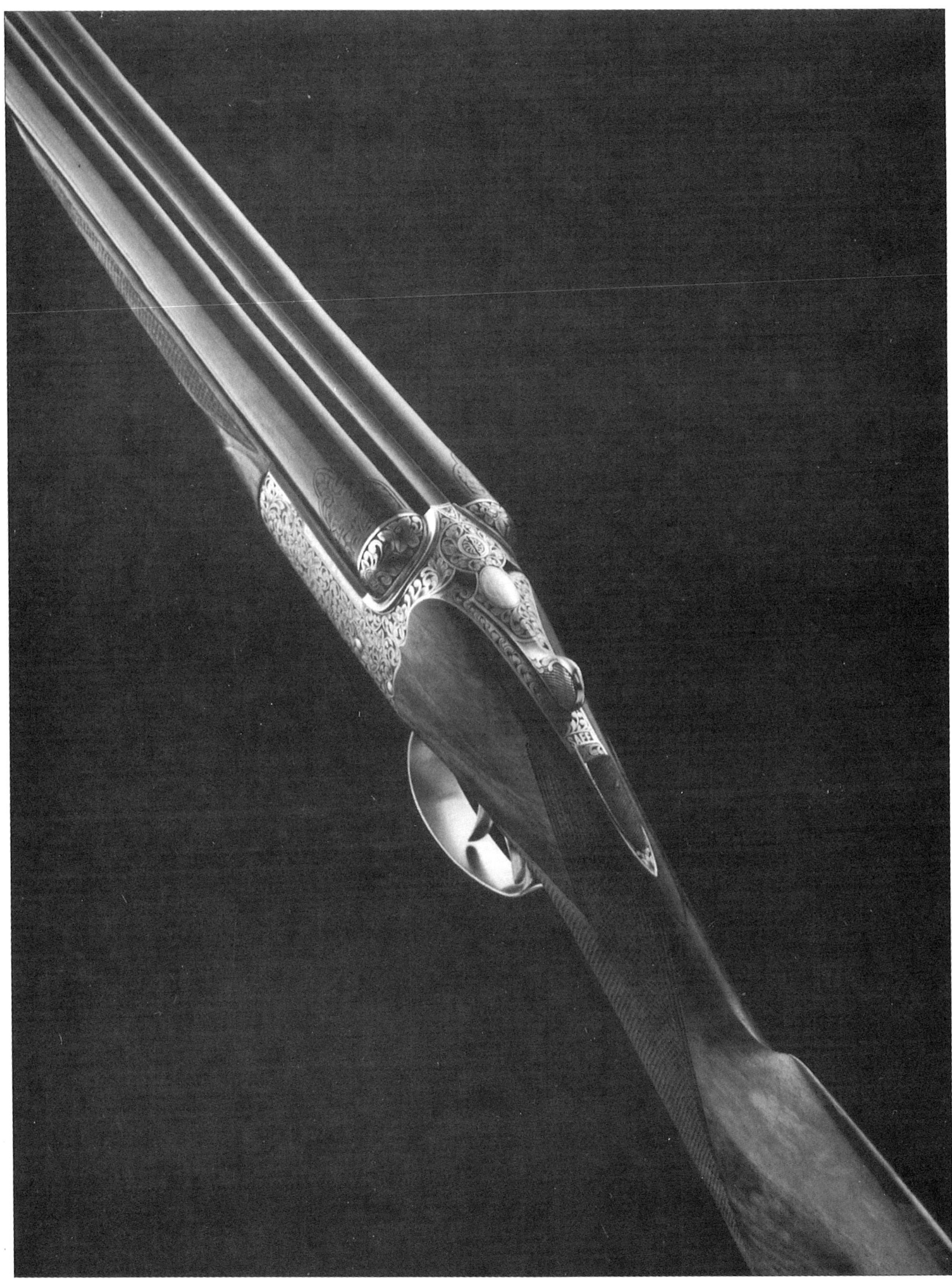

A 20-bore round-bodied gun built for Cogswell & Harrison by Tony R. White. (Cogswell & Harrison)

twenty-six inch barrels with long 2¾-inch chambers. French walnut from trees 300 years old was checkered at twenty-four lines to the inch for the matching stock and fore-end. The major difference between the two guns was in the nature of the action body: While the 28-bore was square in section, the 20 was semi-rounded, giving it an altogether more elegant look and feel.

One major problem with A & D actions is aesthetics. They are frequently of boxy appearance and, as Burrard pointed out, "The lines of no boxlock action can compare with those of a really well-designed bar action sidelock." In the past, all kinds of innovations have been added to the basic design to enhance its appeal. Among the most often encountered are sideplates, as found on some Cogswell and Harrison and many Charles Hellis guns; carved fences, seen on lots of top-grade boxlocks; and the most common device of all, the fancy back. This was done by filing curves into the otherwise straight line at the back of the action. Westley Richards often added a series of scallops, while Daniel Fraser created a bow shape. But my favorite is the long, asymmetrical curve that Daniel Leonard built into the guns he made for W. J. Jeffery. Regardless of how well they are executed, all of these features leave something to be desired. It wasn't until I came upon the pair of single-trigger 12-bore boxlocks Tony built for Manton & Company

that I felt I had seen a truly beautiful box-lock. The action bodies were rounded, with fancy backs. The curve formed by the rear of the action where it meets the strap was wider than any I have seen on any boxlock. Instead of the normal flat panel or points, the head of the stock is almost cylindrical in cross-section. All of these details flow together to form a streamlined design reminiscent of a Scottish round-action. Tony smiled knowingly when I told him of my impression and admitted that the Dickson and David McKay Brown guns had been "big influences." If the style of the guns is Scottish, the engraving, by Geoff Moore, is just as unmistakably English. Geoff, who has engraved Holland & Holland guns, has created something that resembles Purdey's "extra finish" and features deep leaf acanthus scroll with a silver coin finish against a hatched, matte ground. The overall effect is dramatic without ostentation. It is impossible, looking at these round-bodied boxlocks, to escape the impression that we are seeing the next and perhaps final stage in the evolution of the Anson & Deeley action. William Anson and John Deeley's brainchild has finally come of age 120 years after it was introduced.

Anyone who would like to know more about Tony R. White guns can write to: Tony R. White, "The Old Barn," Shugborough Shooting School, Oakedge Park, Wolseley Bridge, Nr. Stafford, PT17 0HP, England.

PART 3

Birmingham Guns and Industries

BIRMINGHAM GUNS AND INDUSTRIES

PORTAL INTO THE PAST:

THE BIRMINGHAM GUN BARREL PROOF HOUSE

BY VIC VENTERS

Hemmed between the Midland railway embankment and the old Fazeley & Birmingham Canal is a modest Georgian building that has literally shaped the destiny of the modern world. From the portals of the Birmingham Gun Barrel Proof House passed the implements that tamed continents, subdued peoples, wrecked empires, won others, and fought the wars that decided the fates of nations—including our own.

Birmingham's gun trade, after all, girded the might of *Pax Brittanica* at its zenith. Her Enfields armed the soldiers of Antietam, Gettysburg, and Appomattox; her *chassepots* battled Bismarck's men in the streets of Paris. The city's cheapest muskets became currency for the African slave trade; in wealthier hands, her Cape guns slew the great beasts of India and Africa. We have all felt, in one way or another, the reverberations of gunfire from the two-story brick building at the foot of Birmingham's Banbury Street.

At first glance, the Proof House seems little changed from the days when the sun never set on the Union Jack. Visitors today still enter under a painted trophy of arms, then sign in at the guest book, leaving their signatures alongside names like Albert, Wellington, and the Kaiser. Guns are still proved in original cubicles, and the old provisional proof room—illustrated in W. Greener's book *Gunnery*—appears identical to the woodcut carved in the 1850s. Black-powder cannon and muskets are still proved in it, by methods unchanged from the era when those explosions were so constant that citizens dubbed the ruckus "the Birmingham Roar."

The British have an extraordinary talent for making pageant of the mundane, affairs at the Proof House being no exception. On the last Thursday of each month, a flag is unfurled to announce the board meeting, and the guardians—the Proof House administrators—ascend a special staircase to reach the paneled board room, just as they've done since 1813. Under the Proof House coat of arms with motto *Cavendo Tutus* (Safety For All), they forge policy around a magnificent oak table, purchased from the London Proof House in 1927. Clocks built in the 1800s still measure time in a building where time seems to have stood still.

Or has it? Muskets and cannon are still proved, but for re-enactors these days, not real soldiers. Where once a million guns passed proved each year, twenty-five thousand now pass. The "small arms arsenal of the world," as old Brum was known, has seen her gun trade wither since 1900, especially from World War II on. The Birmingham Roar still sounds, but far less often and scarcely as loud.

But make no mistake: Birmingham's Proof House still matters. Together with the London Proof House, the pair guard the reputation of British firearms as vigilantly as Cerberus—no dangers or frauds pass unchallenged. British proof remains the world's best guaranty that the gun in your hands is as safe to shoot as it can possibly be, provided you do your part and use proper ammunition and care.

In simplest terms, proof is testing a firearm in a controlled environment by firing a charge through the barrels that exceeds normal service pressures by almost twice. If the gun is not damaged or altered by the process in any way, it passes proof and is so marked with official stamps—on the action and barrel flats in the case of double guns or rifles. So long as the gun and its barrels are not later damaged, or altered beyond some strict limits, it remains in proof in perpetuity.

A gun can go out of proof in any number of ways, shotguns most notably through damage to the barrel from severe pitting, dents or bulges, chamber lengthening, repairs or damage to the lumps or ejector work, or bore enlargement beyond about .010 inch (or .2 mm). Guns can usually be successfully reproved should any of this happen, and reproving is legally mandatory in England before an out-of-proof gun can be sold or resold.

Proof not only offers a real-world assurance of safety, it has also allowed British gunmakers to craft sporting guns second to none in terms of weight, balance, and aesthetics. Proof is an integral part of building a British Best because the craftsmen know precisely how much metal to remove, how much to leave. By contrast, gunmakers in countries lacking a national Proof House and laws—America, for example—must build in a margin of safety by using heavier actions and barrels, both a bane to good wingshooting, certainly for most live game. The Birmingham Gun Barrel Proof House was born in the Age of Empire, its foundations cast in an atmosphere of rivalry, of both the international and the domestic sort.

The proving process began in England in 1637, after the London Company of Gunmakers obtained a royal charter of incorporation and began stamping guns with its marks of approval. By 1670, proof was mandatory in London, with that city home of the only official Proof House. Because proof guaranteed a certain minimum of safety and quality, England's capital dominated the production and sale of guns, especially fine firearms. It was a monopoly, however, that would not go unchallenged.

Since the Middle Ages, Birmingham had been a center for the metalworking trades—most notably for cutlery, jewelry, buttons, and the edged tools of war. By the late seventeenth century, her metalsmiths were arming the king's army with muskets. Over the next century and a half, Birmingham's gun trade would grow rapidly, eventually supplying most of the components used in the London trade, as well as commanding the production of military and rougher trade weapons. Birmingham also became the chief supplier of complete or semi-complete guns to the London and provincial trades, whose

The Birmingham Gun Barrel Proof House. (Vic Venters)

makers would finish out the guns and engrave their own names on them.

Though the city had a number of private proof houses, her guns were little esteemed for lack of official proof, particularly by London makers who relied on Birmingham components, but who were also alarmed by the threat posed by Brum's increasingly wealthy and influential trade. Disputes between the two centers festered for a century and a half before coming to a head in the Napoleonic era, when the need for vast quantities of military arms became acute.

In 1813, London gunmakers introduced a bill in Parliament to require guns to be marked with the real maker's name and place of manufacture. London, though, had grabbed a tiger by the tail. Birmingham makers, dependent on anonymity, promptly killed the bill. Then they turned the tables, introducing their own bill to create an official Proof House in Birmingham, independent of London's.

In July, Parliament passed the Gun Barrel Proof House Act of 1813, establishing the Birmingham Proof House and outlawing the sale of any unproved guns in Britain. Within six months of the bill's passage, industrious Birmingham had its Proof House up and running—the same building extant today.

For the next sixty years, Birmingham's gun trade blossomed like a rose liberated from the weeds, becoming the undisputed gunmaking capital of the world. In 1862, for example, at the height of America's First War for Southern Independence, more than one million weapons passed through the Proof House, arms destined for the highest bidder, Federal and Confederate alike.

Despite the legitimacy the Proof House bestowed on Birmingham guns, there were troubles on Banbury Street. Proof House historian Cliff Harris called the history of its first fifty years "checkered"—English understatement for an organization riddled with the sort of machinations and intrigue that would have pleased an emperor of the Byzantine Empire. The British gun trade was a contentious, competitive lot, and the Proof House was repeatedly charged with financial mismanagement and favoritism for, or prejudice against, certain makers. In 1855, all its early records were burned by Proof House employees, the exact reason lost forever in the smoke and ashes.

The Proof House did not become truly modern in a professional sense until 1868, when the Proof Act of that year mandated a permanent Proof Master to serve under the administration of a fifteen-member Board of Guardians, men elected to serve from the ranks of registered members of the Birmingham gun trade. They were assisted by six other guardians consisting of local city councilors and justices of the peace. Procedures such as additional proof acts in 1950 and 1978 plus amended rules of proof have continually modernized the Proof House as changing technology demanded. In 1980, Britain became a member state in CIP (*Commission Internationale Permanente*), the international body working to standardize proof in most European countries.

Today, Proof Master Roger Hancox and Chairman Guardian Peter Powell are leading the Birmingham Proof House into the twenty-first century. Before his appointment as Proof Master in January 1995, Hancox had been a guardian for a decade, and was owner of Accles & Shelvoke, the world's largest manufacturer of humane cattle stunners and other cartridge-operated equipment. Roger is quick with a joke and loves digging through Proof House archives, but it's clear this former engineer and entrepreneur is utterly serious about keeping the Proof House on the cutting edge of firearms and cartridge-testing technology.

Peter Powell, along with brother David, is a director at William Powell & Son Ltd., Britain's oldest gunmaking firm still under the same family ownership (since 1812). Peter shares Roger's sense of humor, is energetic and friendly, answers questions from writers he probably shouldn't, and generally exudes integrity from every pore. I have the utmost regard for Powell because he cares deeply for the Birmingham trade, not just his slice of it. He was elected chairman of the Board of Guardians by his peers and serves at their pleasure.

Perhaps the greatest task the pair currently face is overseeing the complete transition from Britain's traditional proof methods to international CIP methods. It's complicated work, the change from measuring pressure by crusher gauges to analysis by transducer. Crusher gauges work by venting pressure in a test gun through small holes drilled in its barrel onto pistons which, when a cartridge is fired, crush tiny lead or copper cylinders. Pressure can then be estimated by measuring how much the cylinders were crushed. Transducers, on the other hand, measure pressure through piezoelectricity, which is generated when special quartz-bearing crystals are compressed, in this case by firing. For most of this century, Britain has relied on the crusher method, thus the entire universe of knowledge, painstakingly built over eighty years, is undergoing radical change and revision.

Roger and Peter have also set about, in their words, "making the Proof House more visible and vital to the average British shooter." The Proof House offers a vast array of services for individual shooters and industry alike, from laboratory testing of all types of cartridges to investigating gun accidents to sponsoring safety exhibits at game fairs around the United Kingdom.

Of course, gun proving and reproving remain at the heart of its mission, and the growing interest in vintage British firearms provides steady business for reproof, about twenty-five hundred guns per year, or approximately 10 percent of guns proved each year these days.

Reproving is a topic that should be of special interest to American shooters and firearm collectors. Anyone who's spent time shopping for English shotguns in this country knows how many out-of-proof guns are lying about, particularly old 2.5-inch-chambered guns that have been bored out to 2.75 inches without reproof. No doubt many of these will continue to give good service into the next century. But some will not. The thin barrels that make proved British guns so delightful afield also make them potentially dangerous when out-of-proof, particularly lower-grade guns built with lesser grades of steel. Toss in high-pressured American loads, and you've concocted a recipe that can wreck an expensive firearm or, even worse, wreck bits of anatomy in proximity to it.

If potential dangers don't bother you, how about a hole in your pocket? Peter Powell puts it bluntly, "An out-of-proof shot-

The Proof House guardians in 1963. (Dr. Paul Brown)

gun is valueless in the rest of the civilized world," he says. "Absolutely valueless. Not only is it potentially very dangerous, but it's illegal to sell."

During my visit to Birmingham in the fall of 1996, Peter and Roger were kind enough to arrange for me to follow a gun through the stages of reproof, of which there are three—viewing, proof, then final viewing and marking. Now, you just can't pack up a gun and ship her off to the Proof House. The gun must first be prepared for reproving by a qualified gunsmith in England—the original maker is best should it still exist. Proof House authorities will not even consider a gun for reproving unless the barrels are on the face, the action and lumps are sound, and any pitting, dents, and bulges are removed and the bore finely polished. Depending on how much preparation work is needed, reproving a gun can run you from about £200 to 400—not cheap but not exorbitant either.

At the Proof House, your gunmaker submits the prepared gun for viewing through the special "receiving door,"

The Proof House guardians in 1996. (Nick Makinson.) Back row, left to right: *Councilor J. E. C. Alden; K.S. Elder, J. P.; E. C. Adams J. P.; T. J. O'Donnell; Mr. Turner; Councilor Hanks; G. Clark; C.G.B. Wild; K. J. Irving, B. A. King, Councilor M. B. Olley, R. C. Brown, R. C. Hale, A. A. Haynes, J. P., A. D. Thornton.* Front row, left to right: *F. J. Wiseman; G. C. Smith; G. C. Lemon (Vice President); P. T. Powell (Chairman); J. B. LeBreton (Deputy-Chairman); R. J. Hancox (Proof Master); G. G. Cross.*

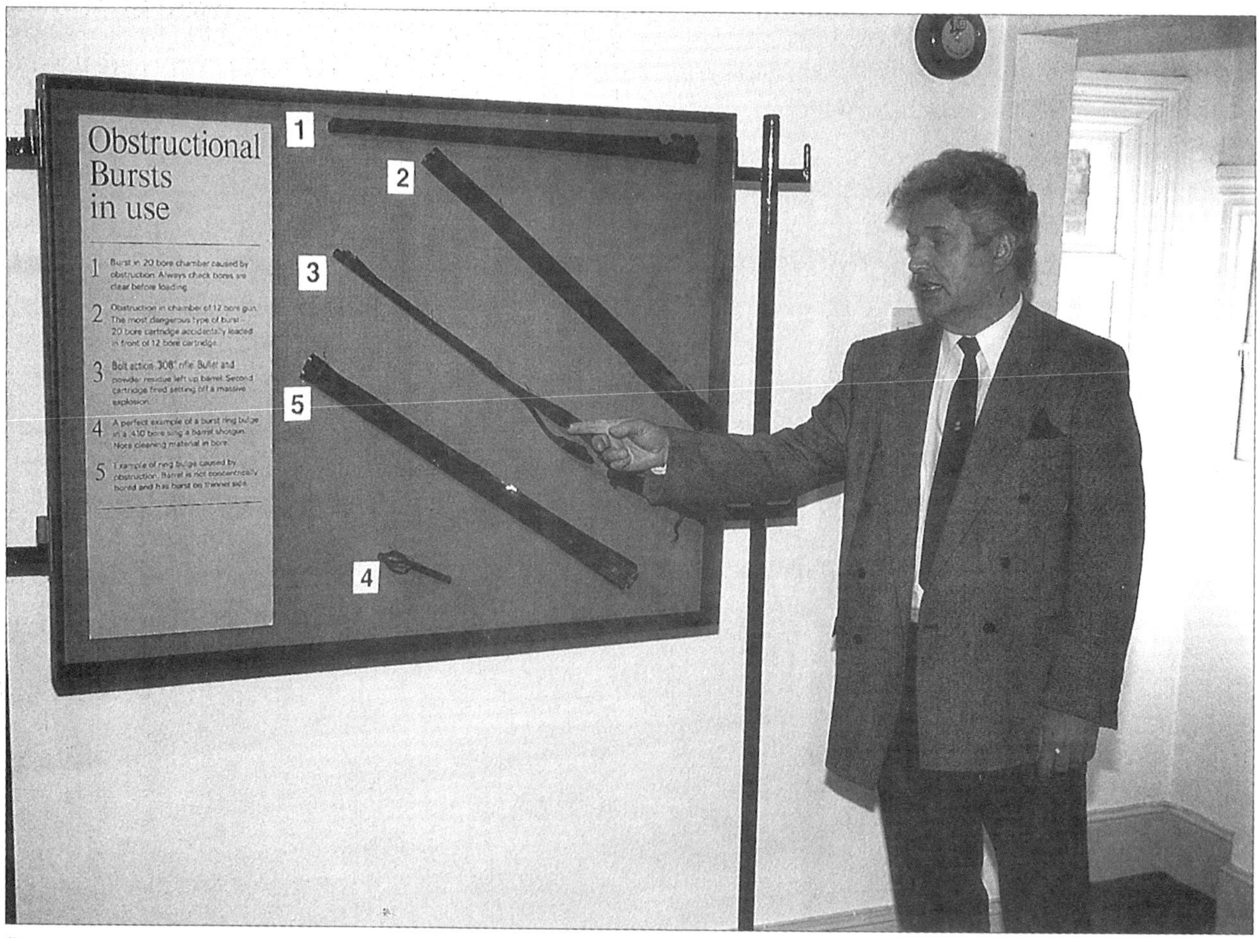

Roger Hancox, the current Proof Master. (Vic Venters)

through which millions of guns have no doubt passed. Here your gun is viewed—examined, that is—by Michael Lynch or Wayne Massey, who check for any of the structural flaws previously mentioned. What's astounding is that the viewing process is entirely visual, relying on the accumulated skills of men who have spent their lives peering down barrels. They can see tiny bulges and dents that few of us could ever detect. Very few properly prepared guns fail reproof, but if they do, it usually happens during viewing. Hancox explained:

It's important to realize a gun doesn't have to blow up or bulge to fail proof. Most of the guns that fail proof actually fail in this examination process. If that happens, they have to be sent back for proper pre-proof preparation. It's very rare for a gun to make

it to the firing process, then fail. That's why viewing is so important.

If judged sound, the gun is turned over to Chief Inspector Pat Hitchcock, who will take it to the firing gallery. Older 2.5- or 2.75-inch-chambered side-by-side game guns will usually be proved at standard levels—that is, at 960 BARS as measured by transducer. The gun is actually marked at 850 BARS, the pressure indicated when the same proof load is measured by a crusher gauge.

The firing gallery is a row of enclosed brick cubicles. While new mass-produced guns are usually proved with their stock on, only the barreled action of a vintage or new best English gun is reproved so as to prevent damage to older woodwork. Inspector Hitchcock clamps the action in a padded vise. Proof shells are loaded and the cubicle door is closed. Pat pushes a rod through an aperture in the wall, places it against the striker, taps it with a hammer, and *voila*, the Birmingham Roar. The process is repeated twice for each barrel.

If the barrels haven't bulged, rivelled, or otherwise teed up, the inspector will check carefully to make sure they are still on the face of the action. Assuming all's well, Pat will take the gun to the marking room, where, appropriately, the gun is stamped with its official proof marks indicating nominal bore size, gauge, chamber length, and the minimum proof pressure. The gun is now reproved, you will be safe, and the proof house has done its job—*Cavendo Tutus*.

The Birmingham Gun Barrel Proof House may be a museum, but don't ever tell the Proof Master that. (Reprinted from *Shooting Sportsman*, courtesy of the author.)

BUYING BIRMINGHAM GUNS

BY DOUGLAS TATE

It is an unquestionable truth that Britain builds the world's finest side-by-side shotguns, but no one pretends they're cheap. The Prince of Wales; his mother, Queen Elizabeth II; and members of Hollywood royalty shoot Purdey shotguns, but we all know you need a king's ransom to buy one. The last time I looked, a standard engraved 12-bore Purdey wouldn't leave you with enough change for a box of cartridges out of $45,000!

Does this mean that all British shotguns are expensive? The answer is yes if you want a new gun. Even Birmingham boxlocks like a Powell or Westley Richards now cost $20,000 and up because of the hundreds of hours of hand labor that goes into them.

However, secondhand British shotguns, particularly older boxlocks, are undervalued—or, as an investor friend likes to say, "They represent an anomaly in the market."

A fair to good boxlock by a Birmingham or provincial maker (the latter almost always made in the Birmingham trade) can still be bought for as little as $1,500, or about one-tenth the replacement cost. Though it is difficult to understand how well-balanced, fast-handling hunting weapons, which double as handcrafted collectibles, can still be bargains, it is easy to appreciate their qualities.

First, they are lighter than comparable machine-made guns, which, as any long-walking bird hunter knows, is a real advantage toward the end of a hard day. Second, they are uncomplicated, with only a handful of working parts that rarely go wrong—who can think of any tool or other piece of equipment that was designed so simply 125 years ago that its form hasn't changed since? A fine gun made by Powell, Greener, or Scott over a century ago is the same thoroughbred animal it always was. And third, they are elegant. When John Ireland said to Montgomery Clift in the film *Red River*, "There are only two things more beautiful than a good gun—a Swiss watch or a woman from anywhere," I like to think he had in mind the slim forearm, double triggers, and straight wrist of the classic English double.

Once you have decided to invest in a secondhand English gun, a good starting point is the provincial no-name non-ejector. These are guns that were built in the gunmaking center of Birmingham for sale by retailers in every corner of England. They usually bear an unfamiliar small-town name and consequently can be bought on a budget. Some of the famous London makers such as Purdey also once offered inexpensive boxlock non-ejectors, but these should be avoided because you will pay a premium for the name. It is ironic that a low-quality gun in poor condition by a prestigious maker will invariably cost more than a superb example signed by a provincial no-name. Guns that do not eject spent cases after firing are considered less desirable in Britain because they cannot be loaded as quickly. While this is a considerable drawback on an English driven shoot, it is of no consequence to the American who hunts over dogs and often conscientiously picks up his ejected cartridges anyway. Shotguns of this description can often be had for as little as $1,300 up to $2,000, but expect to pay more depending on condition, age, and quality.

Boxlock ejectors are more desirable and, as a gross generalization, are better made and tend to have more engraving than comparable non-ejectors. While non-ejectors are often only border-engraved, ejectors are frequently found to have at least some fine scroll engraving, with the maker's or at least the retailer's name engraved in a banner on the side of the action. Webley & Scott and Army & Navy (the latter retailed in London but made in Birmingham) are good names to look out for in a price range up to about $3,500. Some makers offered very high-quality boxlocks that may cost a great deal more. For example, Churchill (some guns made in Birmingham) sold a boxlock which, when new, went for more than twice his sidelock-model guns. These very high-quality guns are recognizable by profuse engraving, wood marbled like the endplates of a rare book, and intercepting safeties. Intercepting safeties are a rare refinement on a boxlock and are recognizable by a small screw visible between the top strap and the rear of the standing breech.

In the same price range as a good boxlock are sidelock non-ejector guns. Often vintage guns from the period before the ejector was fully developed, they occasionally have a transitional look halfway between a hammer and a hammerless gun. They are frequently found with Damascus barrels, which is not necessarily a bad thing if they are in current nitro proof and have good wall thicknesses. If in doubt, use your three-day inspection period to have the gun sent to one of the several English gunmakers now working in the United States: Dale Tate on the West Coast, David Trevallion on the East Coast, and Jack Rowe or Kirk Merrington in the South. In Canada, Les Paul of Roseneath, Ontario, provides a similar service.

The guns described so far are all 12-bores, which was the standard—read only—gun for a male adult in Great Britain, though this is beginning to change. Small-bores were normally made only for women and children, which means they are extremely rare and usually have short stocks of fourteen inches or less. When buying a small-bore over the phone, be sure to ask how much of the stock is original wood and how much is a pad or extension. The scarcity of these little gems does tend to drive prices up, but they can occasionally be found for less than $3,500. Expect to pay a 30 percent premium over a comparable 12-bore.

The vast majority of British guns made for upland birds are chambered for 2½-inch loads, while the standard in the United States is 2¾ inches. Until relatively recently, this represented a dilemma: Should English gun buyers extend the chambers or perhaps shoot light 2¾-inch loads? Although both are still feasible options, depending on the weight of the gun and the condition of the barrels, a third and more attractive solution is to buy imported or American-made 2½-inch shells, which are now available from several sources. The English game gun is now so popular in the United States that over a dozen dealers offer imported cartridges—effectively the same range of brands and loads available in Britain. At least two American companies also offer reloading components and equipment, and another manufactures 2½-inch shells here in the U.S.

Lengthening chambers is no longer necessary and a bit ill-advised. Extending the chambers invalidates the proof marks, and an out-of-proof gun is not as easily sold as one in proof, particularly to collectors looking for originality. If you must lengthen chambers, get the opinion of one of the English gunsmiths mentioned earlier as to whether the gun is sturdy enough to pass reproof, but remember—sending the gun back to England can be expensive, especially if the gun fails and the barrels blow. Although they will not take the pounding of workhorse use with heavy American cartridges, the barrels do last several human lifetimes, given a little tender loving care and fed a diet of appropriate loads.

British Anson & Deeley boxlock in proving cubicle ready for reproof at the Birmingham Proof House in 1995. (Photo Vic Venters)

But what are appropriate loads for the British game gun? William Wellington Greener, one of Birmingham's most famous gunmakers, wrote more than a hundred years ago:

> A safe rule is to have the gun ninety-six times heavier than the shot load. This means a six-pound gun for an ounce of shot; 6¾ pounds for $1^1/_8$ oz.; 7½ pounds for 1¼ oz., and these may be shot with comfort, irrespective of the gauge of the gun. . . .

We ignore Greener at our peril, and anyone stuffing 1¼-ounce loads into a six-pound gun will not only threaten the structural integrity of the barrels and action but will also suffer unpleasant recoil.

When looking at British guns, avoid those that have been ravaged by abuse, neglect, or shade-tree blacksmithing. Look out for worn-down engraving, poor wood-to-metal or metal-to-metal fit, and buggered screw heads. Find out if the gun is still on face and in proof, and make sure barrel-wall thicknesses are above the British gun-trade minimum of .020 inch for 2½-inch-chambered guns. But remain flexible with regard to chokes and stock dimensions, which can always be altered to suit your needs. Even guns with no choke at all can sometimes be recess-choked, and stocks can be bent or lengthened with a leather-covered recoil pad. Buy from dealers after first establishing their reputations, and always ask if the seller is prepared to stand behind a product. A good indication of how reputable an individual is can be gauged by whether or not he is willing to take back a gun at a later date when you may be trading to a more expensive model. Find a dealer who specializes in English guns, and try to establish some rapport. A happy relationship formed now can, with a bit of luck, last for years and give you the confidence to improve and expand your collection when desired.

Remember, each English gun was hand-built by individual craftsmen, and even those with consecutive serial numbers won't be exactly alike. Consequently, no blue book of gun values exists for British doubles. The only way to tell a bargain from a dud is to handle and examine as many guns as possible and read as much as you can.

Most English guns were originally sold cased, with the maker's or retailer's trade label inside the lid, a Brady canvas-covered case for boxlocks or a leather case for the sidelock non-ejector being appropriate styles. Don't be afraid to ask about cases when buying an English gun, but don't be surprised if the gun is sold without its case. Old guns have a way of surviving longer than their boxes. However, a new case can be bought from Brady after first making a paper silhouette of your gun's barrels and sending it off so that the barrel tray can be blocked to your specifications. Reproduction trade labels too can be bought from several sources to enhance the value and collectibility of your newly cased gun.

Recent legislation in Britain has made life tough on gun owners, and many have decided to give up their sport rather than register their shotguns with the police. Consequently, many guns have come onto the market, depressing prices and making guns accessible to overseas buyers. However, *The Times* of London recently published an article on what great investments English shotguns are, so it's only a matter of time before the speculators move in. Now is the perfect time to buy an English gun, but you had better hurry or the investors will have them all locked up!

Any chapter as brief as this one on a subject as large as buying inexpensive English guns poses more questions than it answers. The next step for a potential purchaser is to call one of several dealers who specialize in this type of gun and have some of those questions answered. Try:

Don Gustine
British Game Guns
P.O. Box 5795
Kent, WA 98064-5795

or

Glenn Baker
Woodcock Hill
RD #1, Box 147
Benton, PA 17814

VALUING BIRMINGHAM GUNS

BY DON GUSTINE

"Old Marley was as dead as a doornail.... This must be distinctly understood, or nothing wonderful can come of the story...." With apologies to Mr. Dickens and *A Christmas Carol*, this is particularly appropriate for our endeavor. "Old Marley" could easily be replaced with any of the old gunmakers. They and their way of life have long since passed, and the fruit of their labors can no longer be had for literally pennies per hour. There was a Dickensian flavor to the old gun trade and gunmakers: Though indentured during apprenticeship, they toiled long hours not through conscription but impassioned with pride, dedication, and respect for their tradition. A handful of gunmakers continue that tradition today, but the complexity of society and the cost of goods no longer translate into pennies per hour for hand craftsmanship.

So emerges the secondhand gun—passage, if you will, to an era, a way of life we as travelers can only imagine. The longevity of British guns is testament to the gunmaker's alchemy. However, the value of secondhand British guns cannot be underestimated. While a healthy market exists, the above clearly points to a finite number of available guns. If we accept responsibility for one of these products of gunmaking past, we must sympathetically care for it. The British gunner, and some Americans, comprehend this and dutifully care for their guns, reblacking or refinishing the wood if needed. Restoration breathes life into an old gun, and there is nothing blasphemous about such thoughts. This nonsense of keeping every gun in original condition, no matter what, does not occur to the pragmatic gunner. A balance, though, between the heavens and the nether world is appropriate.

When Douglas asked me to assist in a chapter about the values of British guns, I nearly wished I'd gone the way of "Old Marley." I didn't know whether to cry in anguish, rattle chains after poor old Doug, or aimlessly wander the earth. Having partially recovered, I must warn you that valuing British guns is a greater task than had the three spirits. I offer this advice: Research, examine, and locate a dealer you trust. Value the gun according to the quality, *not* the name. Your research and examination will bear this out. A name sometimes will be indicative of quality, but it isn't always so. Remember that the children beneath the robes of the Ghost of Christmas Present were Ignorance and Want. Here are some points to keep in mind:

1) Small-bores always command a premium due to their scarcity, especially in .410 and 28-bore. In the past, 16- and 20-bores presented enormous value as they could be purchased quite reasonably in Great Britain. However, 20-bores and 16s have seen a resurgence in popularity. Two-inch 12-bores, while disregarded in Britain, have a growing following in the U.S. Seductively light and throwing splendid patterns, they are small-bore sleepers, but rare as well. Small-bores with long stocks should be treasured, as most were originally built for women and children.

2) The advent of bismuth shot will usher in a new age of wildfowling for lovely old fowlers. A return to the marsh will also ignite an upward trend in the pricing of these guns.

3) Single triggers command a premium, though some systems are difficult to adjust and/or maintain.

4) Restoration naturally increases the price. Properly done, the results can be quite special (affordable, virtually new, *sans* the guilt).

5) Any case accompanying the gun will edge the price up a bit, particularly when it is the maker's. Canvas, canvas-and-leather, leather, and oak-and-leather are the most common types, and the prices increase proportionally. Accessories will lend to the ambiance, and to the cost.

The classifications that follow are quite elementary. The price range is purposely broad in an attempt to account for market trends, premiums, and the whisper of change.

BOXLOCK NON-EJECTOR: An odd place to start? This category is really the shy maiden with the handsome dowry, ignored by those always searching for royalty. The non-ejectors, boxlock and sidelock alike, are largely avoided in Great Britain, thus presenting surprising value in the United States. Many believe this class defines poor quality. Remember, quality is where you find it. Be graphically honest about your type of shooting. Do you truly require ejectors? Those who are conservation-minded and/or reload will appreciate the ready collection of spent cartridges. These guns range in quality from "Colonial" and "Keepers" (basic guns) to a fairly high standard and commensurately figured wood. ($850-$4,000)

BOXLOCK EJECTOR: Charm, elegance, refinement, simplicity: All can be had within this category. If one is searching for a high-quality gun, but cringes at sidelock prices, the boxlock ejector leaves nothing to want. Conversely, plain guns with ejectors can also be found. Given the type of shooting once enjoyed in Britain, gunmakers responded and produced a number of these. One is likely to find an excellent selection. Though it is often true, do not expect that ejector guns are always of high quality. Though not as common, pairs have also been made. (Droplocks, while representing ingenuity and elegance, are included here for simplicity.) $1,800-$7,500

BACKLOCK EJECTOR and **NON-EJEC-TOR:** These poor souls are longing for a final resting place. They harken to the Victorian age of shotgunning and the hammer gun. Often times the guns were forsaken by shooters lured to "modern" sidelocks or boxlocks. (Backlocks appearing similar to conventional sidelocks will approach pricing in that category.) Sleek and dynamic qualities usually captivate new owners. These guns survive in the spectrum of grades and present an excellent opportunity. $3,500-$7,000

SIDELOCK NON-EJECTORS: Another undervalued category. Even some best-quality examples may be found. The "maiden" theory applies equally here. Again, these are overlooked in favor of ejector guns and present some of the few bargains around today. The range is from unpretentious to the best. $4,000-$7,000

SIDELOCK EJECTORS: In many ways, this category represents the pulse of the English enthusiast. They are the crowning achievement of gunmaking, combining symmetry and artistic canvas. Essentially, whatever you desire can be found in this category. The finest, plus second- and third-quality guns, serve to bewilder the buyer. A couple of "caveats": All sidelocks are not automatically first-quality, and all sideplated guns are *not* sidelocks. Some of the latter are boxlocks disguised as sidelocks and should be priced accordingly. Pairs of guns are not as common in the U.S. and generally increase the price about 20 percent or more above two single guns. $4,000-$11,000

OVER-UNDER: Quite unusual and seldom seen. Guns by William Baker and the Westley Richards Ovundo are the most frequently encountered. Rarity makes it increasingly difficult to set any sort of price, though examples are found between $7,000 and $27,000.

HAMMER GUNS: Who among us can truthfully say he/she would not like to shoot a hammer gun? Certainly, stories of the "Big Shoots"—King George V, Lord Ripon, and Sir Harry Stonor—fuel our enthusiasm and imagination. Values rise as the age approaches the transition period to hammerless, correlating improvements in gunmaking. The willowy lines are appealing and the guns are quite lively in game-gun variations. Ejector guns are extremely rare and do not fall into this pricing. $1,500-$4,500

NEW GUNS: Few objects become as personal as a bespoke gun. The opportunity to own one allows you to become part of that sorcery that is gunmaking. In turn, the magic will follow you to the covert and perhaps afford some redemption. Boxlock and sidelock ejectors, over-unders and even a round-bodied boxlock ejector are available. The quality is what you would expect from artisans devoted to the craft. $10,000-$40,000.

PART 4

APPENDICES AND REFERENCES

Appendix I

Contemporary documents relating to gunmaking in Birmingham are rare. Rarer still are such accounts from outside the trade. These are particularly valuable because gunmakers writing about themselves tend to be self-aggrandizing and consequently less accurate. The following, from 1913, is interesting because it clearly defines the compartmentalization of the trade. Smirke's observation about "barrels which are made in Birmingham but sent to London to be 'proofed' a practice which is now common" is also fascinating because it raises the question, how many guns with London proofs were actually made in Birmingham?

The Manufacture of Sporting Guns & Rifles.
Report on Birmingham Trades
Prepared for use in connection with the
Juvenile Employment Exchange.

Prepared on behalf of the Board of Trade
by
Mr. R. S. Smirke.
1913

On 10 July 1813, an Act of Parliment was passed to establish a Proof House in Birmingham. It was built in 1813 after plans by architect John Horton.

Introduction

This handbook to the Manufacturers of Sporting Guns and Rifles has been prepared for use in connection with the Birmingham Juvenile Employment Exchange. In its preparation information has been obtained by personal visit to factories and workshops, and by interviews with a number of employers and with working men and women; this information has been arranged and submitted to the criticism of several employers and work people. The handbook is thought to be substantially correct, but does not pretend to be a complete or entirely accurate account of the trade with which it deals, and it is hoped that the criticism and suggestions which must inevitably occur to those who use it will be communicated to the Manager of the Labour Exchange, or the Secretary of the Central Care Committee; a few blank pages are provided in order that notes may be made and preserved for the improvement of subsequent issues of the book.

This handbook is one of a series which it is proposed to issue on the principal trades and occupations in Birmingham. The books are intended primarily as a source of information for the members and helpers of the Central and School Care Committees, in order that they may be better able to discuss the conditions and prospects of the various employments with parents and their boys and girls.

It should be understood that both helpers and parents can get additional information on these trades and trades not dealt with in these handbooks by calling at the Juvenile Employment Exchange, 168, Corporation Street, or at any of the Branch Exchanges in the City.

The Manufacture of Sporting Guns and Rifles

Description

A gun is no longer made by one man throughout, the work being now of an extremely sectional nature. This is one of the reasons why so much of the trade is in the hands of out-workers.

In many instances it takes several men to keep one man fully employed, e. g., on an average, it will take seven "action filers" to keep one "stocker" supplied with sufficient work. The consequence is that most firms are unable to keep workers in some of the sub-processes of manufacture fully employed all the time, and find it better to send the work to out-workers, who may be solely employed by one firm during most of the year, but who take in work from other shops during slack periods. A few large factories carry out the manufacture of the complete weapon, but the greater part of the trade is in the hands of out-workers and "garret masters."

The following list comprises the principal workers engaged in the trade:

1) Barrel welders are men employed in welding steel and iron into blanks or rough tubes. A large percentage of the rough tubes is imported from Belgium. There are in Birmingham only about six men who are skilled hand welders.

2) Barrel turners are employed in turning the barrel from a rough forging.

3) Barrel grinders are men employed in grinding the outside of the tubes or barrels.

4) Barrel filers consist of the men and youths employed in filing, fitting, brazing, and soldering, and building the tubes into finished barrels.

5) Stampers and Forgers are men employed in stamping or forging the action and limbs.

6) Action filers consist of the men and youths employed in fitting the action and lock mechanism to the barrel. In the past the filer completed the whole action himself, but the work is now very much subdivided.

7) Machinists consist of the men and youths employed on all the machine operations apart from barrel turning, grinding, boring, and rifling.

8) Toolmakers make all tools, cutters, etc. for use in the machine shops.

9) Lock filers consist of the men and youths employed in making complete locks and lockwork. A large percentage of this work is now done in the Black Country.

10) Ejector fitters consist of the men and youths employed in fitting ejecting mechanism to hammerless guns.

11) Furniture filers consist of the men and youths employed in filing and the fitting the trigger guards into complete sets of furniture.

12) Stockers are men employed in fitting the rough wooden stocks to the action. Some stockers also screw their own work, but they are chiefly in London.

13) Screwers are men employed in fitting the furniture, etc. into the stocks, and screwing metal parts on to the wood.

14) Finishers consist of the men and youths employed in finishing the stocks or wooden portions of the gun. Some finishers screw their own work.

15) Chequerers consist of the men, women and youths employed in cutting the chequer (i.e. the cross saw-cuts to prevent slipping) on the stock and fore-end. In the past the finisher did his own chequering.

16) Polishers are men employed in polishing the action and lockwork ready for engraving. It is usual, in Birmingham, for the polisher to do the hardening and bluing as well.

17) Engravers engrave the floral and game designs on the action and locks of sporting guns and rifles.

18) Freers finally adjust and free the work.

19) Viewers view and pass the work in the various stages of manufacture.

20) Storemen keep stores and issue parts to the workmen.

It is not an uncommon practice for men to pay rent for their benches in the factory and to take in outside work when their employer cannot give out the sufficient work to keep them fully engaged. The amount paid is usually 1s [one shilling, approximately 20 cents in 1913] per week for bench and 6d [six pence, approximately 10 cents in 1913] per week for gas, with an additional 1s or 1s 6d for every man employed by the worker, and 6d for every boy. Usually, however, gas is necessary only from October to March.

Apprenticeship is the exception, in spite of the fact that many of the firms in the trade would be only too glad to apprentice boys. This is brought about by the fact that the men in the trade for the most part refuse to teach youths, even when offered a premium for doing so. There are many causes for this, one of them arises from the fact that the local trade has been in a state of depression for the past ten years, and is still looked upon by the artisans as a dying industry. For this reason the sons of workmen in many sections of the trade do not take up gunmaking. Another cause of the unwillingness on the part of the men to teach their trade comes from the fact that with few exceptions all work is piece-work, and men are unwilling to lose time in teaching youths.

Owing to the long depression that the trade has gone through, many of the younger men have either drifted in the engineering trades or gone to the colonies. A number of the most skilled men have gone to London. During the most recent cycle boom many youths left the trade because of the higher wage they could obtain by tending automatic machines. Owing to these and other causes there is no surplus supply of skilled labour in the gun trade, and men can get employment with the greatest of ease.

The different processes are as a general rule grouped together as follows:

A)   Barrel making, which is subdivided into turning, grinding, boring, rifling and filing.
B)   Stamping and forging.
C)   Machining.
D)   Action-filing, which is again subdivided into jointing, filing-up, extractor fitting, lock fitting, smoothing, etc.
E)   Lock filing, which includes spring making.
F)   Ejector fitting and snap fore-end fitting.
G)   Furniture filing.
H)   Stocking.
I)   Screwing.
J)   Finishing.
K)   Polishing.
L)   Engraving.
M)   Browning.
N)   Freeing and adjusting.

Those working at *A*, *B*, and *C* are paid piece and day work. Those working at *N*, day-work; all the rest are paid piece work.

METHOD OF ENTRY

Boys start as errand boys to piece or day workers as soon as they leave school. If the boy shows any aptitude, the workman he is under will generally give him rough filing-up of iron or steel work from machinings to gauges, turning pins, etc., on small lathes to do in his spare time, and this will continue till the boy becomes too useful to run errands. He is then regarded as a "learner," and his whole time is spent at the vice. Whether he develops or progresses depends, first on the boy, and, secondly, on the man under whom he is working.

WAGES

THE WEEKLY WAGES OF THE VARIOUS TYPES OF WORKERS (1913) ARE AS FOLLOWS :

DESCRIPTION	AVERAGE WORKER	HIGHLY SKILLED	WOMEN
BARREL WELDER	30s TO 40s		
BARREL TURNER	25s TO 30s	30s	
BARREL GRINDER	30s TO 40s	45s	
BARREL BORER	30s TO 40s	50s	
BARREL RIFLERS	30s TO 40s	50s	
BARREL FILERS	28s TO 40s	60s	
STAMPERS AND FORGERS	30s TO 40s	40s	
ACTION FILERS	30s TO 35s	60s	
MACHINIST OR MACHINE MINDERS	25s TO 30s	30s	
TOOLMAKER	30s TO 40s	60s	
LOCK FILERS	30s TO 40s	60s	
EJECTOR FITTERS	30s TO 40s	55s	
FURNITURE FILERS	20s TO 30s	45s	
STOCKERS	35s TO 45s	55s	
SCREWERS	32s 6D TO 35s	50s	
FINISHERS	35s TO 40s	60s	
CHEQUERERS	20s TO 30s	40s	15s TO 22s
POLISHERS	35s TO 40s	55s	
ENGRAVERS	32s 6D TO 45s	60s	
FREERS	35s TO 45s	60s	
BROWNERS	35s TO 40s	40s	15s TO 25s
VIEWERS	35s TO 45s	60s	
STOREMAN	25s TO 30s		

1) Only about 5 percent of the workers are highly skilled. There is a small trade union.
2) Twenty shillings equals one pound stirling.

The period of training is from three to five years, according to the section and the extent of the course of training. Barrel filing takes from three to five years; action filing five years; stocking, screwing, and finishing, three years.

HOURS

The length of the working week is usually fifty-four hours.

PROSPECTS

The trade is now in a flourishing condition, and demand for English made guns is rapidly growing, especially in the colonies. The trade was a declining one from 1882 to 1907, but it is now increasing, as is shown by the following returns for the number of barrels examined at the Birmingham Proof House:

In 1882 there were about 750,000 proofs.
In 1907 there were about 370,000 proofs.
In 1911 there were about 420,000 proofs.

The returns for 1911 do not include the figures for those barrels which are made in Birmingham but sent to London to be "proofed," a practice which is now common. The returns for 1912 are likely to show a very considerable advance on those for 1911. With rare exceptions seasonal slackness is unknown in all the big factories. The general indications that the trade as a whole is becoming, in many ways, more united point to the probability of a greater expansion both in the home and colonial markets. Gunmaking is probably the lightest and most technical form of craftsmanship of any trade, and is one of the few trades where a man of fifty is generally more sought after than a man of twenty-five or thirty.

It is difficult to say whether in the future machinery will supplant to any great extent the present method of handwork, but it would seem that there is an opportunity for machinery owing to the dearth of skilled workers in this trade. Already one prominent firm has laid down an extensive machine plant for turning out sporting arms, and probably it is only the large initial expense which prevents other firms from following this example.

APPENDIX II

Like many accounts of Victorian gunmaking that purport to be unbiased, the following was probably commissioned by its subjects, in this case Messrs. P. Webley & Son. It is included here because of the detailed description of gunmaking—and particularly Damascus gun-barrel making—as it was in 1874.

The following article appeared in the London newspaper:

IRON
NOVEMBER 7TH, 1874
BIRMINGHAM INDUSTRIES

XIV.—Guns, Rifles, and Revolvers

Birmingham has long been famous for the manufacture of arms. At the time of the great Rebellion her swords were in high repute, and it was for supplying the Parliamentary forces, and for refusing to supply the king's, that the fiery Prince Rupert displayed such severe hostility to the people when he seized and burned the town. In the reign of William III, the making of guns was added to the then increasing industries of the place, and it has since developed to such an extraordinary extent, and the skill of the workmen has been so great, that the trade is now, and has long been, one of the most important staple trades of the many-traded town. It is divided into two principal classes of work—military and sporting. Military arms are chiefly made by machinery, and sporting by hand, with the exception of the action, which is partially machined; and in both cases the processes of manufacture are full of interesting examples of the skill and ingenuity of man in conquering difficulties, and in displaying his power over the apparently most difficult of materials.

For the purpose of the present paper we selected the well-known works of Messrs. P. Webley and Son, of Weaman Street, at which we could witness at one time the largest variety of work in the trade. Our request to inspect the manufactory was at once most cordially granted, and the utmost facilities were afforded by the principals and the highly-intelligent foremen of the various departments into which gun making is divided.

The house was originally established by William Davis, in 1790 (grandfather of the present juniors), as a bullet-mould manufacturer, whose trademark, "W. D.," was well known to every sportsman half a century ago. This formed a foundation whereon the senior partner of the present firm (Philip Webley), aided by his great practical knowledge of the trade generally, was able to extend the business of the house to its present dimensions. The trade now consists of the manufacture of military and sporting breech and muzzle-loading guns, rifles, and revolvers. The gun department being under the management of Mr. T. W. Webley, and the revolvers under that of Henry Webley. Our first visit was made to the gun department, and under the able and thoroughly-qualified guidance and instruction of Mr. Webley, we witnessed the various processes to the greatest advantage. We now ask the reader to accompany us, and witness, in the "mind's eye," the making of a gun or rifle.

To begin at the beginning. The iron used for guns is of a peculiar make, and consists of several layers of iron and steel piled together--both the iron and steel varying in quality according to the quality of barrel it is desired to make. The whole is then put into a furnace, and when sufficiently heated rolled out into square rods, differing in size according to the quality and dimensions of barrel required. "The better the barrel the smaller the size of iron it is made of." In this condition it comes to the welder. Welding is most important in making a gun-barrel. The workman takes a strip of iron, heats it red-hot, places it in a machine, and by turning a wheel twists it to the shape of a screw. Any defect in the iron is soon seen in this process, as in the case of a "fault," the screw is to that extent imperfect and useless. In every gun-barrel of medium quality there are two, and in the best three of these bars, each being twisted in alternate directions, one to the right, the second to the left, and when there is a third, that to the right again. By this means is obtained that varied twist which we see in gun-barrels. The various ways of twisting are known as "plain twist," "stub twist," "Damascus" and so on. The two or three rods are then welded together the entire length, and go back to the mill to be what is called over-rolled, that is, rolled out edge-wise to the required size. The metal is then twisted on a mandrill and welded together on the anvil. When it leaves the mandrill it is a hollow piece of twisted iron, with spaces between each winding. Welding is the process by which it is made into a barrel, and is a very delicate operation, requiring great skill in the workmen, of whom three are engaged at each anvil. The hollow twisted metal is heated red-hot; as soon as it is taken out of the fire, the workman strikes the end sharply on a metal plate on the floor, which forces the heated iron to close, he then places it on the anvil, and all three beat the heated portion with their various hammers. Two of them then take a long piece of steel, called a "float," and whilst the third turns it round and moves it to and fro on the anvil, work the float backwards and forwards, thereby clearing the surface of "scales," and other impurities. This process is repeated until the whole barrel is made. Only about four inches can be welded at each passing through the fire, an uniform heat of that part of the metal worked being absolutely necessary for the production of a perfect barrel.

In illustration of the great changes produced in the process of barrel making, we may mention here that 17 pounds of iron are used in making the two barrels of a best double-barreled gun, which, when finished, only weigh 3½ pounds. The iron used in the best barrel costs 7d a pound; and that in cheap ones 3d.

The barrel has next to be bored—another important process. First it is "rough-bored." In this operation a four-sided "bit," which cuts at each edge, is placed in the barrel; barrel and borer are placed in a machine, and by the use of great power the bit works its way through the barrel, smoothing and leveling the surface of the bore. It is then "fine-bored." In this operation a square bit, "with a wooden spill on one side," is used, which only cuts on one edge, and its cuttings are left on the bit in the form of the very finest powder. A slip of thin paper is put between the spill and the bit to increase the size, and such is the delicacy of this operation, that this simple addition is sufficient to produce the result required. The tubes are then turned at breech, muzzle, and several intermediate parts, to gauges specially made not only to suit the various bores, but to suit the varied requirements for light, medium, or heavy guns, in each bore.

In the manufacture of a specially light pair of barrels the reader can readily understand the necessity for a judicious distribution of metal.

The next operation is grinding, which is laborious—probably the most laborious part of barrel making. It also requires great skill, and much practical experience, but there is nothing specially to describe in the work. The stones used in grinding are from Derbyshire. The barrel is now ready for provisional proving, and on its return from this first test it is carefully examined to see if there are any grey specks—every such speck being considered a defect—or any imperfection which may detract from its value, It is then reset, and finally (as a separate tube) struck up into shape.

For the double-barrel gun two (an exact pair) are now jointed together, and the locking-lump fitted in. That part of the tubes which lies under the rib is then tinned, and the forward parts of the two tubes are soldered together on a parallel, the lump is then bound into its place by iron wire bands. A composition of brass dust and borax is placed round it, and then the breech end of the united barrels is subjected to an intense heat, and the brazing is effectually secured. Instead of the ordinary bungling mode of brazing by the usual hearth and bellows—in which it is almost impossible to entirely exclude dirt, and obtain an uniform heat—the Messrs. Webley have constructed a muffle, which is heated by coke, and the ends of the barrels are placed in the intense heat thus generated, and are never in contact with the coke itself. By this process the brazing is effected in about two minutes; in the common way it takes about ten minutes. This method, however, can only be used when there are a number of barrels to be brazed, as it would not pay to heat the muffle for one or two. The breech end having been thus secured, the barrels are ready for the ribs to be fitted and soldered on, they are then struck up from end to end, with various-shaped strikers, and are then taken to the action-filer, who provides for putting the "action" on the barrels. Then follow in order the furniture forger and filer, who provide the guard, the trigger, &c., the lock forger and filer. Of lock making, Mr. J. D. Goodman truly says:

Till within the last few years locks were entirely the production of hand labour, the several parts were forged on the anvil by men whose wonderful skill became proverbial. They were afterwards put together by filers, to be finished by the polisher and hardener. At the present time the steam hammer and stamp are superseding the forge, and milling machinery is doing much of the filer's work, but in no case, even when machinery is carried to the highest perfection, can the filer by dispensed with; the locks cannot be put together until all the limbs have passed through his hands to receive the final adjustment.

The parts are again taken to the action-filer, who fits on the breech action, to which he attaches the lock, trigger, and guard. It then goes for final or definite proof, with action attached, and is afterwards finally smoothed, and when viewed and found perfect is passed to the stocker.

One of the most interesting operations in gunmaking is that of making the top-lever action for breech-loading guns. Messrs. Webley make a specialty of this action, "which is made either single or double bite; when the latter, Purdey's double bolt is used." They have put down some special and ingenious machines for the purpose of machining it in the most perfect manner. You first see a rough-looking piece of iron, which has been stamped roughly into the form required. This forms the body of the action, and it is first passed between two cutters, which cut it into the exact width. It is then cut to fit on the joint of the barrel. It is now ready for drilling. In this operation the body is placed in a "jig," which is, in fact the pattern in which are the holes through which the drill works and makes the body ready for the bolt. This done, it is placed in another jig, and drilled for the joint holes and slots. It is then passed to another machine, by which the slot is sown out for the lump of the barrel.

It is now ready to be worked on the barrels of the gun. And first a plug, the exact size of the cartridge is fixed into each barrel, and the lump is cut horizontally, and then the ends of the barrels are squared. The next operation is to cut the lump the proper shape, which is done crosswise. It then goes to a machine by which it is cut out for the extractor, and with the extractor which has been properly turned and fitted, it is given to the jointer, who joints the parts together. Then the lock-holes are cut out, then the grip in the lock into which the bolt passes. The gun is now ready for proof. After it has stood this test it is percussioned by hand labour. The workman now puts in the locks, fits in the bolts, puts in the perpendicular spindle, and the lever on the spindle at the top. The whole action is then filed into shape, smoothed, and is, at last, ready for the stocker, whose work is hereafter described.

We have not paused in this progressive account of making a top-lever action to describe any of the machines by which the various operations are performed. They are all self-acting, and one man can superintend several at the same time, for when once set they work automatically. In all the cutting operations the body is fixed into a jig or mould on a moveable table. All the cutters are of the same shape as the pattern to be cut, and some of them are composed of as many as seven pieces. Some of them have a double action, and as the cutter is guided by a pattern fixed on the table opposite to the piece to be cut, the utmost exactitude is secured in all the operations, whether of cutting or drilling. In all cases the best lard oil is used for the purpose of lubrication. It is quite an intellectual treat to see these machines at work.

The stocks are of walnut. Mr. Webley, senior, pays the greatest attention to this part of the gun. He is always in search of good—especially of good English—walnut, which is the best. By constant watchfulness he is able to secure a large quantity of the finest wood for this purpose, and we saw some splendid specimens of walnut on the occasion of our visit. The difference in the value of wood for gun-stocking is great; one stock-piece may not be worth more than a shilling, while another is worth twenty-five. After the tree has been sawn into planks, great care has to be taken in marking out the stocks so as to secure the right way of the grain; and after cutting out, the pieces have to be kept from two to three years in order that they may be thoroughly seasoned.

The rough wood is taken by the stocker, who cuts it into the proper shape; he then lets in the stock, the action, then the lockplates without the inside work, afterwards putting on the inside work, and letting that in also, he fits on the fore-end, and rounds all the wood into shape, and passes it on to the screwer, who lets in the trigger-plate, trigger-guard, &c., and fits the pins and screws to bind the whole together, and passes it to the man who fits the hammers (called in muzzle loading guns percussioning). Barrels are then bored for shooting, and the gun is carefully shot at forty yards for penetration and pattern. Should it not shoot up to the required standard of excellence it is altered until it does. It is then passed to the finisher, who finally makes off the stock, chequers, and smoothes all the work level. The whole is then taken asunder, the barrels are finally smoothed, engraved, and named, at which stage it goes to the barrel browner.

Browning is a very interesting process. The browner takes the barrel and paints on a coat of acid, after which it looks as if covered with rust. This is rubbed off with a wire brush, and it is then boiled in water, and another coat of acid put on, and so on until the work is done, and the figure is completely developed. This operation takes from three to four days for the best guns. For military guns it is much simpler, and more easily done.

The action, locks, and other parts are next polished, then engraved and named, and afterwards case-hardened. The whole is then ready for the hands of an experienced action filer, who frees the action which, in hardening usually swells a little. The gun is then put together by the man who finishes it, and it is then ready for final examination and regulating, and we have a gun fully and completely made.

We were very much struck with the great variety of systems of guns and rifles manufactured by Messrs. Webley, as well as by the many grades of quality, commencing at the lowest, consistent with soundness, and progressing step by step to the very finest work that skill and taste can produce. Amongst the various systems shown to us, we noted, as still being in large demand, the old original double-grip Lefaucheux action with lever over guard; then the same action made self-locking by a very simple addition, patented by Mr. T. W. Webley in 1866, which has been still further improved upon by making it treble-grip, by the addition of a compensating bolt. This is a great advantage, more especially for rifles, and was patented by James Lang, of London. Snap-action guns, both with single and Purdey's double bolt, are made with the levers placed in every conceivable position; on the top, between the hammers; on the side, either right or left, under guard; side of guard or in front of it, and with the bow made open to receive the thumb, known as Purdey's lever. These, again, are all made with or without rebounding (self half-cocking locks) locks, and with lever fore-part fastening, entirely doing away with the old-fashioned bolt. The best of these, by far, is a very neat arrangement of lever, strong and certain in its action, which we did not consider the spring fore-parts to be.

Great attention is paid by Messrs. Webley to the making of double and single sporting, "Express," and long range rifles. The favorite action for double "Express" rifle, being the treble grip, the joint patent of Mr. T. W. Webley and Mr. James Lang. To turn out a perfect double rifle, with both barrels shooting accurately, is the height of gunmaking art. In single rifle, "Express" and otherwise, they use the "Swinburn" breech action, of which they hold a very high opinion, alleging that it has all the advantages of the "Martini" breech action, without its many defects. We annex an engraving of the Swinburn sporting carbine.

For the information of our readers, we furnish illustrations of various systems and forms of lever of breech-loading guns manufactured by Messrs. Webley.

The Messrs. Webley and Son have a world wide reputation as manufacturers of certain well-known kinds of revolving pistols. Among these are preeminently noted the Royal Irish Constabulary pattern, made by them for this force in 1868, and selected by the Inspector-General of the Forces, after a keen competition. This arm has since been adopted, and largely used by the Queensland Government, the Victorian Government, and the Cape Mounted Police. A large number of these revolvers were also used by Her Majesty's officers engaged in the Ashantee war.

Another pattern worthy of especial notice is a revolver constructed about two years ago, which, in comparison with the size of cartridge used therewith, is the smallest yet manufactured. This revolver has been most appropriately named "The British Bulldog," which is stamped on the top strap of each pistol. This weapon has found a great demand in all export markets.

We will now initiate our readers into the mysteries of revolver making. You first see the pistol body, which is a rough-looking bit of malleable iron of the form and shape required. In the centre of each of these pieces of iron is a square hold, which is after several processes, to receive the cylinder containing the chambers of the revolver. The first process is to force a long piece of cutting steel, called a "drift," through this hold, and thereby cut it into shape. Two "drifts," the second of a finer cutting power than the first, are used, and the force required to effect this sometimes amounts to a pressure of ten tons. This forms a "standard," to which all the other parts of the work have to be done, and it must be absolutely true. The next operation is a very beautiful bit of machine work. The piece of iron is put in a block the size of the drift-hole, and by moving it backwards and forwards the sides are planed or milled quite true. This machine also cuts out the recess by which the cartridge passes into the chambers. When one side has been milled it is reversed, in order to mill the other side. This beautiful machine is capable of the most delicate working; in proof of which we saw, on a piece of iron, the name of the workman, which he had cut out as an illustration of its power.

The milled body is next placed in a jig, in which all the action-holes are drilled; then the strap is made for the handle of the pistol, and it is next cut along the top of the strap and round the body, and the slot for the shield-spring is cut in.

In making the cylinder, a round bar of steel is cut into the required length, and a hold then drilled through the center. This center is the standard from which the rest of the work is done. The cylinder is next turned quite smooth, and to its exact gauge. It is then placed in a chuck, and the chambers are drilled. In the chuck are the divisions giving the number of chambers to be drilled in each cylinder, and as each chamber is made, the chuck and cylinder are turned to the next division, and is again drilled, and so on, until all are completed. The ease with which this drilling machine works is manifest from the fact that a six-chambered cylinder can be drilled in from five to seven minutes. The bolt holes are then cut, and then the ratchets, there being as many bolt-holes and ratchets as there are chambers in the cylinder.

This done, we go to barrel-making. A square bar of solid steel of the length of the barrel is placed in a chuck in a lathe, and is slowly drilled through. After drilling about three-eighths of an inch, the drill is drawn out, bringing with it the dirt and refuse. A barrel of four inches and a half in length can be bored in ten minutes. Soapsuds are used in this operation, which are in a bucket suspended over the lathe, and flowing down through a hose, continually runs on the boring tool, and thus preventing it from getting too hot. When bored, the barrel is cut down for screwing, and the screw cut for jointing to the body. It is then cut into shape. Two nuts are fastened on the screw end, and it is laid in a pair of cutters and by a succession of cuts up the barrel, it is finally shaped.

By similar processes the hammer, sear, and trigger are made. Each being put in a jig, having the necessary holes drilled, the sides flattened or machined, and all work needful to make each part fit and work accurately is done. The rounding and pointing the nose of the cock is a very interesting operation.

All the parts being thus prepared, they are put together by the action-maker, and afterwards sent for proof. On returning, the pistol is taken to pieces, smoothed up and sighted. These operations have to be very carefully done, as the utmost accuracy is required in making a good sight. This done, the revolver goes to the stocker, then to the polisher; after it is polished it has to be cleaned and put together, and at last, after all these operations have been skillfully and carefully executed, the revolver is ready for use.

We can certify, from our own personal observation, to the searching tests to which the Messrs. Webley subject all the revolvers manufactured by them; and as a guarantee of the quality and perfection of workmanship, each revolver bears their trademark—winged bullet.

The Messrs. Webley and Son were the only Birmingham manufacturers who exhibited at the Vienna Exhibition of 1873. Mr. Charles Hibbs, the artisan reporter on guns, sent out for that purpose by the Birmingham Chamber of Commerce, gives his willing testimony to the excellence of this exhibit. He says,

The whole gunmaking trade of the greatest gunmaking country of the world is really represented by one firm; the burden of sustaining the credit of England for extensive and various gun manufacture, home and foreign, falls on Webley, of Birmingham. It is not my province to play the critic on the works of any individual manufacturer, but, while carefully avoiding the province of a juror, it is perfectly competent for me to say, what it would be an unpardonable injustice not to say, that in Messrs. Webley's case the gun trade of England is worthily represented.

"An English sportsman who wants his fowling piece to fulfill the conditions of good shooting, easy handling, safety, perfect action, and durability, and at the same time would like it to be a possession he would be proud of; in material and finish, the best of its kind; in form and decoration an object to satisfy the demands of taste; in short, a piece of perfect workmanship from end to end, would here be exactly fitted."

The character of the work is just that which is ordinarily to be found in the showrooms of English manufacturers, and which is well-known in the markets to which English arms find their way. It was, I must confess, an occasion of great pride to me to find, in a miscellaneous collection of articles, no doubt taken from stock, and certainly in no sense manufactured for exhibition purposes alone, work turned out from a house bearing no name of old renown, which would bear comparison with the very best of that exhibited purely for show, by the most celebrated art-producing armourers of the Continent.

Mr. Hibbs adds, "Messrs. Webley show double and single shot guns, sporting rifles, military rifles and revolvers, &c., and an Express rifle, the trajectory of which is so low that it can be fired from 50 to 200 yards with the same elevation of sight."

The Messrs. Webley & Son obtained a medal at the Dublin Exhibition of 1872; also at the Vienna Exhibition last year. We have to record our warmest thanks to the Messrs. Webley for the care, time, and attention which they so lavishly bestowed upon us at both our visits to their extensive and admirably conducted works.

Dr. Langford, LL.D.

CAUTION.

COUNTERFEIT PROOF MARKS.

CAUTION TO GUNMAKERS
And the Public generally.

WHEREAS AMOS ELVINS, of Legge Street, Birmingham, Barrel Manufacturer, was, on the 27th of January last, CONVICTED before the Magistrates at Birmingham, of knowingly selling Two Gun Barrels on which were Marks counterfeited to resemble the London Proof Marks, contrary to the Act of Parliament; and there is reason to believe that various other Barrels have been manufactured by the said AMOS ELVINS, having thereon similar counterfeited Proof Marks, whereby the safety of individuals is endangered.

All persons are therefore Cautioned against selling or purchasing any Gun or Pistol Barrels purporting to have been proved at the London Proof House, without being fully satisfied that the Proof Marks on such Barrels are genuine.

By Order of the Company of Gunmakers of London,

GEORGE RUTHERFORD,

February 4th, 1854.   *Clerk.*

Even in 1854, the term caveat emptor *was not without warrent, as this notice attests!* (David Travallion)

Glossary of Gunmakers' Terms

ACTION BODY or FRAME. The heart of a gun, to which the locks, stock, and barrels are attached.

ACTION BOLT. The primary method of locking the barrels to the action. A rectangular bolt moves longitudinally within the action bar to engage the barrel lump bites.

ACTION FACE. The flat forward surface of the standing breech through which the strikers operate.

ACTION FLATS. The horizontal surface of the action bar that mates with the barrel flats when the gun is closed.

ARTICULATED TRIGGER. A hinged front trigger that swings forward to eliminate bruising when the rear trigger is pulled.

BACK ACTION. A type of sidelock in which the mainspring lies behind the lockwork.

BAR. The horizontal projection onto which the barrels hinge.

BAR ACTION. A type of sidelock in which the mainspring lies in the bar of the action.

BARREL FLATS. The flat surface on the bottom of the barrels at the breech end.

BENT. The notch in the tumbler that is engaged by the nose of the sear when the lock is cocked.

BITE. The slot cut in the rear of the lump that receives the bolt which locks the barrels to the action.

BOLSTERED ACTION. A reinforced action that has additional metal in the angle where the action face meets the action flats. Typical of heavy double rifles.

BREAK OFF. See STANDING BREECH.

BRIDLE. The metal plate found inside a sidelock that provides additional bearing for the tumbler and sear.

CHAMBER. The section at the rear of the barrel that is internally enlarged to accept the cartridge.

CHECKERED SIDEPANELS. The panels on a boxlock immediately behind the action, sunken and checkered for decorative effect.

CHOPPER LUMPS. Lumps that have been forged as an integral part of the barrels, as opposed to having been brazed on.

COCKING DOG. The limb that protrudes through the knuckle of the action and cocks the gun as it is opened.

COCKING INDICATORS. A system to show that a gun is cocked and therefore potentially unsafe. The type most frequently encountered on Birmingham sidelocks are gold or engraved lines along the tumbler pivots. Older models may have protruding tumbler pivots.

COLOR CASE HARDENING. The surface hardening of gun actions and lockplates to help them resist corrosion and wear. It often takes the form of eye-pleasing gray, blue, and straw tones, created by heating parts packed in bone. Ray St. Ledger is Birmingham's master color case hardener.

CONE. The reduction of the diameter in a barrel that joins the chamber to the bore.

CRAB JOINT. The tongue on the stock of a bar in wood by Westley Richards [see definition of bar in wood] that enters a recess in the fore-arm and covers the hinge. Named for its similarity to the joints of the crustacean.

CROSS BOLT. A third fastener that bolts a rib extension to the breakoff. The most common is the Greener, which is round in section; next is the Scott, which is square.

CROSS EYE STOCK. A stock bent so someone with a dominant left eye can shoot from the right shoulder or vice versa.

CROSS PIN. A hinge through the action bar at the knuckle on which the barrels rotate to close.

DAMASCUS BARRELS. Barrels formed by forge welding alternate rods of iron and steel around a mandrill in a spiral. The finished result is an attractive rhythmical pattern that is sometimes acid-etched to increase contrast. Although expensive and often found on best guns, Damascus barrels are today considered suspect unless in current nitro proof.

DETONATING. See STANDING BREECH.

DETONATORS. See FENCES.

DISK SET STRIKERS. Strikers fitted into bushes in the action face. They have the advantage of permitting the bushes to be replaced should they become pitted by escaping gases.

DOG PIN. The pin that holds the cocking dogs in place. The dog pin also provides the axis around which the cocking dogs revolve when the gun is opened.

DOLL'S HEAD EXTENSION. A rib extension that is circular in plan, sinking into a radially curved recess in the top of the standing breech.

DROP POINTS. A teardrop carved into a gunstock immediately to the rear of the lockplate on a sidelock, and at the rear of the side panels on the stock of a boxlock.

ESCUTCHEON. A shield or oval—often of silver or gold—inletted into the stock and bearing the monogram or coat of arms of the gun's owner. Some owners will insist on the removal of their escutcheon as a condition of sale.

EJECTOR. A miniature gunlock built into the fore-end iron that throws fired cartridges free from a fully opened gun.

EJECTOR KICKER. The hammer or tumbler in an ejector mechanism.

EXTRACTOR. A simple mechanism that withdraws cartridges from the chambers of an open gun far enough so they may be removed by hand.

FACTOR. A factor was not a gunmaker as such but someone who rented bench space to gunmakers, bought the raw material they needed, and paid them by the piece. The factor oversaw the making of the gun, and his name would be engraved on it when it was eventually sold.

FENCES or DETONATORS. The demi-spheres immediately behind the barrels.

FILE CUT RIB. A top rib cut with a pattern to minimize glare.

FLAT-BACK ACTION. A sidelock action in which the stock does not extend to the fences but instead reaches to a metal bridge that has a rear edge corresponding to the rear edge of the frame at the bottom of the action, giving it a "flat back." Many of London's best makers built their guns with flat-back actions until the turn of the century. Birmingham sidelocks, particularly the less expensive ones, continued to be made with flat-back actions until well into the twentieth century.

FLETCH. A walnut blank of double the normal thickness with a consistent grain throughout, sawn in half along its length and used to stock a pair of guns. The idea is that the figure in both guns should be as identical as possible.

FORCING CONE. The cone-shaped section of barrel immediately in front of the chambers that squeezes the shot charge of a cartridge into the bore of a gun as it is fired.

FORE-END FASTENER. The device that fastens the fore-end to the gun. In the better-quality Birmingham hammerless gun, this is often the Anson, patented by William Anson (Number 953 of 1873) and consisting of a sprung rod terminating at the fore-end finial.

FORE-END FINIAL. The terminating steel part at the tip of the fore-end. In the Deeley Edge, the finial is decorative; in the Anson, it houses the push-rod release button.

FORE-END IRON. The steel part of the fore-end that forms a frame for the ejector mechanism and carries the fore-end wood.

FORE-END LOOP. The projection beneath and between the barrels that holds the fore-end in place. On Birmingham guns the fore-end loop is also frequently the location of the maker's serial number, as opposed to the retailer's serial number, which appears on the rear of the trigger guard.

FRAME. See ACTION BODY.

FURNITURE. The trigger guard, trigger plate, triggers, or almost any small part that requires bluing, perhaps including the base plate of a plain Anson & Deeley boxlock.

GREENER CROSS BOLT. A round bolt that moves laterally in the standing breech to engage a circular bite in the rib extension.

GREENER SIDE SAFETY. A type of safety situated on the left side panel, as opposed to the more conventional top strap. It was almost wholly restricted to use on Greener guns among the Birmingham makers.

HIDDEN THIRD FASTENER. A projection between the ejectors that mates with a bolt in the action face. It supplements the underbolts, thus adding strength, but is less of an impediment to fast loading than a rib extension. This feature is usually an indication of high quality.

HOOK. The circular cut in the forward lump that hooks the barrels to the cross pin.

INTERCEPTING or BOLTED SAFETY. A method of preventing the fall of the tumblers in the event the sear is jarred out of its bent. Recognizable in a boxlock by a small screw on the side of the action in the angle formed by the top strap and the fences.

JONES UNDERLEVER. A double screw grip operated by an underlever. The barrels have two underlumps into which are cut two opposing slots. A "T"-shaped rotating bolt engages the slots in the lumps, pulling the barrels down on the bar of the action. The system was patented by Henry Jones, a Birmingham gunmaker (Number 2,040 of 1859), and was used on many hammer guns before the development of the snap action. Even after the snap action was in common use, the Jones underlever was employed on double rifles and big-bore fowlers because of its strength.

KNUCKLE. The rounded front to the action bar that receives the rear of the fore-end and through which the cocking levers protrude.

LUMPS. The downward projections at the rear of the barrels into which bites are cut to receive the action bolts.

NON-EJECTOR. A gun in which spent cases are not ejected when the gun is opened but rather are extracted from the chambers so that they can be removed by hand. Typically, but not necessarily, an inexpensive gun.

PINS. Screws.

PISTOL HAND. A buttstock formed like a pistol grip, as opposed to the more conventional straight hand stock. Pistol hands are common on wildfowling and live-pigeon guns and are relatively rare on light game guns.

REBOUNDING HAMMER. A hammer that bounces back a fraction of an inch after striking the firing pin. When used with spring-retracting firing pins, the rebounding hammer made it possible to open the gun without cocking the hammers and reduced the risk of accidental discharge when the gun was closed.

RIB. A raised metal strip laid between the barrels of a gun as an aid to sighting.

RIB EXTENSION. A rearward continuation of the top rib that mates with a slot in the standing breech between the fences.

ROUND-BAR BARRELS. Barrels that, unlike chopper lump barrels, have no lump integrally forged. Therefore, lumps must be added by means of a dovetail and brazing.

SEAR. The part of the lock that releases the tumbler when the trigger is pulled.

SETTING UP. Assembling a gun from separately made lock, stock, and barrel, particularly in the muzzleloading era. Many of the firearms made in Birmingham during the Napoleonic Wars were "set up" or assembled in London.

SIDE CLIPS. Forward-facing projections on the sides of the fences that mate with machined surfaces on the rear and side of the barrels to eliminate lateral movement. Common on pigeon guns and double rifles.

SIDE NAIL. The large screw in the center of the lock plates on a sidelock gun by which the lockwork is attached to the gun.

SLEEVING. A method of repairing barrels by inserting new tubes onto the existing breech ends.

SPINDLE. The rod connecting the top lever to the underbolt.

STANDING BREECH, BREAKOFF, or DETONATING. The part of the action perpendicular to the bar that houses the top lever spindle.

STRAP. The finger of steel inletted into the top of the stock that carries the safety.

STRIKER. Firing pin.

TRIGGER PLATE. The platform on which the triggers are mounted.

TUMBLER. The component on the inside of a lock by which the mainspring acts on the hammer. The tumbler substitutes for the hammer in hammerless designs.

TUMBLER PIVOTS. The axles on which the tumblers rotate. Their exterior surfaces are often engraved with a line—sometimes inlaid with gold—that acts as a cocking indicator.

VENTED BREECH. A groove milled around each striker hole and a lateral groove across the action face that allows escaping gases to be directed away from the breech in the case of a primer failure.

BIBLIOGRAPHY

1. Printed books and periodicals.

Abridgments of Patent Specifications. *Class 119, Small Arms 1855-1930.* Oceanside, California: Armoury Publications, 1993.

Akehurst, Richard. *Game Guns & Rifles, Percussion to Hammerless Ejector in Britain.* London: Arms and Armour Press, 1985.

Allen, G. C. *The Industrial Development of Birmingham and the Black Country 1860-1927.* 1929.

"ARTIFEX" and "OPIFEX" [Greener, C. E., Greener, W. O.] *The Causes of Decay in a British Industry.* London: Longmans, Green, and Co., 1907.

Bailey, De Witt & Nie, Douglas A. *English Gunmakers, The Birmingham and Provincial Gun Trade in the 18th and 19th Century.* New York: Arco Publishing Company, Inc., 1978.

Baker, David. *The Royal Gunroom at Sandringham.* Oxford, England: *Phaidon,* a Christie's publication, 1989.

Baker, David. "Conversations with Harry," in the *Sporting Gun,* May 1992.

Baker, David. "The Machine Made Classic," in the *Sporting Gun,* March 1993.

Blanch, H. J. *A Century of Guns.* London: John Blanch & Son, 1909.

Boothroyd, Geoffrey. "William Baker, Inventor Extraordinary," in *Game and Gun,* May/June 1993.

Boothroyd, Geoffrey. "The Birmingham Gun Trade," in the *Shooting Times & Country Magazine,* October 4-November 8, 1969, [published in six parts].

Boothroyd, Geoffrey. *Boothroyd's Directory.* Amity, Oregon: Sand Lake Press, 1994.

Boothroyd, Geoffrey. "Cashmore's Patent Nitro Action," in *Guns Review,* March 1995.

Boothroyd, Geoffrey. "The Needham Ejector," in the *Shooting Times & Country Magazine,* March 8-14, 1990.

Boothroyd, Geoffrey. "Charles Osborne of Birmingham," in the *Shooting Times & Country Magazine,* May 26-June 1, 1988.

Boothroyd, Geoffrey. *Sidelocks & Boxlocks.* Amity, Oregon: Sand Lake Press, 1991.

Boothroyd, Geoffrey. "The Tale of a Tolley," in the *Shooting Times & Country* magazine, March 21-27, 1991.

Boothroyd, Geoffrey. "Tolley—the wildfowler's gunmaker," in the *Shooting Times & Country* magazine, August 28-September 3, 1986.

Burrard, Major Sir Gerald. *The Modern Shotgun.* Volumes I, II, and III. London: Herbert Jenkins, 1931 and 1932.

Crawford, John A. & Whatley, Patrick G. *The History of W. & C. Scott, Gunmakers.* Rowland Ward, London: 1991.

Crudgington, I. M. & Baker, D. J. *The British Shotgun, Volume One, 1850-70.* Southampton, England: Ashford, Buchan & Enright, 1990.

Crudgington, I. M. & Baker, D. J. *The British Shotgun, Volume Two, 1871-1890.* Leatherhead: Ashford, Buchan & Enright, 1992.

Dunham, Keith. *The Gun Trade of Birmingham.* Birmingham, England: Birmingham Museum and Art Gallery, Department of Science and Industry, [Newhall Street], 1955.

George, John Nigel. *English Guns and Rifles.* Harrisburg, Pennsylvania: The Stackpole Company, 1947.

Goodman, John Dent. *The Birmingham Gun Trade.* Robert Hadwicke, London: Published in the Birmingham and Midland Hardware District, 1866.

Goodwin, J. "The Newdigates of Arbury . . . Early Memorials of the Birmingham Gun Trade," in *The Gentleman's Magazine,* February 1869.

Grant, David. "Smallest of the Best," in the *Shooting Times & Country Magazine,* June 21-27, 1990.

Greener, W. W. *Modern Breech Loaders, 1871.* Cassell, London: Peter and Galpin, 1871.

Greener, W. W. *The Gun and its Development.* London: Arms and Armour Press, 1910, [reprint of the ninth edition].

Harris, Clive, ed. *The History of the Birmingham Gun Barrel Proof House,* 2nd edn. Birmingham, England: Guardians of the Birmingham Proof House, 1949.

Hewitt, E. M. "The Gun Trade of Birmingham," in the *Victorian History of the Counties of England.* Warwickshire, England: Warwickshire pp. 226-232.

Izon, John. "The Birmingham Gun Trade," in *The Birmingham Post,* 16 to 22 October, 1952, [an article in five parts].

Kelver, Gerald O. "T. Ketland and Company, Birmingham and London," in *The Gun Report,* February 1987.

Latham, Sid. "The Birmingham Trade," in *American Rifleman,* February 1951.

Langford, Dr. LL. D. "Birmingham Industries—Guns, Rifles, and Revolvers," in *Iron,* 7 November 1874, XIV.

McIntosh, Michael. *Best Guns.* New Albany, Ohio: Countrysport Press, 1989.

Neal, W. Keith & Back, D. H. L. *British Gunmakers, Their Trade Cards, Cases and Equipment, 1760-1860.* Warminster, England: Compton Press, 1980.

Newland, Mike. "William Greener—A Dyed in the Wool Muzzleloader," in *Black Powder,* 1991.

Purdey, T. D. S., Purdey, Capt. J. A. *The Shot Gun.* London: Adam and Charles Black, 1938.

Richards, W. A. "Black Country Guns and the Slave Trade," in *The Blackcountryman,* Winter 1975, Vol. 8, No. 1.

Sharp, Henry. *Modern Sporting Gunnery.* London: Simpkin, Marshall, Hamilton, Kent & Co., Ltd., 1906.

Shelton, Lawrence P. *J. P. Clabrough & Bros., Gunmakers.* Fair Oaks, California: Far West Publishers, 1978.

Shelton, Lawrence P. "Unsung Shotgun Manufacturer," in *The Gun Report,* May 1981.

Smirke, R. S. "The Manufacture of Sporting Guns and Rifles. Report on Birmingham Trades, prepared for use in connection with the Juvenile Employment Exchange." H.M.S.O., 1913.

Smith, D. M. "Birmingham's Gun Quarter and Its Workshops," in the *Journal of Industrial Archaeology,* Volumes 1 and 2, August 1964, pp. 106-119.

Taylor, John. *African Rifles and Cartridges.* Long Beach, California: Safari Press, 1994.

Taylor, Leslie B. *A Brief History of the Westley Richards Firm.* Stratford-upon-Avon, England: Shakespeare Head Press, 1913.

Teasdale-Buckell, G. T. *Experts on Guns & Shooting.* Southampton, England: Ashford Press, 1986.

Timmins, Samuel. "The Industrial History of Birmingham," in *Birmingham and the Midland Hardware District.* London: Robert Hardwicke, 1866.

Venters, Vic. "Winds of Change in Birmingham," in *Game & Gun,* Volume 1, Number 5, March/April, 1993.

Venters, Vic. "William Powell & Son Ltd," in *The Double Gun Journal,* Volume 4, Issue 4, 1993.

Wise, M. J. "On the Evolution of the Jewelry and Gun Quarters in Birmingham," in the *Transactions of the Institute of British Geographers,* 15 pp. 59-72, 1950.

Various issues of the following periodicals were also referred to: *Arms & Explosives, The Field, Game & Gun, The Sporting Goods Review, the Gunmaker, Shooting Times,* and *British Sportsman.* Also consulted were numerous auction-house catalogs from Bonhams, Christie's, Sotheby's, and so on.

2. Unpublished manuscripts, found in the various libraries in Birmingham.

Anon. "A Century of Gunmaking, B.S.A. from 1861 to 1961."

Greener, Leyton. "The Saint George Gun." 11 August 1972.

Newland, Mike A. "Information on the Gun Trade." 1989, plus numerous other notes on a variety of Birmingham gunmakers.

Nie, Douglas, "Birmingham Gunworkers, circa 1767-1800."

Stanton, Lorraine E. "The Birmingham Gun Trade: Dead or Alive?" Birmingham, England: University of Birmingham, 1976, undergraduate thesis.

White, Helen and Trudgeon, Rodger. "Birmingham's Gun Quarter: A Skilled Trade in Decline."

Young, Dorothy W. "History of the Birmingham Gun Trade, up to mid 1935", Birmingham, England: University of Birmingham, 1936, master's thesis.